⤚ The Story of the Lake ⤙

The Story of the Lake

A Novel

Laura Chester

Faber and Faber
BOSTON • LONDON

F
che

For George Miller Chester

With special thanks to Jean Lindsay Johnson, Chapman Chester, Mason Rose,
Danny Frye, Christine Schutt, Kenny Buchanan, Cia McKoy, Helen Chester,
Jill Barrett Johnson, Bernice Abrahamzon, Augie Pabst, and Betsy Uhrig,
for their stories, advice, and loving support.

First published in the United States in 1995 by Faber and Faber, Inc.,
50 Cross Street, Winchester, MA 01890.

Library of Congress Cataloging-in-Publication Data

Chester, Laura.
    The story of the lake : a novel / by Laura Chester.
        p.   cm.
    ISBN 0-571-19861-9 (hardcover)
    1. Summer resorts – Wisconsin – History – Fiction.   2. Family –
Wisconsin – History – Fiction.   3. Lakes – Wisconsin – History –
Fiction.   I. Title.
    PS3553.H43S75   1995
    813'.54 – dc20   94-48570
                                                                          CIP

This is a work of fiction. All characters are products of the author's imagination and do
not represent any person living or deceased. They pass through the pages of this book
representing the passions, attitudes, and prejudices of past generations. Some of the
letters, poems, songs, and obituaries herein were taken from the author's family archives
and transformed to suit the purposes of fiction.

Jacket design by Mary Maurer
Jacket photographs from the collection of the author

Printed in the United States of America

PART ONE

When the light on the water spreads like liquid gold leaf, I am reminded of one of the great pleasures of my childhood – standing by this window with my grandmother and watching the sun go down. At that moment I am filled with a visual elixir of sun-burning water and feel the desire to be nowhere else.

My grandmother moved swiftly and was known to drive fast – "There goes fearless Helen in her Peerless," one of the first cars made – and nothing seemed to stop her from anything athletic. She even played tennis in a long white dress and led the field on horseback. Still, she had a kind of patience with me as a child that never put me in a rush. Her energy wasn't filled with anxiety, and she always had time to talk or read a book. I believe through her manner she taught me to behold, and that everything should be done for beauty.

I loved to sit with her in the blue-green study at the far end of the house. The wall curved and the room reminded me of a ship. A convex mirror bent the dimensions even further, and the watchful eyes of Great Grandmother Felton in her oval frame followed me about the room as I touched the spines of the leather volumes or spun the giant globe that looked as ancient as the Constitution, flame-burnt brown – it stood on its pedestal and whirled at an angle in actual imitation of the earth.

In this room I felt aware of our own planet turning, that we were indeed in orbit as the globe rumbled round. It seemed amazing to spot our exact location in southern Wisconsin – that this was the land of black earth, where glaciers had deposited their richest treasure of topsoil and lush vegetation was unequaled.

My grandmother spent time every day at her desk, for she believed in the nature of correspondence. Those were the days when etiquette began with the fountain pen and written expression was honored. She still wrote to school friends from Rosemary Hall and to others as far away as Zurich or the Dordogne. I loved the fine cream-colored paper she used, her shiny black pen with the golden tip, and the expert slant of her script.

Because I was the oldest granddaughter, I had certain unspoken privileges – my grandmother took me into her confidence and told me the stories of the lake. But sometimes it was even better when we were very quiet, when she would do her work and I'd do mine. I didn't have to ask her to unlock the middle drawer of her desk or to remove the flat leather box. She simply handed it to me without admonishment, and I carried it over to the rose-colored love seat, then pressed the brass button that opened it up.

The box was lined with a dark purple velvet, and the seven precious gems were each sunk into place. Gazing at the glitter of the gems all together put me in another world, as if an essence had been released and I was under its spell, as if I could hear the planets revolving, each one on a different note in the cosmos, like the sound of our glasses filled with water – rubbing round the rim, making the crystal sing out at each level.

I took up each gemstone and held it to the light, entranced by the individual color and cut – amethyst, citrine, garnet, alexandrite. My grandmother taught me their names, just as she taught me each leaf as we rode – black oak, elm, maple, and poplar. I liked the splashy aquamarine best, then the tourmaline and smoky topaz. Holding each one I felt a different sense of mystery, and sometimes, when I dared hold all the gemstones together, listening to the sound of her pen as she wrote, I became as quiet as if we were in church.

I remember the pile of letters that arrived after Papa's death. Only then did I feel the oppression of her correspondence, for she felt she had to answer each one – sympathy cards, outlined in black. It was my very first funeral, the first time I'd seen my father cry.

Now both grandparents are gone and the generations seem to blend together, but it's as if the good qualities have thinned or crudeness has thickened, as if each generation has gotten weaker, less aesthetically tuned. The house is basically the same. A few portraits have been replaced by lesser works that don't harmonize with the architectural dimensions, and throw the big room slightly off balance. The furniture, the Oriental carpets are still there, only the mood is different – that reverence, that gracious mood of calm is gone, or perhaps my own capacity for wonder has lessened, making me long to have that box of gemstones back in my hands.

I asked Aunt Carol about it. She knew I'd been particularly close to her mother, and I mentioned how Gramma had once casually promised the box of them to me, but this made my aunt appear rattled. She went into her study, no longer used for quiet correspondence or for the study of ancient Greek myths, but for family business transactions. Where there had once been order, my grandmother's desk was now piled high with magazines and catalogues, postcards stuffed in all the slots.

Then my aunt remembered that she had found that old box of semi-precious gemstones a while ago, but she had passed them on to my cousin Vernon, for his boys to play with – "You know how children enjoy that sort of thing. I don't think I could ask for them back now. They have such a good time playing marbles with them."

Marbles, I thought. They play marbles?

I had loved those gemstones because they were beautiful, beautiful and useless, a private treasure, certainly nothing to be tossed about the rug.

"But maybe we can find some other memento," she went on, rummaging through the desk, though I wanted to get out of there. I didn't want to witness any more of this now. But then, opening a side drawer, she seemed to find something, and turning, she produced my grandmother's black fountain pen.

CHAPTER ONE

O pen up another deck of cards," Jon Bloodgood called out to his partner, Merrick Wells, as he entered the *Nogowogotoc Cannonball*, a private red and yellow club car that would take these commuters by rail back out to their summer lake homes. In the one hour and ten minutes it took to get from Milwaukee to the Wahcheetah Station, these gentlemen would manage to get in a few fast card games for fairly high stakes, and the fresh pack guaranteed no marked cards. Though none of this select group would suspect any other, it was the custom of the commute to let the old pack fly, rippling out the window along the gravel and steel rails still hot from the mid-August sun.

Back home at Broadoaks, Merrick's daughters, Helen and Isabelle, were washing down the statue of a waterboy that stood in the center of their mother's English garden – larkspur, dahlias, roses, phlox. It was a robust little statue with hard tufts of hair, tirelessly holding out his shell filled with water – the girls tried to get him completely wet, no dry marks on him, but slick all over like a seal.

Isabelle, five years older, was more careful in the way she wiped the liquid over the waterboy's torso. He seemed almost alive to her, and she imagined her touch might offend him. Perhaps he was trapped within the limits of his form and had to put up with their attention. But just then, Isabelle's chow appeared with another half-dead chicken from Vintry's. Helen turned on the dog, "Oh no! You're a bad, *bad* girl, Tai Fung. This time you're going to get it."

Isabelle also knew what Mr. Vintry had threatened, but she didn't know how to prevent Tai's raids without caging her pet and making a true beast out of her. Then up came Helen's pug, Pompeii, carrying a dirty old sock in his mouth. The faun-colored pug looked stupid as well as knowing, embarrassed as well as very proud.

As soon as the shiny black brougham turned in at the drive, both girls ran to meet their father. Helen got there first, as usual, and climbed onto her father's lap before he'd had a chance to descend, but Isabelle's upset won his attention. "Tai's going to be shot. Mr. Vintry said so. Pompeii probably led her over there."

"Don't blame him," Helen defended her dog, who now yapped and twirled about the new arrivals. Bloodgood was amused by the fresh little pug, though Merrick Wells had hoped for a more convivial welcome, since he'd been trying to encourage his friend to consider Caroline Felton and the joys of family life.

"I don't think anyone's going to have to suffer the death penalty over this," Merrick assured his daughter, "except, perhaps, this rangy looking capon," which Tai still held firmly in her jaws. Tai was a very loyal animal, yet aloof. She did not crave petting like Pompeii, but Merrick had always been taken with the chow precisely because she paid little attention to him.

"Tie the bird around her neck," Bloodgood suggested. "That usually teaches them, once it begins to rot."

Isabelle ran for the kitchen, while Merrick calmly extricated the bird from the dog's blue-black mouth. The darkness of the chow's eyes seemed to concentrate, giving her an even more wolf-like expression. The pug stopped his antics and regarded the exchange with the utmost solemnity. With a snap, Merrick Wells broke the capon's neck. "Where's your mother?" he asked.

"She's over at The Readers. Will you flip me, Uncle Jon?" Helen loved this feat of gymnastics. She would bend over, put her hands between her legs, then grabbing them, he'd yank – and she'd somersault over, landing flat on her feet. Helen smiled up at their visitor, always eager to please. In that way she was much like her mother, though Sarah Felton Wells had never had her daughter's energy or spirit.

Isabelle was clearly like her father. She had his delicate proportions and sensitivity of mind. She was also a bit homely compared to Helen, whose sweetness of appearance disguised the determination within.

"What scandalous novel are the ladies of the lake devouring now?" Jon Bloodgood wanted to know.

"Nothing much. Some British poetess. But speaking of that, Sarah's been writing some verse herself these days, and it's not bad, flowers in the Alps and that sort of thing. You should get her to read you a couple."

Indeed, Sarah Wells had an ear for the euphonic. She was fond of everything that was elegant and harmonious. Broadoaks was known for combining the beauty of the country with all the comforts of town. There was a graciousness about the large, brown-shingled house, balanced on either side with its wide, welcoming porch. Hosta bloomed along the borders of the herringbone walkway, and the window boxes overflowed with white and pink petunias.

Sarah had just finished decorating the foyer at Broadoaks using a cream-colored material with an oak leaf pattern. There were dark green rugs that seemed to keep in the coolness, preserving it like a cave stores wine or a dense glade shades you from the heat. The house was a refuge from the Wisconsin summer climate, though the sight of the lake alone was cooling.

Jon was ascending the steps to his guest room when he spied Sarah's buggy bouncing down the drive. Quickly he returned to greet her. She descended like some newborn thing, wearing a mint-green dress of voluminous lawn, delicate pink ribbons laced through the bodice. "Ah, the most beautiful, most gracious and good," Bloodgood began his typical eulogy, "the finest, most fashionable dove in the entire aviary."

"Jonathan, don't tease me. I am nothing but a dupe!" Sarah's face was flushed, and she seemed strangely flustered. "Can you imagine, Harriet Hawkshurst bribed one of the gardeners for a bag of my seed corn!" This tiny, delicate corn had such pale, milky kernels you could eat it raw. "She got hold of it last summer, planted it this spring, harvested her first batch, and had The Readers for luncheon. I can't tell you how she relished my upset."

"Why, Sarah," Jon teased, "I didn't know you were seed proud."

"Well of course I am." She was proud of her husband, her children, and her home, but especially proud of her garden. Sarah Wells had been known to order every single item in the seed catalogue, and Kurtz, her gardener, managed a work crew of ten.

"Anyway, we'll eat lightly tonight. The girls are going to join us, and here – " she lifted a small ceramic jug. "I just went over to Ulrich Farms, fresh cream for dessert. *Schaum torte*, isn't that your favorite? We don't want it to spoil." So off she swept toward the kitchen, where Isabelle and Helen were each relating different versions of the chicken-sock story.

Over dinner they savored a freshly opened bottle of white wine, an excellent *Deideshaimer Langenmorgan*. "I tell you, Wells, this Liebenau store is really headed somewhere. Merging's the only way to go. You could turn Felton's into the biggest drygoods operation in the entire Midwest."

"It is the biggest in the Midwest," Merrick replied.

"That doesn't mean it couldn't be bigger and better." Turning to his hostess, Jon added, "You'd think with that much gray matter, he'd wake up to the ways of the future." Jon liked to kid Merrick about being three-fourths brain.

"What are the ways of the future?" Helen asked.

"You have to be *grabby*" – he snatched at her arm, and she squealed.

Fraulein Reusner, who always joined the family for casual dinners, maintained a rather dour expression, for she didn't think the girls should hear conversation about business.

Merrick only shook his head. "That's what they say, greed and speed. But I think endurance stands for something, don't you, girls?"

"Come, come, let's have no contests," Sarah urged.

Merrick was the first to admit that Jon could usually beat him at tennis, or even golf, and Jon usually pulled up much bigger perch than he did, but he believed that he could probably out-stand him. "What do you think?" he asked the girls.

They were both delighted by the challenge, for they had often witnessed their father out-standing larger, more powerfully built men, who hobbled away aching and groaning after a fairly short stint on one foot, while their father continued to stand there. He might have been small of stature, but he had a fierceness of mind that made him well-respected in this world of moguls and magnates.

William Felton, Sarah's father, had noticed this quality as well as Merrick's unusual thoughtfulness. Years ago, when Felton's Department Store burned to the ground, the old man had arrived at the scene in his nightclothes, and Merrick had offered his galoshes. Felton accepted, and soon asked the young man to give up the law and come help him rebuild the store. He had also introduced him to Sarah.

When the store reopened, railroad lines running into Milwaukee gave special rates to customers coming from a radius of a hundred miles, and some seventy thousand people thronged the store that first day. The new Felton's was a true trade palace, the finest of its kind. A huge mahogany triple fireplace stood as a symbol of the store's hospitality. On frosty mornings, when the wet and chilled ladies of Milwaukee appeared, it was the solicitous Felton who ushered them up to the glowing logs to warm themselves. It was his habit to stand with his hands behind his back, bowing graciously to the elite and plain folk alike, while Merrick Wells sat in an office upstairs making radical yet certain decisions.

Before coffee and dessert were served, Sarah asked, "Who'd like to go for a boat ride?" It was that splendid hour of the evening, and the girls were up in an instant, flying down the slope to the lakefront. They loved to ride out onto the water when the sun made a pathway of flaming orange and they could imagine it leading to somewhere. Sarah also liked to cruise in the silent electric launch, trailing her fingers in the warm lake water, which always seemed to be so smooth at this hour.

Merrick headed the launch along the shore past their next-door neighbor. "You know they're calling Moore 'the Sultan of Salt' in the *Sentinel* these days," Bloodgood announced. The amber-colored house, Springwood Lee, was even larger than Broadoaks. "I guess he's quite a man. With the exception that he's Catholic, Irish, and a consumptive."

"Jon," Sarah warned.

"Your own mother used to say she'd rather see Caroline marry a Jew than a Catholic," Merrick reminded her.

"You shouldn't say such things."

"I didn't," he responded.

As they continued around the curve of the bay, Bloodgood began shifting his weight, rocking the boat a bit in his effort to catch a glimpse of the Ulrich mansion as it appeared and disappeared amongst the elms that surrounded it.

"Look at all those bloody beasts." Jon pointed, for Ulrich had begun raising sheep and the herd covered the front lawns of Topside. "Delusions of being a gentleman farmer, I suppose."

Heinrich Ulrich had raised his three sons in this thirty-room monstrosity, described by one journalist as "neo-nothing." The eldest son had disappeared on a hunting expedition in Kenya, and Frederick had moved abroad, having earned the sorry reputation of being a dandy with a drinking problem. That left only Joseph.

Merrick considered his wife's expression as they approached the Ulrich boathouse, a gray cement construction with a red-tiled roof.

"I think it's lovely that he's tending sheep. Though when the wind blows in our direction," she confessed, "it can be a bit overpowering. I'm inviting him to our party for Caroline next Friday. We must try to get along with our neighbors, darling."

Heinrich and Merrick did not see eye to eye on the formation of the Milwaukee Water Commission. It was actually part of a bigger issue, the limits and liberties of free enterprise, and as far as Merrick Wells was concerned, Ulrich understood little about limitation of any sort.

He was down on his dock repairing the rudder to his E boat. When they cruised over close enough to say hello, he stood up with his hands on his hips. "So, what do you think?" He waved his hand toward the sheep. He was aware that this herd was causing a commotion on the east end of the lake. There were even rumors of filing a petition, though no one wanted to be the first to take that step.

"Are you breeding for wool?" Sarah asked. She was always disturbed by this gruff, stocky man, with his glowering expression and bull-like chest. Before he could answer, a bundle of sheep rushed in a swell up the hillside.

"I'm sure they're very fine animals," Merrick acknowledged, "but they keep a good many of us awake at night."

"Looks like they're making mud out of a fairly decent piece of property," Jon Bloodgood put in.

"I have no use for property that's not being properly used. What good is green grass if it's not being eaten?" Heinrich looked at Sarah in such a way that made her feel that she too was going to waste. "Now I don't have to pay some damn fool to keep it cut. Plus, I rather like having my own flock. It's a bit like having my own religion."

This shocked Isabelle. At fourteen, she had entered a vague religious phase, and she believed this comment must be blasphemous.

"They don't bother me," Helen piped up, smiling at her friend Mr. Ulrich. "They never keep me awake."

Heinrich leaned down in her direction and said, "That's because you, my dear Helen, are the only one on the east end of the lake who goes to sleep at night with a clear conscience."

Bloodgood had to laugh, while Merrick shook his head, lowering the lever that moved the boat forward. "Baby lamb braised in beer's not bad, I suppose."

"Oh, Popa," Isabelle cried, "don't say that. Look at how innocent they are."

CHAPTER TWO

S ome men cannot have enough wine in their cellars to please them, and some cannot own enough acreage to suit their sense of privacy. Almost in protest of the dominating influence of the big beer family on the lake, Merrick Wells delighted in cultivating his wine connoisseurship. Heinrich Ulrich in turn purchased every piece of available land until his 25,000 acres nearly surrounded Broadoaks.

It had begun as a kind of hobby, relief from the pressures of Kreuser Beer, but Heinrich went on to build up Ulrich Farms until it was the largest dairy breeding industry in the area. His Holsteins became internationally renowned, winning enough blue ribbons to cover the walls of his office.

It only seemed natural to open a milk and cheese operation that would butter most of the bread in Wisconsin. Neighbors came and helped themselves to his pure, fresh cream that whipped up in a couple of strokes. Ulrich's huge stretch of pastureland not only fed his cattle but also gave him the even greater pleasure of spaciousness necessary for the hunt.

It was seven o'clock in the morning when Sarah Wells rode her gelding over to Topside. Helen trotted her pony alongside. Sarah felt that Helen was far too young to participate in a hunt, but Merrick insisted that the girls be allowed to pursue their individual interests.

Riding sidesaddle down the long, winding driveway, Sarah was about to begin offering precautions, but the child looked up at her mother with such admiration. "You're good enough to come. You *should* come, Mama. You'll have a terrific time, I promise." Helen rode in the boyish manner, with jodhpurs and a smart caramel-colored jacket buttoned closely at the waist, her mother's ten-pearl pin holding down her white cravat.

They were setting up tables for the hunt breakfast, and the sound of a piano could be heard coming across the lawn. Heinrich left the gathering to greet them. Reaching down, Sarah said how pleasant it was to hear Chopin before breakfast, but Heinrich felt he had to apologize for his son's display. "Just warming up his fingers for the reins. I hope you're coming with us."

"Looks to me like a predominantly masculine group," she replied, which made her femininity even more disarming. He helped her dismount, and her smallness increased him. Taking in an extra breath, he seemed to enjoy the morning air. She saw that Addie Graf and Stephanie Barber were both there. They were wearing long riding habits, not unlike her own, and would jump sidesaddle, a feat that was beyond her sense of bravery or balance. "Don't let them distract you," she warned, glancing at the women. "I'm leaving Helen entirely in your hands."

Ulrich placed one of his large, weathered hands on Helen's shoulder and said something that startled Sarah. "All children should be girls. There would be much less regret." Then he called to his groomsman, "Jack! Hold this horse for Mrs. Wells."

The little bow-legged man spun in her direction. "Morning," Jack said, gathering the reins. He quickly took charge, smoothing the horse's flank with a firm hand. "Now this is one fine piece of horseflesh." The swarthy little man had always favored her gelding.

"Don't worry, Mama, they're dragging the scent now."

"Wouldn't want little missy hatcheting up no body," Jack teased Mrs. Wells about the mask and the brush. "You'd be surprised what she can take, though. Plenty of girls are rough."

Sarah's eye traveled out toward the two long buffet tables set up before the main house. The help was stretching out the gleaming, starched linen. After the ride there would be quite a feast – bear-meat sausage, wild duck eggs,

13 ✍

ginger-pear tart, a large assortment of muffins – but Sarah was not the least bit hungry. "You must promise me, Helen, not to take the larger jumps, but to go around through the gates. Shadow's smart, but he isn't a hunter."

Her black New Forest pony could jump like a deer, and he loved to run. Surely Shadow could keep up with the rest of them, Helen thought.

The child promised, crossed her heart to put her mother at ease, but Sarah was ill at ease that morning. She felt a tenderness for her daughter, as if some remnant of the girl still dwelt within her, and just seeing how Helen rubbed her pony's ears, and how the animal responded with a nudge that pushed the child off balance, making her laugh, gave her mother such a pang that she knew if she followed the feeling any deeper, it would lead straight to some maternal terror. She turned and there was Heinrich approaching again with two glasses of sherry. A crew of stable boys held the horses, while the gentlemen in their traditional coats and high hats drank and joked with each other. "No, no," Sarah said, for she did not drink even in the evening. "You *will* remain stable." She persisted in her concern, though he hardly looked like the kind of man who'd be affected by two small glasses of sherry.

Helen took hold of Mr. Ulrich's sleeve. "Is it true you have to fall off a horse three times in order to be a real rider?"

"That's what her father told her," Sarah explained.

"At least three times, but not while you're with me."

Sarah Wells was not a stunning woman, and yet she had a mild, soft graciousness about her that was instantly appealing to most of the men who met her – but Heinrich was not used to being moved by the sight of anyone. "We only have one saying we abide by, right?" He took the double reins to his majestic, prize-winning thoroughbred, Tyack, and swinging up into his saddle he recited, *"Uphill fast, downhill slow, on the level – let 'em go!"*

Sarah had to step back, admiring the dark bay hunter that stood almost seventeen hands. Heinrich had taken him to the International Show in London and had won first place, outshining the Kaiser as well as the king of England.

Tyack began to rock in place while Heinrich held him in, reluctant to get going with Sarah standing there. "You know," he said, "there are just a few automobiles in this country, and over twenty million horses, but you can look forward to the day – "

"When only zoos will keep horses, and man will be an emotional invalid," Lionel Hewitt finished for him. Lionel was Ulrich's great friend. He ran a tannery in Chicago, and during the summer they sailed together on the lake. He came along on these rides not because he was an avid equestrian but because Heinrich always joined him during bird hunting season, a sport that required more silence and patience than Heinrich generally had. It was a reciprocal exchange, mutually begrudged, and the sacrifice bonded their friendship.

"Lionel," Sarah reached up to take his hand while his groomsman tightened the girth on the other side. "I've been meaning to have you and Marjorie for dinner. Jon Bloodgood is with us, and we're having a small party on Friday for my sister. You remember Caroline, don't you? Heinrich," she called after him, "I hope you will come. And do bring Joseph." She knew that would please the girls.

But Heinrich had already turned his horse and acted as if he had not heard her. Signaling the release of the hounds, the haunting sound of the horn bellowed across the lawn, startling Sarah Wells. The group was off down the driveway, and when Helen turned to wave good-bye she was already far from her mother, who stood there alone watching them depart. Her young daughter seemed so reckless, far too athletic and forward for a girl. She saw how Helen trotted up next to Joseph. He was six years older, about Isabelle's age, quite a handsome, fine young gentleman.

"Look who's here," Joseph glanced down at Helen. "Are you to keep me company?"

"Only if you can keep up." She smiled, looking straight ahead, posting a little faster than the rest of the larger horses.

"We're going all the way to the Prime Woods, you know. That place is full of spooks. When I was just your age," he began telling her about the ride he had taken with his father – Heinrich had gone one way, and he had gone another. It was close to dusk and very difficult to see, when all of a sudden in the middle of the woods, Joseph had come upon a massive, all-white deer with a great big rack, and large, muscular neck – "I thought I'd seen a ghost!" he exclaimed. Even the memory of it seemed to haunt him. "But then, I was just a child." He poked her with his riding crop, amused by this charming girl's crush on him.

She sensed it, and her pride was vaguely insulted. It made her feel a bit testy. Helen had her mother's wavy brown hair, but she had bright blue eyes, and there was something saucy about her that was matched by the jogging of her pony and her fanciful cap with three feathers sticking out the side.

"Are you going to enter the show this year?" Joseph asked. His father was organizing the seventh annual Nogowogotoc Horse Show. "I imagine you'd do first rate. That pony of yours is quick."

"Yes, but he's naughty, and he hasn't any manners," she responded, letting Shadow burst into a canter. The gravel drive swerved up and over the canal that wound through the expanse of the lower property. As the horses clattered over the cement bridge, she spotted a great blue heron lifting up from the marshy foliage into the brightening morning gray. Her heart seemed to lift off with it, for Joseph had spoken to her, quite naturally too. Perhaps he would even do the relay race with her, or the spoon and egg, where you needed a partner – her fantasies flying, she maneuvered her pony closer to her old friend Mr. Ulrich, as if to seek protection.

"So how's my girl," Heinrich asked as they jogged their horses down the road. He had no girl child of his own, and he liked to think that she could have been his daughter, what with the masterful way she rode. "How do you like these old canals? Ever paddle a boat through here?"

"Mama said that Grampa Felton was offered this land, but he thought it was too swampy. Your house isn't sinking though, is it?"

"Ha," he responded. "Not yet. The most glorious city in the world, you know, has nothing but canals running through it. No horses there, I'm afraid. No streets." He tried to make light, but his heart might as well have sunk into the black depths of his own winding canals with their dark scent of waste. It was the first time in sixteen years that he had fixed upon a woman, and he was possessed by the vision of Sarah riding up that morning, in her natural linen skirt laid so carefully to the side, with her small brown boot tips sticking out, and her hands almost folded as if her mount needed no physical direction, but responded to her unspoken wish.

It was surely a lot of foolish nonsense. He was probably only disturbed because his anniversary was approaching and that brought back memories – BEER BARON MARRIES BEER BARONESS. What a match they had made. So satisfactory! For Hilda had been an heiress to the Raifstanger Brewery, and the entire population of Wisconsin had received their announcement not as mere news but as if royalty were marrying royalty.

"Don't you get lonely out here in the winter?" Helen asked Mr. Ulrich. It was hard for her to imagine anyone liking Nogowogotoc Lake with a blizzard whistling over it, all the piers pulled in, dark nights and long bone-chilling drives, terribly few parties.

But Heinrich liked the cold. "It invigorates me." He was not the socializing sort, but he had almost said yes to Sarah that morning. Instead he had turned away from her as if her invitation had not registered. Better not provoke such things. As he thought about it now – thought of watching her all evening, perhaps dancing with her, for she would be his hostess and she wanted to make amends, wanted everyone on the east end of the lake to get along – he was sure that her arrival that morning had been intentional. She had ridden right up to his front door in her finest riding habit with that innocent, sweet expression on her face, using Helen as a pretense, of that he was sure. He kicked his horse onward, for only at a gallop could he remain firmly in the moment, making those instantaneous decisions that gave his mind and constitution a singular freedom – allowing him to act with a pureness of thought, unhampered by any pondering. Excited here *en masse* with the thudding of the horses' hooves all around him, he felt the power of flight – even the bright green corn seemed lush and promising, while the entire past closed shut like an album of sepia-toned photographs.

The farmland opened up to a prairie field, and the first stone wall was still far ahead. Helen had plenty of time to decide, and she took it, not quite against her mother's wishes, for it wasn't a big jump, and easy for Shadow. She leaned forward and patted him on the shoulder, her reins gathered together for a moment. She was feeling the exertion, a little pain in her side, but she wouldn't let on, and was only sorry that she had to wear this close-fitting jacket. The hounds were apparently after something real, for there was a sudden, unplanned change in direction. The excitement of the pace, the group thundering together was powerful to her. She took the next wooden fence with certain ease. Glancing sideways, she saw Joseph take a clod of mud on the cheek, but he was looking at the hem of another young lady who had joined them on the road, Alicia Bosquet. From Helen's point of view she seemed a most competent rider, but she was horribly beautiful, her dark auburn hair caught back in a hair net.

Helen sought out Mr. Ulrich once more. She was sure that her friend was not "rude and self-serving," as her father had said, for he was building a huge grandstand for the horse show coming up, and everyone in the village would enjoy that event. He had the tallest pair of silos in the country. That was something. All that grain went to feed the cows that gave food to so many people. Dulcie-Mooie alone gave four hundred and fifty quarts of milk a week and twenty-two pounds of butter. Mr. Ulrich had also erected a horse barn with an indoor ring where Helen had learned to jump. It came naturally to her, and the next fence was easy – it was only a two-and-a-half-foot strip of brush that bordered the entrance to Crooked Lake Farm, Mrs. Orten Prime's property.

They took off down her drive now, galloping through an *allée* of maples. One careless rider got knocked down by a low-hanging branch, but his bay stopped nearby, and he was able to catch him. Sweeping himself off, the man quickly remounted.

Heinrich took an unexpected left into the woods, following the hounds, for someone had spotted a real fox and there were cries of "Tally-ho!" The wooded path ran for miles over the Kettle Moraine. There were Indian mounds back here in the shape of panther and turtle, and supposedly someone had even once found a human skull.

The lead horse crashed into the stream and all the others followed, lurching through the water. Helen gave a shout as Shadow sank up to his belly. Sprays of water soaked her boots and the calves of her jodhpurs. Alicia Bosquet lifted her black boots together, while Helen's pony paused mid-stream to violently paw water on her horse's face. Joseph laughed at the impertinence, but Alicia, quite alarmed, bent to scold the youngest rider. "What are you doing there? Can't you move that pony on?"

As they rose onto the bank, scrambling through briars, mud was flying, and the men were shouting that they had him now, had the fox securely on this two-mile island, and Helen wondered if she would actually see the kill. There was such gleeful confusion as the horses clashed together, men and horses pushing up against each other there on dry land.

Heinrich split them into groups, waving to both Helen and Joseph to follow him as one party headed off around the north end of the island, another to the south. They took the trail that cut across the island, though it looked less well maintained. Branches whipped at their faces, and Helen had to shield her eyes. Kicking to keep up with him, she cropped Shadow on, for Joseph was right behind her. They took a sharp right just as the trail dipped down, and she saw a slim birch tree had fallen across the path. Mr. Ulrich yelled a warning, "Heads up!" as Tyack took the jump, but the log lay up to Shadow's shoulder, and though the pony's heart sailed into it, and Helen leaned forward with all good intention, her mother's warning pulled her back with just enough hesitation, so that the pony's hoof caught upon the slick white bark – she felt herself plowing, her left hand out, heard the thud of the animal on the hard ground beside her, felt the snap in her thumb before she struck full force, crushing the wind from her chest with a cry that was a slap of both pain and stupidity – rolling backward on the ground, all of this in an instant – as Joseph's lathered girth flew over her.

CHAPTER THREE

*I*sabelle had heard that it was possible to canoe from Nogowogotoc Lake all the way to the Mississippi River, and she wanted to see how far they could get. Each summer she got to choose an adventure, and her father accompanied her. Now Merrick Wells unfolded the panels of the large, stiffened map, and they examined the lake country together, plotting their course from the Broadoaks dock.

Angeline, the cook, was completely devoted to Mr. Wells. She was up by five o'clock that morning to make them their breakfast and a picnic lunch. Bowls of hot oatmeal awaited them with a pewter pitcher of warm maple syrup and fresh cream from Ulrich Farms. The mornings were cool now, as if the beginning and end of each day cinched in the warm, billowy noontime weather. Angeline seemed to take pleasure in any sacrifice, whether it be sleep, food, or personal comfort. She would gladly give up her portion if anyone at the main table wanted a third helping, but Isabelle sensed in this masochistic trait a subtle form of fishing, and indeed Merrick Wells played his part in the scenario, for he was quite dependent on this grim German cook, and showered her with culinary compliments. "Incredible scones. These are perfect, Angeline."

She was pleased that he liked them, but grumbled in response. "You're not eating very many." Angeline also thought Isabelle needed more weight on her bones. Nothing seemed to cling to her frame, but that morning she was far too excited to eat.

"Do you think I'll need a jacket, Popa? I suppose I should take your old hat with the visor." Her outfit looked like something taken from the mud-room closet. "Must I really eat this horrible oatmeal?"

"That porridge is good for you!" Angeline asserted. "Go on now. You try it."

"Why don't you eat half," Merrick drew a line across the top with his knife.

"And put some currant jelly on one of those scones," Angeline instructed. "I just make it yesterday." The fresh wax sealer had been popped from the glass, and the little round mound of jelly eased out. Angeline liked it when Mr. Wells ate breakfast in her kitchen. She liked to fuss over him, pouring him more coffee before he had taken three sips. "I suppose someone's going to be in bed all morning," Angeline scolded. Angeline did not like to pamper Helen and for this, at least, Isabelle was grateful.

Helen had sprained her wrist and broken her left thumb, receiving a battery of black and blue marks from her fall. Isabelle felt the whole commotion had been intentional somehow, a device for gaining unnecessary attention. The younger sister had been brought into Broadoaks on a stretcher and examined by a doctor who carried a large, ceremonious bag, while their mother's sighs had fluttered about the room with remembered premonitions.

"I wouldn't call it so terrible," was Merrick's response. "It could have been worse, and things do happen." He had a fatalistic bent and believed less in protection than in the inevitable forward motion that unreels a life almost before a child begins breathing.

Sarah Wells thought that accidents could be prevented and that that was her job, but now she had to do everything she could to make her youngest more comfortable. She sent Isabelle running up to the third floor to fetch more pillows, and then there was the healing bath of Epsom salts, and the special veal-bone broth, followed by Helen's absolute favorite – white cherries, while her mother sat on the window seat overlooking the lake and read *Little Women* out loud. The pug was also indulged. He nestled down into the covers looking guilty but content. "Pompeii," Helen cooed, spoiling him with strokes. "Pompeii needs so much love."

So this day trip alone with her father was more than well deserved. For what did Isabelle earn in the way of attention by simply staying home and being bookish. She knew she was not as modest or as good as she appeared, for she often felt nasty, and she longed to reveal some of this inner turmoil to her father. To think she would have the entire day with him, alone.

"Now make sure you don't spill this picnic in the river." Angeline was always full of warnings. She was a small, severe woman, with amazingly strong hands that could open any stuck jar. Flour seemed to be pounded deep into the creases of her fingers, the way earth etched the hands of Kurtz, the gardener. "You've got two roast halves of chicken, some hard-boiled eggs. Don't go and squash these garden tomatoes. Here's some wine for your father – oh, *schnapps*, where's the corkscrew?" She rushed to find the implement, adding another large linen napkin and several ginger cookies, folding it all in neatly.

Looking out the window, Isabelle could see that her father had already pulled the canoe from its stand in the boathouse and eased it out beside the pier, placing the paddles perpendicular to the caned seats in preparation for her arrival. "This is plenty," she thanked the cook, and then running – "I've got to go!"

The outer skin of the canoe was a dark forest-green canvas. Merrick held the boat close to the pier while Isabelle lifted her skirts and carefully placed one foot on the bottom, inching her way across the honey-colored ribs. The canoe was long and thin and could easily tip. Once her father was seated, she pleaded, "Now let's stay dry. I don't think we need any more upsets in this family," but as soon as she had spoken, she felt the undesirable presence of her mother coming through her. Why not tip if it meant living life more fully?

Merrick pushed off from the pier with a long wooden paddle. He sat in back where he could guide the course of the boat. They set up a rhythm, five strokes on a side, so that neither arm would get too tired, and then, shifting, they made an arc of droplets in the air. She liked to see the paddle digging into the green lake water.

"It looks like we've got a perfect day," her father said, as if to congratulate her on the selection.

"And to think Mama wanted me to go in town to be fitted for a dress." There had been much talk about a party at Mr. and Mrs. Lionel Hewitt's, to celebrate the horse show at the end of the summer season.

Isabelle was old enough to be invited, but she had displayed no interest, and this displeased her mother. "I don't know what kind of girl would rather go canoeing like an Indian."

"I wish I *were* an Indian. I wish we lived in a tent."

Sarah feared her older daughter leaned toward the eccentric. Isabelle liked to sympathize with anyone oppressed.

"Mr. Hewitt used to see Indians right here on Nogowogotoc," Isabelle told her mother. "He saw smoke from their campfires right on our property. I just wonder where the Potowatomi are now."

"I'm sure they've moved up north, where it's wilder," her mother reasoned. "They don't like civilization. And I really can't have you acting like one." This seemed unfair, for Helen was the unruly daughter. "If you keep this up," Sarah persisted, "you'll end up like my sister." She meant an old maid, a spinster, a weight and embarrassment for the maternal family – but Isabelle loved her Aunt Clickey, who was as nervous and excitable as Sarah was calm.

"Mother wishes I'd been a boy," Isabelle announced to her father. They were halfway across the lake, heading for the Nogowogotoc River. She dug her paddle into the water with such force he was afraid she would tire herself out. Merrick understood that Isabelle was at that age when emotions take on an exaggerated life of their own, and any little feeling can become overwhelming.

"I'm sure your mother loves you just as you are."

Isabelle almost laughed. "Oh Popa, how can you notice what goes on? You have so much to do. Helen has her projects, and no one dares stop her, and Mother has her garden. I simply don't fit." She paddled along for a while, thinking. "You know that watercolor Mama bought from Emily Groom? That big, beautiful bouquet? Well, I'm like that one flower, dangling from the vase, about to drop on the floor."

"But that flower is what makes the painting interesting. Otherwise it would be totally lacking in tension."

"But when you're a girl," she turned back to regard him and the boat shifted slightly, "it's not nice to be always so interesting. Especially under

Mother's scrutiny. I wouldn't mind it away from home." Now Isabelle was inching closer to the subject she wanted to discuss.

"There's the opening." Her father pointed out the mouth of the river, and they both rested for a moment, laying their paddles down across the frame. Merrick gazed down into the water and saw a large school of walleye. "Blazes," he said, "I should have brought my rod."

As they moved down river, seaweed caught on their paddles. Approaching a low cement bridge, Merrick called out, "Watch your head," as their boat went gliding beneath the echoing archway, and swallows dove from their mud-clinging nests, soaring out into the shock of daylight. Merrick Wells was partial to each of his children in different ways, one being so similar to him, the other opposite in nature.

In most families it was the younger child who had to make an effort to keep up, but Helen was the leader, and this seemed unnatural to Isabelle. "She takes such glee in beating me at everything. I was just teaching her jacks, you know those little metal things, where you pop up the ball and scoop up the jacks, but she not only learned it, she won the game too. She beats me always! It's just not fair."

"It's not fair that she wins?"

"It's not right that she takes such pleasure in beating me. She's nearly triumphant, and gloats about it too."

Merrick agreed that that must be hard to take. "Perhaps you should have someone your own age out for a visit before school begins."

"Potter could come. We've been writing all summer." Isabelle was forever sitting on the end of the dock waiting for the mail boat to arrive. "I suppose we'll have to keep corresponding. She's getting ready for Miss Baldwin's School back east. Popa, do you think I might go next semester?"

"Well," he paused, "I haven't given this any thought." He had to push through the marshy curve in the river where the sediment had risen almost to the level of the boat's bottom. Isabelle gripped the wooden bar that ran across the bow.

"I just want to feel *hungry* for something."

"Do you think you're being too well fed? Intellectually, I mean. That doesn't speak too badly for Milwaukee Downer."

"I don't know, but just sitting around here all summer, I feel like I'll spend the rest of my life on some great big cushion. I feel so . . . *drowsy*."

"So you don't like the easy life either. You know your mother's world and mine are really quite different. One of your greatest handicaps is going to be overcoming your advantages. Most people have so many obstacles to surmount it keeps them very busy, but you could have time on your hands. When so much is given, it's difficult to find out what you want out of life."

She didn't know what she needed, she only felt she did not belong at the Hewitts' party with Alicia Bosquet inspecting her shoes. "Mother hates me because I'm the laughing stock."

"Your mother doesn't hate you, darling. She just wants you to look nice."

"She wants everything to look nice."

"Is that so bad? You might think of going to this party as a kind of challenge. You can still be yourself and dress as you like, but you should try to develop a little self-confidence. Maybe then I could trust you to go away to school."

This gave Isabelle hope. Her dark brown hair, parted in the middle, was pulled back with a string, as if she were ready for study. She wore the same oval, metal-rimmed spectacles as her father. Ribbons and finery and lace did not suit her, but she did want to please him more than anything in the world. "I'll go if you want me to, Popa."

All of a sudden they heard the blast from a shotgun, and Isabelle dropped her paddle in the river. Her father had to dish it out just as the current picked up and their boat threatened to turn sideways. Merging with the Rock River, they saw a low barge on the far bank. It held two slovenly looking, bearded hunters and their big, surly dog. The sight of the men was alarming to Isabelle. They were nothing like the elegant hunters she was used to tolerating. They were drinking whiskey from a jug, and the mongrel seemed to sneer as they cruised on by. Merrick lifted a hand in greeting, before the larger one called, "Big tree down 'cross there. Your little lady better be wearing her high rubber boots," and then they laughed as if picturing her up to her hips in mud. They couldn't seem to get over it. Merrick did not respond, but pushed the boat on with even deeper strokes, and Isabelle's matched his, eager to get away.

Once out of sight of the hunters, Merrick pulled out his spy glasses. He was hoping they could just drift for a while, and he could spot some unusual birds along the shore. He kept a list in a notebook in one of his many pockets, and he was eager to find a yellow-bellied sapsucker, *Sphyrapicus varius*, a small, elusive bird of the woodpecker family, but they only saw some small green herons and red-winged blackbirds, nothing unusual.

"Don't you wish we lived on a river?" she asked. "Lakes are so stagnant."

"Our lake isn't stagnant. It's spring fed."

"But you could *drink* this water. It's heavenly, isn't it? *All rivers begin in the clouds.*" Large cumulus clouds were now staggering above them. In Wisconsin the weather often changed five times a day. "They're just like stiffened egg whites, aren't they? Slipped from the bowl?"

"More women in this family seem to be interested in poetry. First your mother and now you."

"But that's different," Isabelle complained. "She doesn't want to look at what's ugly or unpleasant, and you have to if you're going to write."

"I see." He smiled, though from her forward position she could not perceive his amusement. "Looks like those gentlemen back there were correct." He pointed out the large trunk of an elm that had fallen across the river. "Must have been struck by lightning. We'll have to portage around. Back paddle, pry!" he instructed, for the Rock had a good bit of rush to it. Isabelle panicked and stuck out her paddle to catch the bow from smacking the horizontal trunk. There was deep brush on both sides of the river, and her boots were only ankle high.

Merrick thought it best if she took off her shoes. There was no one around, and she could hoist up her skirts. She did as she was told, and he was discreet and didn't look at her slim white calves as she stepped from the boat into the cold rush of water. She made a quick retreat back into a warm little pool that had formed a muddy inlet, while Merrick pushed the canoe up through stiff brush onto the bank. Together they would have to carry it, but as he helped her onto the spongy ground, she saw the horrible clot on her ankle – "Oh!" she shrieked. "Look – get it off of me, quick! Do something, Popa."

He grabbed the shaker of salt from the picnic basket and after a vigorous application, he plucked the tiny bloodsucker off with a fork.

Isabelle examined the spot, feeling faint, while Merrick unscrewed the metal thermos of cider. It was cool and sweet, and it served to revive her.

Paddling onward, she could not help wondering why God had made something so repulsive, unless it was necessary to offset the beautiful. The glittering surface of the water was lovely but deceptive, for there were slimy, horrible creatures down below.

Isabelle confessed that she had watched their yard man hatcheting that capon the other day. Blood had sprayed all over his shirt. "But I couldn't shame Tai for bringing it back to us."

"She's a natural killer, that dog."

"But that's part of her beauty, don't you think? That she is such a dog, not just a silly pet, like Mrs. Valenschein's terrier. He wears a ruby-studded collar and a blue silk jacket for her garden parties. And those men back there, I bet they take pleasure in seeing things drop from the sky."

"They probably need the food."

"I suppose, but I would wager they also like to kill. Tai was bringing us an offering."

"Maybe it's just instinct for a dog."

"I think it's necessity," Isabelle answered. "It isn't sport, or fun, but necessity." She paused, realizing something.

And her father knew – if she wanted that, she would have to find it for herself. He could never provide it.

CHAPTER FOUR

No one could tell if she had recovered adequately to be riding or if she was simply too willful to be denied. In any case, Helen Wells had talked her father into letting her participate in the Ulrich Farms Horse Show, though he did make one concession to his wife – Helen could only ride in a single class, any one of her choice.

Isabelle decided not to attend the show, for the sun had been making her feel ill and she had never been even the least bit horsey. Her father also decided to stay home in order to catch up on his personal mail. Sarah would have to sit in their box alone, but she was eager to witness the mysterious costume Helen had been preparing with Fraulein Reusner. It was a glorious day for the event, clear and warm. The country spectators began arriving, filling the twenty-plank bleachers. The forty boxes constructed in the grandstand had been washed a pale blue-green, which seemed to set off the colors of the ladies' dresses.

On arriving, Sarah was immediately deserted by her daughter, who ran off to find Jack, while Fraulein Reusner was instructed to quickly follow the child. Everyone, it seemed, had someone to sit with, and suddenly Sarah Wells felt slightly resentful of her husband. He should have been there to escort her. She nodded calmly to her many friends and acquaintances, stopping to chat with the reclusive, horse-loving Montgomery Ward. He was a short, stocky man with a Teddy Roosevelt mustache. He parted his hair in the middle, and Sarah always thought he looked as though he wore a pair of little horns. "I can't seem to pry the girls away from your latest catalogue," she told him, getting a whiff of the half-smoked cigar he clenched between his teeth. "They're discovering things they need that I never knew existed."

"That's the point," he said, unwilling to get into a real conversation.

Sarah moved on. Mr. Schraeger, the pork packing prince, was sitting with Mr. Schultz and his family. Even a few politicians were there, the governor from Madison and the mayor from Milwaukee. The grandstand was comfortably covered by a green-and-white striped awning, though most of the women also carried parasols, which they tilted for effect as much as for shade.

When Heinrich Ulrich noticed Sarah Wells sitting unattended, he sprang from his seat and rushed across the ring, insisting that she join him in the judges' gazebo. "Please," he insisted, "you can't sit here alone. You'll get a much better view, and it would please me."

Sarah was grateful for his attention, and could not think of why she shouldn't accompany him. She felt piqued to be sitting by herself with no one to talk to, and Heinrich made her feel like the guest of honor. She took his arm and let him lead her around by the gate and across the dusty ring. He assumed a very cordial air – "Now watch your step" – as they climbed the makeshift boards up into the gazebo. She almost felt that she should turn and curtsey as a response to this show of gentility. He was a strange, awesome man, not the customary gentleman, and it put her slightly on guard.

Heinrich explained to her that one of the main purposes of the show was to encourage local breeding. "We need more and more plain, good stock, not just for farm work and riding, but for driving and coach. Almost all the farm entries are county."

"I heard you turned your horses out to pasture, so more visitors could board." She considered that a true act of hospitality. He nodded, glad to acknowledge the fact, as if he had only intended to please her. At that moment she saw beneath his tough, almost brutish exterior, down to the well-concealed softness within.

For a moment Heinrich was glad, and the sensation was so unusual that he felt he must stand and pace around the gazebo, not only to organize the other judges, but to order his own careening thoughts. When he sat back down, he said, "Mrs. Dickenson, over there, had her groomsman spread an Oriental carpet in front of her brood mare's stall. Jack thought his stable was being turned into a brothel." He immediately regretted sharing this vulgar anecdote.

Though such an allusion might have put her off, she actually found that his mentioning the unmentionable excited her. This man's physical presence seemed to cast a net that entrapped her. The best she could do was to remain very still and let the feeling pass.

Quickly changing the subject, he told her that he would not be competing with Tyack that day, but that he would give a jumping demonstration later in the afternoon. Tyack could easily take a jump of 5'10" and had been known to clear a six-foot pole.

Passively Sarah absorbed all this information, but then turning to the gate she cried, "Oh my!" as a wicker pony cart containing three little girls in pink, yellow, and blue signaled the beginning of the show. The girls wore matching bonnets and wide ribbon sashes that rippled behind them as they bounced around the ring. Sarah reached to touch Heinrich's arm, and pulled him slightly closer.

Alice Prime had organized this part of the show. A polished George IV phaeton with two high-stepping hackneys entered the ring followed by a parade of ladies and gentlemen in a variety of horse-drawn vehicles – park drags and gigs, buggies and buckboards, an old restored British road coach painted a dark green, and finally, a six-in-hand of Shetlands pulling a miniature gilt-painted carriage with an equally tiny princess waving from inside. The entire audience gave a cheer of delight. "Now where is Helen?" Sarah scanned the audience. "I *hope* she is watching."

Just then a bright blue Cadillac cabriolet attempted to join the procession, but the automobile's entrance was blocked by Jack at the gate. Heinrich stood up. Picking up the announcer's megaphone, he shouted at the driver – "Go get a horse!" The crowd applauded, for they had not come to witness the interchangeable parts of some new-fangled machine, though plenty of curious boys gathered around the automobile.

Sarah was endeared even further to Heinrich when she commented, "Don't you think a horseless carriage is an unfortunate sight?"

"It's a kind of amputation. You cut out the vitality and you have mere power without life."

His tone both comforted and disturbed her. She found it difficult to focus on the first class of the morning, Suitable Stallions, led by their careful groomsmen. Jack walked out with a bit of a limp, but he was the proudest man in the ring, parading Heinrich's sorrel, Dance Card.

But now the audience was ready for a contest, and the show seemed to gather momentum. There was a whooping from the railbirds as Alicia Bosquet entered the ring on her saddlebred, Sensation. There was also a murmuring from the box seats, both awe-inspired whispers as well as frowns of disapproval, for she was wearing a bright green silk jacket from Paris with a matching split sidesaddle skirt, while the other six contestants were dressed in conservative dark brown, plain navy, or gray, with boiled shirts and simple bowler hats. Alicia's hat was rakishly set with a peacock feather hanging past her shoulder. "Look at that brooch," Sarah commented. It was said that the jewel box of Miss Bosquet's tack room almost matched the splendor of her personal gems, and the sight of her that morning gave every man a thrill, no matter how inappropriate she was.

"I'm afraid my Joseph's fallen under that woman's spell."

Sarah seemed to sympathize, but added, turning to him, "Can one control such things?"

Alicia's horse *was* marvelous, especially when it began to "rack on," lifting and placing each separate foot, a smooth gait that was popular in the show ring because of its artifice. Ulrich, however, disapproved of the breed. "No real lady would ride such an animal." He didn't care for the high carriage of the tail, achieved by cutting and bracing, nor for the exaggerated step acquired from heavily weighted shoes, but he had to concede with the other judges that her horse was both strong and collected, the best of the group. She had guided that power and tension in a seemingly effortless manner, and he had to appear magnanimous presenting her with the cup.

On receiving the trophy, Alicia winked at Mr. Ulrich, and his opinion of her was underscored. "That was a most unpleasant duty." He sat back down next to Sarah. "Now this is more to my taste." It didn't matter so much in the Open Jumping Class what the horse or rider looked like. Performance was everything. The hunter could even leave the triple bar rocking as long as the pole didn't fall. "This shows the true heart of an animal," he insisted, but Sarah was distracted, wondering if Helen were all right and if Fraulein Reusner had found her.

Joseph Ulrich entered the ring and took the first jump in a perfect arc. Heinrich pointed out the importance of timing the takeoff and landing, so that they were equidistant from the jump itself. "Amity never falters," he said of the mare. "Actually, jumping is judged on a horse not getting too high. It's a tendency they often have." Heinrich refrained from clapping when his son left the ring, though his eagerness showed in the way he leaned forward, both elbows propped on his knees. The next rider took the high-crossed poles and the railroad gate exceedingly high. No one heard a single nick, but the effort seemed ungraceful. The final entry spooked over the triple bar, and the rider hit the ground with a thud. When the boy didn't move, Joseph cantered his horse back into the ring and sprang down to assist him, but the stunned rider managed to get back onto his feet. Another four entries followed, but no one was surprised when Joseph won the Hilda Ulrich Memorial Trophy, an ornate piece of silver with an angel on the lid.

Alicia Bosquet had managed to change costumes as well as horses before the Lady Hunter Class began. She was now dressed entirely in bleached white linen, and Sarah speculated, not unkindly, on how long that would remain looking so clean. The outfit was striking against the black sheen of Alicia's four-year-old. She did look comfortable and secure mounted sidesaddle. Two women from out of state shocked Sarah by straddling their mounts like unabashed men. "Everything's changing, too fast for me," Sarah said to Heinrich. What was becoming of the natural modesty of women?

He was now focused on the next rider, whose horse made low, clean flights over the seven varied fences. He pointed out how the gelding kept his forelegs tucked up high, and Sarah appreciated his expertise, saying how grateful she was to be out in the ring with someone so knowledgeable.

The words they exchanged were brief yet empowered with a special intensity. The day seemed finer than most days, the sun brighter, more warm, the bonbon he offered lemony, delicious. She breathed deeply and noticed the delightful, earthy smell of everything about her. She felt uncommonly well. Completely alive.

Finally the children's classes began. Ulrich asked her if she would judge the Lead Line Class. The children were four to six years old, all dressed up in hunting attire, with caps and coats and breeches. The youngest boy stood in his stirrups as he passed the gazebo and called out, "Look at me!" There were six contestants and only five ribbons, but Sarah insisted on giving something to each child – blue, red, yellow, green, and two pink.

The German polka band began to play, and keg after keg of Kreuser Beer flowed. One farm couple began to dance on the sidelines and another followed suit. Sarah felt like hopping up and clapping along. The smell of grilled bratwurst and roasted corn filled the air. Heinrich poured Sarah a glass of spring water while he moistened his mustache with beer foam and sat there grinning. He reminded her that Helen's class, Children Under Twelve Jumping in Costume, was the next event, and Sarah felt her stomach tighten.

Libby Keikhaefer, the first entry, rode into the ring as an Indian princess. This chubby little girl was all flying pigtails on her pony, Teepee, whose name must have been the inspiration for her outfit. She dropped her bow when her pony balked before the chicken coop, but she was good-natured and simply shrugged her shoulders and trotted on out. Then there was a very convincing Abraham Lincoln, followed by Mr. Lapham's grandson riding around the ring dressed as a frontiersman. He had a real rifle hooked to his saddle and wore a coontail cap.

Riding was one of the few sports in which both boys and girls alike could compete on equal ground, Merrick Wells had reminded Sarah that morning, but she didn't know why they should pretend to be equal as children when as adults they certainly were not. She felt it might encourage Helen's passionate nature, and that she would ultimately be disillusioned. But now Sarah forgot all her reasoning when her daughter galloped into the show ring riding bareback as a Cossack!

She came racing around the ring so fast observers had to pull back away from the rail. She held a cardboard sword on high, and her billowing pants and white sleeves blew, while a little round cap hid her hair. Sarah sat there paralyzed, though the crowd seemed to love it – how that youngster could brandish her golden sword, how fierce she looked with her tight red vest and long black make-believe mustache!

Sarah fell back into her seat and wished she had had the forethought to warn somebody. How could Fraulein Reusner have encouraged this? Helen circled Shadow at a full gallop, and with her one good hand, she turned the pony toward the jumps. She never once lost her balance, quite a feat for a bareback riding jumper only ten years old.

Jack could be seen holding on to the gate, following each jump as if he were astride. He knew his girl could do it. No doubt he was muttering some secret communications, but Helen heard nothing as she circled the ring, taking jump after jump till all six were completed.

The only trouble now was that the pony wouldn't stop. Shadow clamped his bit firmly in his teeth and persisted at a runaway gallop. The little Cossack took her cardboard sword and smacked him over the head, breaking the sword in two. Laughter rose with the dust that circled the ring, while large tears formed in Helen's eyes as she whipped around and around. She knew she would be disqualified. With only one good hand, she did not have the strength to stop her pony. Normally, she would have sawed him down.

Jack leapt over the gate into the ring as they approached once more, stepping out to raise his arms up – "Hey!" The pony responded, coming to an abrupt halt that threw Helen onto his neck. Jack grabbed the reins and gave them a good yank. "You gol' darn rascal. I'm gonna take a bite out of yer misbehavin' ear!" But then he turned to Helen and said, "His blood got up, don't worry about it. You was the winner all right, except for this bum."

The crowd was in agreement, for they rose and gave her a standing ovation. Jack released the pony, and Shadow jogged on out, while Helen turned and waved to the audience, feeling the confused elation of victorious defeat.

Her mother, Sarah Wells, was exhausted.

CHAPTER FIVE

*W*hile Helen was flying about the ring before an audience of hundreds, Isabelle was having a private conference with her father. Merrick Wells had decided, and Sarah had agreed, that if Isabelle applied and was accepted, she could join her friend Potter the following semester at Miss Baldwin's School back east.

They were together in the living room that also served as his summer study. A large mahogany desk with a two-shade Tiffany lamp sat before the window seat where Isabelle liked to sit.

"I've always wanted you to have your own independence," her father began, "and I think you should have some experience handling financial matters yourself. It will be good practice."

Though Isabelle was thrifty, with a good mind for math, proud that he trusted her maturity, the child in her still wanted her father to take care of these things.

"When your mother and I were first married," he went on, "your Grandfather Felton was extremely generous. He gave us this summer house as a wedding present, and throughout the years he's passed on the department store holdings to your mother and Aunt Clickey. Now I want to do something of the same. Gradually, of course. This October, for your fifteenth birthday, I plan on depositing one hundred thousand dollars in stocks, bonds, and cash into your account. I shall do the same for Helen in April."

This bit of news sobered Isabelle, dampening her excitement about going away to school, as if this exorbitant gift were a weight, a burden, bordering on the ominous.

"I think it's extremely important for a sense of family harmony," her father wrapped up the discussion, "to always give the same amount to each child. I've seen more family grief come from financial favoritism, and of course I love you both equally."

"Yes, Popa," Isabelle acknowledged.

He got up from his chair rather stiffly and walked to the window that overlooked the lake. Almost as an afterthought he added, "But I love your mother most of all." A white-breasted nuthatch was walking headfirst down the bark of a tree just outside. "I hope you'll accompany her to the party this evening. I had to decline the invitation. Hewitt knows how I feel about the tannery, and what they're doing to the river."

The Hewitt Tannery of Chicago had bought out a large Milwaukee firm, and there was no indication that the pollution would stop. A nauseating stench rose from the sewage and untreated refuse that was dumped right into the Milwaukee River. Grease fires had even been seen burning on the water. Merrick Wells was using his legal knowledge to set up a Water Commission, and in turn he was receiving some negative social pressure from certain powerful families on the lake.

"I'll go tonight if you want me to, Popa, but given the situation, I don't see how it's a favor to you."

When Sarah and Isabelle were ready to go that evening, Merrick came downstairs to inspect his daughter. "Let me see you. My, you look lovely," he beamed, and she was almost convinced, turning in an awkward circle. She wore a delicate gown of white mulle, and her brown hair was swept up from her neck with a large navy ribbon pinned to the back of her head. "You might surprise yourself," he kissed her cheek, "and have a tolerable time."

"I'm only doing this on a dare," she reminded him.

"Yes," he chuckled, "an exercise in social courage. Well, we all need that."

"Constance Hewitt should be there. We can eat together, I hope."

"Don't ignore all the young gentlemen. You don't want to break too many hearts."

The carriage was waiting outside, and a single thought flew through Isabelle's mind as she turned to join her mother – that if ever a heart were broken, it would probably be her own.

Turning out of the driveway they took a left on the narrow gravel road that connected the four large properties on the east end of the lake. Leaning toward the open window, she caught a glimpse of the Vintrys', and then farther on, the large metal gates to the Hawkshursts' house. There were no stone pillars before the entrance to the Hewitts' summer place, and Isabelle liked the lack of pretension. Only a small wooden sign hung from a horizontal oak limb, reading Hewitt's Point. The Hewitts' driveway wound back through the woods for at least two miles, and as they approached the white clapboard "cottage" that rose from the bluff, the lake could be seen on either side of the point, with spangles of moonlight all over it.

When the coachman opened the door to their carriage, and Isabelle heard the music from the orchestra, she believed she was going to be sick.

"Don't be ridiculous. It's just that you haven't eaten. Once you're inside, it will be so gay, you'll forget all about yourself."

But Isabelle clung to her mother's arm, and on entering the party, there was such a splash of light and song and conversation, she felt overwhelmed by the dizzying swirl. She groped for the first familiar person she saw – Auntie Maeve talking to her Aunt Clickey.

"That woman ought to be suppressed! Oh Sarah, *finally* you're here. And Isabelle, what a dream! Where did you get that exquisite gown?"

"At Felton's," she answered, and the women all laughed, for of course she had gotten it there.

"Is Jon Bloodgood behaving himself?" Sarah asked her sister, for she had been hoping that something might develop. Caroline Felton would be twenty-eight that year, and Jon, being a bachelor and close family friend, was a prime possibility, in fact, their only hope.

"One is never bored with Jon in the vicinity," Maeve Peckham laughed, and her keen social eye scanned the party. There he was, almost telepathically lifting his glass to her.

Maeve turned back to Sarah. "I was just saying that I got a letter from Elsa Field the other day confessing the most dreadful things. I think she has fixated somehow on our Jon, though he's given her no encouragement whatsoever."

As Maeve went on, Aunt Clickey took Isabelle aside to compliment her on her dress, and to assure her they were not making fun of it. "It's the prettiest gown in the room. But isn't this fun? Do you think you'll dance? I hope I will." Isabelle thought her aunt's mood seemed exceptionally high, and it was hard for her to imagine how the rather rotund and boastful Jon Bloodgood could have a helium effect on anyone.

"So what do you think, do you have your eye on some boy?"

Isabelle had to admit that she could barely focus, though she was beginning to adjust to the pace of the party. As long as she did not have to move, she would be all right. But there were so many bits of conversation going on in all directions, it was confusing. "Harriet is such an old worry wart," she heard Bill Hawkshurst laugh, inciting a few others to laugh along with him. "I tell her she's only allowed to worry on Wednesdays." Mrs. Valenschein was going on about money, how it didn't mean a thing to her, except for the pleasure it gave others by spending it. Mrs. Hewitt told an out-of-towner that she must make their place her home, while another woman contradicted the offer and said confidentially, "Do no such thing. She thinks she means what she says, but she'd resent it if you stayed. I know her."

Aunt Clickey seemed all eagerness that evening, as if she could not bear to stand still, her eyes springing about the room in time with the music, but then she spied Frank Schraeger. "Oh dear," she said. "Maeve has become so matter-of-fact since breaking off with that man. But my, he does look glamorous. Don't you think so?"

Isabelle was not impressed by what other people considered handsome. "Frankfurter" Schraeger had a semicircle of women around him – he was sipping alternately from two glasses of champagne, as if he could not decide which goblet to drink from.

"I hear he's very different from his father. Old Mr. Schraeger's only interest in life is pigs. Since they're asleep by nine o'clock, so is he."

"They're smarter than you'd think," Isabelle inserted, and for a moment her aunt thought she was referring to the Schraeger family. "If you put twenty-four pigs in a barn, they'll split into groups of twelve. They never dung where they sleep like most animals."

Aunt Clickey gave a little shriek of amusement. "Wherever do you learn such things! Really, you amaze me."

Maeve came up and joined them, whispering to Isabelle, "You must watch where you leave your heart. Falling in love is something that can be absolutely controlled, and you simply mustn't let yourself fall in love with an undesirable person."

Isabelle wondered if the handsome Mr. Schraeger hadn't been a bit too desirable, and therefore a dreadful mistake. It was said that the Schraeger meat packing plant had found a use for every part of the pig, save the squeal. Perhaps that was reserved for Frank's women.

"Isabelle, darling," Marjorie Hewitt swept up and whisked her away, just as Jon Bloodgood approached her two maiden aunts with a humorous swagger, as if wondering which one of them wanted to dance with him the most. Socializing seemed so complicated to Isabelle that she longed to sit down somewhere. Luckily she was delivered right into the arms of Constance Hewitt.

"Now you girls must cheer each other up," Mrs. Hewitt chastised them, dashing on in her effort to circulate.

"Mother thinks we're both melancholic," Constance explained, "that we should have a homeopathic effect upon each other. If she only knew," Constance beamed, "I've never been so happy in my entire life." Constance, though four years older, pulled Isabelle off to the side like an intimate. "I really must talk to you. I have such an exquisite burden to unload. Let's go take a look at the buffet."

A large autumnal centerpiece graced the table, using the purple-streaked, crinkled leaves of kale, orange and yellow flowers as well as gourds and nuts – one of Tommy Wolff's creations. On either side there were platters of stuffed squab, breast of partridge, canvasback duck Cumberland, mounds of wild rice, *pâté de compagne*, tiny muffins, diced beets, and a tree made of Brussels sprouts. Tiny maple leaves were carefully pressed onto each Gebhardt cake, and to the side there was a small rowboat containing clams, shrimp, and cracked lobster tails on ice.

An exuberant laugh came from the center of the dance floor. Both Constance and Isabelle turned and stared. Alicia Bosquet was wearing both of her bright blue ribbons, earned just that morning, on either shoulder of her crimson dress. Her sapphire necklace and earrings matched the color of the ribbons, and with her auburn hair she was the most dazzling woman in the room.

"It's a good thing she didn't win a third," Isabelle remarked. "Where would she put it?"

"Joseph Ulrich certainly seems interested."

"She must be at least two years older." Isabelle did not think much of the match, but her comment struck a nerve.

"Why is there always such a fuss made over a man's height and a woman's age? Not to mention religion and social standing. My mother has limited my possibilities down to none. But don't you worry," Constance took Isabelle's arm.

Joseph came and stood to the side of the grand piano. The girls saw him pour an amber-colored liquid from his silver flask into the punch cup he was holding. His thick yellow hair looked perpetually tousled, and his eyes began to scan the room before they stopped upon Alicia. He confessed to Colin Hewitt, "My, but I'm strong for Miss Bosquet. She's the whole damn menu, including the drinks!" The two boys drained their cups. Then, setting them down, they approached the animated dance floor.

"Do you think you'd like to dance with Colin?" Constance asked her friend.

"Certainly not," Isabelle was mortified. "I mean, I just want to sit here and listen to your news. Please."

"You promise, cross your heart, you won't tell a soul? Not even your sister?"

Isabelle promised. The only thing she had to tell Helen was that Joseph Ulrich had other amorous interests. She had no empathy or understanding for Helen's crush.

"Well," Constance whispered, "Father bought a car. A large car for traveling between here and Chicago."

Constance seemed breathless, and Isabelle thought this attitude very queer. "Is it so horrible to have an automobile? My father has a very open mind about them."

"Oh, not at all. It's a wonderful car. It's an all-white Winton, with green leather seats and a bulb horn klaxon, but what's really amazing about the car isn't the car," she paused, "it's the man who drives it, Haven Rose. I believe I've fallen in love with him."

"You've fallen in love with your chauffeur?"

"Oh, but Isabelle, you don't know him," Constance insisted. "You've never seen a kinder man. He's so generous and thoughtful. Handsome too. I can't stop thinking about him."

"Well I do like the sound of his name." Isabelle tried to be encouraging, though she could already hear what her mother would say, and her mother's friends. Was love really worth causing such a scandal?

"We've only recently spoken about it," Constance went on, no stopping her now. "We were both so amazed that the feeling was mutual. He does want to do the right thing, to be aboveboard and responsible."

Isabelle believed the only right thing for him to do would be to resign immediately and flee his position, but an unshakable sincerity entered her friend's voice.

"You must try to understand. Look around this room. Look at Mitzi." Her younger sister was dancing with a loud and slightly drunken boy from a wealthy Chicago family. He looked like a boor, though Mrs. Hewitt thought him charming. "Do you think he could ever possibly make my sister happy?"

Isabelle didn't believe one found real happiness in a man. It was something one found within oneself. "But would this Haven of yours fit in? Do you think it's fair, I mean – wouldn't it be awfully difficult for him too?"

"He's not afraid, if that's what you mean. He's more of a gentleman than any man here, of that I can assure you. He wants to be a doctor, to do things for people. I want to be with him every day for the rest of my life. I can't tell you how completely I feel this."

Constance was lost in her own thoughts now. Isabelle's mother stood alone in the doorway, gazing out at the dancers. Mr. Ulrich came up and spoke to her, and after some discussion, she seemed to acquiesce, and they began to do a slow fox trot. He appeared to be a little out of practice, as if stiff and rusty from disuse, but Isabelle also noticed that her mother's soft and flowing manner seemed to put him at ease.

Sarah Wells looked up into Heinrich's face. "I've been so worried about Helen." Sarah knew that he cared a great deal for her daughter, and this encouraged her sympathy for him. "I just wish I could teach her how to be more cautious. She has no idea. Children don't realize they can hurt themselves."

"Or hurt their parents by hurting themselves." His face took on a pained expression. It was difficult for him to enjoy himself. "I've been meaning to tell you, the Hunt Committee decided no children under the age of sixteen will be allowed to ride up front anymore, only behind with the groomsmen where there isn't much excitement." The groomsmen often followed the hunt in case one of the gentlemen fell or needed assistance. "I wasn't so afraid for her this morning," he continued. "The pony was confined within the ring. But what bothers me is that I was the one who gave her that animal."

"Oh, but she adores him! She wouldn't part with him for the world."

He smiled down at Sarah, exerting a slightly greater pressure against her lower back. She glanced about the dance floor to see if anyone noticed, but she caught no one's gaze – no eyes noted her. After all, there was nothing unusual. It was just that Heinrich was so much larger than her husband.

"You didn't tell me this morning," he said in all seriousness, "what you think of that Bosquet girl."

"I don't like to say unpleasant things about anyone."

"Joseph seems quite taken with her."

"That's most unfortunate," was Sarah's reply.

"My sentiments exactly. *Reinheitsgebot* – if he'd only think of that." This centuries-old purity law strictly forbade the use of any artificial ingredient in the making of good lager.

George Bosquet's paternal ancestors had been French traders and trappers. His mother's side had been prominent in the lumbering industry in Quebec, but his mother had a dash of Indian blood, and some of that savage spirit had obviously been passed on to Alicia. In any case, there was too much gossip surrounding the family. George Bosquet, also a widower, had recently announced his engagement to an actress from New Orleans who was blonde, petite, and a bit of a tart. Alicia was furious because the woman was not much older than she was, and the marriage put her inheritance into question.

Mr. Bosquet, not present at the party, was a relative newcomer to Wisconsin. He had built the most outlandish mansion on the lake, an exact imitation of some castle on the Rhine, and he had spelled out the name of the property, Bon Pres, with white stones and coleus all along the bank. Surely his daughter would be lacking in any practicality, not to mention good taste or common sense.

Heinrich did not dare mention to Sarah that he had his eye on Helen for Joseph. He realized that such a proposal, while Helen was still so young, would be a shock to her mother, but he believed that it was a marriage he could heartily encourage, a match his son would never regret. "It was very pleasant having your company this morning," Ulrich said awkwardly as the song came to a close. He walked Sarah from the floor to the far side of the room, near the closed porch door.

His uneasiness was endearing to her. "I enjoyed it too. You know so much about horses. I felt like I'd taken a course."

"I haven't been around women much since Hilda passed away. Not for sixteen years, to be exact." A long time for a man in his social and economic position, but the more people tried to set him up with some appropriate lady, the more he withdrew from society altogether. Lionel Hewitt understood him perfectly, and never allowed Marjorie to waste her matchmaking skills on Heinrich.

But now he felt stifled, as if his necktie were binding. He asked Sarah if she would take a breath of fresh air with him, and for a moment she was worried – it seemed as if he were having some sort of attack or palpitation. But out on the porch he regained himself. The stars were brilliant pricks of light scattered amongst the turning leaves.

"*Adorned with a celestial diadem, the night sky turns her head.*" She walked over to the railing and looked out across the water. "I do love Indian summer – don't you?"

"Yes," he said, "but Sarah . . . " He offered her his coat, because the evening air was cooling. Suddenly she felt that it was getting late, and glancing toward the illuminated window panes she thought to excuse herself, but he put a hand on her shoulder. "Don't leave." He spoke in such a manner that she felt it was a command, not a mere suggestion. She turned to him then, and in a sudden flash of feeling, he leaned down and clumsily embraced her.

In her confusion, and willingness to please, she patted him on the back for reassurance, but it was not comfort that he sought, and he believed she was hiding her true feelings. He took Sarah's shoulders in his hands and held her at a distance, as if trying to take possession of her face.

She understood in that moment that he was seized by a passion she could not possibly consider, for it would disrupt her entire sense of self – her world, her life, her family. "Please," she said. "Don't do that."

"It's intolerable," he said. "I'm in love with you. I have to know one thing. Are you happy?"

"Of course I am," she said, stepping back. "You must put this out of your mind. You're a strong man, a very strong person, and you must try to control yourself." She turned to walk back into the party, but just before entering she paused to look at him, and he appeared so bent and dejected, it made her miserable too. "Dear Heinrich," she said in a whisper. "Perhaps in some other lifetime."

This did not help the inner wound he was covering with the mitt of his hand. Of course she was happy. A wonderful marriage. Lies, he believed, self-deception and lies! He would never set foot at another lake party for as long as he lived. He felt like unhitching his horse, riding it out into the water until they both went down. But as he stood there thinking these confused and angry thoughts, a blaze of light exploded on the far side of the lake, climbing up instantly and spreading to illuminate the sky with a ghastly brightness.

Others ran onto the porch to investigate, cries of shock and disbelief rose up with the spreading thunder of fire as trees caught sparks and started dancing like humans, trying to throw the flames off. It was the Bosquet mansion – layer upon layer just peeled away – even a burning flag could be seen writhing in the light and an enormous height of smoke blotted out the starry sky. The music inside the party teetered and then stopped as people flooded out to look on, transfixed. "Good Lord," someone uttered, before the panic began. "Get the boats! Someone ride to the firehouse!" Alicia was pulled out onto the porch to witness the disaster, and she clung to the balustrade and shrieked – a cry that was almost convincing, except to Heinrich's savage ears. Joseph dragged her away, signaling for his carriage, while Constance Hewitt rushed out the back door in hopes of finding Haven Rose.

CHAPTER SIX

*A*licia did not have to look beautiful in black for long. It was the end of the summer season and soon she would be off to finishing school in New York State. Only a handful of prominent people attended her father's memorial service. No one wanted to be too closely associated with the mysterious fire or the horrible death of the old man.

Representing his family, Merrick Wells went to the funeral alone. He had not given up his legal practice completely, and he had done a bit of work for George Bosquet. Merrick was always pleased to draw up the occasional will for a friend, not that Bosquet was an intimate – it was only that Angeline, Merrick's cook, was sister to Bosquet's caretaker, and he turned out to be one of the prime suspects in the Bon Pres fire. Merrick had to substantiate the character of his servant, for she claimed her brother had been with her that evening, eating *lebkuchen* and playing *schafskopf*. Because of his position of confidentiality, Merrick Wells did not reveal that Bosquet had intended to change the nature of his will, and that his daughter might well have been aware of that. There were rumors that when Alicia reached the site of the fire, she had not uttered a single cry of concern, but had insisted that Joseph help her by moving two stone lions that she feared would be crushed by falling timbers.

At first the police assumed that Bosquet had fallen asleep with a cigarette in hand, for he smoked a great deal, but then the detectives stumbled upon a jar near the west end of the house and it smelled distinctly of gasoline. Alicia had been dancing at the Hewitt's that evening so she could not have been involved, but Marjorie Hewitt pointed out that their chauffeur had driven their gasoline-powered vehicle over to George Bosquet's the morning of the fire. Haven Rose had waited in the driveway while Constance spoke to Mr. Bosquet about initiating a building fund for a village hospital.

"Mr. Rose, it turns out, is not just an ordinary driver," Mrs. Hewitt informed her husband, "but a student of medicine with social ambitions."

The presence of the automobile run by petrol was certainly a disturbing link, until Constance Hewitt came forward to reveal that he could not possibly be guilty, for just as the fire started, she had run out to find him in the garage apartment, where he had been studying in his robe and slippers.

"Why on earth would you have disturbed Mr. Rose?" her mother wanted to know, incensed by her daughter's lack of discretion. "I've never heard of such a thing."

"Because I thought he might help. I thought he could drive somebody over."

"And be a hero, I suppose," her brother, Colin, put in, though to Constance he had already achieved that status.

Apparently Constance's impulsive action was considered a more remarkable crime than the setting of a fire or the snuffing of a life, Mrs. Hewitt was about that ashen.

When Haven Rose arrived for the family conference, Marjorie Hewitt took offense that he was not wearing his uniform, only a coat and tie. He looked entirely too presentable, in fact, he appeared quite distinguished for such a young man. His face had a noble openness about it, and though he was blond, his eyes were a warm hazel brown, and his countenance mild and loving, especially when regarding Constance, who had apparently been in tears, pleading with her parents before he arrived. Lionel Hewitt was almost inclined to believe his daughter as he took another look at this well-mannered young man. He had a very soothing voice and a particularly nice way of putting things. Lionel could hardly remember having noticed him before.

"I'm sure this must be difficult for you to understand," Haven spoke first to Mrs. Hewitt and then turned to direct his plea toward her husband, "but you must believe that I love your daughter more than anything in this world. We both want to have your blessing."

Haven went on to explain his future plans, and Constance added, "He's going to be a doctor, Father. We're going to build a hospital, right here in the village."

One look from her mother silenced her, for as far as Marjorie Hewitt was concerned, Constance was still a child and in no position to marry, least of all someone beneath her. "Well, I'm glad we've had a chance to learn more about Mr. Rose's qualities and intentions, but your father and I feel that he must finish his medical training before this goes any further."

"We thought a year in Switzerland would be just the thing," Lionel added, with an encouraging twinkle. "Let time be a test to your love."

But when Haven agreed to their stipulations, Constance ran from the room. He had to excuse himself and go in search of her, then found her sobbing in the kitchen garden, where the last of the pear-shaped tomatoes had begun to split open with late-summer ripeness. She didn't even want to talk to him, and begged him to leave her alone. But he took her hand and gently pulled her down next to him on the curved concrete bench, placed between two lavender bushes. "We can give it more time," he encouraged, but she kept her back slightly twisted, for she felt he had not stood up to her mother.

"Time to keep you away from me," she cried. "You don't know what she's trying to do. No one is good enough. We'll never get married."

"I don't believe that," he answered.

She looked up at him, startled, as if it were the first reasonable thing she had heard that afternoon. His confidence nearly won her over, and his calm tone reassured her. She rested her head on his shoulder, and he kept it there with his hand. She could see that his thoughts sank deeper and deeper as if searching for the bottom level of the lake. It was as if the rope of his sentiments became even more secure, exposed to the tightening element of water, and she was anchored there.

But Constance wanted their love to live in the sun, on the good solid earth. The garden was filled with warm yellow sunlight. Black-eyed Susans sprang up along the edge of the garden, and there was the pungent scent of tomato leaves. She wanted to bring him back into this brightness, to take his hand and walk with him beside the fresh-mown fields of alfalfa. Her heart was glad for a moment, there in the sun. She believed she could accept her parents' wishes, if Haven was with her, and he thought this was right.

But as soon as Constance left for Europe that fall the young chauffeur was dismissed without notice. Lionel Hewitt, overlooking the awkwardness of it, claimed they simply didn't need a driver in the winter. He tried to offer the boy two thousand dollars as compensation, but Haven Rose refused.

Merrick Wells got wind of the situation, and decided to become more up to date, purchasing a dark blue Simplex car. Isabelle wrote to her friend in Lugano:

> My Dear Constance,
>
> I have such good news. Recently I overheard my father telling Mama that he thought your Haven was an exceptional person. Those were his exact words, and he rarely hands out undeserved praise. So it may come as no great surprise to you that my father has hired your sweetheart as his own private summertime chauffeur.
>
> Father went so far as to tell Mama (and this must be kept in strict confidence) that he intends to put Haven through medical school. He can study in the winter and drive us in the summer. A fair exchange, don't you think? My father was in a somewhat similar position when he courted Mama. He was not in the social register. But Grandfather Felton had a very open mind, perhaps because he also had humble origins and came from a family of farmers. Anyway, as we say in our home state – "The cream always rises to the top."
>
> Still, I must add that we all have a genuine regard for your Haven. Indeed, he has won the hearts of everyone who's met him, and I'm entirely happy for you.
>
> > With fondest wishes,
> > Isabella Wells

Despite this one note of optimism, autumn descended with a mood of darkness. When the winds changed off the lake, the chill was felt through thickened layers of woolen clothes. Nighttime seemed to move in on the daylight hours as if to compress them, and the ground itself was impenetrable.

All of the wooden piers had been removed from the lake, and the launches and sailboats were safely stored up high in boathouses. Lawn chairs and tables, umbrellas and beach toys were kept well under cover. Life itself seemed to have shrunk back away from the edge of the lake, leaving it bare, exposed and unadorned, as if it weren't a place fit for human beings. The north wind whipped across the unobstructed water, over the burnt out stub of Bon Pres.

Heinrich Ulrich, one of the few gentlemen who remained living on the lake throughout the winter, always said that he liked the isolation. It made him feel as if it were truly his domain – wild, like it was when the Indians lived here and had sweat lodges, rolled in snow. He liked to think of the sweating, smoky bodies of the men all together, while outside the cruel Wisconsin weather ripped into all that was vulnerable.

When Heinrich contemplated the unfortunate demise of George Bosquet, he could not help but hope that Alicia would sell the ruined property and try out another socially prominent area in the East where she could hobnob with others of her ilk.

Every morning Ulrich took a brief horseback ride to inspect one area of his farm, before driving to the train that took him in to the brewery. He was considering joining forces with a Mr. Michael Perelman, who owned Milwaukee Malt. Ulrich had always bought his supplies from Perelman, and he had proved to be an excellent business associate. It seemed natural to combine their interests in this way. Ulrich would still maintain controlling stock, but he had found a growing need to delegate some authority, at least until Joseph came of age and was in a position to take over the brewery.

The decision was a wise one, as it turned out, for Kreuser Beer remained the top-selling lager in Milwaukee, though Raifstanger, his wife's family brewery, was most popular nationwide, Mahler Beer coming in a close third. Kreuser maintained the most rigorous standards of excellence, with experts performing bi-weekly taste tests. The best hops and grains were used in the huge copper fermentation bowls – and it paid off, quality always did.

From the height of his saddle, Ulrich plucked a chestnut from its spiked burr, rolling the dark, oiled nut in his hand. He touched its light matte spot. Absentmindedly, he rubbed the luscious red-brown nut across his mouth before hurling it far away as he could. As a boy he had hammered holes through these nuts, pushed a string through and tied a knot, twirled the bead around and around before letting it haul through the air. He remembered seeing his two sons playing in the leaves beneath this tree when Hilda was still alive. The boys were intent on their play, creating an outline for a house, making a leaf pile for a bed, falling over and over again.

Frederick had made his mother a necklace of chestnuts, and she had worn it every day until the shiny brown beads began to look dull and shabby, as if life had sucked the living oils out of them. Even then she saved the necklace, having just discovered she was pregnant again. There was something about the feel of those chestnuts, all together, that made her reflect on the stirring within – smooth, dark, oiled, cool.

Perhaps because of these memories, Heinrich liked being alone during the late fall season. Soon enough there would be a skating party with a big bonfire roaring on the ice. About once a month he would be wrangled into attending some social event in Milwaukee, but, for the most part, he was entirely content to work hard all day and come home to Topside in the evenings. He relished his late nights by the open fire with his brindle Great Dane, Thor, asleep at his feet. Mildred often brought his dinner in on a tray, and he ate in the little living room, in his big brown leather armchair with the golden studs running along the edges, his feet up on the stool that Hilda had covered with needlework: *Isz was gar ist. Trink was klar ist. Red was wahr ist. Lieb was rar ist.*

Now that it was December and the lake had frozen, Heinrich looked forward to using his ice boat. The lake was perfect for it now, for there had not been any real snow, and the surface was completely slick and black, having frozen on a windless night. There was not even a single ripple, just this glassy smoothness.

As he walked down to the boathouse, the wind almost felt like thrown knives. Thor whined and ran up and down the shore, but did not venture further when Ulrich gave the command to stay. A groaning boom followed Heinrich out as he pulled *The Comet* onto the ice. He had purchased this ice boat from Lionel Hewitt, who rarely came up to the lake in the winter. *The Comet* was an all-mahogany creation with brass railings and a red cockpit. The twenty-eight-foot spar held six hundred square feet of gaff sail, and once out on the glassy surface, the six-foot runners went zinging across the ice.

Zipped into his fleece-lined, canvas-covered outfit that fit snugly from neck to ankle, with a matching helmet and round rubber goggles, he took robust pleasure in the ever-present cold. The whip of the icy wind cleansed Ulrich somehow. The runners of the boat made equidistant slashes, singing out with their tuneless cries like two strange birds traveling parallel, bound to each other and yet estranged, never really coming together.

Ulrich's hands pulled hard on the straining line that held the wind-filled sail, shooting the boat across the lake in a minute. As he went, a booming voice from a colder depth cracked and struck like winter lightning, making the icy heavens roar. As he turned the boat and sailed past what was left of Bon Pres, he couldn't help but think that Alicia was to blame. But just as he had this thought, the wind cupped up behind him and lifted the boat onto a single runner. He felt dangerously close to flying into some other realm, and took his eyes from the disaster area.

CHAPTER SEVEN

Y ou must let me drag you to a couple holiday parties," Joseph urged, for now that he was home from school for Christmas break, he wanted to have a good time. He liked to visit with his father, but he actually preferred spending time with the Raifstanger cousins in town. They were such an enormous extended clan that their mere excess made him feel that he really had a family to encompass him. "Weren't you surprised at Jon Bloodgood's engagement? I always thought Helen's Aunt Clickey was in love with him. That must have been quite a shock."

"I'm sure they took it all in stride," Heinrich responded, with a bit of a laugh. Caroline Felton had apparently accepted the news without grace and fled for southern California, but Sarah Wells had risen to the occasion and was having a large prenuptial dinner at her father's home in Milwaukee. Both Heinrich and Joseph were invited. "I don't intend to spoil the festive mood of other people. But you must go and enjoy yourself. You're young, and you should be out and around. I suppose you have your eye on some new young lady?"

Joseph did not tell his father that Alicia Bosquet was staying with friends in town and that she had also managed an invitation.

The dinner party for one hundred and fifty had all the excitement and anticipation of the season. It was the first day of winter and the longest evening of the year. Six hundred crystal glasses were set out on the full-leaved tables. The ivory-colored tapers were ready to be lit, the front hall festooned with garlands of evergreen, a Christmas tree in every room, each holding small beeswax candles that had to be continuously replaced, filling the halls with a luxurious smell of warm honey. There were little red velvet holiday bows tied to the limbs and mica-thin stars, but the grandest thing of all was in the living room. The chandelier had been turned into a hanging Christmas tree, and all the most precious miniature ornaments hung there out of reach – hand-blown glass fruit and crystal snowflakes, miniature oil paintings and carved sailboats, wooden apples for hospitality, antique salt spoons, clip-on birds with feathered tails, and tiny musical instruments. Helen's favorite was a little brown rocking horse with bright red reins and glassy eyes. It was only four inches high, but perfect, with a real leather saddle and silver stirrups. She imagined herself very small, sitting up there on the miniature pony, overlooking the entire *fête*.

Sarah Wells was in her element. She wore a long red velvet gown with satin bows along the inseam and little red tassels with thread-covered beads rustling along the bottom of the hem. Old Grandfather Felton sat back in his chair and let her take care of the mixing. The rich coloration of the Oriental carpets joined the warm glow of the hand-rubbed wood and lent a cozy winter atmosphere, luxurious and glimmering. The fireplace was flanked by a pair of massive six-foot columns with ram's head capitals. Spirals of evergreen wound up them, ending with crowns of holly.

Merrick descended to the *cave* in the basement in search of some special dessert wines his father-in-law had been hoarding. From that distance he could hear the muted tones of "*Oh Tannenbaum, oh Tannenbaum, treu sind deine blatter,*" as a merry group sang by the grand piano. Joseph was one of them. He liked to sing. He loved the Christmas season, and, standing there in the great hall, he could keep his eye on the entrance, as if he were dazzled by the marble wainscoting topped by the burgundy majolica tile – but Joseph was not really interested in these architectural treats, he was on the lookout for late comers. Alicia had not yet arrived.

Evergreen boughs had been spread at the entrance to the house, and the smell of snow on crushed pine mixed with the scent of mulled cider – sticks of cinnamon, and bobbing allspice. There was a pleasing combination of ages at the party, little Helen Wells being one of the youngest. When she caught sight of Joseph, she ran up and kissed him. "I wish your father had come. Isn't he feeling well?"

"He gets a bit low this time of year," Joseph admitted, "though I'm sure you would have cheered him up."

"I knit him some socks for Christmas. Four needles! Would you take them out for me? They're red with green ankles and toes, not too perfect, but very warm. I have something for you too," Helen added, but Joseph touched her shoulder as if to say – just a minute. Then he rushed to greet that beautiful girl who was lingering beneath the mistletoe.

Helen had made all of her Christmas presents, gathering tiny pine cones and berries and nuts to make miniature wreaths for her special friends. She had made a rather large one for Joseph.

Soon the candles were lit on the long dining-room tables, and the guests moved in to find their place cards, engraved with gold and sprigs of holly. Each place setting had a red velvet package with dark green ribbon containing a crystal apple or dove or pear. Helen received a crystal horse head, which sat, truncated, before her plate and made her feel quite special.

The meal began with a terrapin soup, served in an enormous tortoise shell. No one spoke of Caroline Felton. She had sent a bitter telegram from the Huntington in Pasadena – "*Good luck to the bride who steals a beau, for her wedding day shall be buried in woe.*" Disturbing.

Isabelle was not surprised that she had been seated next to her sister, for her mother did not trust her to carry on a conversation. She whispered to Helen privately, "Aunt Clickey was probably lucky."

Alicia had been placed between the two most eligible bachelors, Joseph

Ulrich, still boyish and blond, though he was now almost six feet tall, and the dark, robust Walter Schraeger, who had already finished Princeton and was learning the family sausage business from the ground floor up. Alicia paid both boys equal attention, while her eyes flirted with one of the Raifstanger cousins farther down the table.

"At least they didn't put us with the old, queer ones," Isabelle muttered, and Helen gave her a jab, for she didn't want to be distracted by her sister's sour comments.

"Can't you get in the spirit?"

The spirit of what, Isabelle wanted to know, for she did not believe that Christmas had anything to do with a showy production or with lavish gift giving. She intended to distribute food and mittens to the poor on Christmas Day, and she had only asked her parents for a magnifying glass.

When the boar's head, stuffed with pheasant and grouse, was brought around, Isabelle declined and sipped her mulled cider as if it alone could sustain her. She nearly stared at Alicia's rust-colored gown with the yellow topaz necklace. Isabelle wondered why these jewels had not been lost in the fire. She distinctly remembered Alicia wearing sapphires that night. Isabelle found herself picturing Alicia with a flaming torch, madly running from room to room, intent on destroying something. She imagined Alicia torching the curtains while hauling off her *cache* of jewels. Even her long, lustrous hair was streaked with fiery tones, and there was something odd – the way she over-reacted, laughing wildly at ludicrous jokes. In any case, Alicia seemed so far advanced that it made Isabelle anxious about going off to school. Would all the other girls be so worldly?

Alicia dabbed her mouth, not covering her glass when more champagne was poured. "I swear they're trying to finish me off at that finishing school," she protested to her end of the table. "Rules, *rules*, rules."

"So they haven't taught you Lesson Number One?" Walter asked, and Joseph Ulrich wanted to hear what that was. "That rules were made to be broken, of course."

"*Ha*," said Joseph. "That's some attitude. Does it extend to the law as well?" Joseph had been drinking too much. He turned to Mitzi Hewitt on his left and muttered, "I wonder if Schraeger Sausage can follow a recipe."

"Excuse me?" Walter leaned forward, and Alicia had to take his arm.

"Now boys," she insisted, "I won't have you blowing foam off the top of your heads. I hate to talk business. Let's think of something else. What do you think of the French Impressionists? If it weren't for the men, I'd go study in Paris."

"I heard they're all fortune hunters over there," Mitzi answered. "As soon as they found out about Lindsay, they immediately assumed her father owned gold mines and cattle ranches."

"Oyster beds under the sea!" Alicia bubbled, but suddenly her face became sober and she said in all seriousness, "I would never marry a Frenchman."

This seemed to please Joseph Ulrich, as if she were considering him, but Isabelle wondered why Alicia was prejudiced against the French when she had the same Gallic blood.

Alicia scanned the table for approval and most of the gentlemen gave it, though several of the young ladies looked slightly embarrassed by the current subject, considering it was a prenuptial dinner, for they had been taught not to show any interest in such things or people would think them forward. "Of course, I'm in no hurry," Alicia added. "It's so easy to make a mistake when you act impulsively."

"Young women today don't pick their husbands with their hearts," Walter told the table at large. "They're much too smart for that nonsense." Isabelle wondered what wisdom would deliver any young woman into his arrogant domain as the large Schraeger ham was brought around, along with potatoes Dauphine, followed by a sirloin of beef with horseradish sauce.

Soon the conversation shifted to a round of toasts, "Hear hear," and glasses were smashed in the fire. Maeve Peckham seemed to have a perpetual blush, even though many of the salutations were not directed toward her. "Here's to one of the last great dyed-in-the-wool bachelors, though his colors are bleeding badly!" There were hoots of laughter, for soon Jon Bloodgood would be no more than they – mere husbands, captured, tamed, domesticated animals, though Maeve was considered quite a catch.

After the flaming plum pudding and the sweet dessert wines, the mood became even more boisterous. Walter Schraeger got up and stood on his chair, putting one foot on the table to make a bawdy toast. Alicia leaned toward Joseph and enflamed his pride by saying, "You're certainly the most mature man here. Can't you say something flattering about Maeve?"

Joseph stood up, half-drunkenly, to announce, "After the rather austere fare at Choate, these divine indulgences seem as well deserved as the bride must seem to Mr. Bloodgood. May his appetite only increase!" The room seemed to find this hilarious, "Well said," though he had not intended humor exactly, and Alicia seemed delighted with him. Before they rose from the table he asked her, "Will you sit with me tomorrow at the wedding?"

Alicia didn't have a chance to answer, for Sarah Wells came rushing up – "Please give my regards to your father." And before Joseph had a chance to kiss Alicia's hand, she had been whisked away, while his cousins hustled him off in another direction. He had to stay at their Lake Shore Drive home that evening. He was in no condition to travel back out to the country, and a fresh snow was falling rather heavily. He wanted to crawl into some soft, warm feather bed and sleep the sleep of baked apples.

Heinrich was disturbed when Joseph didn't return to Topside. He used the absence of his son as a convenient excuse for attending the wedding the following day, denying to himself that he was drawn to the event because of Sarah Wells. He knew that the pain of seeing her would be well worth it, for his love wound was like an annoying low-grade infection and he wanted to feel it flare.

The wedding ceremony itself aroused a certain bitter mirth in Heinrich. He sat beside his son and the Raifstanger clan, his late wife's family. The procession into the church was headed by a crossbearer and sixteen young boys, followed by the ten homeliest women Heinrich had ever seen, all dressed up in black – they constituted the choir. Then came the bridesmaids and ushers, ten of each, followed by the bride, given away by doddering old man Felton, who actually stopped to greet friends on his long journey toward the altar. "Push him in the right direction," Heinrich muttered to his son, but Joseph had his eye on Alicia as she glanced across the aisle at Walter Schraeger. "Quite the high Episcopalian performance," Heinrich whispered to Mimi Raifstanger on his right, for the bishop was magnificently decorated with a white satin robe and a hat over a foot high. The bishop and his two assistants moved around the altar, bowing frequently, as the bishop put off his high hat and put it back on again at least every three minutes. The congregation was expected to remain on their knees whilst this continued for forty-five minutes, and there was not much else to help pass the time but to marvel at Maeve's long train, which seemed to attach to the top of her head and trailed behind her for fourteen feet.

After it was all over, and the crowd stood briefly at the front of the church, Sarah Wells overheard Heinrich telling Montgomery Ward, "I suppose you could call it beautiful and dignified from one point of view, ridiculous from another," and she was tempted to go and have a few words with him, to let him know what she thought of such comments after all the effort she'd made to retain her social dignity in the face of this difficult alliance. Sarah still felt hurt for her sister, and though she carried that pain invisibly, she thought Heinrich might at least show her more concern, but he was not even trying to seek her out, and that wounded her pride as well.

Returning to Topside by sleigh that afternoon, father and son sat covered with a thick camel hair blanket. It took several hours for the two dark bays to cover the distance, and it was a good chance to talk. "I guess Maeve Peckham recovered fast enough from her affair with Frank Schraeger," Heinrich laughed. He had never thought much of Jon Bloodgood, and he believed that most women were fickle and did not know their own hearts, let alone minds. "I would bet when Jon asked her to marry him, it was the first time the idea had occurred to either one of them. No reason to think of her cousin, who was supposedly smitten with the man. One big happy family." He chuckled. "Another well-suited, appropriate match."

"Father, you sound so spiteful," Joseph remarked, a bit grouchy himself from all the festivities. "Have you forgotten what it's like to be in love with a woman?"

"No," his father snapped. "I haven't forgotten." They sat there in silence for a while. "At least your mother was always trustworthy. You can't say that for too many women."

"It's not high on the list of charms."

Joseph was obviously growing up, and the thought both gladdened and irked Heinrich. Perhaps he would have been more pleased if his son had matured in a way he could admire. But the boy seemed soft and coddled, even though he had never had a mother to spoil him. Arriving home, he decided that a little ice fishing might be in order. "We could use a simple dinner, don't you think? Fish is always cleansing to the system."

"But it's already dark," Joseph protested, "and it's freezing outside."

Heinrich did not like that sissy attitude, but he knew he could only teach through example, not preaching. He had learned that much at church today. He remembered how Joseph had wobbled out onto the ice as a child, sucking his mitten, scarf knotted, cheeks rubbed to a bitten shine, how he always complained of aching ankles. "Tell Mildred I'll be back in an hour with fish for the four of us." He bundled up in his ice-boating outfit and took his pole, auger, and hatchet from the closet before heading down to the lakefront.

As he walked outside, he noticed the delicious scent of burning cherry coming from the chimneys. The fresh four inches of powder had mostly blown to the far side of the lake. With the invigorating cold in his lungs he felt that he could finally breathe, perhaps for the first time that day. Heading for the shanty Morvan had constructed, far out on the ice, he noticed a circle of birds to the right of the boathouse and thought he should investigate.

As he rounded the small promontory, he made out something that alarmed him. There was the head of an enormous stag, lifting out of the frozen water, its twelve-point rack held high in the air, as if it had been trying to swim and had frozen in its last effort to save itself. One of the birds descended and settled on the antlers, while another seemed to peck at an open eye. This incensed Heinrich, who ran at the flock, nearly slamming into the frozen muzzle. Up close, the tongue looked rubber pink, and hoarfrost could be seen on the rigid jaw. He felt he had to free the magnificent animal. Taking his hatchet, he slammed into the ice, hacking and chopping in the most violent manner, trying to loosen the stag. Finally, he was able to pull the stiffened body from the frozen lake, leaving behind the black water of its grave. Water splashed on his leggings and gloves, instantly freezing, as he dragged the stiffened creature to the bank. He sat down there beside the frozen stag and put his head in his hands, for he realized that it had been a senseless gesture, one more futile task in a long, endless life that was no longer really worth living. He felt the darkness penetrate as well as the cold. Even the ground was frozen solid, and there was no way to bury the animal.

CHAPTER EIGHT

*T*wice Alicia invited Joseph Ulrich to come meet her at some grand cotillion in New York, but he was unable to attend, and now she wanted him to be her escort to a Service Club Ball. He was disappointed at having to write no once more, for he had made arrangements to go home. He was going to surprise his father for his fiftieth birthday, and he had already bought his ticket. But Alicia wouldn't let it rest. She called Joseph at school and taunted him. "Maybe Walter Schraeger will be available over Easter. He knows how to fly his own plane."

"Schraeger's almost engaged to Lucy Smythe."

"Almost?" Alicia responded. Either one *was* or one *wasn't*. It was apparent that *almost* meant nothing to her.

Her response set off a panic of desire in him. He fought that impulse while wanting what he wanted, which was Alicia's dark, unattainable sparkle, which felt like the gift of night itself, with all of its blasted allurements. She was now a very wealthy girl, and back east there was no scandal associated with her name and the horrible demise of her father.

Taking the train home was an extravagant gesture, but extravagance was still the rule in those days. Morvan had actually been trying to wire Joseph, but had missed the boy by a matter of hours. Joseph arrived late, and left his trunk at the Wahcheetah Station, walking the six miles to Topside. He felt strangely

51 ⇜

heady that night, going along the gravel road dusted with moonlight, tickled by his own crazy plan. It was a radiant spring night. The moon was almost full, slightly lopsided, and the sky looked like it had been streaked with white watercolor paint.

There were no lights on in the gatehouse, and Joseph began to wonder if he should awaken his father. At first he had imagined what a surprise he would be, standing there, singing "Happy Birthday," but the train had been delayed and now it was way past midnight, and his father did not appreciate the unexpected. Perhaps it would be best to wait. He could still surprise his father in the morning, when he tended to be in a better mood.

In any case, Joseph felt confident humming along the road. Down by the canals the sky was open, just low shrubs and an occasional cluster of birch trees. Soon the black-eyed Susans would begin to grow here, and purple loosestrife would come into bloom. The cool smell of mud rose up from the ground, as if the earth itself were coming back to life. The cedar trees, fragrant with moisture, nourished his senses. He craved these smells on coming home. The very atmosphere here was different – gusts of wind off the water filled with mulch smells and rain – one inhalation seemed to contain his whole history.

Resting on the bridge that passed over a canal, Joseph watched the moonlight wobbling on the water, losing himself in that delicate balance. But then something startled him, an animal coming up over the bridge. It stopped a yard away and looked directly at him, dragging its long, hairless tail on by – an opossum, nothing to be afraid of, but it quickened him.

Hurrying up the hill where the elms became dense, he was eager to get to the edge of the lawn where the sky opened up again and he could see the family home rising out of the ground. It was an impenetrable monster of a house that defied him. It almost looked like an enormously heavy bird, trying to beak its way upward. One light anywhere would have made it his home, but it was completely dark, all the windows even blacker than the massive walls that surrounded them.

Suddenly Joseph felt like the student he was, excited and foolish. He decided to climb in through his bedroom window. There was a porch that went out from that room, and it had a ladder that went part way down. He made a tremendous leap and grabbed the bottom rung, chinning himself up to get a foothold. He felt grateful that Thor had not awakened the entire house, for that old beast was a perceptive watchdog.

As he lifted the window and stepped over the sill, he did not feel the relief he had hoped for. The room smelled strangely of graham crackers and gunmetal. That must be the lead soldiers, he thought. Searching around his bed, he groped for the lamp he had made himself in wood shop. Even at that moment he was proud of his handiwork. It was supposed to look like a pump, and when you primed the handle, the light went on and off. The bedroom seemed smaller than he remembered, and his plaid woven bedspread looked worn.

He could have tried to lie down and get some sleep, but he thought he would have better success with a glass of warm milk. Their housekeeper, Mildred, had always heated him some with a teaspoon of honey as a soporific. He was all wound up from the trip, and he figured he would creep downstairs, but as he passed his father's bedroom, feeling his way along the wall, he noticed that the door was wide open, which was not normal, because his father always slept with the door bolted from the inside. He felt alongside the door for the light button and the room was instantly illuminated – a perfectly made bed and empty bedroom. Heinrich was either away on vacation, which would be a disappointment, or he was staying in the townhouse. That was probably the case. Joseph could ring him in the morning and drive the phaeton in town, possibly take his father out for a special luncheon at the Milwaukee Club and then dutifully visit the brewery.

Still Joseph wanted that glass of warm milk, and he wandered down the long corridor to the head of the stairs. He knew the old house so well he didn't have any trouble seeing, even in this dimness, but descending the carpeted steps, he was aware of another curious smell – a powerful but natural perfume – and he wondered if his father had been entertaining some woman. The idea was distasteful to him.

At the bottom of the steps, the scent came up to him in an even more distinct, wide way, a sweet confusion of odors. There beside the tall grandfather clock, he punched in the lights to the big room – it was intoxicating! The whole immense front room was filled with flowers, buckets and baskets and huge arrays of breathtaking arrangements of flowers, everywhere, all over the room, on the mantels and tables, even on the floor, but there on the piano was the most lovely assortment of all, placed so abundantly and yet elegantly together. It drew him over to the piano where he naturally sat down and began to play the first thing that came to mind, *Jeux d'Eaux*. He wasn't even thinking as he began the music, letting it play for him, as if he were entering the liquid intuitions intended by Ravel.

The piece had always been one of his favorites, and he was sure he played it better than he ever had. He played without any restraint, for now he was sure there was no one to wake. Filling the house with this sound of water, fountains bubbling and pulsing, splashing over stone, this musical flight of wind and water, a transcendence of natural sound, he felt as if he were being washed by it, flowing out of and into that music.

53 ⤺

But then something stopped him. He couldn't go on. It was as if he had heard his father's verdict – that music was a wonderful talent to have, but that he should consider his future profession. It was then that he saw in the arrangement above him on the Steinway a little white envelope with his name in black ink, Joseph E. Ulrich. He looked around and saw that all the flowers had envelopes hidden amongst them, and that each bouquet held his name. Odd, since this was his father's birthday. Perhaps they had made some mistake. The first message that he read was written by his father's best friend:

Dearest Joseph,

I am very deeply grieved at the news of your father's passing. He was one of my dearest and closest friends, and no friend can ever mean so much to me again. We are heartbroken at his loss, for Marjorie and I both loved him, and we shall miss him dreadfully.

Lionel Hewitt

Joseph snatched at other envelopes, tipping flowers as he went, jerking them off and tearing them open – he did not know what he was reading or what anything meant, but his father was supposedly dead, or so all these people seemed to think. Mrs. Valenschein hinted that the death had been committed by his father's own hand, because she said that God would surely grant him forgiveness. Reading that, he didn't know why or how, but he was certain that his father was gone.

Almost to overcome that moment, he was seized with the thought that his father was lying in his mother's locked bedroom, which he had never in his life been in. He was sure that his father was up there, lying in state, as white and as bloodless as a bar of soap. Weeping and choking, he raced back upstairs, for even if he had never gone in there, he certainly knew where his mother's room was.

He banged on the door, but it was firmly locked as always. He then remembered that his father kept a pistol in his bedside table, so he tore back into his father's room, and there it was, a polished, perfect hunk of revolver, loaded, yes, he checked that, then he raced back to his mother's door, held out his arm and aimed, shooting right through the metal, and then as if he simply wanted to unload it, he repeated the shots until the gun just clicked.

He pushed open the door and stood there. The musty smell was at first overpowering, but he had imagined this room for so long, he felt that he must have dreamt the exact replica of what he saw before him at the moment he turned on the soft lamp light. He felt he had lived some other life in this room. Well of course – he had been born here. Is that why it seemed so familiar – the creamy, ornate furniture with pale blue ribbons painted on, those cane-back and cushioned chairs. Even the faded hooked rug seemed familiar, and the canopy over the bed. The flowered curtains were closed and a suitcase rack was there at the foot of the bed. He saw a sepia-tinted photo of his parents together in a tarnished, blue-black frame. They looked so young and healthy. But then he noticed the French doors that led out of the bedroom. The shades were drawn down the length of them and when he opened them up, at first he thought the room was bare, but he managed to find the light chain, and then he saw the small dust-covered harpsichord. Just one flat Indian rug and this instrument, one watercolor on the wall, a painting of a woman reclining on a summery *chaise longue*, reading a book as she leaned up on her elbow, very simple yet pure, absolutely pure.

As he stood there looking at the harpsichord, tempted to lift the lid, he thought he heard a sound downstairs and he froze, like a statue of ice. He was sure death was down there, coming upstairs to get him, but then he turned from ice into lava, burning, murderously hot, and he knew that he had to hide, but where? He made a dive to get under the bed, but damn if there weren't a hundred hat boxes under that bed. He could hear a man's footsteps coming up the carpeted stairway, very slowly, deliberately, God!

He thought of the bathroom, the bathroom! He could lock himself into her bathroom. He raced in there and bolted the door before he had even gotten the light on, but then he turned on the light and knew that something was wrong. He forgot all about the man on those stairs. He did not even hear him at that point, because something was wrong, the bathtub. The bottom of the bathtub was wet, and one of the faucets was dripping in the basin, and then he saw a smear of brown blood on the floor and his father's garnet signet ring in the soap dish.

He flung open the door – there was Morvan with a rifle pointed right at his head. He had never been so glad to see anyone in his entire life. Morvan was pretty shaken up himself. It took him a minute to lower the gun, because as he said later, he had been instructed to shoot on sight anyone who ever violated that room, and it was hard to break a man of his loyalty. Joseph was the first offender. His father's offense apparently didn't count. Since she was his wife, and it was his home, he had a right to bleed himself in her bathroom.

"You shouldn't of come here," said Morvan. "He was a good man. A good man. Don't hold hardness against him." Morvan led the boy down the stairway to the door. On stepping outside, they saw the sun was about to appear, and Joseph sensed the fresh-born odor of softening earth beneath the sweep of a luminous sky.

CHAPTER NINE

*F*rom the raw air that claimed late April, Sarah Wells stepped into the gush of the greenhouse. It had been two weeks since Heinrich's death, and she felt she didn't love her husband anymore. Perhaps she never had, for his mere touch now repelled her, even the way he held his knife and fork, and ate with such precision. The sight of his spindly legs and thinning hair, his delicate, round spectacles, made her turn from him in revulsion. His mentality left her cold, like the chill outside, the deep mud chill. Only now did she realize what Heinrich had been offering her – true masculine passion, with all of its horrible earthiness and heat, like the fecund air of this greenhouse, where the peat scent rose to enwrap her. How could she have lied and said, "Of course I am happy." How could she have spoken otherwise.

Beneath the glazed roof of glass panes, Kurtz was working at the far end of the building, pushing flat wooden sticks down into the long lanes of flat beds. He marked the name of each variety with his own shorthand, *Snaps, Zins, Glads*. He motioned to Mrs. Wells to acknowledge her presence, but kept to his work, absorbed and at home beneath the weathered, whitewashed frame of the place. He was smoking a hand-rolled cigarette, and from twenty feet away Sarah felt the emptiness inside her reaching out for that sweet, comforting smell. Coming closer to the flats, she saw the seedlings were a lush mass, and the smell of growth almost bloomed in the air. The forced warmth made her glow as she stood on the cement walkway beneath the sprinkler system and recalled the pressure of Heinrich's hand on her lower back as if it had made a permanent impression. Why had she been so rigid? What if she had returned his love. Would he still be alive today, or was it simply pride to think she was ever that important? Why didn't people come together more simply, like that stack of red clay pots, and yet she knew how easily terra cotta crumbled, from dish to shard to dust.

"Good morning," she said, coming closer, inspecting the on-going work. "I suppose some of these will need to be transferred to the cold frame." The soil in the cold frame was embedded with lead-covered heating coils. Gradually the small leafy plants would acclimatize to the harsh Wisconsin weather, and by June her garden would be far ahead of most.

Gustav Kurtz was her treasure, her prize employee, and he did not need directions. His thumb was not green – it was gold, black gold, rich as the earth he nourished, coaxing and working his flowers. His mere presence seemed to make the plants grow more profusely, as if they meant to honor him.

The Garden Club ladies were always astounded by the magnificent order of Sarah Wells's garden and by the unusual varieties Kurtz found, including some rare Egyptian lilies, which he had placed in the marl of a man-made marsh, contained by a sunken basin. The tall stalks bore three-foot circular leaves and enormous pink blossoms. Last year he had begun several rows of phosphorescent moonflowers that opened only at night. His dinner-plate dahlias were exactly that size, and his vegetables, arranged in a veritable mountain, always won first place at the fair.

Their garden was a work of art, and it was on this level that Sarah understood it. But now she did not feel like beginning the usual small talk about the progression of colors, and what they might expect according to the almanac. Without thinking, she looked up at the warm, gray, sweet-smelling smoke that curled toward the sun-bright panes. "I'd like to try one of those, Gus. May I?"

Kurtz was not surprised by her request. He already had an extra cigarette rolled in his pocket. His thick, dirt encrusted fingers seemed so large and close when he lit the cigarette for her. Neither of them said a thing.

She did not inhale, the sensation of smoke so foreign to her. She was shocked by the taste and coughed slightly, puffing the smoke out with some satisfaction. "It makes me feel better, somehow."

"That's why we do it," Kurtz responded.

"It seems wrong to feel badly when spring's just beginning. When new life's starting up."

"Winter has not really left us."

"Neither has death." She knew she was stepping over some invisible boundary, speaking to her gardener as if he were a confidante, but she had never felt so without friends, true friends, and she sensed that she might find some relief in this sun-filled place, where she could warm the chill that inhabited her.

Kurtz did not speak for a moment, carefully plucking. "It's all in the cycle. You learn that." The cycle of growth and decay. His fingers seemed like instruments made to turn over earth, while Sarah Wells only approached her garden with a small, special scissors and a wicker basket in order to clip the clean, colorful blossoms she loved to arrange. She was not eager for the feel of loam beneath her fingernails, or to thrust her hands up to the wrists in mud. She was fouling herself now just by holding this cigarette. She held it out, not knowing what to do with it. He took it and crumbled the red hot embers between his thumb and forefinger, sweeping the bits of paper and tobacco off the path with his boot. There was something fierce about Kurtz that disturbed Sarah. She knew he had lost many dear to him, and perhaps that had hardened him somehow. He had been raised by his *grosspapa*, who had taught him the secrets of gardening and the earth. Kurtz had married early, but his wife and twins had been taken in a diphtheria epidemic. It was then that he had sailed for America, having one more familial connection in the Milwaukee area. Kurtz had put in several years at the Kreuser brewery, but he was much happier now living in the country.

"I thought I put death in the cupboard when I come to the New Country," Kurtz confessed. "But I know now different. You don't leave this behind." The words he spoke had an awkwardness, in contrast to the sureness of his constantly moving fingers. Each little poke of the dibble made a hole that received the roots of another seedling, which was then patted down securely. "Each person we love," he said, "clings to us. Is tied with a knot, even after. Like a kite you could say. Like the tail of a kite."

"Perhaps we need that weight to climb."

"Exactly," he answered, looking up at her. The intensity of his face startled her, for it was something like Heinrich's, no pretension or craft, nothing civilized about it, that look that sprang straight from this connection to earth, from the layers of rotting humus that gave back abundant life. "But you cannot fly away from it." That was all he had to say. He was not an airborne person.

The two dogs had been waiting for Sarah at the greenhouse door. The little pug leapt then ran under the chow, who spun around and grabbed him by the folds of his scruff. Their antics always made Sarah smile. Pompeii cocked his head and looked up at her with that comic-sad expression. "*Mooshie*," she said as an endearment. "And my dear, good girl. My *best* girl." These were her words for Tai, who looked up at her mistress with calm sobriety. It was as if the chow had been born ancient.

As Sarah picked her way down the drive, the soft earth felt rubbery beneath her feet. She let the words of her latest poem repeat themselves, over and over, until her mind felt somewhat soothed:

The cypress trees stretch forth their arms
To meet the gale on windswept shore
But when they guard our Sacred dead
They fold them in calm reverence
And stand like sentinels with bowed head.

She saw the men filling the ice house with the last blocks of ice cut from the middle of the lake. The ice would be covered with a blanket of sawdust, stored, and used throughout the summer. She did not like that stale smell of cold, but it was amazing how well the darkness and thick wooden walls preserved the integrity of ice. She hoped her own inner chill would not remain so constant, for she already wanted to coax the weak warmth of the sun to enter and make her feel alive again.

As she approached the main house, which had not yet been properly opened, she saw Merrick in the driveway, fussing with something. Then she saw that he was in his wading boots, his trout creel slung over his shoulder. He was wearing the old blue-and-gray plaid shirt she had given him years ago. He waved, but she barely returned the gesture. She found herself looking at him as if he were a stranger, an oddly familiar stranger in a lure hat.

"I thought I'd try my hand," he walked up to her with his fishing rod, and the spell of estrangement was broken – "see what I might catch from the bank. You smell like tobacco, Sarah." He seemed both alarmed and surprised, looking at her with curiosity, but she did not feel like explaining herself.

"I was over inspecting the progress at the greenhouse." She looked absently out toward the lake.

"I suppose Kurtz told you his news."

"No, nothing unusual. What do you mean?"

"About the will, Ulrich's will. I was going to discuss it with you on the ride in town." But now she wanted to walk along beside him on the muddy way down to the lakefront. The lawn opened up with large oaks on either side to frame the view from the house. It seemed unlike Sarah Wells not to bother about the ruination of her shoes, but her husband was not going to warn her if she didn't care. He was in a slightly aloof mood himself that morning.

The stack of white pilings lay ready to construct their summer dock, and the water looked clear and very cold, lapping the shore in a kind of staccato. The shoreline seemed wilder than it did in the summer, when it was tempered by wildflowers and decorative grasses.

She glanced at her husband's worried expression and felt an old familiar fondness for the man. He had not shaved that morning, and the graying stubble on his cheek caught the light with tiny sparks. She felt like touching the blue-gray flannel of his collar, as if it were her last chance to make tender, human contact, as if he were about to leave the earth for other heights or depths. She felt a pang for him, for he was also a victim of all these emotions that had been put into motion by a man who was no longer around to assume any responsibility.

Merrick Wells was a completely responsible person, good and smart and kind. He was a strict but loving father, who encouraged his daughters in every possible way. She thought of him holding Helen on her Shetland pony when she was just two years old, of how proud he was of Isabelle's accomplishments, for she had made highest honors her first marking period at Miss Baldwin's.

Indeed, her husband was the most decent, upright man in Milwaukee. He was concerned about others, about conservation and the state of the world, he was an honest civic leader, well-respected and admired by most, but he was not a passionate person. She detested herself for stopping there, for what, in comparison, did she have to offer? Why should it concern her so.

"It seems your friend Mr. Ulrich left our Kurtz quite a handsome sum. In fact, he's his own man now. Two hundred and fifty thousand dollars. Can you imagine?"

Merrick seemed to find this amusing, though Sarah was flushed by the mention of Heinrich as her special friend, as if her husband sensed the truth, but this sudden disclosure took precedence and allowed her to appear ruffled by the startling news concerning their gardener.

"Why on earth?" she seemed mystified. "I don't understand."

"You remember it was Ulrich who brought him from Germany and finally found him a position with us. Well, it turns out that Gustav is his bastard half-brother. Same father, though Kurtz kept his mother's family name. Now he's a fairly wealthy man by most standards."

Sarah was taken aback. "Will he leave us?" she asked. "He didn't say a thing."

"Actually, he wants to stay on. I wouldn't be surprised if we end up having the only lake gardener with his own chauffeur, but as he said, he's settled here, and as long as he has time to do research, he'll be happy to oversee the garden."

"This is all very odd." Sarah was overwhelmed.

"Life would be odd indeed if it weren't very strange. Even you, my dear, seem different these days. Has something been bothering you?"

She leapt at the chance to sweep her feelings away, out of the light of his scrutiny. "Oh, it's nothing, it's just an end-of-winter mood. This time of year's so unsettling. When the snow melts everything looks so shabby, don't you think? I never feel easy until the gardens are planted, and I worry about Isabelle. She seems so content to be apart from us."

"Well, you know she's always been reserved, and a scholar, so she's in her element. And she does have poetic aspirations, I might add. She sent me some poems the other day. I think they're quite excellent."

"Oh?" Sarah was offended. "Why didn't you share them?"

"She asked me to keep them in confidence. Rather shy about it, unlike you. I only bring it up because it seems the poetic temperament needs solitude in order to create, and I thought perhaps that was what you've been craving. Either that or some new inspiration." He began to thread a small white mealworm onto his hook, adjusting the spaced lead sinkers on the line. "Maybe you'd like to take a trip abroad," he suggested, stepping into the water and casting far out, reeling the bait in slowly.

She felt another pang at this unexpected suggestion. Did he actually want her out of the way? Suddenly she felt a strange longing for him. He did understand her so thoroughly, and he cared very deeply, she knew, not only for her physical needs, providing everything she might desire, but also for her emotional well-being.

"Life would be dull here without you," he went on, "but I'm going to be doing a great deal of work in Chicago this coming year, with the purchase of the Liebenau stores, and it would be good to expose Helen to the art of Italy and France. Of course, you could also take Reusner, so you wouldn't feel stifled."

The idea of a trip was thrilling, but it also made her anxious. "I think I'd be afraid to go without you," she protested. She yearned to reach out toward him, but he took another step away from her into the crackling clear water.

"Perhaps if I helped with the itinerary you'd feel more secure."

Old wet leaves were matted along the bank. Her eye darted from spot to spot, from the new blades of crocus to a scattering of twigs. Then a robin alighted on the ground, another sign of spring. Merrick suddenly seemed so charming in his old flannel shirt and canvas hat. She knew him and loved him like the most comfortable pair of shoes. She would be loath to live without him.

PART TWO

CHAPTER TEN

$\mathcal{E}$ veryone out at the lake seemed somewhat carried away. Perhaps it was the release one felt in early summer or the engagement party mood, but marriage was certainly on everybody's mind. In fact, that single ceremony was central to all else in this summer society, and the rituals leading up to it were clearly prescribed.

Aunt Clickey was spending the month of June with her sister, and Sarah had arranged a house party for Isabelle. Broadoaks was filled with excitement, so many spirited girls in their summery hats and dresses, flying in and out. They had a million ideas about everything, but especially liked discussing the young group of gentlemen staying over at Joseph Ulrich's.

Isabelle, on her way back from the garden, carried a bow-shaped basket of beet greens. They were having their main meal at noon, and though no one had asked Isabelle to perform this chore, she had needed a few moments to herself. Her mind filled so quickly with all the noise and commotion, and socializing made her tighten up. Isabelle thought her aunt was better suited to the younger generation than she was herself. The heat pressed on Isabelle's temples, leaving the few stray hairs there limp and damp.

"Your mother certainly has a gift for putting a party together, don't you think? She always has, so effortless. No one could ever accuse her of being overly organized, but actually, I believe she is. And we're attracting so many nice boys. Do you ever get over to Princeton? It's not far, I've heard. Isn't Bryn Mawr considered their sister school? Your father must certainly like that."

Isabelle could see, looking from the front porch, through the house, on out toward the lake, that two young gentlemen were out in a canoe with her sister. Isabelle's eyes narrowed as she perceived the pretty scene out beyond the float. Helen, though only sixteen, was perfectly self-confident, no shyness about her. She was the one they all paid attention to, all of the men. She would waltz right in and take Isabelle's beaux, not that they were ever rude to Isabelle. She straightened her shoulders and remarked to her aunt, "No one asked *me* to go in a canoe."

Aunt Clickey was sensitive to Isabelle's feelings and deftly changed the subject. "Don't these greens look splendid, but they'll wilt in this heat. We must take them in to Cook – she'll be so pleased." But Angeline only growled, as if she didn't have enough to do. Isabelle was horrified when Angeline proceeded to explain how she had prepared the midday goose. At dawn that morning, the poor fowl had been placed in a pot of warm water, and slowly, very slowly, it had been steamed to death.

"I've never heard of anything so cruel," Isabelle exclaimed.

People should be so sensitive to other human beings, Angeline thought. She told everyone to get out of her kitchen – she had work to do.

Just then Helen led her boisterous group up toward the porch. They came running up the slope, and Helen's cheeks were flushed, her chest heaving beneath the pale blue shirtwaist. "I won," she laughed, touching the porch steps as two young men came racing behind her.

"I wouldn't call that fair," the taller one said to her. "We had to pull up the boat."

"You have to give a girl some advantage," Helen explained away the handicap. "Oh Isabelle, dearest," Helen kissed her sister on the cheek, "we just had the most lovely paddle through the Ulrich Canals. We saw a snapping turtle and a mother mallard. What are we having for luncheon?"

Isabelle too had seen the drab brown mallard with her little ones trailing as if spaced on a thread. She had also felt the slowing swish of seaweed as it dragged beneath the bow, and seen the green mass of waxen water lily flowers that sucked their muddy juices up through those tubular connections, but usually she went canoeing by herself.

"You know Max Farwell, and this is Leonard Faithorne." Helen beamed, inhaling, as if relishing the lime scent of his Lilac Vegetal. "They used to be roommates with Joseph Ulrich at Choate. Now they're all together at Yale."

Max Farwell was a stubby, slightly overweight chap, in contrast to the tall, thin Faithorne, who had maintained an air of elegance despite the events of the morning. Though Isabelle did not speak, Leonard took her hand and made a gracious, minimal bow, asking with a smile, "Is your sister always so aggressive?"

"I suppose, as an older sister, I have never presented enough of a challenge, so it seems natural that Helen must test herself against the rest of the world."

Farwell lifted his eyebrows. Taking his friend by the sleeve, he said, "The only way to catch a girl like that is to go in the opposite direction."

Sarah called her young guests to the table by tapping a small square xylophone. The five notes were pentatonic, so she could strike any sequence with the padded mallet and it always sounded euphonic. On hearing the call, the girls came in from the porches and down the stairs. "You boys *must* stay," Sarah pleaded with them. "We need some gentlemen at the table."

She placed the more attractive Leonard at the foot next to Isabelle. Potter came to her rescue and sat on her left. Lindsay Esser was there, Mitzi Hewitt, Leslie Anderson, Biddy Hawkshurst, and Teensie Brumder. Some of the girls were from Isabelle's alma mater, and some were the daughters of Sarah's friends. In any case, it was a fairly convivial group, and everyone, save Isabelle, turned to her left or right and began a conversation.

After a delicate cream of celery soup, the goose was brought around. Sarah noticed that her elder daughter refused the main course, and she tried to cover up Isabelle's strange behavior by telling her end of the table, "They say a vegetarian diet is most healthy. Isabelle has always been advanced in her ideas, but don't let that hold the rest of you back. This should be exquisite."

"I don't eat anything with a face," Isabelle murmured, and Farwell laughed, claiming *he* didn't eat anything unless it liked to gambol or cavort.

"They've got a new dietary menu over at the Bifford Hotel," Mitzi Hewitt put in. "But the Chosen People have gotten possession of that place." All of a sudden it seemed as if everyone at the table had something to say.

"Did you hear Joseph Ulrich and Alicia are engaged?"

"They don't eat pork, because it's unclean," explained Potter.

"They say he was only her second choice. Poor Lucy." Walter Schraeger had finally made up his mind, and none too soon, for there were rumors circulating about Lucy Smythe's delicate condition, though no one would say more in polite company.

"You don't mean little Lucy from Spruce Lake!"

"Best to keep them on your side if you go into business," Farwell put in. "Those boys know how to bring home the bacon."

The less Isabelle spoke, the more constricted she felt, until she believed she couldn't even reach out to take a sip of water.

In contrast, Helen's upset on hearing the news about Joseph took the path of vivacious hilarity. She called down the table to Leonard Faithorne, "Why don't we play a round of croquet? We could play partners," as if it were *her* house party. "Isabelle, won't you join us this time?"

But no, Isabelle was ready to retire for an hour as she always did after luncheon, eager to continue with her volume of Coleridge. She knew Helen could entertain her guests.

Potter followed, asking, "What's wrong?" But Isabelle just waved her off. She even felt estranged from her own best friend, and thought she might burst into tears. At the moment she wanted no part of any of them.

Isabelle watched from the window as the group departed. The girls in their colorful dresses wove through the tall oak and hickory trees that rose majestically across the lawn. They seemed like so many fluttering butterflies to her. Someday each one would be caught and stuck with a pin, left to heal on a black velvet background – dry, beautiful, lifeless, wed.

She went to lie down on the swinging bed that hung on the porch facing the lake. The horsehair mattress had a comforting crunch to it, and the steady creak of the chains was soothing to her. What a relief to rest her head upon a soft, flattened pillow and not have to listen to such chatter. Words, she felt, should be savored, not bandied about.

Angeline broke Isabelle's restful mood when she popped through the open porch door to announce, "I wouldn't go swimming if I were you. I just saw a ten-foot snake come out of the drainpipe."

Isabelle lifted her head to look at Angeline, and noticed that the afternoon light had suddenly shifted darker, lighting up the color of everything. The purple loosestrife seemed brilliant against the teal blue of the lake. The sky itself was an ominous yellow. Isabelle heard a rumble of distant thunder before the wind picked up and pushed the fresh June leaves back to expose their silvery undersides.

Rushing into the house, she helped the servants, who were already slamming shut windows. Then they pulled back the wicker porch furniture and closed the French doors. Fierce rain was coming in sheets. These summer storms were often sudden and violent, but also exhilarating to Isabelle's oppressed nerves.

Over by the tennis court, where the others were whacking croquet balls about the lawn, the darkened sky made the oat fields more golden, rippling beneath the rush of wind. "My hat!" Biddy cried, as it blew toward the poplars. Helen urged the entire troop to run for the barn. The scent of moistened dust rose up as raindrops started pelting, pockmarking the drive. Then they really had to run for it.

Inside the hay barn they stood and watched the rain as it came on, moistening the lime-whitened floor of the stable. The sweet, oily smell of worked leather was coming from the tack room. Most of the horses were still out to pasture, but Leonard left the group and went over to the dark bay hunter and buried his face in the horse's mane as if inhaling the very essence of the animal. Helen was taken by the gesture. She went over and joined him, suggesting that they climb into the hayloft to wait out the storm.

Some of the girls needed coaxing, for they were not as sprightly as Helen, but no one wanted to stay downstairs alone, even if it were a bit risqué, climbing up into the cozy darkness of bound bales. The afternoon took on the look of near-night, and they were all enlivened by the energy in the air, yet the hayloft seemed close and protective. "I'd like to go swimming in the rain," Farwell said.

"That's a terrible idea!" Lindsay Esser reeled, as if he wanted to drag her in too, clothes and all.

"Why's that, my dear?" he wanted to know, moving closer to her. She gave him a little shove. The bales of hay were stacked at different heights, and Helen's ankles were at the level of Farwell's eyes.

"If lightning were to strike, your body would get charred," Lindsay admonished, and everybody laughed, imagining old Farwell burnt to a crisp like an overdone bratwurst. Another crack of lightning struck and all the girls screamed.

"I love a good storm," Helen admitted. Leonard Faithorne was sitting beside her. He was so well-mannered, perhaps because he grew up in New York City, not a country person. "You can tell how close the strikes come," Helen explained to him, "by counting the seconds from the flash to the boom. Each second is about one mile."

He looked at his watch and said, "That gives us very little time." When another bolt hit in the vicinity, Leonard took advantage of the moment to slip his arm around Helen's waist. She was aware of the gentle pressure of his hand in contrast to the pricks of the hay bale beneath her, and she kicked her small feet quickly back and forth. Leonard was so tall and calm and good looking. How could she ever have been so absorbed by Joseph Ulrich? Her heart still felt saddened for him, for she was sure he was making a mistake. She had heard it could be a curse to get what you wanted, and surely Joseph had longed for Alicia long enough.

Back at the house a black carriage pulled up in the drive. The gray horses were drenched and the driver was soaking. Mr. Liebenau and his son jumped from the compartment and then made a dash for the safety of the porch.

Merrick Wells had recently been doing a good deal of business with the Liebenau family from north Chicago. They owned a department store chain that Merrick was in the process of purchasing. Samuel Liebenau and his son, Joshua, would be staying at the Bifford, though certainly they would have been guests at Broadoaks if the house had not been full.

"We weren't expected till tomorrow," Mr. Liebenau explained as Isabelle received them, "but the storm was so severe. We were hoping to wait it out."

"Of course. Please come in," Isabelle urged. Looking up at Joshua Liebenau she felt stabbed by the intensity of his hawk-like eyes. She went to rouse her mother, but walked in the wrong direction. Then, leading her guests into the living room, she offered them lemonade instead of hot tea. She made her way to the kitchen, but forgot what she had come for – Angeline had to snap her out of it.

"What's the matter with you? Didn't I see company? Do I have to cook another goose?"

"Lemonade, thank you," Isabelle gripped Angeline's arm, "and some of your ginger cookies. That would be excellent. Should I bring it? Or should you. Oh!" Isabelle gasped as she glanced in the mirror that backed the china pantry cupboards, catching a glimpse of herself amongst the rose crystal goblets and trying to revive her hair.

When Isabelle returned to the living room, the storm had passed, and Sarah Wells, who had heard the commotion of arrival, had returned downstairs. She wanted to take the elder Mr. Liebenau down to the boathouse to see the electric launch. Joshua stood at the end of the room as if he were waiting for Isabelle. She had never felt so thrilled or helpless, but, oddly enough, she wanted to be there, to talk.

Carefully placing the tray down upon the oval mahogany table, Isabelle said, "Please, won't you sit?" trying to imitate a method of hospitality that did not particularly suit her. "Or will you help yourself." He assured her that he usually did just that, and with relief, they both gave in to informality. She felt as if the shell of her cocoon had suddenly cracked open and was about to expose another kind of creature altogether, folded, fresh, and neatly moist.

"I've heard a great deal about this lake country," he said, "but I had no idea it would be this dramatic." He spoke as if he wanted to plant a fire somewhere. "The colors are marvelous. Everything's gray and boring in the city. Tomorrow I'll set up my easel."

"So, you're a painter. I knew it," Isabelle exclaimed, though she had actually imagined him an actor. But no, this did seem to fit his visionary eyes. "My sister and I were both painted by Frank Benson. He stayed here, at Broadoaks."

Joshua scanned the sky out the window. The lawn was littered with nuts, twigs, and leaves from the storm. A red squirrel raced about collecting the spoils. "I'd like to paint you," he announced, and this surprised her. "You have very unusual features."

Isabelle could feel his eyes running over her face, over her unusually full lips and tidy, arching eyebrows. She sat up straight, and his eyes seemed to finally light upon her earlobes. She knew she was not beautiful, her figure was delicate, yet he seemed to find her entirely worth looking at.

"My sister is much more pretty," she admitted.

"I'm not interested in common prettiness. I can imagine painting you in the wind before a storm. The sky would be a yellow-gray, and you'd be wearing something black. Do you have a cape, or robe? That might be good."

Isabelle wished that he wanted to paint her in white or blue, but she didn't want to appear disappointed. "You know, I once saw a lightning ball," she revealed to him, eager to feel free in conversation for once – she felt as if her new wings were glistening. "It struck the ground right out there, and rolled across the lawn. No one else saw it, but it burned a path. No one but Popa believed me."

"I believe you," he asserted. "Your father's a remarkable man. I can tell you one thing, I'm glad my father found him, or the other way around. I suppose you've heard we're selling the store. People rarely charm my father, but perhaps that runs in your family. Anyway, I have little interest in retail. Dogskin gloves," he said, as if he could smell the faint odor of foul fur coming from the men's department. "So what do you like to do?"

"I write poetry. That is – I'd like to be a poet."

"Ah," he responded, "a poetess. I can't imagine what a debutante would find to write about."

Isabelle felt offended. She put down her glass on the prettily painted tray. "You don't know me very well, do you."

"I'm afraid I wouldn't know you even if I *knew* you," he laughed, and she had to smile, for he was probably right there.

Instead of holding back, she had to admit that yes, she had almost come out the year before. "You see, if I'd had a brother, he might have been my escort, but since I have none, I asked my cousin, Alcott Allen. I could tell he didn't want me as a partner, so what could I do? Mother always does things so naturally. She said, Oh, just pick anyone, it doesn't matter, but I thought it such a dreadful position to be in, I defaulted altogether. A mysterious brush with influenza. Do you think that was terrible, a wicked thing to do?"

"I think it was rather ingenious. I doubt if many girls would go to such great lengths to get out of their ball gowns."

The suggestiveness of his approval shot a new feeling through her. She did not want to put this man off by making herself out to be the wallflower she was. "But many of the lake party dances are quite gay – you'll be coming to ours on Saturday, won't you? It's a good thing the rain came this afternoon. Tomorrow they'll be laying the dance floor."

"I don't dance," he said abruptly. "What kind of dancing is this?"

"Oh, the typical ballroom, but there is one figure that a lot of us enjoy." Here she began to describe what she had only observed in the past. "Each girl goes and chooses a partner, and she harnesses him up with ribbons and then drives him about the floor. It is rather fun, partly athletic. Then finally, all these different teams of horses come together and perhaps form a circle – then everyone changes riders."

"I can't say I'd like to be harnessed by anyone, though if some lovely lady were to drive me out into the woods . . . "

Isabelle, not knowing how to answer such a forward remark, stood up and walked over to the window. "Well, the sun is out now." She saw her mother escorting Mr. Liebenau up the front path between the greeny-white globes of hydrangea. When Joshua stood up beside her, he was at least five inches taller.

"I'm serious about that portrait," he said. "But you must tell me something. Where do you get *your* inspiration? Do you listen to some muse?"

"Oh, that was in ancient times," she responded, turning to the cut glass knob of the door. She felt like a modern woman.

CHAPTER ELEVEN

*W*hen Joshua Liebenau returned to Broadoaks on the following day, he glanced in Isabelle's direction but did not come forward. He let his father do all the talking. "That's some hotel, really a fine hotel, no scrimping on provisions over there, ha ha." The old man was in a particularly good mood. "Half of Chicago is up here! The Gimbels and Florsheims are right down the hall."

"Mixing business with pleasure, no doubt." Sarah smiled up at him. That was always permissible in Nogowogotoc.

Sarah and her guests were standing on the front path between the two rows of hosta when Joseph Ulrich pulled up in his red tallyho, a large pleasure coach drawn by four black horses. This handsome monogrammed carriage had his father's initials painted on the door. There was a padded beige velvet interior, a mahogany bar, and even a ladies' W.C.

Decked out in a bright blue uniform, Jack took the reins in one hand and held up a long polished trumpet in the other, giving it a tremendous blast. Pompeii, the pug, went hurtling toward the house, and the party of girls came swarming out to greet the young gentlemen from Ulrich's. Joshua Liebenau stepped back, as if socially on guard. He barely acknowledged Isabelle's presence.

Alicia was in the carriage amongst the boys. She leaned out of the window and waved for everyone to join them. "We're going to climb the lookout tower," she called, and Joseph chimed in that he had something to tell them.

"Alicia always needs an audience," Lindsay whispered to Potter before they ran back inside to fetch their hats. Leonard Faithorne appeared particularly keen on including Helen in the outing. It was only because of his persistence that she agreed to take part. Alicia always made Helen feel small and insignificant, a sensation that was unusual for her.

Isabelle observed the young Mr. Liebenau regarding the gathering with amusement, as if he were much more mature and worldly-wise. She overcame her usual timidity and rushed up to Joseph and nearly pleaded with him, "Wouldn't it be nice to include my father's young friend? He's come all the way from Chicago, and he *is* just our age."

Joseph was the kind of fellow who liked to include everyone. He went right up to the newcomer and held out his hand, introducing himself. "Hope you'll hop aboard. We've got more food and company than we know what to do with."

"Where are you going?" Joshua seemed aloof. Isabelle felt he was consciously avoiding contact with her, as if he didn't want the others to think they had any association. His reserve made her feel hysterical. She even broke character and interrupted their conversation, "Joshua," she announced, "is an artist."

"We're going up to Lapham Peak," Joseph said, as if she hadn't spoken. "We'll be back this afternoon."

Joshua touched his chin as if trying to figure out what the risks might be. It was clear to her now that he simply needed to establish some contact on his own. He had a few quick words with his father as the girls began piling in, then he asked if he could sit up on top, beside the driver. He didn't glance in Isabelle's direction to encourage her, so she followed the others into the carriage.

"Perhaps he wants to blow the horn," Farwell chuckled, but Helen came to the newcomer's defense, and said that she would like to ride on top coming home.

"You get a whole different feeling for the scenery," she explained. "It's especially beautiful at dusk. I love those in-between hours, don't you?" she said to Leonard. "Sometimes I go horseback riding at dawn."

"These buggies have been known to tip," Lindsay told them. "We need our weight downstairs."

Normally Joseph would have been sitting up above with Jack too, but now he held Alicia's hand.

Looking at Joseph's happy face, Helen felt a contrasting sadness, for she missed her old friend Mr. Ulrich, missed the gruff affection he had always shown her. Though Joseph was now ready to take on the responsibilities of the brewery, he seemed so much younger and softer than his father. Helen could hardly imagine him filling the position. The old man had always seemed so sure of himself. Perhaps it was that inner certainty that had allowed him to nurture the wildness in her. He had understood her passions, for they were made of the same material, rough wool, while Joseph made her think of the silk stretched over a top hat. Her own father was like boiled white cotton, starched and pressed. Max Farwell was a bit like seersucker.

In a certain sense, she felt Mr. Ulrich had been like a father to her, and that would make Joseph a brother. She did feel sisterly toward him now, protective, yet accepting of his own true nature. He would have to make his own mistakes.

"Did you know you can count fourteen lakes from the top?" Alicia squeezed Joseph's arm. She was in a heightened mood. She had gotten her new outfit at Bergdorf's, in New York, a far cry from Felton's, Milwaukee's finest, which was perfectly adequate for the rest of the girls. But Alicia always did look well put together, in the latest colors and fashion. No one could fault her. Even for a casual tallyho picnic like this, she wore a smart red jacket with octagonal black buttons, polished boots, and a long pleated white skirt.

"Do you really think it's safe to climb all the way up?" Teensie wondered. The horn sounded from above as the carriage rumbled down a narrow lane where a herd of cows was being moved from one pasture to another. They were clogging the way between two dense rows of hemlock.

"We don't want to rush them, or we'll curdle our cream." He leaned out to touch a large, flat forehead, but the cow shied away.

The padded interior of the carriage made Isabelle feel claustrophobic. She wished she were sitting by a window, for she had nothing to hold on to as the tallyho began to climb. It was a warm, windless morning, and yet Isabelle felt buffeted by some inner element. She was thrilled that Joshua had joined them, but hurt and confused by his lack of attention. Had she merely fabricated all that had taken place the day before?

She had never thought much about her muse, but now she realized that throughout her college years she had been infatuated with one particular English teacher who had singled her out and encouraged her talents. Isabelle had written many love poems to her, in fact, her feeling for this woman was akin to inspiration, and yet the subject of her quatrains had always been disguised, and her schoolgirl crush had been mainly from a distance, nothing that was ever openly spoken about. Now all of that seemed an embarrassment to her, a remnant of some old, raggy blanket. Last night she had written a real love poem, and her muse was most certainly a man.

Once they arrived at their destination and all piled out, Joshua seemed to stand apart from the group. His stance did not permit her to approach him. The lookout tower stood there, demanding that they climb it. Some ceremony was supposedly to take place on top. But a strange thing happened to Isabelle as she began to ascend the wooden planks of the tower – it was as if she were losing some inner control, and she became weaker and weaker with each step. She tried not to look out at the landscape, which was receding and spreading out far too wide. She tried to concentrate on the number of steps in each level, twelve, and then she could turn, inching her way around to the next set, an agony of movement. By the top she felt dizzy and numb.

The other boys and girls were joking and squealing, trying to count the fourteen lakes that were supposed to be visible. Finally, Joshua came and stood by her side. Perhaps he was as miserable as she was. She felt foolish, silent, afraid to look out, but he made her feel better when he leaned down to speak to her. "I'm not sure which is more dreadful, a fear of heights or a fear of depths. Of course, the latter is more rare and less easily observed. I personally don't like going down. In fact, I think I'd prefer to walk down this thing backward."

"Yes," she agreed, as her knees seemed to buckle and she let herself down very cautiously upon the built-in bench that was protected by the cockpit of the tower's top.

Recklessly Joseph leaned far over the edge, and then, hopping up onto the end of the bench, he turned to face the group. He took Alicia by the hand, and drew her up beside him. "We have brought you all up here this morning, our dearest and closest friends, because it is the highest point we know of in the vicinity, and that seemed appropriate for this announcement." He paused, searching in his pocket for the small gray box. "I didn't want to ask this question until I was certain of the answer."

"How dull," Farwell commented, but Leonard nudged him to be still.

Joseph then faced Alicia and asked with playful formality, obviously rehearsed, "Alicia Bosquet, will you marry me?"

"Of course, darling," she answered, holding out her hand for the five-carat diamond he slipped onto her finger. There were *oohs* and *aahs* over the size and cut of the stone. Isabelle was afraid they might kiss now, but Joseph did something even more shocking. With the help of the flagpole, he climbed onto the railing. "Till August!" he yelled, jumping down with a thump. "Now let's go make a fire and grill up some bratwurst."

A few of the girls were cautious, but the majority of the group went skittering down the steps, though the ground below looked like the bottom of a well. "Here, let me help you," Joshua took Isabelle's hand, descending the steps backward as if it were a ladder. His skin felt clammy, not too secure, so she also held onto the railing – painfully, deliberately down. She couldn't tell if he was only pretending to help her in order to disguise his own panic. Even when they finally reached the bottom and were standing on bedrock, she felt as if some protective covering had been ripped right off and she was still exposed. Joshua gave a sigh of relief, for no one had noticed. The other girls were busy spreading blankets, and the boys had taken to the woods in search of long sticks for grilling sausage. There was punch and Kreuser beer, German potato salad, watermelon, grapes, and pastries for dessert.

"Is anything the matter?" she asked Joshua, settling down next to him.

"No," he answered. But then smiling, "Does it show?"

"You know, I feel like I don't belong here either, and I grew up with these people."

"I caught seventeen cisco yesterday afternoon," he said to change the subject as another couple joined them.

"Popa says we have the best fishing in the whole Midwest. But then, the rod and reel were invented in Nogowogotoc. Not to mention the corkscrew and the kite boat, and just recently the reinforced cement block."

"Really," he scoffed, "you're a veritable suitcase full of information. Why don't you pack it up and come back to Chicago?"

She didn't answer this, for his tone was slightly punishing. She stood up, prepared to go and help herself to the picnic. "Popa says fishing's more sporting if you use a red lure. Or was your purpose simply to catch as many fish as possible?"

He still had not mentioned her portrait, and she felt it would be far too forward to bring it up. Perhaps he no longer saw her as inspirational. The climb had left her feeling wilted. "Why don't we get some food?"

"I don't eat sausage," he responded, just as their host circled by. Joseph felt embarrassed that there was not an alternative. Bratwurst was the typical summer fare. He had not anticipated this. "Some salad and melon would be fine," Joshua assured her, and Isabelle wondered if he expected to be served. She had no intention of waiting on him.

Walking off, she selected a stick for grilling. The stinging warmth of the fire and the smell of the hickory, the hot mustard and toasty buns, all were appealing to her, as if she had come back into herself. Returning to their cloth, she waited to begin, for he still had not made a move to help himself. Finally, he rose with an irritating lethargy, and after selecting a few morsels, he went to join another group of boys who were sitting on a slab of granite, uphill.

By the end of the meal, the boys began spitting seeds at each other to the girls' disgust or delight, Isabelle couldn't tell which, but she noticed the pink bits of flesh left lying in the dust. She did not want to make herself sticky with melon juice, but felt like stealing off by herself for a stroll. A solitary walk would help her maintain her equilibrium, and yet other couples were now beginning to pair off, and Isabelle wondered if she shouldn't chaperone Helen, who had taken Leonard's arm and was leading him over toward a familiar path. Their mother would be scandalized if she knew.

"I'm going to show Leonard our camel tree," Helen called back to her sister. "We'll be right back." Now Isabelle certainly couldn't follow.

"What's a camel tree?" Leonard asked.

"Oh, you'll see. It's just this old bent beechwood."

"Maybe it's an Indian marker. I once saw two trees intertwined like this. Neenemoosha." He showed her with his fingers. "That means sweetheart."

"Yes?" she beamed, skipping ahead of him. "Well, I always rode this tree as a child, whenever we came up here. Do you like to ride?"

Leonard gave a modest laugh, for he had never mentioned his passion for horses, possibly because he did not like to brag. He was more than a competent rider, he was captain of the equestrian team at Yale.

He didn't realize that the one thing Helen sought in a man was a true athletic companion, someone who could keep up with her, possibly even beat her once in a while. Leonard would be staying at the Ulrichs' for another two weeks, and there were so many things they both wanted to do. He loved tennis and he was also interested in hearing more about Felton's. His family was involved in banking, but he wanted to pursue an avenue other than Wall Street, something that dealt with material goods.

"So you appreciate quality merchandise? I'm sure Popa would love to show you around the store. That is, if you can stand the heat in Milwaukee." She led the way down the path, going deeper into the ravine. "Watch out for poison ivy – there's a great deal of it here."

The path forked and Leonard took the opportunity to steal off in another direction as she continued. "The store *is* beautiful. I'd love for you to see it. Say, maybe we could use father's sailboat in the regatta. Would you like to?" When Leonard didn't answer, she noticed he wasn't following her. She quickly turned and raced after him. "Wait for me!" Catching up, she looked concerned. "What's the matter? Are you mad?"

"No, just disturbed," he took a chance and slipped his arms beneath hers. "Disturbed by your loveliness, I'm afraid." Lifting her slightly, up toward him, he softly, very gently, gave Helen her first kiss. She was stunned by the tenderness of it. Somehow she had imagined it would feel harder, more rough.

Joshua, meanwhile, had changed his sullen mood. He came over and suggested to Isabelle that they also take a walk. He said that he had noticed a path on the far side of the granite slab, a more deserted area beyond the lookout tower. "Why don't we explore," he suggested, giving a look that was thrilling to her, but now she did not trust him – she didn't believe he cared anything for her, and this made her skin prickle with confusion.

She found herself making small talk as she followed him down the overgrown trail. Vines caught at her dress, and she tried to be cheerful. "Did you have enough to eat? Weren't those berry tarts delicious?"

"Yes." He looked back over his shoulder. "I *love* berry tarts."

She couldn't help thinking he was making fun of her, but she continued in a similar vein. "I hope this good weather continues."

But then he said something disturbing. He asked her if she had written him a love poem. Isabelle stopped in her tracks, and he turned toward her also. She wondered if he were clairvoyant. He looked down at her chest, which was obviously heaving. She felt startled by the directness of his gaze. "No," she answered. "I haven't written anything lately," though she could feel the blood rising in her cheeks.

"Well, perhaps you should," he said, stepping closer. He could tell he had an effect on her. Putting one hand boldly behind her back, he let his other hand press against her breast, and he held it there, with intention. No man had ever touched her before and when she struggled to free herself, instead of breaking away, she found herself pressed even closer. He held her firmly against him, making her submit to the humiliating embrace, for he had no intention of actually kissing her, and she felt as if she were dropping.

On returning to Broadoaks, Helen and Isabelle found their mother visibly upset, and both of them felt immediate remorse, but she had not been thinking about them. Soon the entire tallyho party became sober and still.

"Oh, this is dreadful! I'm so glad Colin and Mitzi weren't with you."

"Mother," Helen begged. "What on earth's happened?"

"Marjorie Hewitt," Sarah cried, hiding her face in her handkerchief.

Just that afternoon, Marjorie Hewitt had been playing bridge with her foursome of friends, and after considering her hand, she had said, "I pass." Within moments her cards were scattered on the floor – Marjorie Hewitt had passed away.

Helen burst into sobs, while Sarah wondered aloud what on earth they could do, how could they ever help relieve poor Lionel's suffering.

But Isabelle only had one thought – Now Constance and Haven can marry.

CHAPTER TWELVE

C olin Hewitt began each day of his life with a big bowl of oatmeal. Raising the family flag was also one of his morning chores. He liked handling the heavy canvas material. It reminded him of unfolding the sails to his E boat, *The Meteor*, how he hauled the tremendous mainsail up the mast, hand over hand. He craved the sound of rippling canvas, especially when all the humidity had been banged out of the air and light seemed to spank the water. He enjoyed the feel of the soft gray weathered rope going through his fingers, how he looped the line to hold it, controlling the power of the wind as it connected to the even movement of the hull – gliding across the water.

Joseph Ulrich had been Colin's crew for the past six summers, and they had been best friends since childhood. There was no need for them to fabricate conversation. Sometimes they spoke and sometimes they just sat there, letting the breeze air out their minds, letting it soothe them both with a sunfilled peacefulness they could not seem to find elsewhere.

But even when they chatted about inconsequential things, Colin kept his eye on the weather. A true diagnostician, he was constantly considering the small shifts of wind that came across the surface of the lake like ruffled feathers. Joseph had been made to understand that even the slightest adjustments – tightening a sail or raising the centerboard – could create a more effective balance, making the difference between winning a race and coming in second.

It was the end of the summer season, and not wanting to jinx themselves, neither of them spoke about the Valenschein Cup. They had a chance to retire it. Colin and Joseph had won the race the past two summers, and they knew everybody was expecting an upset, especially the Spruce Lake boys. Getting ready for the race, most of the boats tied up to the Lake Club pier, Colin tried to ignore their comments. "The catch to it is, you don't just have to win it three times, which is difficult, but three times in a row, which is impossible."

"Let the truth be seen on the water," Colin muttered as he stepped onto the flat bow of his boat, jerking up the sail to show his lucky number, eight.

All of Nogowogotoc's sailing families were either on deck or on dock now that Skipper's Lunch was over. The Lake Club was playing host to the annual Northwest Regatta of the Inland Lake Yachting Association. It was the final two-point race, and there were so many entries crowding the bay that the sails of the E boats almost touched.

Colin nodded toward a neighboring boat. "Now there's a unique combination." Leonard Faithorne was standing on the deck to *Bottoms Up* in his immaculate white flannels and dark navy blazer. His striped tie and tidy cap made him look like the captain of some college team, but he was only crewing for the undaunted Helen Wells. "Impeccable taste doesn't always make for the best sailing," Colin added dryly. Colin was dressed in more casual attire, an old white shirt unbuttoned at the collar, worn khaki pants, and no shoes. His arms and neck were tan and his thick brown hair blew back in the wind. He couldn't help shaking his head as he heard Helen giving instructions. She was urging Leonard to raise the boom – "Can't you peak it up another couple inches?"

A large stopwatch made a weight in Leonard's pocket. He checked the number of minutes left before the race began, and then, getting the boom between his legs, he yanked even harder on the halyard, giving it all his weight.

Suddenly the old line snapped, and, unsecured, he fell backward into the water with a splash, while the sail slithered down onto the boom and draped itself over the surface of the lake. Observers on the pier began clapping and cheering while Helen scowled. What a soggy sight he was, climbing back on board.

Meanwhile the judges' mahogany steam launch was floating near the starting line, its small brass canon all set up and ready to fire. Getting ready for the gun, Colin tried to attain the best starting position. Unfortunately, Schraeger's boat, *The Pirate*, was close beside him now. Colin ignored his friendly wave, and looked up at the skull and crossbones on Walter's flag. How appropriate. He knew Walter's boat was a good one, for he had sailed it himself during an exchange race, where each man drew lots for another's boat. *The Pirate* was light and responsive. Colin had won in that boat, but now he wanted to steer clear. He was sure someone would try to run him into a marker buoy just to disqualify him.

"What do you think Lucy sees in that guy?" Joseph asked.

"Love doesn't *see*, it gropes," Colin answered. "I can't figure out this blasted weather." He scanned the sky while simultaneously trying to avoid a boat that was angling toward him. That morning it had looked like a good day for sailing, with a steady wind of about ten knots, but now the air felt sodden, and the sky had a peculiar yellowish cast to it, especially in the west above the darkening border of trees.

"Jack said the horses were lying down in the pasture this morning," Joseph reported, and now seagulls could be seen flying inland from Lake Michigan — both indicated that a heavy storm was on the way, yet no one seemed particularly concerned.

Colin was getting serious now, vying for position, with only thirty seconds to go. It was tricky tacking back and forth with so many boats crowding the buoy. Skippers were shouting, "Ready about, hard to lee." Colin knew a good start depended on perfect timing as well as some luck. Today he had both on his side when the explosion sounded from the starting gun and the boats were released toward the number-one buoy anchored across the bay.

Though at least five boats had a similar advantage, within minutes certain crafts seemed to move ahead. Colin knew the lake extremely well. He knew the position of every sandbar, where the weeds grew close to the surface, and where the wind might get trapped because of an inconspicuous inlet, but there were always unexpected elements. "We've got to watch out for *The Gremalkin*," number twenty-seven, from Lac La Belle. "Did you check out that bamboo mast? It should make her very light. Damn." He could see the boat steadily gaining. He had to remain slightly ahead in order to keep the wind fully in his sail. Colin knew he could depend on *The Meteor*, for his boat had been custom built at White Bear Lake, and the polished hull almost slipped over the water. The bleached sails were perfectly stitched, stretched out against the increasing wind, as pleasing as the very best linens, washed in rainwater and line dried.

Colin kept watching the sky in relation to the water. He felt the atmospheric pressure bearing down, and it made him uneasy, tense. He had not really grieved in the last few months since his mother's death. In fact, he had not felt much at all. But today he felt the weight of something bearing down on him. Instead of succumbing to sadness, he tended to joke. "Too bad Mean Marjorie isn't around to see me now."

Marjorie Hewitt had often watched the sailboat races from the point, peering through a spy glass. The boys had made a decent come about and were second in position tacking around the buoy. Second place had never been sufficient for his mother. "Sometimes I can still feel her breathing down my neck. Mother love." Colin flattened the sail a notch, putting his foot against the sideboard as the boat heeled over slightly. "It does seem a shame, as if I'd never experienced Christmas or sex or cognac or something."

The boys both laughed, not really admitting to the loss they felt, having gone without that essential ingredient for a happy life – the first milk of human kindness, a mother's unconditional love. They sailed in silence for a while, gaining on *The Gremalkin*, which was now in the lead by a boat's length. Sometimes Colin felt that he could will himself to win, as if some mental faculty made his boat glide faster, but it was hard to compete with something new-fangled like a bamboo mast, and Walter Schraeger was not far behind.

Marjorie Hewitt had been known for being bossy and cold. In many ways Joseph Ulrich had had a more breezy boyhood because he had never known his mother. When he and Colin took off to row around the lake, eating cookies and grapes, experimenting with tobacco, they often forgot their life preservers. Anchoring in the bay, they would dive off the stern – the smell of lake water, full and round, the sunlight crackling into bits of brightness – and when they finally came in, no one was there to scold Joseph for disappearing. No one had even missed him.

Colin, on the other hand, had always felt that he had this big, hard knot, this mother knot inside of him. But now that burl of bitter wood was replaced by an empty space, like a vague, bad dream. "It's as if I can't hold on to anything. I keep groping for something but it disappears."

Joseph was startled by this description, for he had had that sensation all his life. Alicia was the first person to give that void some substance, even if the substance she created was a curious mixture of longing and pain, inevitably considered love.

Colin could never imagine loving a woman. He only felt irritation in intimate situations, and he doubted if he would ever find a girl who could tolerate his moods.

"Things are going to change in my life," Joseph said. "I'm going to have about ten children and fill up that old house. Don't you ever want to have a family?"

"Ready about," Colin said perfunctorily as they came around the second buoy, both of them swooping to avoid the swing of the boom. Now they would have to tack across the lake, but Colin knew just how to go. He sat precariously on the lee side, splashing his shirttail. "We're certainly going to miss you at the Rooster Club. In fact, I don't know what the ladies are going to do without you, left high and dry."

The Rooster Club was composed of twelve young men who got together and frequented the infamous Everleigh House. After choosing one of the beauties in red or black satin, each boy was escorted to his choice of room, either the Chinese or the incense-perfumed Persian room, with their erotic paintings on the walls. There was also a College Room and a double-decker

Pullman Room. Colin often chose two girls. It gave him more release and he did not have to focus his affections on either one, thereby making it less personal. Joseph inevitably chose the Golden Room, with its golden piano and cuspidor. What his friends didn't know was that he never touched the prostitute. Though he had sworn off playing the piano since his father's death, he permitted himself that one illicit pleasure here, while the lovely brunette danced about the room, disrobing from her already scanty costume. He did like to see her breasts swinging down, for he was a normal boy with normal appetites, but he didn't feel right turning himself over to a whore. He wanted to save that moment for Alicia.

"I've had it with the Midas touch," Joseph chuckled as Colin began hauling in the mainsail and instructed him to do the same with the jib. They jibed to the leeward, and both boys ducked, deftly switching sides.

"I always picture Alicia in a big, gilt frame," Colin responded. "She does have rather expensive taste."

"Worth wasting a fortune."

"Two fortunes," Colin corrected. "At least you won't be strapped. I'll never forget last winter when I took her out in your father's iceboat. You really thought I was running off with her, didn't you."

Joseph looked a little grim, remembering how desperate he had felt. He hadn't thought it very funny, though Alicia had been in such high spirits, coming up the frozen hill holding her stomach – she hurt so much from laughing.

"Anyway," Colin went on, "I'm not the one you should worry about." He sensed Walter Schraeger's continuing interest, and there had been rumors, but Joseph didn't have a doubting mind, so Colin just let it drop. What did he know about romance anyway. Joseph at least appeared happy, and Alicia *was* a delicious-looking girl. But as far as Colin was concerned, no woman was worth suffering over.

After taking the third turn they began heading downwind, the whisker pole set to keep the jib sail out. The boat moved evenly, flat and steady. There was something almost effortless about their course now, though they were being pushed along by a fairly strong breeze. Walter Schraeger had not shown too well in the second turn, but as the wind freshened up, he showed better speed and was still an aggravating contender.

Colin's grandfather had taught him about the ways of the wind, and his father had also won many races. Perhaps his nautical skill was an inherited gift. Artistic traits often ran in families. Sailing was a true combination of brains and brawn, but Colin considered it something of an art as well. There was an elegance to a proper turn, something painterly about the angle of the boats all together, their sails bellied out in the wind.

A strange assortment was out on the water watching the race. Tommy Hawkshurst had a sailing canoe with a lateen sail and a sliding seat. He could shoot his weight out over the water whenever the heavy puffs struck, and then there was *The Turtle*, a nearly round sailboat that seemed more amusing than effective. You could hardly tell if it was coming or going. Hans Jansen rode by in his motor-propelled rowboat, waving at the sailors as if racing were a joke. Everyone liked Hans, but not at times like this, when his wake disturbed the steadiness of the sails. When they had first seen his boat without oars, they could not believe their eyes. The motor looked like a coffee grinder with a pinwheel on its tail.

Colin motioned to the far end of the lake, toward a mean-looking sky that was approaching at a menacing rate. He moved without hesitation, and began yanking down the main sail, gathering it together in his arms. "Fasten it tight. Hurry up! I *knew* this was coming."

"What are you doing?" Joseph asked, but one hard look from Colin told him to just *do* it. The other boats were flying past them now, making use of the wind the storm was pushing in front of it. Joseph tried to ignore Walter Schraeger as he hooted and waved.

"When it hits," Colin instructed, "give the jib a little slack. Then we'll gauge it. Now get down, get under the canvas – she's really coming hard." The storm was more than the typical thunderstorm, but an actual tornado ripping across the lake, and the other boats were not prepared for it. Their good humor at having passed Colin and Joseph turned quickly from joke to dismay. With a loud cracking sound, the bamboo mast of *The Gremalkin* bent like a reed and then shattered. The storm broke the masts of five other yachts and turned the sails of the others. Shouts could be heard, and sailors were struggling not to get trapped beneath the heavy canvas. One fisherman's rowboat was tossed like a cork up onto the shore of Broadoaks, where a seven-pound walleye was wriggling on the lawn. There were cries from the spectators, who were frightened or in trouble, as the wind continued to whip across the surface of the lake, driving torrents of rain along with it.

Finally Colin and Joseph came up from under cover and saw others struggling to climb onto the bottoms of their boats. Joseph spotted Tommy Hawkshurst tangled in the lines to his capsized canoe and without thinking, he kicked off his shoes and made a dive for the boy, who was flailing beneath the weight of his clothes.

Colin had the jib sheet, and one hand on the tiller. Alone, in the storm, he began to pass the whole lot.

Joseph got a grip on the front of Tommy's shirt and hauled him to the safety of the committee boat, which was cruising the shoreline for trouble. Then he crawled up into the big boat as well, and saw that Colin was actually moving ahead by simply using that one small sail.

No one else was paying much attention. No one could see that Colin's eyes were filled with tears, that at the moment of crossing the finish line, he tasted the salt and sadness of his own triumph. He had finished and won for the third time, despite all odds, but he had lost his mother God damn it – that was the simple truth. He lay down on the bottom of the boat and wept, for he wished his mother were still alive, barking some gruff admonishment – how he was a fool to try and finish that race, what was he trying to do? He could almost hear her speaking to him, but he felt something else inside himself now, as if she wanted to inhabit him with a strange, curious warmth, as if she were finally showing her impossible love and her belated admiration.

All the racers had to drag their heavy sails onto their porches that afternoon, hanging the canvas sheets out on the porch hooks to dry before flaking them neatly and stuffing them away in big gray duffel bags. No one had been seriously hurt, though Joseph was considered a hero, having probably saved Tommy Hawkshurst's life.

That evening, at the black-tie trophy dinner, there were close to forty cups and bowls, platters, pitchers and champagne buckets, all sparkling along the linen covered table. But when the commodore rose to present the Valenschein Cup at the end of the evening, hoisting it high in the air and announcing their names, "Colin Hewitt and Joseph Ulrich," the entire room rose and broke into applause. "These boys," he went on, "these sailors, have won this thing for the third and last time. Here it is – it's yours, to keep." The tall, elegant trophy, designed by Tiffany's in New York, stood at least three feet tall, with sea horses rising on either side to serve as handles. The commodore held it out to Colin, the skipper, and he came and took it in his arms.

Colin's happiness was apparent. "There aren't too many things in life you can really hang on to. But now that I've got this in my hands, I don't mean to let it go."

The Valenschein Cup held fourteen pints of champagne. The boys filled it that night and didn't need any help draining it. Colin let Joseph's chauffeur drive them home, while he laced his arms through the rearing arms of the trophy and embraced the buxom sterling form.

CHAPTER THIRTEEN

*J*oshua Liebenau had come and gone, leaving Isabelle in a state of deflation. Nothing much mattered or appealed. She felt stifled in the house, and yet desired no excursion, spending most of her time on the creaky swinging bed. No one but Angeline bothered her.

Angeline was certain Kurtz was trying to poison them. He had given her a cabbage from the garden, and she had carried it home in her arms, but as soon as she lay it in the soapstone sink, a long black snake slid from the leaves, disappearing down the unplugged drain. She had also been complaining about one of Helen's old dolls, and how it kept staring at her. No matter how many times she put it away in the closet, it seemed to reappear. Helen had always had a penchant for teasing, but Isabelle could not believe her sister was still interested in riling up Angeline. She was preoccupied with more important things.

Helen had written to Leonard every other day during the month of July, and her efforts had been more than reciprocated. Now he had returned for the Ulrich wedding, and a corsage of lilies had just arrived: "*Living blissfully in the past, and hopefully for the future. I am, in the present, as ever, Leonard Faithorne.*"

Both girls had become like exaggerations of themselves, Helen leaping even higher, and Isabelle withdrawing back into the dark wedge of the doorway.

"Her tendencies have simply gotten hold of her," Sarah spoke to her husband as they prepared for the ceremony. She began powdering her face with the delicate puff and asked Merrick to fasten the tiny top buttons of her pistachio-colored gown.

"She only needs to get involved," Merrick commented. "She needs to feel useful. Some cause. She *has* shown interest in suffrage."

"But that's so unladylike," Sarah protested. "Did you know she's been receiving correspondence from Margaret Sanger in New York? The one who made such a scandal in the papers. Do you think Isabelle's giving her money? I can't imagine why she'd want to prevent babies from being born when she doesn't even have an escort."

Merrick was secretly pleased that his daughter might be developing a precocious sense of philanthropy. But Isabelle had developed other passions as well. Her father had noticed her response to young Liebenau. Sarah had not permitted herself to even consider that match, and Merrick only hated to see his daughter pining, breaking her heart over nothing, but words of warning and comfort were useless. "How rare it is," he said to his wife, "to fall in love with the right person. I think I was extremely lucky."

"Why darling," Sarah said, surprised, and turning from her mirror, she took him in. "Did you know you're one of the few men in our set who's not overweight?" Normally, Sarah might have described him as frail, but now he looked trim and elegant in his evening clothes.

Merrick was wearing the lapis cufflinks and studs that William Felton had given him as an engagement present twenty-four years before, and he wondered if he would pass them on to Leonard one day. It would please him to have Faithorne as a son-in-law, and yet he had refrained from speaking of it to Helen. There was nothing so damning as too much approval.

"At least Helen is following in our path," Sarah added, meaning the straight and narrow path of sensibility where a partner was chosen, not by a visceral response, but with certain essential things in mind – religion, class, taste, education. There were problems enough in making two people one without adding insurmountable obstacles.

"I think Isabelle must only be encouraged to follow her own inner course. Even if it means going to New York and working with this Sanger person."

"I'd agree to almost anything if she'd get off of that porch bed. She simply doesn't know what to do with herself, now that college days are over and she hasn't any prospects." Sarah seemed pleased with what she saw in the mirror and she fastened a diamond crescent moon to the bodice of her dress.

"I always say the best remedy is doing something for someone else." Merrick was ready to go now, enough said. He didn't like to hear his wife downgrading Isabelle, as if she disliked her own daughter. He feared it was his own qualities in the girl that turned Sarah the most.

"But how could she have any beaux," Sarah went on in her own vein, "the way she acts, so gloomy. She didn't even care that she has nothing to wear for the fanciest event of the season."

"At least she's not an expensive child." Merrick opened the bedroom door in order to end the conversation. "Be happy she agreed to go."

The tents set up on the Ulrich lawns had been brought from North Africa, colorful embroidery stitched all over the brilliant stripes. It was a stunning effect, but hardly the picture of purity most girls would want to present on their wedding day.

"Alicia does everything with flair," Mrs. Valenschein spoke up in the bride's defense as the guests began to gather in the parking pasture. Who else but Alicia would have thought to get a string of camels to carry her guests down to the lakefront ceremony. All the women were inspecting each other's gowns. One striking young lady wore a silver lamé, with little silver leaves in her jet black hair. Joseph's Aunt Teckla wore a pale yellow cape gown with small purple orchids cascading from its ties.

Finally everyone took a seat and, as if on cue, the surface of the lake became calm just as the sun began going down, throwing a hot orange light across the water. A flock of white doves was released from the boathouse and then the crowd turned to see Alicia being carried in a golden sedan chair, accompanied by fourteen bridesmaids.

"It must be everyone she knows," Merrick commented. He and Sarah had a good view of the ceremony, as they had arrived early and were up toward the front. Sarah was enjoying the spectacle, but Merrick whispered, "Don't you think it looks more like a pageant than a wedding?" his eye drifting to the new bride of Walter Schraeger, Lucy Smythe, a lovely, delicate-looking girl. Walter had his hand on her shoulder, as if he meant to keep track of her. She was wearing a simple pale blue dress with an empire waist to conceal the fact that she was now showing.

"Poor Lucy." Sarah noticed the direction of his gaze. "It is such a shame. You've never seen a nicer girl. But at least they did the right thing."

It was clear from a glance that Lucy was hopelessly in love with her dark, handsome husband, while he seemed perturbed by the sight of Alicia carried in the magnificent chair. Alicia looked like some kind of queen with her veils of white silk, a small gold aigrette clipped to her hair.

Joseph stood by the altar in his cutaway, encircled by hundreds of pots of agapanthus, stacked to give the illusion of pyramids. As Alicia stepped from her chair and held out her hand, he moved forward and drew her close to him. Then, carefully, he lifted her veil, and a sigh went through the audience – it was like the forbidden glimpse of some dazzling immortal – but even the bride had to turn and smile when the call of a baby elephant could be heard trumpeting in the distance.

The ceremony was traditional and short. As soon as the couple kissed, the orchestra up the hill began playing, and everyone fled the splendor of the sunset to the even greater opulence of the hors d'oeuvres tent, where unusual dainties were being served on skewers by Bedouins in golden sandals. There was a man with a monkey doing tricks for amusement and a woman with a giant snake. Isabelle found Constance in the crowd, staring at the creature. "Isn't it alarming?" Constance shuddered.

"It gives me a chill just to look at it," Isabelle agreed. Hearing this, the woman coiled the thing around her bare midriff until Isabelle had to turn away.

Constance and Haven had married earlier that summer, a small church wedding, but there was something about it that Isabelle would have called "spirit," an equality of spirit that had appealed to her. "In your service," Isabelle remembered, "you both promised the exact same thing, didn't you? To love, honor, and protect." Alicia had promised the typical honor and obey, and both girls had the same thought – they could not fathom Alicia obeying anyone, least of all Joseph Ulrich.

"They should have said – Honor and *Oh Baby*." Constance smiled. "But he does look like the happiest bridegroom, doesn't he?" Her comment seemed to want to remedy the situation.

Joseph and Alicia had their first dance, and then members of the boisterous Raifstanger family pushed onto the dance floor, crowding the couple with congratulations. By the end of the evening these cousins would be singing "*Hoch so sie leben,*" and urging the orchestra to strike up a polka. The members of Joseph's extended family could not relate very well to Alicia's sense of style, though they displayed their own version of excess. Irma Raifstanger wore the most magnificent jewels around her neck, but they mostly disappeared beneath the folds of her double chin, and Merrick in his discreet, droll manner commented quietly to Jon Bloodgood, "What a terrible waste of good diamonds."

Bloodgood hooted over this, but it was obvious to Merrick that his friend was disturbed by the behavior of his wife. Maeve had apparently arrived a bit tipsy, and she had already consumed a good deal of champagne. Uncannily, she noticed them observing her now and wandered in their direction, her glass held out as if her husband might replenish it.

Years before, when Maeve Peckham had married Jon Bloodgood, the newlywed couple had been plagued by a curvaceous blond woman who claimed to be Bloodgood's common-law wife. The general sentiment was that Maeve was unhappy and that Jon had seriously disappointed her. Who could blame her for drinking after what she'd been through?

"This is just your kind of party, isn't it, dear?" She missed her husband's cheek with an attempted kiss, then said in a lowered growl to Merrick, "Rather tawdry, but voluptuous. I keep expecting some creature to escape. I can't imagine what they're going to serve for dinner – deviled ostrich eggs?" Then off she wobbled in search of more champagne.

Constance Rose was whisked onto the dance floor by Haven, who insisted that Isabelle would also have a turn as soon as he could get back around. Isabelle smiled at him. She had always liked Haven and his melodious, soothing voice. You could have a real discussion with Haven.

Walking over to the edge of the tent, Isabelle helped herself from the fountain of punch. She did not care much for champagne, though it might have made her feel more sociable. Her thick heels sank slightly into the earth – she was unused to these shoes and she felt she could easily tip. Joseph had agreed not to have kegs of beer at the wedding, though certain members of his family were apparently chagrined. Alicia had insisted on Moët Chandon, and the caterers had come from Chicago.

"Do you know what she spent on the invitations alone?" Isabelle overheard Harriet Hawkshurst. "More than a thousand dollars. *Maquet de Paris*."

Suddenly a gong could be heard, and a line of veiled dancing girls wove through the party enticing them on to the dinner tent. Each person had to find his own place card, and the search created a bit of a hubbub, though there were several servants directing the guests to their tables as if they knew all the locations by heart. "Oh, Sarah." Mrs. Valenschein waved. Sarah made her way through the crowd and saw that they were both seated at the same table, but then Mrs. Valenschein whispered, "June Schraeger was fooling with your place card. See here? She took the card of that girl," one of the more well-endowed young females, who had been placed to the left of Henry Schraeger, "and she put *you* there instead."

Sarah felt vaguely insulted. "I must be terribly safe and untempting."

"Oh, don't take it like that. It's just that you're considered so scrupulous."

Then everyone settled down and began the first course. "You could say that it goes with the theme." Mr. Schraeger seemed suspicious of the green Ethiopian pancake accompanied by a highly spiced meat dish, but once they had taken a bite, they found it delicious. Heaping platters of vegetables followed, accompanied by something called couscous. The spit-grilled baby goat had been done in the Algerian manner of a *mishwe*, tender and aromatic with fresh sprigs of rosemary.

A honey liqueur was offered at the end of the meal, but most of the party continued drinking champagne as the obligatory toasts went on. Joseph's college friends got up and sang song after song. Another recited a bawdy poem: "*There once was a girl named Ann Hauser, who thought no man could arouse her . . .*"

Laughter seemed to rise higher and higher until Lionel Hewitt stood and clinked his glass, then everyone gradually became quiet and subdued. "With so many of us gathered here together tonight, we can't help but think of those we love who are missing. I personally feel the presence of my dear friend, Heinrich Ulrich, right here amongst us, and I'd like to raise my glass to his memory, and to thank him for giving us Joseph. To the bride!" he concluded, and there was a unanimous "Hear hear," before everyone rose and drank to Heinrich Ulrich and Alicia Bosquet, a combination of souls that would normally insist on separation as much as any oil and water mixture.

Isabelle's table, placed by the outskirts of the tent, remained animated. Mr. Schultz was recalling how he had walked behind their farmer's plow as a boy, and how he had found enough arrowheads to fill a shoe box. "Lionel there and I used to trade," he confided. "One red one was worth two blues."

But Mr. Hawkshurst had to add, "Those Potowatomi Indians are so dirty and ignorant, great beggars, you know."

"That's not true," Isabelle blurted out.

"You must admit, " Hawkshurst challenged the entire table, "they didn't know anything until the white man showed up. They didn't even have the wheel. They just dragged things around from place to place, using up the game wherever they went."

Isabelle had done a paper on the Potowatomi, a local tribe known as the Keepers of the Fire. She believed they had gotten a raw deal. "Most Indians know more about nature than we do."

"I'm sure it must have seemed like paradise here a hundred years ago," June Schraeger put in. "Can't you just imagine it – birch-bark canoes floating by against the autumn scenery?"

Luckily, the music started up and many couples began to swirl out onto the dance floor. Mr. Hawkshurst asked the lady on his other side to dance. Isabelle wished that she hadn't come.

She overheard her godfather, Jon Bloodgood, talking to a friend from the all-male Phantom Club. They were standing by the edge of the tent, smoking. "You know," he began, "before I got married, I could always tell where I was in a relationship by the smell of my cigar." The men seemed to gravitate toward one another, Isabelle noted, and perhaps that was natural. "When you first meet a woman, and she happens to get a whiff, well, she just can't get over how good it smells. Pretty soon, it's only tolerated, and finally," he made a face of disgust, "she calls it nasty, and you're banished."

Isabelle had remained silent, glued to her seat, but now Mr. Schultz wanted to be congenial. Unfortunately, he picked another sore subject. "So what do you ladies think about this voting nonsense?"

Isabelle hesitated, and Mrs. Schraeger spoke up in her eloquent and inoffensive way. "Now Howard, you know that we women have good common sense. I'm sure you'd never consider my opinion nonsensical."

"But you are not the common woman, my dear."

"The present situation is indecent," Isabelle asserted. "It's as shameful as slavery."

Mr. Shultz seemed to gulp in air with his wine on top of a guffaw when he heard this. "I suppose, young lady, you feel equal to a bunch of female darkies," the old man went on, goading her. "I have never in my life liked to see a woman wanting, but there is such a thing as wanting too much." He patted her knee, and his mere touch repelled her.

Mr. Schultz also excused himself, and then Isabelle felt exposed with no one on either side. Mrs. Schraeger seemed to take in her mood and moved over a seat, explaining, "You know, so much depends upon the tone. What you say is not so important as how you deliver your speech. You can get your ideas across if you coax a man." But Isabelle didn't feel like cajoling anyone. She gave Mrs. Schraeger a pathetic look, not wanting to argue with her as well.

"I know you come from an opinionated family," the older woman went on, "and I must say I admire your father's position on pollution." Schraeger Sausage was no longer throwing pig parts into the river, mainly because of Merrick Wells. Mrs. Schraeger had a small beaded purse filled with hundred-dollar bills that she intended to donate to the Water Commission. "Would you mind slipping this to your father?" she said. "Just say it's from an anonymous admirer, for a worthy cause."

Isabelle did promise, taking the beaded bag in her hands. She decided to use this as an excuse to rise from the table. With a great deal of effort, she willed herself to stand and walked away from the tent, instinctively heading for the lakefront. The swelling noise of the party lifted in a wave, and she felt great relief to be apart from it. She thought she would sit on the bench at the end of the pier until she saw all the boats tied to the dock there, a cluster of drivers waiting for return. So she wandered around the perimeter of the vast grounds, trying to find the Ulrichs' rose garden. There was a lovely weathered-gray gazebo somewhere that Joseph's mother had built. Sarah Wells insisted that she wanted to copy it. The moonlight would be wonderful on the blossoms, Isabelle thought, but as she approached this little hidden area tucked away from the open expanse of the lawns, she realized that someone else had gotten there before her. She was shocked to hear Alicia's voice speaking to some man, not her newlywed husband, but someone familiar. Her tone was both intimate and angry.

Isabelle stood behind an elm tree, horrified that she might be found out and accused of spying, but she could not help listening now.

"Well, I must say, my princess, this is really some get up. Are you going to depart tonight on a lotus covered barge?"

"Don't forget, you had your own little pink posy wedding, not so innocent, I might add. Now it's my turn to celebrate."

"Retaliate, you mean."

"Everyone's in a wonderful mood, except you. I'm having a marvelous time."

"Just don't forget who you are. I'd like to have you right here, before he even has a chance. He hasn't yet, has he. I thought so."

"I'm sure he'll make an excellent husband. I wouldn't want to depend on *you* for more than a little fun."

Isabelle did not want to be a witness to this, but she was paralyzed, afraid she might gasp when she finally took in a breath.

"I will always remember you as my first," Alicia said coquettishly. "That's considered quite special, in a woman's life at least."

"You're brazen," he said, and then Isabelle heard a slap. It was then that she realized it was Walter Schraeger. There was more tussling, as if he were gripping her upper arm and Isabelle imagined him making the twist marks of a snake bite, squeezing the golden bracelet that curled around her flesh. Isabelle thought of all those roses with their thorns. She imagined him pressing a long, hard stem against Alicia until she cried out, pressing the velvety petals against her mouth while also drawing blood – staining the recent whiteness of her wedding gown.

Isabelle was desperate to flee. She heard nothing for a moment, and then, glancing around the elm, she saw that they were kissing. In that moment she believed she would be invisible, so she quickly retreated, nearly tripping on her hem and cracking one heel from its base.

Panting on the fringes of the party, she walked slowly around the ring of lantern light until she felt a bit more stable. Joseph was dancing with his great-aunt Irma, looking all about for Alicia. The candlelight seemed to illuminate his curly golden hair, and she was reminded of a golden retriever, so eager to please, good natured, well-mannered – admirable qualities, but there was something about his innocence that irked her, for she thought people should know the truth, that they should seek it out, confront it, even at the expense of pain. This was like a lopsided fairy tale.

Max Farwell came up and asked Isabelle to dance. "Your sister is already *occupée*," he said, but Isabelle declined because of her broken heel. "Oh, your *heel*," he laughed. "Have you been grinding it into your victims, Arachne?"

She didn't feel like being a part of his repertoire of jokes, though she already was. To the others he called her "the spider." Taking refuge at her mother's table, Isabelle listened to Lionel Hewitt recalling stories about his old friend Heinrich Ulrich, how they had each bet a million dollars on the race of two raindrops down a windowpane. "I know Ulrich had his faults, but then all of us do. I liked him and he liked me. People don't need high society as much as they need a good friend." It seemed he missed Heinrich more than he missed his own wife. Perhaps he did not mention Marjorie because the recollection of that loss might throw a shadow across Sarah's lovely countenance.

But Sarah was not feeling the least bit gloomy. Even their speaking of Heinrich seemed to buoy her up. She had always enjoyed Lionel's company. "For someone who is supposed to be retired, you're certainly giving the term a black eye."

"What I do isn't really work. Making money is fun. Colin's taken over the Milwaukee branch, and I guess I can still take care of Chicago. But I tell you, if I knew I was going to live this long, I might have taken better care of myself."

Isabelle saw that Helen was dancing with Leonard, looking up into his eyes. Isabelle was happy for both of them, for she genuinely liked Helen's young man and believed, if such things were possible, that they would make a good marriage, one she would be happy to witness. But still she wondered how anyone could tell the real thing, pick it out from the different lights that shimmered on the water – True Love, like the moon herself, disguised by all the globes that illuminated the launches down by the dock. Isabelle sat there musing over a quatrain from one of her recent poems.

In sorrow, dream, of days long past –
An unforgotten spring –
When love was pledged but later lost
Like bird upon the wing.

Suddenly Alicia reentered the wedding party in a change of outfit. Rushing up to Joseph in all apparent innocence, she acted as if she had been away applying fresh makeup for his admiration alone. Isabelle watched Walter Schraeger's expression as Joseph twirled her around, pressing his lips to her cheek. In a moment the eight-tiered wedding cake was brought out and placed upon a cleared, round table. Joseph did not notice that his older brother, Frederick, had just arrived with a handsome male companion. Isabelle had never seen a man so tall and thin.

Alicia seemed aglow now, knowing all eyes were fixed on her. But Walter turned his back and went off to shake hands with the long-absent Frederick, while the wedding couple held the silver cake knife in preparation for the cut. Exclamations of alarm seemed to merge with hilarity as everyone observed the white frosting of the cake parting to reveal dark chocolate beneath, with a black forest filling, Alicia's favorite. It almost looked the same color as her hair, which had been hennaed more lustrous for the occasion. They fed each other crumbs of the moist, dark cake, then quenched their thirst with elbows linked, drinking down goblets of champagne.

Frederick, a fleshier, more sanguine version of his younger brother, snapped up a bottle from one of the silver trays and waltzed out to pour them some more. "Big brother is back to serve you. May I kiss the bride?" He smacked the air on either side of her face then turned to his effete-looking friend. "Ravishing, isn't she?"

"Freddy! How wonderful for you to come all this way." Alicia beamed, trying to make up for Joseph's lack of response. Frederick had not even been formally invited.

Frederick swiveled on his heel as if to absorb the entire party. "I guess I'll have to take care of the family farm while the children are running about the continent." He raised an eyebrow, as if he could actually smell the cow manure.

Joseph, regaining his composure, clapped his brother on the back. "I'm glad you could make it, old fellow. Quite a surprise. Sorry we don't have much time to catch up."

As planned, the couple darted for the lakefront, where a steam launch was awaiting them. Most of the young people followed, and were delighted to see lanterns placed all along the bank spelling out Alicia's nickname, *Bijou*. She turned at the steps and threw her bouquet. Helen sprang up and caught it, though Alicia had intended it for Mitzi Hewitt. The couple left the pier beneath a hailstorm of rice, thrown to shower them with luck and fertility, but most of the grains fell into the water, and Alicia brushed the white rice from her shoulders and hair as if she did not want too much good fortune to cling to her.

CHAPTER FOURTEEN

*W*ith the distribution of the Ulrich will, Gustav Kurtz had become a very wealthy man, though he still considered his occupation to be that of a simple gardener. He had the same gruff workman's manner, and begged no apology for his appearance. With his large, square hands he tucked inch-high seedlings into rows, all at an equal distance from each other.

Instead of being damaged in transition, the tender plants seemed to thrive – the moment of transplanting like communion for him.

Ever since Merrick Wells had deposited the two hundred and fifty thousand dollars in the First Wisconsin National Bank for safekeeping, Kurtz was determined to maintain the same style of life he had always known. Why shouldn't he have the same concern for his gloxinia, cineria, and begonias? He still wore the same black hip boots, and dragged the hoses around from place to place, winding the ventilators of the greenhouse up or down depending upon the weather, but at least one thing was different – he was no longer asked to put in a fence post or mend a gate. He had made it clear to Mrs. Wells that he was not a maintenance man.

On a drizzly morning in late May, the crew was sitting around the potting shed, cleaning and stacking the terra-cotta pots, wiping the metal counter of sifted soil, and smoothing the boards of debris. As Kurtz sharpened tools, the foot-propelled stone sent sparks shooting out into the darkness of the shed while the men traded stories of the Old Country. Otto, from Dusseldorf, now eighty-two, liked to remember the family he had worked for, and how Frauline V. would come into his greenhouse and kiss the flowers each morning. "One day I put out the *Mimosa pudica* – you know how sensitive dat is, and when she come by and go *smoooch*, dose leaves just folded and drooped, like dis," he dangled his hand and the gardeners all laughed. "Now you done it! I said. You killed it!" The gardeners were all in agreement – a woman was no more welcome here than she would be on board ship.

Kurtz had one personal preoccupation – he was obsessed with creating an all-white amaryllis hybrid. For years he had worked diligently toward his goal, and today a new blossom had opened. He held the pot up toward the light, inspecting the bloom for a streak of rosy red, running like a trace of blood in the petals of the flower. He wanted to drain this delicate beauty of her sanguine tint, allowing her to live like an angel, in pure white hallowed perfection.

The men admired his scientific methods, which were actually rooted in German folk wisdom. He made the mulching of the soil work like magic, and kept insects from destroying the plants by interweaving certain pungent varieties such as garlic, white geranium, and marigolds. Building up the beds for better drainage, he fertilized the transplants with a dilution of cow dung, and planted according to the phases of the moon. The tuberous plants needed to be placed in the earth during the contracting lunar cycle, while the flowering plants that opened upward benefited most from the phase of expansion.

His men were expected to maintain the same high standards he set. If any one of them was found dragging a hoe over a new tomato plant, mistaking it for a weed, that was the end of his career at Broadoaks. But if he performed well, there was no age set for retirement. Even Tai and Pompeii were expected to behave in the garden, and the neighboring children who entered by the metal gate had to respect the established order, though Kurtz was always happy to show them how to pull up a carrot by holding the greens close to the top, rocking it slightly back and forth in order to ease it out. He was generous with visitors and gave them wooden pint baskets to gather berries from the hay-strewn beds, for he liked to see the pleasure on their faces when they dared to sample the luscious fruit.

Most of the city folk moved out to Nogowogotoc in early June, but Alicia and Joseph Ulrich were to live year round at the lake. Kurtz winced when he heard the sound of her Packard limousine as she was driven up to the greenhouse. Standing, he caught sight of the deep burgundy of the luxurious car that continued to idle in the pooly yard. The car was lined with a soft, dove-gray kidskin, and there was a gray Persian lap robe flung over the seat.

Rapping twice at the greenhouse door, Alicia stepped into the warmth of the glassed-in structure. Pausing there, she seemed to be entranced by the large lavender orchids that grew in baskets of sphagnum moss. The lanes were filled with abundant flats ready to be transferred to the cold frames – delphinium, dahlias, calendula, zinnias, and early dwarf snaps, which were already blossoming. Alicia stooped to pinch one, making it open its gaping mouth, and then smiling up at Kurtz she admitted, "I always did that as a child."

"Are we still a child?" Kurtz grumbled, turning his back on her, for he did not like sacrificing even one of his blooms. "Leave that umbrella by the door." He would not have her swinging that about and knocking his plants.

"I'm here to pick up my wedding present," she explained. "Did Miss Wells ever tell you? You know she was always very fond of my Joseph," Alicia went on, but he gave her a disgruntled look that said, I wouldn't know. His loyalty was such that he never spoke about the family. "She promised us the most unusual thing," Alicia paused, trying to look past him, "a flat of forget-me-nots. Isn't that quaint?"

Kurtz turned and led her down the walkway to a mass of tiny blue flowers. He was grieved to give away even one of his twelve flats, for he liked an even number. Alicia actually thought the gift sentimental, but in collecting the common perennials, she hoped to get some advice on his more exotic bulbs.

"I heard you have a wonderful source for lilies," she ventured, her gloved hand brushing a fluttery maidenhair fern, and then glancing above – "I just love those violet orchids. Something like that would look splendid in my new solarium. It's so hard to know what to hang."

Kurtz was not about to give away any of Mrs. Wells's favorite flowers. He had caught hell enough one time when Otto had shared a bit of their seed corn.

"You see, I'm redecorating my house," Alicia went on, actually taking him by the arm, so that he could smell her perfume, a scent that reminded him of overripe peaches, "but I'm trying to upgrade the gardens too." Kurtz felt uncomfortable, for his men had closed the door between the potting shed and the greenhouse and he did not care to have this much privacy with her. "I received the most unusual Oriental poppies," she continued. "They're almost as big as my umbrella over there." She nodded back toward the door, releasing him finally. "No one else around here has anything like them. I thought you might be interested in a trade."

Kurtz was slightly intrigued by this offer. "I could take a look. But I'm busy right now. I've got to get the men back out to the garden." He felt trapped, and Alicia seemed to enjoy his discomfort.

"While we were on our honeymoon, I fell in love with the most beautiful nude. We're going to put her in the middle of the fountain, in the circle out front. I want to grow my poppies around it."

"You'll have to have other plantings for later in the season," he responded. "A garden is an orchestra. You have to compose."

"I wish I could have more of your advice. If only you could find enough time to design this one little garden. I know you're a gentleman farmer now. I hope you get to do whatever you want."

"Yes," he stopped her. "I do what I want."

"I think you should focus more on your research. You know, if you liked working over at Topside, I'd support you in that."

"I'm a gardener," he answered, "not an arsonist."

Alicia was momentarily taken aback, but she quickly regained her composure. "I hardly think *you're* one to fling any mud. As appropriate as that might be."

Kurtz was silenced. He had not meant to say anything. He simply did not like to feel her manipulating him. He could never stay under the Ulrich roof like a kept half-person.

"What do you know anyway," she said, walking away. "If he was innocent, he never would have burned."

"I'm sorry," Kurtz answered, keeping his eyes averted.

"Don't be sorry." She turned her attention to a potted bay-leaf tree. "It's just that things aren't always what they seem. I can tell you're completely devoted to Mrs. Wells, aren't you." She plucked a leaf and rubbed it between her fingers, sniffing it, then dropping it to the floor. "I suppose if she told you to plant a tree upside-down, you'd do it in an instant, without question."

"Without a question."

Her opinion confirmed, she seemed relieved, almost ebullient. As she turned to walk down the cement pathway, he followed with her flat of forget-me-nots. "Why don't we pick out some daisies," she suggested. "They're my favorites, actually. Does that surprise you? And you know I'd love to have one of those orchids. That one with the cute little faces. Aren't they exactly like kittens? I'm sure no one will miss just one of them." Kurtz continued to follow, stunned by her requests. "May I?" she asked. He did not say no, so she helped herself. Reaching up to unhook a basket, she placed it on the counter. She seemed exceptionally strong, as if her new acquisitions had given her this force that led her to confront the gardener with a strange, broad smile before taking hold of his arms and kissing him squarely upon the mouth.

Alicia found it amusing that Gustav Kurtz had been Heinrich's half-brother, an heir to the Ulrich fortune and yet still a hired man. Alicia felt she and Kurtz had something in common, somehow they were both on a similar plane, impostors of sorts, neither of them quite legitimate, but doing exactly what they wanted, getting their own way, because they were both single-minded. She felt a kinship of spirit, which he obviously didn't share, as though the darkness of their individual backgrounds served to set off the colors of their lives – Kurtz with his flowers, and Alicia with her fabrics. Topside was in a state of upheaval.

During the six-month wedding tour, Joseph and Alicia had purchased special wood for new parquet floors and shipped back three marble fireplaces from Carrara to replace some of the heavy dark wooden ones, which Alicia insisted were a fire hazard. She could never forget the sight of those chimneys after the burning of Bon Pres, how they had remained standing there like specters.

On returning from their honeymoon, Alicia struck up an immediate alliance with Joseph's brother, Frederick, who was in no hurry to leave the family home. Alicia and he spent hours going over swatches of material and samples of paint. They both agreed that the house was too dark and depressing. "You need lightness and levity, *mon bijou*. Did you know there's even a dungeon in the basement?"

"That's nothing but a water cistern," Joseph insisted as he walked into the living room. He was tired of his brother trying to stir things up.

"Next you'll be telling me there's a closet I can't go in," Alicia teased, dragging her husband out to the front of the house where she admired the stone-carved hop vines, for they identified Topside as the home of a great brewer, but she didn't like the soldiers etched onto the front-door glass. "I feel like I have to be on my guard entering my own house. They look so judgmental, just like your father. And you know I can't tolerate a scowl. Wouldn't a nice depiction of fruit be more cheerful?"

"I don't know," Joseph seemed worried over these changes, as if he had to live up to some image of the past. "I don't see anything wrong with them. They never bothered me."

Frederick pointed out that the soldiers *were* wearing knickers, completely out of date. And then he went on about the living room – it was far too somber. "When you open the door, you expect to hear a *groan*, the visual equivalent of a dirge, old boy. Too bad you don't still play the piano. Some music might brighten the mood of this room."

"And these tapestries are from some other century," Alicia added.

"But we grew up with these things. That was Mother's," Joseph pointed to the dark blue-and-green wall hanging.

"If you wanted such a masculine house," she wheeled around, "why did you marry a woman?" In a fury, she marched up the stairs. Then leaning back over the banister she cried, "I refuse to entertain in that big ugly room. Maybe you should go back to having your stag parties."

"Naughty little roosters," Frederick commented, sitting back in the deep red velvet of the couch with his midday glass of sherry.

"Listen, Fred," Joseph began. "I'm sure you realize how difficult the first year of marriage can be."

"Why should it be any easier than the last? You and I need to work things out too." Frederick meant to contest their father's will unless Joseph gave him his fair share. There was no need to involve litigation if Joseph saw things from a gentlemanly point of view. "Father obviously wasn't in his right mind. There was no apparent cause for suicide, no financial disaster, no loss. He was simply deranged. Why else would he want to cut me out of his will? I'll have to assume that at least the farm is mine until we get this settled." Frederick knew that his younger brother didn't want further investigations. Joseph's main concern now was for his marriage, which had not gotten off to the smoothest start.

Joseph craved his new bride, but her fiery domination often made him feel like less than a man, and he could not always perform with her, which infuriated her further. When he failed, she would turn on him and make insinuations that turned their coupling into some kind of contest, which only brought on more disappointment.

"You know I adore you," he reassured her that night. "You're very desirable. If it really means so much to you, go ahead with the living room."

"Oh, darling, you never should have married such a mean, bad girl. I just want to see you happy, and I'll never make you happy."

"But I *am* very happy," he responded, looking exhausted and miserable. "You should keep your mind on business. Let me deal with domestic things."

"But I have been planning our annual *gemütlichkeit* picnic," another German family tradition that she didn't understand.

"You mean the one where all the men traipse barefoot through the daisy field? Will you hire that little brass band again?" He sensed she was only feigning interest, maybe mocking him now, but Alicia did want things to be decent between them. She only wanted him to be a bit more appreciative, to admit that she did have a talent, a keen eye for color and illusion. She knew just how to hang a Venetian silk drape to give a room a softened quality. She loved Fragonard paintings, and she borrowed his palette for the exotic fish she had painted on the walls of her bathroom.

Frederick began to take more and more liberties in the house, in part because Alicia encouraged him. He liked to come into her bathroom while she pinned up her hair. "Some people might call this vulgar," Frederick commented, turning on the hot water faucet so that water spurted from a cupid's tiny member, filling up her black marble bathtub, but Frederick could appreciate celestial plumbing.

Embroidered fans covered the walls of her dressing room. Frederick wandered in and sat down at her vanity, rearranging the clutter of bottles on the mirrored surface, but when Joseph appeared, Frederick gave Alicia a ghastly look and slipped out.

"What's wrong with you?" Alicia asked her husband. "You know Freddy means no harm." But Joseph just stood there, arms crossed, surveying the walls of the dressing room.

"I was just thinking how fortunate it was that all these fans were at the public library the night of the fire."

"Why remind me of that horrible time?" She came up to him then, letting him encircle her with his arms. She had collected these fans throughout her childhood, and each one carried some import. Joseph looked inappropriately wolfish as he began inching up her dressing gown.

"It doesn't suit you, that hungry look."

"Even lambs need to eat sometimes," he answered, grazing on her shoulder. Nothing was entirely natural between them, and Alicia knew that was mainly her fault. She had to let him have his way with her once in a while or things would get ugly between them. He did have a manly, strong body – she

101 ↰

was not repulsed. She simply could not conjure an image of desire in relation to him and had to keep her imagining elsewhere.

Even as he lifted her and carried her to the pillows of the high, canopied bed, she could not help thinking about Walter, how he held her wrists and scruffed her neck. With Joseph, making love was like some exhausting foot race, where he was desperate to win – the whole focus on the finish line, reaching that ribbon of completion – while with Walter, his aim was to prolong her pleasure, and she had to overcome the resistance he established. He was clearly in charge. It was always on his terms, but that made her feel more excited. She wanted to be controlled.

Still, she could enjoy the physical sensations as Joseph lay down beside her, stroking the unrestrained flesh of her breasts. Apparently, he wanted to take her from behind, and though he acted somewhat apologetic, she knew she could accommodate him best this way, for she didn't have to really reciprocate. She gripped the large square pillow to her face and let him hold her buttocks as he rode her like an animal. Strangely enough, this was comforting to her, for it confirmed what she had always known – that men were beasts and would always use women perfunctorily if they had the chance. Joseph fell into a heap when he was finished.

He could not figure out why she remained so difficult, even after they had success in bed, not realizing that if he became less accommodating, she might not take such advantage of him. She had gotten the upper hand, and Joseph soon discovered that it was easier to say, "Whatever you want, dear," though that was not at all what she needed. She disliked the lack of contest more than anything.

PART THREE

CHAPTER FIFTEEN

Sometimes Helen could hardly believe that their love had become so ac-
cessible, that there was so little conflict to overcome. Her summer days
spent with Leonard were almost lived in another element, as if they floated in
a daze of pool-warm water with no resistance to either hot or cold, just this
perfect lulling temperature, where the two of them existed without dispute.
More and more she recognized him as her perfect partner. When they played
tennis together, they almost always won, for she was a steady, good player,
and she could count on Leonard's lob, his height at the net. Whenever he
smashed a ball between opponents, he would say "I'm sorry," or "Excuse me."
She liked that combination of unexpected aggressiveness with his confident,
gentlemanly manner. But sometimes in the evenings, alone with him, his politeness became a source of aggravation to her. She felt wilder, more daring
beside him, and she wanted to tip their perfect balance, as if testing his ability to recover.

Now that the country had joined Great Britain and declared war, Leonard
wanted to finish up his last term of business school and join the American
Volunteer Ambulance Corps, stationed in France. Helen found herself imagining life without him because it helped create the inner desperation she
needed. She liked to fabricate unwarranted jealousy because it brought him
closer to her.

The vista of the lake opened to the night as they approached the shore
through the dark oak trees. Leading her down the herringbone walkway
through the moonlit balls of hydrangea, Leonard had an unusual urgency
about him. "I want to row you to the middle of the lake," he said, and she
sensed he had some plan.

Why the middle, she wondered. Why not all the way across? He was more
charming when he didn't try to be, she thought. In many ways Leonard was
similar to her father – reliable, learned without being pedantic, scholarly
though a thorough realist. She depended on Leonard's clarity of mind, for he
was not only bright, he had a special integrity that impressed her. Her love had
deepened in layers, not so much out of longing but through genuine respect.

She respected his honesty, fidelity, kindness. He would make a wonderful father. She admired his unusual range of knowledge, for he knew the names of all the constellations and told her fabulous myths about the heavenly bodies that made her feel as if she too were a heroine. He could recognize the bright song of a chestnut-sided warbler and repeat its message for her – *Please, please, pleased to meet'cha*. And he was one of the few young men who understood her father's passion for wine. She was glad they shared that sensibility.

Tall, thin, and upright, Leonard was protective and yet not overly demanding. His countenance was akin to that of a young Briton, and reminded Helen, fondly, of a dazed field animal, sitting up, considering his natural surroundings as if he wanted more time to chew. Often he hummed a little tune, forgetting he had company, amused by his own inner thoughts. Usually she appreciated the way the two of them existed, whether speaking or silent, active or still. Almost always she felt they were compatible, except when this other thing got hold of her.

Tonight, beneath the moon, out on the warm lake water, trailing her fingers across the surface, she felt restless and asked, "May I row, too?"

He seemed momentarily disappointed, for he had wanted her to be more receptive to his plan, which he had conceived and considered over and over until it took on its own reality, which did not match up to the actual evening, for the stars were not as brilliant as he'd hoped. If she wanted to row, well then he had to acknowledge that this was the woman he loved, though the size of the waxing moon left him feeling more exposed than he might have imagined, and he felt a physical urgency growing in him now, which he knew he must keep concealed.

Putting that energy into his rowing, he had almost felt at ease until she wanted to sit beside him. He was afraid that might be too much, for he had never been so taken with a girl before, and found it difficult to keep from brushing her leg through the layers of her dress as she sat down beside him on the middle plank. He did not sense that she might have similar desires, which she could hardly describe, let alone name. It was so tempting to have her there by his side, pulling on an oar, matching his efforts as they both dug into the water. He placed one hand behind her, as if to lend support, but he resisted the temptation to move his hand farther around to where he might caress the natural movement of her breast.

That he did not pursue this very impulse made her impatient, especially once they'd reached their destination and their oars began to drag, the boat drifting in a semicircle. "Looks like the center to me," she said.

He teased a wisp of hair that had fallen across her cheek, and she moved her head, for his fingers were tickling. She didn't realize that she wanted him to hold her, to kiss her in a more earnest way, for him to exert his masculinity and dominate her own strength for a moment. Instead, she felt this disgruntlement, which made her click the toes of her shoes. "I don't know what to think about Isabelle's antics."

Helen's older sister had decided to sit out on the raft as a protest that week, refusing to eat, sleeping on the bare, hard wood of the float, and she had gotten a terrible sunburn. She had announced that she would stay there until suffrage was granted, and the *Sentinel* had come out to take photos. On the third day she had gone into a faint.

"I think what she did took real courage," Leonard said, though this was not what he wanted to be talking about.

"She doesn't care much for food, never has. So what difference does it make if she goes without for several days. To tell you the truth, I believe she was trying to draw attention to herself."

"I wouldn't be surprised if you have the vote a bit sooner because of women like Isabelle." He spoke in such a kindly manner that Helen knew he wasn't chiding her. "It's a social issue. You have to reach the papers if you're going to make a change in the minds of the majority."

"My Aunt Clickey used to tinkle a little silver bell at men who spat on the sidewalk. She and her friends got *them* to stop, but now the same men smoke cigars." Helen was also on the side of suffrage, but she wanted everything done yesterday. She felt that women should already be doing all that men did – building, teaching, exploring.

"Did you know you're the most beautiful girl in the entire world," Leonard said to her.

She knew she was not, but she didn't contradict him.

"Will you marry me?" he asked, not at all as he had planned, for he had wanted to present her with the family diamond, and he had forgotten it in his room. He had anticipated a cry of happiness, that she would throw her arms around his neck, and he would be allowed a more intimate kind of kiss, but instead she bowed her head and appeared thoughtful.

"You surprise me," she admitted. "I'll need some time to think."

He couldn't imagine what she needed to ponder, but he didn't like her making light of such a question by adding, "Are you including Pompeii in the proposal?"

He had always had trouble with that fresh little pug, its face like a pushed-in piece of pâté. On first meeting the dog he had asked her, "Will its breathing improve?" She had found his irritation with her pet most amusing, but had insisted that he accept the pug-pig side of her, for he would have to embrace all aspects of her nature.

"So my darling isn't in such a big rush, as usual," he summed up the mood. He could always participate in the war effort while she continued her studies.

She knew she would be Leonard's wife. She just wasn't going to say yes to him that evening. She didn't want to make things too easy for him, or they would never attain the proper intensity. She had known he would be her husband for some time now. She had known it since the night of the Ulrich wedding, when she had seen him walking toward her table to ask her to dance, his eyes intent upon hers. She had known right then that she wanted to see this man walking toward her for the rest of her life. That moment, more than this, had been the revelation.

She simply felt they had to bear this bit of misery a while longer. As he rowed her methodically back to shore, the water lapping against the sides of the boat, moonlight stirring about them, she wanted him to seize her, for him to taste her lips as if fresh-skinned peaches were being passed from mouth to mouth, but Leonard was feeling rather formal.

She could sense his discomfort as he rowed, and she knew her hesitation was almost cruel, but she also believed this moment of resistance would wed them forever. He let her off at the end of the pier, and she listened to his nervous *hum-tee-tum-tum* as the hull of the rowboat slid up onto earth. He pulled it forward and flipped it over, clapping the two oars together upright.

She did not want the evening to end this way, so suggested they sit on the white wooden bench that was bolted to the end of the pier. The planks were damp with moisture, and he wiped the bench with his handkerchief before she sat down. "Tell me a story from your childhood," she urged. She loved to hear him talk about New York.

Small brown bats were swooping out over the water, snatching mosquitoes from the air, and he wanted to let her know that he was not offended by her response, that he was confident still. "You know, I never thought I'd meet someone like you," he confessed, not taking her hand as he might have. "I always thought I'd get stuck with Babbs Markham or Polly Peck, one of the girls from dancing school. Boy, I hated that ordeal. All the hawk-eyed mothers watching from the balcony. Everybody anxious. Why do girls always want you to play tea, or be the father? I figured when the time came, I'd just have to keep on pretending, you know, to play the part expected. But now it seems natural just to be here. I can't imagine it any other way."

"Nor can I," she took his hand, giving it a squeeze. He turned with surprise and happiness to look at her. "But Leonard, there's something else," she added, looking up at him with tears in her fiery, determined eyes. "I want to go with you. I want to drive an ambulance to the front." She seemed overwhelmed by her own suggestion.

"And what would you do if I said no?"

"I wouldn't believe you."

"Oh," he laughed. "Well, we'll have to think about *that* for a couple of days." He had turned the tables, and now she too had to laugh a little, startled by his taking her advantage away, but admiring him all the while. "Farwell and I wanted to take a bicycle trip. This might be the perfect time, give us both a spell to think things over. We were planning on going to Madison."

"But that's so *far*." Suddenly she felt desperate, deserted. Their summer time together was too precious to be apart. Now it would be her turn to suffer.

Both of them were in a subtle state of torture during that week. Helen was anxious that she had used the wrong strategy, that Max Farwell would introduce him to someone truly beautiful, as he was always threatening to do.

The image of their marriage, so precious to Leonard, tossed about in his mind like an irritating pebble. He had taken the ring along on the trip, lest he forget it again, and it burned in his pocket like a tiny, brilliant flame. The right answer, he hoped, would be like the lulling lake water, soothing his entire being.

Four days later, returning from the capital, Leonard rode down the gravel drive to Broadoaks on his rickety black bicycle with its loose front wheel, while Farwell walked – he had had another blowout by the garden and was not going to bother patching it again.

Leonard shouted, "*Oooh-aaah*," to anyone who cared to hear that he was back, and Helen burst from her room down the double flight of steps, banging out the front screen door, leaping down the two steps to embrace his dusty form in her powder-blue-and-cream colored dress. She nearly knocked him off his bicycle to the amusement of Farwell, who had scoffed at Faithorne's fears, while encouraging him to be sensible and remain a free man.

Leonard had never looked so good to Helen. Taking his mud-flecked sleeves in her hands, she kissed his smudged and scratchy cheek. Then looking up into his eyes she did not hesitate, but released her response and whispered, "Yes."

"Yes?" he answered. "You mean, *yes?*"

"Yes," she confirmed.

"You'll marry me?"

"Yes," Helen told him, laughing at him now.

"Definitely yes?"

"No," she shook her head. "Absolutely yes."

"When?" he asked her.

For that she had no answer. She would have to ask her mother.

"Soon, I hope," he persisted, as if he had acquired a new spirit of energy. "I popped my wheel eleven times."

She leaned forward and murmured, "I love you so much." Then she noticed that Farwell was listening, and she looked to the ground, still clinging to Leonard's arm.

"I could use a cool drink of something," he suggested, and she was taken aback, realizing that she would now have to start watching out for the welfare of another human being. Of course she would run to fetch him something right away. Farwell had already placed his damaged bike against the servants' wing and was heading inside for a ginger beer. "Wait," Leonard caught her. "I have something for you."

He brought from his pocket a tiny pair of deerskin moccasins with Indian beads sewn onto them. They were just the right size for her old doll, Butterfly-Beau, and she suddenly longed to be a girl again. But just as she felt this tug from her childhood, he reached into his pocket and presented her with the ring, a beautiful round diamond with many sparkling facets. She held the two presents together in her hand and then burst into tears. He let his bicycle drop and held her. She clutched the leather just as tightly as the stone.

Isabelle joined the dinner table a little late that evening, returning from a suffrage meeting in town. She came in full of her own exuberance, her hair in disarray. "I have a scoop," she said between mouthfuls, not picking up on the mood of the room. No one could guess what was inspiring her now, so she told them outright, "Springwood Lee – it's for sale! It's not on the market yet, because Mr. Moore has tuberculosis and they aren't sure how to proceed. Did you know he's moving to Switzerland?" For once Isabelle seemed to have an appetite, perhaps because she hadn't asked what she was consuming – larded sweetbreads smothered with chanterelles. "I'm just holding my thumbs we get some nice neighbors. Can you think of anyone, Popa?"

"What about your sister, and Leonard," he suggested in his most casual tone. Indeed the idea had just occurred to him.

"Popa!" Isabelle was shocked. For Springwood Lee had always had a rather scandalous history. Patrick Moore had kept a luscious fan dancer in the gatehouse, and when she became pregnant, he had hired a eunuch to marry her. Even then she wouldn't give up her career, she was such an exhibitionist.

"We're engaged," Helen explained, unable to hold back any longer, and finally Isabelle understood.

Though her mouth was full of mushrooms, she rose to kiss her sister, and Leonard sprang up to embrace Isabelle as well. Then, turning to her father,

Isabelle had to confirm this. "You mean Helen will live next door to us? What an idea! Just imagine," she turned back to her sister, "no more Waldheim Spa." That was their private little joke. Isabelle had been allowed to play with Tommy Moore after he had become legitimate, until the boy showed her a shocking photograph of an enormously fat woman plastered with mud. That had strained the relations between the two families.

"Think – we'll finally get to go into that playhouse," Helen added, for this had been one of the chief frustrations of her childhood, living so close to such a glorious construction and not being allowed to go in. Once or twice Helen had peeked in a window and seen the child-sized stove and little upright piano. It even had a tiny treadle sewing machine, a three-foot china cabinet with miniature goblets and bone-handled silver. Small wicker rocking chairs were placed out on the porch.

"I've always admired Moore's skeet set-up," Merrick put in, as if this were the deciding factor. Angeline brought around a platter of prairie grouse, and Merrick offered Leonard one of his more special wines, a Steinberger '93.

"Don't forget the widow's walk," Sarah added. "Wouldn't that be a grand place to watch a regatta?"

But Leonard was hesitant. He hadn't even thought about this. And he worried whether they could manage Springwood Lee, for it was a twenty-room cottage, and the grounds were even more extensive than Broadoaks, with a gymnasium, loft, gatehouse, and bathhouse. After dinner he took Merrick aside and told him he didn't think they could afford such a place. Merrick explained that the house would be a wedding present, and when Leonard still expressed concern about the enormous upkeep involved, Merrick only answered, "Don't worry. I'll endow it." Not much more was said.

Grouped in the palm-banked recess of the vast Felton fireplace, the bride and groom made a charming picture. There was a spectacular luminescence from the Tiffany window that day, and the prisms of gold favrille glass shimmered with magenta and yellow beneath the hand-blown sconces of the grand Milwaukee home. Helen also looked full of color and light. She could feel her lucky sixpence in the toe of her shoe. Aunt Clickey had given it to her. Helen was not superstitious, but she had also accepted "something blue" from her mother, and "something new" from Isabelle. She would always treasure her bridal hanky because Isabelle had picked it out herself.

Helen wore an exquisite gown of white satin, trimmed with old rose point and Duchese lace. It had belonged to her late grandmother, Julia

Felton. Helen's long tulle veil was caught with orange blossoms and she carried a bouquet of lilies of the valley, while Isabelle wore a gown of larkspur blue and held a muff of mixed sweet peas.

Pillars of foliage linked by ropes of white chrysanthemums stretched to form an aisle to the improvised altar. Above the kneeling couple was a large horseshoe of small white roses. Percival Defoster played the wedding music – he even managed to help cover up when Leonard dropped the wedding band, and it rolled across the room and nearly threatened to go down the grate, saved by the quick foot of cousin Alcott Allen.

Standing in the bay window the couple received their guests. A profusion of roses filled the air with their perfume. Aunt Clickey could not help but congratulate Leonard on the fumbling of the ring, for every wedding needed a near disaster – it was those awful little moments one remembered the best and recalled with inexplicable glee.

Standing in the receiving line, Merrick leaned behind his wife and said to his tall son-in-law, "Remember when we met on the *Cannonball?*"

"Of course," Leonard said. "Going into Milwaukee."

"And you told me how you'd just made the acquaintance of the most remarkable girl."

"Who just happened to be your daughter." Leonard beamed.

"I remember how you told me what a bright, intelligent young woman you thought she was."

"Indeed." Leonard smiled, for he remembered it very well.

"I thought it very odd," her father went on, "how you could be so blind."

Leonard was taken aback by this comment, but he did not let it sour his mood, for he knew in his heart that he loved Helen Faithorne for much more than her exceptional beauty.

After the excitement had settled and the couple sailed for France, Merrick found time to write his daughter a note:

My dearest Helen,

Isabelle is extremely well and trying to please her old father by learning to play golf. She seems perfectly happy settling things, as she says. I did not know she had anything to settle, but she seems to be very busy.

We got to watch three people take a dip in the frigid lake the other day, but we contented ourselves with watching their agony without emulating them.

Your mother was very anxious to send you a night letter suggesting you be careful, but I doubted the efficacy of telegraphing advice of this character, so was able to prevent the suggestion from being forwarded to you by wire.

I miss my little daughter a great deal, but am confident you are doing what you must, and I'm pleased that you have begun your own life in earnest with a wonderful man by your side. Nothing could make a father more happy.

Months later, Helen wrote her sister from Paris.

Darling Isabelle,

Your description of the early morning sun filling the verandah and the meadow in a golden mist made me terribly homesick for Broadoaks. I hope and pray that by next summer we'll all be together.

Tonight, I feel like a lemon pushed through a sieve and my letter probably has acquired certain acids of that fruit. This war business has a curious effect on most of us. We forget some of the most familiar names and subjects. Just the other day I was trying to think of one of my favorite authors, the one who wrote Tess of the D'Urbervilles, *and I couldn't come up with his name. One gets mental aphasia. I suppose it's the complete absorption in the moment and the strangeness of new surroundings.*

It is killing how many men in the street salute Leonard. He is the best-looking private you ever saw, and his bearing is so commanding – they often don't notice that he hasn't the insignia of an officer, he has such a good-looking uniform.

Wednesday I had a dreadful day chauffeuring for the Red Cross using the heavy old Studebaker that barely crawls up the hills, and I told Miss English that I thought it a poor reflection on our organization. Her response was to give me the worst truck in the place. She gave my car to Anne, but then it wouldn't even start, and I had to tow her home, the climax of a series of petty, unjust tyrannies.

The Germans are gaining ground but the Americans are covering themselves with glory. Some shells fell within a few blocks of me today and the explosions were so loud, I jumped in spite of myself. People go about their business the same as usual, and just give vent to a few curses now and then, like – "Ces sals Boches." Need I translate for you?

My heart aches for the poor wives who will suffer as the war goes on. I think if I knew the old cannon was going to get me shortly, I'd be much more worried about Leonard and all of you than I would be about myself. These have been days full of inspiration, and I shall never forget them.

Never before in my life have I held such a position of responsibility, or felt so truly humble and insignificant. I guess we are all pretty small cogs in the greater scheme of things.

Your loving sister,
Helen

Though the family had moved back in town for the winter, on the fourth Saturday of September Merrick motored to Nogowogotoc for one last peaceful day of fishing. That morning by the porch he had been stopped by the cheerful song of a Rufous-sided towhee that had been puttering about in the leaves before the front steps, singing – *Drink your Tea. Drink your TEA*, and Merrick had suddenly thought of his mother, calling up to his sickroom where he had lain as a boy. During those months of convalescence he had learned how to sew, knit, and embroider, and he had always maintained, *The more dextrous the hands, the more nimble the mind.* But as a boy he had not been able to bear the ghastly concoctions his mother had brewed. He had poured the teas into his pitcher, later asking his nurse to freshen up the water, for he liked it clear and cold.

Merrick actually preferred the autumn for fishing, because the fish that sulked in the depths during the hot summer weather now renewed their appetites as they instinctively prepared for colder times, and the solitude of the lake was appealing. All eight hundred and eleven acres of water were undisturbed by the other summer residents, no gentry or tourists, sailboats or steamers, and the bay on the northeast end of the lake was one of the best locations for fishing. He could have caught a significant number from the dock, but he preferred rowing out to feel the greater isolation, and to know he was unavailable to either telegraph or caller.

Angeline had accompanied him to the country, and she had fixed him a special bag lunch. He would catch them some nice perch or walleye for supper, and then they would return to Milwaukee later that night. But at sunset, Angeline came down to the dock to scold him for not coming in. She stood at the end of the pier and called out to him, but Merrick Wells was slumped over in his rowboat. Only a string of black bass trailed behind him, moving beneath the surface with vague undulations.

CHAPTER SIXTEEN

$\mathcal{T}$he following spring, when Isabelle took Angeline out to Broadoaks to open up the summer home, the furniture was still covered with large white cloths that kept the dust from settling on the fine upholstery. This ritual of maintenance, performed by Angeline each autumn, gave the place a ghostly look. "Nothing will ever be the same," the old woman kept saying, yanking and folding sheet after sheet. "We loved him, and we'll go on loving him. But nothing will ever be the same."

Picking her way through the familiar forms of furniture, Isabelle felt a chill, starting in her arms and creeping up into her back. It felt as if she were trying to find the exit to some cemetery while the tombstone shadows kept lengthening all the while. The summer before she had been so happy with her father, playing golf and honeymoon bridge, just the two of them. She had teased him about his spats, and timed his evening stroll up and down the front corridor when the weather was too hideous to go out. She thought of the oddest things – how he liked his cucumbers carefully peeled, so that a good tint of green was still visible. How easily the life force could slip from the body. Even her pen could not make sense of it.

Since her father's death, Isabelle felt even more removed from most people. She had to make a mental effort to cross the gap, self-conscious in her conversation, as if she were editing her words as she went. Nothing came naturally, and she was beginning to sense that a normal life would not be hers. She had no inclination to marry or raise a family. Pregnancy did not sit well with too many women, she thought. She had never seen her sister looking so pale and listless.

Helen had just returned from France, three months pregnant, while Leonard had stayed to continue his service. That in itself was an adjustment.

"I feel like a plant that's been ripped from the soil," Helen told Constance Rose. "Are you as miserable as I am?"

Constance did feel queasy, but she didn't like to complain.

Isabelle, standing in the doorway, did not understand all the fuss. "If you feel like sleeping, why don't you sleep?" She could see no reason for fighting it.

"But this isn't like me!"

Constance agreed that she felt peculiar. "But eating a little something all the time seems to help. Haven says that we should indulge. We should try to imagine the pace of a cow."

"I know, with a big green pasture." Helen made a face at this cud-chewing occupation, which did not appeal to her at all. She didn't mind most of Dr.

Rose's suggestions, for she knew that he meant well. He had prescribed raspberry leaf tea, tepid lavender baths, and a normal amount of exercise, but that meant no strenuous athletics, only a regular morning walk. She was not supposed to bend over from the waist, and she was supposed to eat lots of leafy greens and fresh calf's liver. She was to avoid any circular motion, such as winding yarn, for it was a common belief that such activity could wrap the umbilical cord around the baby's neck. So far Helen had not even felt the baby move. She simply felt nauseous and exhausted.

"We could certainly use your help planning the hospital bazaar," Constance suggested. "We're going to start building this spring."

"We've been raising all sorts of money," Isabelle put in. "I told you about the Euphoria Society – Max Farwell began the Loiterers Club in response to ours, but all they do is sit around, gossip, and spit."

"They call us the bright bachelor maidens, but we hardly look like maidens anymore," Constance said cheerfully. "Do you think you could help us with one of the booths? Haven thinks we should get women from the lake to pair up with women from the village. He thinks it's high time we broke down the snob barrier. Maybe we could pick names from two different bowls."

Helen admired the impulse, but not the method. "That might seem a bit artificial. You can't really make advances like that overnight, by shuffling people together. We *are* two different decks."

It was hard for the poor country women to feel comfortable around the ladies of the lake. They were intimidated by the wealthy women who carelessly arrived on the morning of the bazaar with boxes of priceless bric-a-brac for the white elephant table. How casually they plopped down their treasures – a tarnished tiara beside a hand-carved cane with a dagger hidden inside it, a full suit of Japanese armor, not to mention the sheer, luxurious gowns, castoffs from previous seasons. The village women almost felt like objects of amusement themselves when they displayed their desire for the magnificent discards.

It had been decided that the village women would be in charge of selling homemade food as well as the raffle for "the smallest pony in the world," no bigger than a dog. All the children had been saving their nickels for a chance.

On the morning of the event, local farmers set up tables to sell rounds of cheese and early summer produce, while the ladies of the lake were in charge of the booths arranged on the north side of Main Street. Each booth was labeled a different day of the week – *Monday* had floral wreaths, bags of sachet, and dried herbs. *Tuesday* offered hand-painted clothespins and homemade soaps, some carved into rosebuds. *Thursday*'s table had embroidered aprons and handkerchiefs, while *Friday* displayed irresistible baby items, hand-knit booties, blankets, and buntings. *Saturday* boasted doorstops and hand-crocheted fly swatters, and *Sunday* had copies of the Bible. You could have your name engraved on the cover in gold leaf.

"I think it's wrong to have freaks on display," Lindsay Esser said to the members of the *Wednesday* booth. She was referring to the six-legged calf that had just been led by – two additional legs dangled from its hips.

Helen confirmed her opinion, but Constance Rose, now six months pregnant, surprised them with her attitude. "I think it's only natural for a fair like this. It's part of the fun, to be shocked." And it was true, most people were drawn to the gruesome. Haven himself had set up a stereopticon show of the San Francisco Earthquake disaster, and there was also a Globe of Death Dancing Pavilion that was sure to be a hit. Helen had organized a Rat Maze made out of hanging bed sheets, and the new owners of Ulrich Farms had brought over two of their dairy show cows, which would be milked before a small Swiss chalet with Whitey Simmons out front yodeling. The German garden replica was ready to serve *kaffe kuchen*, and later in the day there would be *frankfurter mit kartoffelsalat*.

Helen had recovered from the early months of her pregnancy and felt stronger than ever. She was in charge of the money in the *Wednesday* booth, which was offering ladies' summer hats. "I wouldn't be surprised if we make over two thousand, if we sell everything here," Helen ventured to say. "That would be enough for an ambulance."

"She thinks she's still in France," Lindsay teased.

"Anything we make will be wonderful." Constance tried not to focus too much on the material outcome. She was already feeling a bit oppressed by the heat, and wondered if it would be all right if she sold sitting down.

Helen was in a swirl of activity, arranging her coin box, labeling hats. She wanted everything to look just right before the band began playing from the Lac Le Beau gazebo, which signaled the official opening of the fair. People had come from as far away as Menominee Falls, and many women were already lined up to pounce on certain items.

Helen was convinced that their hats would be popular. "I think we should charge more than twenty for this one." The large straw hat had a tiny stuffed bird beside a real bird's nest filled with three speckled eggs, blown and glued in place. "I've always liked to play store," Helen admitted. The others laughed and had to agree – it was probably an inherited trait.

They had an abundance of bonnets decorated with flowers, organza, feathers, and lace. Constance plopped one funereal-looking hat down on her head, lowering the exotic black veil. Helen told her to take it off – "You look ghastly" – and then the brass band started up and a loud steam whistle sounded from the fieldstone station. People were eager to spend, knowing the proceeds would benefit their own small town hospital. Joseph Ulrich had donated kegs of beer, and he bought back the suit of armor Alicia had donated. A big bunch of red balloons swung by, followed by children with cones of scraped ice splashed with blueberry syrup. John Reeves drove his tallyho drag through town, serpentining amongst the crowd, whooping it up and hollering.

By noon, the women in the *Wednesday* booth were thoroughly tired, operating only on the energy generated by too much excitement. Constance was feeling almost faint and wanted to get a bite to eat, when Max Farwell wheeled up with his crew, blaring the horn to his fancy cabriolet. Hopping out of the open-air car, one inebriated man pulled a big wad of money from his wallet and waved the bills in the air.

Helen found their antics in very poor taste. They didn't need this kind of attention. But the brazen big spenders swayed before the milliner's booth and insisted they each needed a summer hat. In a moment, feathers and ribbons hung down in front of their faces, tickling mustaches. The largest man of the group slapped the tiniest hat on top of his head. Grabbing a purse from the table, he minced about while the others roared, and then they scooped up aprons and tied them on too. Helen didn't know what to say. Constance had taken their money, and the men had not even asked for change. Helen watched as they plucked the *Wednesday* sign from its hooks and held it up just as a photographer materialized. They must have known that the editor of the *Free Press* would love to get a good spoof photograph. As he quickly set up his big black contraption, the men turned their trouser pockets inside-out for full effect. Just as the photographer was about to squeeze the bulb, his camera steadier on its tripod than the men were on their feet, Helen rushed out and yelled, "Don't do this!" But as she reached for the dishcloth that covered the box, the man squeezed the bulb and got the shot – there she was in the foreground, frowning, obviously pregnant, the bonneted buffoons behind.

"Why do you have to ruin everything?" she demanded of Farwell. "You just come in here and act like this!"

"I was trying to support your venture," he said sheepishly, falling to one knee and trying to kiss her hem. She jerked it away. "We're going to give back all the hats, so you can sell them again." A cheer went up from his crowd. They all ripped the carefully sewn bonnets from their heads and mashed them back down on the counter.

"Perhaps we can tidy these up," Constance whispered to Lindsay, fingering one of the hats the men had abused.

Haven appeared with three cups of lemonade. He had heard the commotion and wanted to see what was going on. As soon as Helen saw him, she burst into tears, for she no longer had her old equilibrium. Haven would normally have stopped to comfort her, but Lionel Hewitt's chauffeur appeared at the corner, shouting, "Dr. Rose, come quick! Mr. Hewitt's been stung!" The boy's face was flushed, his voice high pitched with excitement.

Haven didn't wait to hear more, but grabbed his black bag and ran after the boy. He knew Lionel was allergic to bee stings and might only have minutes to live. Jumping into the Daimler that was idling before the bank, he told the boy to step on it – they didn't have a moment to lose. Perspiring, Haven drew serum from a bottle, wishing he could be behind the wheel, but sensing the young driver's tension, he tried to stay calm. "I used to drive for the Hewitts," he said.

"I know," the boy responded, driving faster than he ever had. "Someday I want to do something too."

It took them five minutes to get to the entrance. They roared past the sign and went flying down the driveway, dust billowing behind them. Haven got ready to jump from the car, which stopped with a scatter of gravel arcing onto the lawn. A workman ran up and pointed to the garden – Lionel was lying on his side, shaded and fanned by two house girls.

"Stand back," Haven ordered and they gratefully withdrew. He administered the shot and Lionel moaned. The old man rose up onto his knees like some kind of beast that refused to go down, vomited, defecated, and began to breathe, gripping a handful of earth in each hand. As he collapsed onto his back, he saw the huge morning glories on the chicken-wire fence, trumpeting a heavenly blue.

CHAPTER SEVENTEEN

L earning about etiquette," Lionel Hewitt explained to his son, "is a lot like learning about sex."

"Oh?" Colin scoffed. "Then I suppose I shouldn't have any manners at all. Really, father."

But Lionel continued as if Colin hadn't spoken. "The main difference is that learning etiquette isn't much fun." Lionel felt that his boy only needed instruction, advice, that was all. He was used to his son's rather rough way of speaking, and attributed it to Colin's extended bachelorhood. He had been somewhat hopeful about the boy's interest in Lindsay Esser before these more recent rumors began. "There are certain rules we all must learn, the sooner the better."

"Good Lord," Colin interjected. "Just because we're stuck in the same house out here."

Lionel leaned forward and put both fists on the desk before him. "You have no idea of what you're doing, as usual."

"As usual," Colin repeated.

"Just taking and using, taking and using. It's going to backfire someday." Lionel then proceeded to the point he had wanted to make. "I don't like your behavior with the summer girls. It's inappropriate and it must stop immediately."

"Where have you been hearing this truck? Not from the respectable Mrs. Wells."

Sarah had been making regular visits to Hewitt's Point for luncheon or tea and Lionel had been her escort to various social affairs that summer. It irritated Colin that they had so quickly become a twosome. So what if he had taken a liking to Lolly Jones. What healthy young man wouldn't have the same response. She was one of the two girls brought up from Chicago to help with the housekeeping. "You were the one who hired her. I suppose you didn't notice anything in particular."

"Nothing worth losing one's head about."

Blame it on the midsummer heat and humidity, but it was almost more than Colin could bear, watching her sweep the front porch in her white cotton smock dress, her large breasts swinging from side to side. Her foamy brown hair was heaped and pinned up, small strands falling down around the base of her neck, which gave her an appealing, disheveled look. She had been working very hard, creating a flush in her cheeks and a glow of perspiration on her brow. Colin could not help staring.

Clearing his throat several times so he would not startle the girl, he said, "You know there's an art to that, if you get the hang of it."

"Sweeping?" she asked.

"Would you like me to show you?"

"You don't think I do a good enough job?"

"I'm not saying it's terrible, it's just that you can always do better if you practice."

"Well, I've had plenty of practice at this," she said smartly, stopping for a moment to lean her cheek against the handle. She was tempted to hand the broom over to this good-looking rich boy. She would like to see him working for a change.

"May I?" he positioned himself behind her as if he were a golf pro, teaching her how to putt. Clutching his hand over hers, he pressed himself against her, and helped her sweep a little pile of dust and leaves to the edge of the front porch steps. He could feel her buttocks moving before him, step by step, sliding sideways in rhythm, and when they stopped, he let his hands move up onto her arms, brushing lightly across her breasts.

Lolly turned and said, "You shouldn't play games."

"Why not?" he asked, sensing her ambivalence.

She suddenly seemed vague, not really thinking, as if the heat had seized her mind and squeezed it. "I don't know, maybe because I don't know the rules."

"There aren't any rules to this game." He followed her as she began her retreat to the kitchen.

"Everything's got rules," she said, and he liked that, her quick response.

"You're right," he agreed. "Absolutely right. We simply need to pick our sport. What about curling? They use a broom for that, on a long lane of ice."

"Well, I don't think I'd have time for curling," she said, turning at the swinging door to stop him from following, but her lightness of mood signaled a certain giving in. "And I don't think you'd find that much ice around here, not in the whole state of Wisconsin."

"So what were you doing up there?" his father wanted to know. Lionel was sure he had heard his son's voice up on the third floor in the servants' quarters. "You don't know what kind of trouble you'd get yourself into if you got that girl into trouble."

Colin wanted to play the whole thing down, for he was not about to stop his dalliance with Lolly. Lindsay Esser worked him up to a pitch in a cerebral way, while his response to Lolly was visceral. "I took them a bucket of ice," he answered honestly. "Because it was so bloody hot. It's impossible to breathe up there. They don't even have a fan and there isn't any cross draft."

"Our summer girls have always used those rooms. I've heard no complaints." Lionel was defensive because his housekeeper, Mrs. Knutson, had recently hinted that the rooms were not very pleasant. She was more outspoken now that Mrs. Hewitt had passed away.

"I'd hate to propose a quality in your own flesh and blood that you seem to find so lacking, but I was simply being thoughtful."

"I see." Lionel looked up with his blue-gray eyes, knowing that Colin was not likely to do something nice for anyone unless he intended to get something in return – a good quality for a businessman to have, Lionel thought, but not a husband or a son.

The night Colin had crept up the narrow curving steps that led to the third-floor rooms, it was still ninety degrees at midnight. Lolly and her helpmate, Antoinette, were both sitting on their wrought iron beds, fanning themselves with pleated newspaper. When Colin tapped on the door, Antoinette jumped, for they were only wearing sleeveless bodices and short bloomer pants, but Lolly signaled her to hush.

"It's the ice man," Colin whispered. "I've come to cool you off."

"That's a likely story," Lolly whispered to her roommate, but her heart was pounding. Colin had been on her mind. She cracked the door and saw his bucket of ice chips.

"For you, Madame." He made a bow, struck by the unadorned look of the place, for there wasn't even an armchair or a picture on the wall. The floorboards were painted a dismal gunmetal gray, and a brown coil rug lay between the two beds. Each girl had a small cardboard trunk, that was all. A bare bulb hung from the ceiling. "You could certainly use a breeze up here."

"It's not so bad, really," Antoinette apologized. "This is the hottest night so far."

"Well here," he set the bucket on the floor and sat down with a crunch on Lolly's horsehair mattress. He pushed the bucket toward Antoinette. "Help yourself." She plucked a chip from the top and looked as happy as if she had been treated to an ice-cream sundae. Then he offered the bucket to Lolly.

"Oh, thank you, kind Sir," she said, running a piece of ice over her forearms.

Taking her cue, Colin selected a large piece of ice and rubbed it over Lolly's shoulders. It felt shocking, delicious. Cool trickles ran down her chest and back, moistening her top. He went up onto her throat, sliding the ice chip up and down in the groove of her neck as she leaned back on her elbows. She didn't think she could trust him, but she felt relatively safe with Antoinette in the room.

After a while, Colin asked, "Would you rub a little on my temples? My mother always did that when I had a fever." Lying down, he looked up at her with a little-boy look that made her feel overly confident, maternal. "Ah," he sighed, "that'll help bring my temperature down." He smiled, closing his eyes, and Lolly lifted an eyebrow, glancing over at Antoinette. Both girls tried hard not to giggle.

"My, my," she nursed him, "you really *are* sick." She ran ice over the pulse points of his forehead and wrists. "I think he must be delirious." Playing along, Antoinette lay a moistened hanky on his brow, but then Lolly scooped a handful of the chilled ice water and splashed it onto his stomach.

When Lindsay Esser appeared the next day in her brand-new green electric car, Lolly stayed in the kitchen. Mrs. Knutson was busy with the laundry – the sheets had to be washed and line-dried every day – so Antoinette went out to receive the visitor, offering the lady a mint iced tea. Lindsay accepted, more out of politeness than thirst.

Lolly kept thinking of Colin's lean, muscular arms. When he had lifted his nightshirt to receive the cooling effect of her tickling ice cubes, she had taken in the spicy ginger scent of his cologne and the memory was still swimming around her. She was dazed, even slightly intoxicated. She kept remembering how he had grabbed her when she shocked him with ice water, but he had not really gotten angry. He had even stayed around to tell them jokes. Saying goodnight, he had stroked the top of her head, saying that he'd see her in the morning.

Mrs. Knutson entered the back screen door with a wicker basket full of laundry. She assessed the situation with her typical, "Good grief, it won't do you no good to keep mooning over that one. In fact, you better stay clear away. He's always had a mean streak, ever since he was a child. Certain people are born nice and some people are born mean, that's God's plain truth. Just because He loves 'em all the same doesn't mean you've got to."

Antoinette poured the sun-warmed tea into a tall, thin glass with octagonal sides. "She's wondering where Colin is. I told her he was probably out sailing, but she said I must be mistaken. How do you like that? She *is* awful elegant, though. She drove herself over."

"Let's hope she doesn't hit a tree." Lolly pulled at the puffed white top she had tucked into her bright red skirt. She felt foolishly over-dressed now, and wanted to go change.

"You sure you don't want a better look at her?" Antoinette picked up the tray. "You look real nice too, very festive." As if Lindsay Esser and Lolly Jones were in some sort of competition.

Lolly knew she wanted to change her life, and felt frustrated by her lack of any real opportunities. It didn't seem fair that she would have to work all her life, while this woman could do what she wanted. *Why don't we pick a sport* – she remembered his words – *Sure*, like washing, sweeping, or ironing.

From the kitchen window she could see the young woman walking over to the bluff where the wooden steps went down to the lakefront. She was not even waiting for her tea. Then Lolly saw Colin come bounding up the steps, taking the lady's gloved hand. He checked his watch and acted surprised. Then they walked along together, laughing and talking. It struck Lolly that this woman was his equal, and she wondered if he were more attracted to that.

Mrs. Knutson snapped her out of her mood, telling her to help fold the laundry. "I've seen that boy put a firecracker up a little lame chipmunk." The old Swedish woman kept folding one pillow case after another, smoothing out the pile.

"Colin wouldn't do that," Lolly tried to dismiss her.

"I'm sure you don't know what he'd do."

Lolly could not keep from looking out the window, though she couldn't bear to witness how Colin held Lindsay's hand and acted like a perfect gentleman. At least the young woman was not well developed, only willowy, blonde, and very beautiful.

Colin and Lindsay were expected at the Ulrichs' for an afternoon croquet match. Alicia had invited three couples to play round robin.

"I guess we'll be fashionably late." Lindsay smiled up at him, settling herself down on the porch swing as if they had all the time in the world. "I'll just rest here in the breeze while you're getting ready."

Only then did Colin realize he was supposed to change clothes. He leapt up the stairs, pulled on white linen pants and a clean white shirt, his crimson-and-white school tie. Glancing in the mirror, he grabbed his jacket, not noticing that his shoes were slightly scuffed.

Lindsay smiled as he appeared. "You look so healthy," she admired, as if her words put the finishing touches on him. "My skin's too sensitive for the sun, but I must say it makes a man look rugged. Would you like to drive?" She offered him the keys. The car had been a birthday present from her father.

Colin, unfamiliar with the vehicle, began with a lurch, but Lindsay complimented him on his expertise. She had graduated from Mount Holyoke College and she did not miss a trick. "Your father always finds the nicest-looking summer girls. Our summer help is always so gruesome."

"My father tends to have good luck. Did Antoinette make you some tea?" He wanted to steer away from the mention of Lolly, and Lindsay did not take it any further.

"I hope we beat Joseph and Alicia. They've been practicing all week with this new English set. I think Morvan even rolled the lawn for today. You'll have to make up for my incompetence."

But he did not find her lacking at all. "I'm sure we can win if we put our minds to it. Just watch the ball, and have no sympathy for your opponent, that's the main thing."

Lindsay and Biddy and Lucy all made a fuss over Alicia's new living room. It was feminine, sumptuous, and comfortable. "You amaze me," Lucy said. "I wish you'd help me over at our place."

Even Walter praised Joseph for his lenience. "There aren't many men who'd give Alicia free rein. You should be proud of her."

"I am," Joseph answered, ushering the group out to the lawn. Morvan had set up a keg of Kreuser beer and each man was offered a large glazed stein. The women sipped lemonade and snacked on cucumber sandwiches as they sat together beneath the lawn umbrella, catching up on local gossip. "That's extraordinary," Biddy said to Lindsay. "You actually drove over and picked *him* up?"

"Curiosity got the better of me. But I didn't see anyone, not really."

"It won't amount to a thing," Lucy assured her.

"Besides," Biddy added, "it doesn't hurt a man to look."

"It certainly does," Alicia asserted. The rest of the women turned to their hostess, who was bound to inform them of some disquieting truth. "Women might fall in love with their ears, but men fall in love with their eyes. Haven't you noticed?"

"I wish I'd notice *somebody* noticing," Biddy complained.

Alicia glanced toward Walter Schraeger, who met her look with a smile from across the lawn, but then he shifted and nodded to his wife, who quickly bowed her head, for she had taken in the unspoken contact.

Out of hearing range, the men were sharing their own lewd anecdotes. "Someone said you have a rather fabulous piece of topography over at Hewitt's Point." Walter nudged Colin. "Have you made a map? Or is she one of those unexplored continents?"

Max Farwell rubbed his hands together. "When do we get to witness this wonder?" Colin took Farwell aside until both boys were hooting, and Alicia hopped up, wanting to discover the source of the hilarity.

Picking up her white straw hat, she began swirling slips of paper – "Come on now," she called. "We'll each pick a partner." Colin reached out, but she said, "No, no," holding her hat away from him. "The girls, I mean. We're doing the picking these days." Alicia offered her bonnet first to Lucy, who was pregnant for the third time, and Colin was put out that she had chosen him. Lindsay got Joseph, and Biddy, Max Farwell. That left Walter for Alicia, as planned, for his name had not been in with the others.

"I want green," Lindsay cried, as if it desperately mattered, scooping up the ball with the matching mallet.

"Black is my lucky color," Max insisted.

"Joseph, dear, will you get everybody straight? Why don't you and Colin start, then we'll play the next round."

Joseph took over naturally, and had the first group line up. "Whoever gets closest to the center line leads," he instructed. Colin came within inches.

"Lucky me," Lucy said. "You'll have to make up for my handicap." She wished he didn't look so severe.

"It's only a game," Walter yelled from the sidelines, noting his wife's distress. But Colin never had a good time unless he was winning.

"You should have seen the time I played Joseph's father," Alicia told the group. "No one told me I was supposed to let him win. Besides, I would never let a man win on purpose, would you?"

Biddy said that she always let a man win. "It's my only strategy."

"No one ever dared beat him before," Joseph added from the sidelines, slightly defensive whenever the subject of his father arose.

"*Heinrich Ulrich has a big stick*," Alicia began, reciting the childhood rhyme until Joseph gave her a look that said – that's enough.

"But darling," she pleaded, looking about for support, "he *was* awfully scary."

"I hope we're playing poison," Max put in, "otherwise I'm going home."

"Just don't whack my ball in the bushes this time," Biddy warned, reminding him that she was his partner – luckily, not for life.

"Will you help me with this?" Alicia asked Walter, handing him the tray. "I have no idea what Mildred's up to." She led him over to the side door, and as soon as they passed into the study she took the tray and set it aside. "Oh darling, I've been absolutely dying for you. It's so hard being this close and having to pretend."

Walter kissed her on the mouth but only briefly. She wanted his passion to match the intemperance of her own. "I lost Nicole," she complained. "I don't know what I'm going to do."

He looked confused, for he had forgotten the name of her personal maid. "Is that what you wanted to tell me?"

"No, not exactly." She became her most coy, kittenish self, slipping her arms around his waist, leaning back so he had to hold her. "I just wanted to be alone with you for a moment. Is that so terrible?"

"No, it's not terrible. You're the most delicious, desirable woman in the entire world – how could any man resist you?" He kissed her again, but there was still a lack of abandon.

"What's wrong?" she asked.

"Nothing's wrong. It's just I don't think this is the best time or place, not with Lucy here. There's no need . . . "

"Listen," she tried another tack. "Joseph's going to a convention in St. Louis next Friday. We could have a whole weekend together. Stay with me, please."

"Darling, I can't this weekend, but we'll have our time, I promise." He did find her tiresome when she tried to set things up. "Patience is rarely coupled with beauty, is it, *mon bijou*?" But just then a burst of activity was heard from the lawn, and Walter made a move to return to it. Alicia retreated to the kitchen for a moment.

Having to restrain her desire made her irritable, angry. "I'll play badly," she thought. "I'll miss the wickets altogether, and he'll lose."

Lolly was beginning to sense that Mrs. Knutson was right – there was something dangerous and unpredictable about Colin. He could hurt a girl without provocation, but he was also very tender at times. It frightened her when he suddenly turned harsh or vulgar. She never knew what to expect, a gentle caress or a coarse word, but he had been pushing his advances further and further. "Taking unwarranted liberties," as his father might say. Colin liked to come up behind her when she was making a bed, and flick up her skirts as if to inspect her.

Just that morning she had turned to slap him, and he slid his hands under her arms and kissed her neck, but then he got rude, insulting. "Boy, do you smell sporty. Don't you girls have a bath?"

"Leave me alone. I'm working."

"But you're always working."

She gave him a weary look that said – that's not my fault.

But then Colin had another idea. "Why don't we go swimming tonight. Can you meet me at the boathouse at eleven? I'll bring the towels so you can just slip out."

Colin crept down to the boathouse with his own worn bar of soap. Sitting on the bench in the changing room, his bare feet on the cool cement floor, he could hear the bell from across the bay marking the hour, and he counted each stroke, eleven. Soon he heard Lolly coming down the steps. He waited in silence as she approached. When she peeked in and whispered, "Colin?" his only response was to say, "Come here." She carefully crept into the darkened chamber, afraid of stepping on something. She gasped when he ran his hand up her leg without any preliminaries. He then pulled her down onto his lap, and scolded her for keeping him waiting. "But you're divine, worth waiting for, aren't you."

"What if somebody comes?"

"We're safe," he assured her. "Why don't you undress? I want to see that beautiful body in the moonlight."

"I can't see a thing."

He unfastened her top, and as she stepped out of the layers of skirts, he stood up behind her and cupped her large breasts, admiring them. "The lake should be like a bathtub." His eyes had already adjusted to the dark, and her skin seemed to gleam with white softness, the globes of her buttocks picking up the faint light.

"But I can't go out like this," she protested. "Where's a towel?"

He let her wrap up, but at the water's edge, he insisted she drop it on the shore. "You want to have something dry when you get out. Now let me get you all sudsy." She didn't point out that he was still in his bathing suit, and he didn't mention that Max Farwell and a buddy were hiding behind the weeping willow on the bank. Colin led her out into the water. That spring his father had dumped a load of sand, which made entering the lake a little easier, at least on this side of the pier.

"I'm scared," she said.

"It's shallow enough. Lie down." She sat down, very cautiously at first, but then she felt less exposed underwater. He gently eased her back, a knee on either side of her, until her thick brown hair became a sodden mass. He drizzled water over her upper body before taking the bar of soap from the pocket of his suit. Sudsing her up, he pushed the slippery meat of her big breasts together. The water now felt warmer than the air.

As he slid his hands over her body she began to moan, but he told her, "Be quiet. We don't want to wake the old man." He wanted the torture of it to intensify her feeling, and she could hardly stand it, his strong, sure hands running over her belly, but when he ran the bar over her floating mound, whipping it to a lather, she cried, "Colin, it stings."

He stopped, and she lay there, quivering, on the verge. He was listening, but then he asked, "Don't you know how to swim?"

"No!" She didn't want him to stop. "This is my first time in the lake." She felt so urgent, left hanging. She wanted to kiss him, to hold onto him – she would have even let him come into her then – but at the same time she was afraid he might do something horrible, like produce a slippery fish and wipe it against her. He seemed to have some secret plan.

"I'm going to walk out to the end of the pier," he said, and she tried to keep him from leaving, but he slid out of her grip. "You can either walk out to the ladder – it's not over your head – or you can follow me."

"Colin, don't leave. I think something's moving – " in the water, she meant, but he acted unconcerned, going over to pick up the towel. She splashed out of the shallows, reaching for the towel he was holding up, retreating like a matador. "Don't," she cried. "Give it!"

At that moment Lionel Hewitt could be heard coming down the steps. "What's going on down there?"

Max Farwell and his crew would have to remain still.

"Just taking a dip," Colin called. "I'm coming right up." He instructed her to crouch. "Stay down or he'll see you. Don't say a word." Colin tossed her the towel and ran for the steps to stop his father from descending.

The rumors about that evening finally reached Lionel's attention, and he was forced to let the summer girl go. "It's really a shame," he told Colin. "She was such a hard worker. Taking advantage of one's help is like taking advantage of a child." He was less stern than he was disappointed, and that tone was even harder to take. "Someone who is almost at your mercy, who hardly feels she has the right to refuse."

Colin didn't answer, but thought – She could have refused.

Mr. Hewitt was about to return the girl to Chicago when Alicia Ulrich announced to her husband that Lolly might serve her needs. "Now that Nicole's gone, I think she might be perfect. All she needs is a decent uniform, and a little sprucing up."

"I'm not sure that's such a wise plan," Joseph responded, for the scandal involving Lolly Jones was now common knowledge.

Alicia seemed to read his mind, and was incensed by his attitude, as if the girl were now ruined and it would reflect on them. "You can't blame *her* for what they did! We should at least give her a second chance."

Joseph considered the responsibility of such a situation, but seeing the look on Alicia's face, he relented. "You're probably right. It might help settle things down."

Alicia was capable of remaking people as well as rooms – she had such excellent taste in material.

CHAPTER EIGHTEEN

*T*hough Constance Rose had never felt particularly close to Colin, she still cared about her brother's welfare. She wanted him to marry someone who would soften him. Though he did appear drawn to Lindsay Esser, it seemed as if his interest was held in check for some reason. Perhaps Lindsay herself was too cool and aloof.

Constance noticed that when Lindsay helped herself to the massive preparations of the Lake Club buffet, her brother broke into a smile, for Lindsay only took the tiniest morsel from the enormous poached salmon. All of her portions were dainty. She was the kind of girl who believed you should always leave something on your plate, and it made Constance feel horribly hungry.

The dinner-dance theme was a "Hobby and Sportsman's Ball," and Constance, now eight months pregnant, felt somewhat conspicuous dressed up as a balloonist. She had a helium balloon rigged to a wicker basket that hung around her pregnant waist. Colin sported the typical nautical garb – a striped sweater from Marseilles, white cap, no shoes, and a coil of lanyard over his shoulder. Max Farwell was there in his hunting pinks, and Walter Schraeger showed up late in his well-worn aviator's outfit. Mitzi Hewitt's fiancé had been misinformed and he had come dressed as a clock. Lindsay was in a brand-new tennis outfit. Her round collared shirt, cable knit sweater, and pleated skirt were immaculate. Constance saw that she wore a ruby the color of pigeon's blood on her right fourth finger, and when the girl glanced in Colin's direction, it was clear that she would like to wear another gem on her left fourth finger as well. Constance looked down at her own bare ring finger. She had removed the simple band because of her increased weight. Now she felt she must excuse herself from the table before dessert was brought around.

Haven teased her by saying she mustn't float away, but when she rose from the table she felt weighty, ridiculous. Though she knew he did not mean anything, tears welled in her eyes.

Walking up to the ballroom after a second helping of linzer torte, Haven saw Lindsay waiting by the door. "You're a vision," he said, dazzled by the whiteness of her tennis outfit. "Who're you playing with these days?"

"The partner of my choice prefers not to play mixed doubles. I can't really blame him. Women aren't so strong."

"Well, you shouldn't be playing singles."

There was Constance, standing out on the ballroom balcony, alone in the dark. He went out and tried to persuade her to come in, for the music was starting, but she was having problems with shortness of breath. "It's the baby," he told her, "pushing against your diaphragm. Try to stand up straight and breathe deeply."

But she still felt miserable, trapped in her rigging. She wanted to be released, to go home early, but he only led her back inside to the padded bench that ran around the dance floor. "Look," he nodded, "Colin's asking Lindsay to dance. She told me he wouldn't play tennis with her. That's not a good sign."

"He doesn't like to lose to a woman," Constance explained. "He'll play up to set point, then walk off the court. I've seen him do it. And Lindsay's such a dear – she makes up some excuse. He couldn't find a nicer woman."

Lindsay had asked Colin to enter the club tournament with her, and he had responded, "Why me? You could pick anyone and win." It was becoming more and more obvious that Colin was a confirmed bachelor, though Lindsay was not sure she believed in such a thing. In her curiosity, she had asked him if he had a notion for the future, and he had said how he didn't like to plan.

Biddy Hawkshurst was dressed up as a butterfly catcher and she kept putting her net over various heads. "Caught one!" she yelled. Haven was snared, trout creel and all.

"Don't expect me to be too graceful in these wading boots." He wanted to accommodate some of the single girls, for there was nothing so heart-rending as a group of wallflowers, especially when they were decked out in costume.

Lindsay's tennis shoes were not especially good for dancing. She was tempted to kick them off so she could glide over the dance floor, but Colin kept her so on edge, she didn't want to stop to take them off. She found herself saying things she instantly regretted. "Are you going to stay late?" As if she hoped to remain with him the entire evening. And then, without thinking, "Alicia said something that made me wonder."

"I'm sure it's nasty, but probably true. What did she say?" He had enough vanity to want to know what anyone said about him.

"She said you couldn't stay with anyone for long. Not that I believe that."

"If you're not really with anyone, how can you stay with them?"

"I see," she said, stopping, though the music continued. The soles of her tennis shoes seemed stuck to the floor. "Will you excuse me?" She walked off the dance floor with perfect equilibrium, but then pushed through the double swinging doors to the powder room.

Constance followed and found her sobbing on the *chaise*. "What on earth did he say to you?"

"It's not that," she cried. "It's what he never *does* say. He simply doesn't care for me. Not at all!"

"He's horrible," Constance said in a very low voice. She rarely said anything against anybody, so her verdict had condemning weight. She saw no need to make Lindsay suffer like this. It was as if he did it on purpose.

"I have to get out of here," Lindsay looked up, and her eyes were red and bleary. She looked as if she might climb out one of the windows and flee.

"Colin would never make you happy," Constance tried to console her. "I feel sorry for him, not you. Will you help me out of this contraption?"

It was hard to see how to unfasten the thing. Constance was sure to get Most Original Costume, though Isabelle's outfit was pretty ingenious. Their friend had dressed up as Cupid's Victim, wearing a voluminous white night-gown with jutting lace sleeves, a broken arrow penetrating a stain of fake blood – fairly dramatic. Isabelle had intended for it to relate to her poetry, for she was not keen on sports, but now she felt ludicrous, unable to carry it off, especially when people asked, "Who's the hunter?"

With her harness unhitched, Constance tried to step out of the basket, but then stopped as if stung and just stood there, eyes wide. She began a strange sort of breathing. "Oh, no," Constance whispered. "I'm not ready for this. Get Haven." This was not supposed to happen for another five weeks.

Lindsay raced from the powder room, flashing through the doors, almost colliding with a big game huntress. She didn't give Colin a single thought, but ran out onto the dance floor and grabbed Haven by the arm. He under-stood and was out the front door in an instant. It was the most effective exit Lindsay could have hoped for – she felt aloof from the attention of the crowd, elevated by emergency, singled out. Surely Colin would see her helping his sister as they supported her down the steps and into the sedan.

"Looks like Lindsay's playing midwife tonight," Alicia said taking Colin by the arm. Turning, they began a slow box step. She was dressed up as a painter from Montmartre, with a black beret and paintbrush behind her ear. "Lolly's turned out wonderfully for me."

Alicia had gotten Lolly to tell her in detail what had happened that night by the lakefront, and this confidence had created a bond between the women.

Colin knew that Alicia could hold certain things over him and he didn't like her having too much advantage. "Don't you think your affections for flight are becoming a bit obvious?" Colin lightly accused her.

"What do you mean?" she responded, following the direction of his eye. "You can't mean Baron Von Braunschweiger over there. Walter and I are just friends."

"Everybody needs special friends, I suppose," Colin winked at her. "Where's Joseph tonight?"

"Joseph," she responded, as if he had just occurred to her. "He sprained his big toe. He's always doing something. Sometimes I think he does it on purpose so he won't have to come."

"Maybe he wants you to stay home and baby him a little."

"Well, I'm not a nurse. No one ever mothered me. He's all wrapped up in the brewery, anyway. Do you know what he considers a profitable evening? I wish someone would dance with that fallen angel over there." She was referring to Isabelle. "What on earth is she supposed to be, a goose? He has his driver take him out to different intersections in Milwaukee and then he counts the number of vehicles that pass."

"What for?"

"To decide where the best location for the next tavern will be. And when he finds a spot, he buys up all four corners so there won't be any competition." Alicia looked up into Colin's intense blue eyes. "Lindsay's not exactly your type, is she. But now there's my friend Dana. You might enjoy meeting her. Come, dance me over to the doorway."

Dana had just arrived from Pittsburgh by train, and Alicia's driver had brought her over to the club. "Dana!" she waved, and the attractive young woman scanned the room to find the voice.

"You didn't tell me this was a costume party," Dana complained, kissing the air on each side of Alicia's face. She had dark brown hair, bobbed short and stylish, and she wore her traveling clothes, a summer suit and an olive-colored trench coat. Her features were small, yet striking. One could tell she came from a very good family, Dana Ash. She had that manicured, slightly bored look of self-confidence. Apparently she also had a head cold, for she took out her handkerchief and blew her nose.

Colin did not know what had happened to the old heave-ho, but suddenly he wanted to drop anchor. He felt stupid standing there with no shoes on, especially when her eyes traveled down to the floor.

"I don't always dress like this," he confessed. "I do own shoes."

"In fact, his family owns a tannery," Alicia laughed. Dana found this amusing, but turned away from Colin, as if she imagined he would now disappear.

"You know, I'm just not in much of a party mood. Why don't I go get a good night's sleep, and we can visit in the morning. I just want to get rid of this head cold."

"I'll take you home," Colin offered. "My boat's right here."

Alicia thought this an excellent idea, assuring Dana that she would be in the best of hands.

"I can't say I trust traveling by water," Dana told him. "I prefer the good, solid earth. But if I haven't any choice, you have to promise not to tip us. I'd probably drown."

Colin assured her that the boat was impossible to turn over. "You can inspect it from bow to stern." He offered his arm, walking her down the fifty wooden steps that ran alongside the Lake Club.

She thought the boat looked a little low in the water. "And the lake's so dark. Won't we get lost?" At least she admired the new red leather of the seats, and the steering wheel made out of polished mahogany.

"This might be a little loud," Colin warned her as he turned on the ignition. The engine made an impressive roar. Then, shoving the bow of the boat out into the darkness, he flipped on the beam that illuminated the water and pushed the control lever slowly forward.

Placing her hand on the cylindrical handle, she was able to move the light around, and this amused her – how it seemed to get lost in the night sky, but bounced along on the surface of the water. "Are those birds?" she asked.

He didn't want to tell her what they actually were, so he claimed they were only swallows, eating bugs. "Do you play tennis?" he asked her.

"Not really, just golf. Do you have a decent course around here?"

"Sure, we have plenty of golf fanatics. Last winter they even used red balls in the snow. But my clubs are all rusted up."

"And my racquet's completely out of tune," she laughed.

He felt relieved that they wouldn't be in competition.

"So tell me about Wisconsin. Will I have to eat sauerbraten and listen to *oompah* music?"

"Probably. They say Milwaukee's the most Europeanized city in America, but I think it's like any other Midwestern city, only more so. It grows on you, gradually, like a beer belly."

"Well, lakes are nicer than oceans. I'm afraid of waves. And I've never liked salt on my skin."

"It can help you float, if you're lost at sea," he responded, but seeing her expression, he quickly changed the subject. "I think my sister's giving birth tonight. I can hardly believe it – I'm going to be an uncle." He felt strangely happy, for he was certain he would marry this woman, Dana Ash. Everything now seemed to matter. Everything seemed important. "They thought she might come early. Her husband's a doctor. Actually, he was our first chauffeur, but that was years ago. You see, our mother died, and – I'll tell you all about it."

"Interesting," she said, thinking he was daft.

"He thinks it might be twins, because he heard two heartbeats. I hope they get boys."

"Why boys?" she wanted to know. "I think it would be best to have one of each and get it over with."

"There's Topside," he pointed out the dimly illuminated lawns of the estate. Colin guided the bow of the boat up toward the pier, curving it in an arc so the impact wouldn't jar her. He then tossed over the protective fenders, jumping out, pulled the line tight, securing it to the pier cleats. "Let me take you up Alicia's ramble path. She'd love for you to see it." White water lilies were faintly glowing in the marsh, and at the beginning of the path, fragrant mock orange and honeysuckle created a bower of perfumes. The path wound along in a serpentine fashion, past the Ulrich canals, little benches placed along the way as if to encourage romantic lingering, but Colin didn't have the nerve to stop.

"You're quite a nature person, aren't you."

"Do you prefer the city? I work in Milwaukee and I haven't found much to commend it."

"I think the country's disturbing. You never know what to expect." She took the arm he was offering, for she suspected there were dangerous creatures lurking in the bushes – skunks, maybe badgers, even muskrats.

Colin would have liked to pick her up and carry her in his arms, but then the jungle spell was broken as the civilized expanse of the well-mowed lawns appeared at the end of the walk. She seemed relieved to see the house lights.

"May I see you tomorrow?"

She seemed surprised. "I'll have to see what Alicia has planned. She told me Nogowogotoc's exhausting."

"And I'll have to check on my sister. Who knows, I might be an uncle right now."

Mildred opened the door, and Colin could see Lolly coming down the steps, looking a little bleary. He was afraid she might ruin the whole thing, but Mildred collected the new arrival's raincoat, and Joseph was there at the top of the stairs. When he saw Colin, he called out – "Wait up, I need to talk to you." He hobbled down the steps, greeting Dana with a hug, then took Colin by the arm and led him back outside. "I've had the most hideous day. First I broke this blasted toe, and then the most bizarre accusations. They say they *think* – it's because of my silo, it's so tall – good grief!" He laughed from exhaustion. "They think I'm in contact with the Kaiser! That I've got a radio in the top of my silo. Can you believe it?"

"Joseph Ulrich, a spy? A traitor? Good job! Certainly they can't be serious."

"I invited them to climb the damn thing and take a look, right there, but of course they didn't want to do that. So – " he took a deep breath, "I've decided to enlist. I'm every bit as much of an American as anybody else."

"You don't have to convince me. In fact, you don't have to go that far. Can't you just make a donation to the war fund? *Every nickel every dollar helps to make the Kaiser holler.* I guess we can't call Milwaukee the old Midwest Munich anymore."

"But I'm serious. I want to go over and fight."

"Now? But you're disabled!" Both men laughed. Colin had not gone overseas because of a lower back problem. He almost envied Joseph's decision to get going, and yet now for the first time in his life, Colin believed he had a reason to stay put. "I'll come over first thing in the morning. We can talk more about it."

"Come have breakfast," Joseph suggested. They gripped each other's arms.

Dana was still lingering at the bottom of the stairs, and Joseph asked her if she would like some brandy. She seemed eager for a glass. "Was everything all right? I hope Colin was a gentleman. He's my very best friend, so you're going to be seeing a good deal more of him."

"I hope that won't be a chore," she said.

CHAPTER NINETEEN

*T*he exaggerated heat of the empty greenhouse reminded Helen of gas jets left burning in daylight. There were not any flatbeds teeming now. All the plants were at their height outside, and Kurtz had spent the morning in the cutting garden securing the taller flowers with string and wooden stakes.

He brightened when he saw her coming down the walkway, and quickly crushed out his cigarette – he knew she couldn't tolerate smoke, especially now that she was pregnant. Helen looked preoccupied, worn and downcast. He liked it when she came to him for comfort or advice, but he didn't like that frown of concern. "You need a peppermint candy," he advised, shuffling on back in search of his tin.

"It's just too hot to be alive," she protested.

"Come back here," Kurtz invited her into the cool, dark potting shed that lay at the end of the greenhouse, open to the breezeway beyond. "I was just about to gather some chicken eggs."

Helen had always liked to help with that chore as a child, but now she couldn't bring herself to respond. She just eased herself down into the metal rocking chair and gently bounced back and forth.

"Remember how the chow liked to lick up the broken ones? You even used to drop one, on purpose."

Yes, she remembered, smiling a bit now. It was restful just to be there with Kurtz. "I should get a chair like this, for when the baby comes."

"You don't have a rocking chair?" He seemed incredulous. "That's the most important thing!" He shook his head. He was always muttering how modern folk didn't know how to live. They did not know how to take care of their children, or how to properly eat. You only used the very best produce if you wanted to create a satisfying meal, just as a truly beautiful dress could only be made of the finest material. Kurtz was known for his frugality, but he also believed one should spend a little more if it meant getting the very best. Sarah Wells had always shared this attitude, but Helen seemed to worry constantly about money.

"American people make a big mistake. They buy lesser goods but in greater quantity. What good is that? You need one fine chair. You sing and you rock – the baby sleeps." He picked up a ripe golden tomato from the sill and wiped it off. Holding it up, he offered to cut her a slice. "No acid in these. You spread a little sugar, and delicious. I tell you."

Helen accepted the slice from his large, weathered hands, and slurped it down gratefully, bending forward so as not to drip on her dress. Her appetite had become a kind of tyrant, and she was tired of thinking about food, always food. She had come over to the garden because she craved *haricot verts* for some reason. She liked them especially thin, and there was a good second crop. She wanted Winnie to grate up some *carotte rapé*, and perhaps make a diced-beet vinaigrette. Living in Paris had influenced her eating habits. Simple wartime rations could be turned into a feast if herbs were used and courses properly prolonged.

"Can we go take a look at your home garden?" Helen asked, for that always cheered her up.

Kurtz had made a special little garden by the side of his farmhouse, which contained an exact replica of his home town in Germany, including the house where he had been born and the church where he'd been confirmed. The entire miniature countryside had been landscaped down to scale – the tiny bread store only three inches high, the smithy, the schoolhouse, all the features of the terrain, the hills and quarry, the big river. He never wearied of his little garden. "When I get tired I come out here and rest in the homeland. It makes me feel young again. But come, let's see about those chicken eggs."

Opening one swing-down drawer after another, they collected the unattended brown eggs, still warm in the rounded straw of their nests. In the third compartment, Helen had to slip her hand beneath the ruffled feathers of the hen before it made a dive for the chicken coop floor. It always excited her – the feel of the warm egg and the fear of getting pecked, though usually the chickens only cooed, as if caressed by the intruding raid.

"I keep hoping to find a gold one," he teased.

"Me too. If only we had a great big nest egg. Isabelle and I want to start a fresh-air camp for city girls. They would come in the summer and experience nature. We'd have horses, and a garden, and we'd teach them self-confidence, how to swim and canoe and tie knots. Everything." Helen's enthusiasm grew with the details.

"Then what happens?" Kurtz asked. "The month of September?"

"We thought about that," Helen answered, and she did look serious. "But don't you think they might gain *something*, at least? Maybe someday we could offer scholarships, to the brighter girls. Help them change their lives."

"What's holding you, then?" Kurtz closed the last of the chicken coops.

There was a sprinkling of lime on the old cement floor, fresh whitewash on the wooden walls. Hollyhocks crowded the panes with their bright pink blooms, and Helen realized at that moment how much she loved this place, how dear the country was to her. "A few of us formed a group," she explained. "We're called the King's Daughters. I don't like the name, but that was the vote. Anyway, we're trying to raise money to buy some land, around Crooked Lake. But there was this horrid article in the paper. It made our project seem like a hoax. *What purpose would such a camp serve society in general?* There are plenty of people who think it's unladylike, encouraging young women to sleep outside on the ground. New roads are more important."

"Ideas are like seeds," Kurtz said to her, as she set her basket of brown eggs down in the breezeway. Leaning back against the weathered gray of the door she looked pretty as a flower in her pale-yellow smock dress She had always been his favorite, ever since she was a girl. So impassioned, she could get anything accomplished. Kurtz liked that, her energy, her strength of will. He wondered if her temperament would make it easier or more difficult when it came to the birth. She looked ripe to him, ready to fall.

"We took Angeline home for a visit last weekend. She was worried about her brother and wouldn't stop bothering us about it, but her neighborhood has become so depressing. It isn't a good German neighborhood anymore. Most of the Germans have moved out and there are only Poles and some Irish, but Angeline had these two little nieces – it came out that they steal lightbulbs and trade them for food. Their father kept saying how he never touched alcohol unless he had a cold. But he obviously gets a sore throat every other minute. It really was a ghastly situation. The girls were so eager to hear all about the woods, until Angeline started telling them stories, how the lake out here is covered with fire. She hasn't been the same since Father died. Those poor, poor girls," Helen shook her head.

"Do you think you can save people suffering?"

A darkness dropped over Helen's face. So he also thought she was just trying to be a "do-good." She put her hands on her belly and felt the baby kick. Suddenly she missed her father. He would certainly have been supportive of a venture like this. The article in the paper reminded her of the hospital bazaar – how you work so hard to raise money for something, and then someone comes along and makes fun of you, saying it's only female sentiment born out of guilt.

"I think it's all right, to do things," Kurtz told her. "Why shouldn't young girls know the earth, sleeping out. I believe you have a very good plan."

"You do? I was afraid you thought it silly, or impossible. I'm going to write a response to that article today. It made me so mad."

"Maybe I could write something too," he suggested.

"Would you?" she asked. "You mean, I could quote you?"

"No, not like that. I will write you a bill."

Helen stood there, not understanding.

"I want to buy you the land," he said, simply. "You see, I have the money." He could tell she didn't believe him. "It's been waiting for this, just like you have been waiting." He liked to picture his fortune spilling from the doors of the big gray bank. "Maybe I brought golden coin from the old country," he winked, "sewn into my underwear like Brewmeister Ulrich." He thought this a terrific joke. "How much is this land around the crooked lake?"

Helen did not even want to say, for he couldn't possibly have that much savings. "Fifteen thousand dollars."

"Is that all? I was thinking of thirty. That way you get started. You buy tents. You buy boats. You said you want horses. Whatever is needed. Believe me, I have this. For the baby," he added, "a gift for the newborn – you can think of it that way. Any easier?"

She understood now that he was serious, and she threw her arms around his neck, finding it more than a little awkward in her present state. "Oh, Gus," she cried, "that's the most wonderful present anyone could ever give me! I've got to tell Isabelle." She ran from the greenhouse. When she stopped to catch her breath, the muscles in her abdomen were cramping. But she was exhilarated, high, full of light.

"So this is how the man must feel," Isabelle said to herself, sympathetic to her own state of torment, waiting. Her feeling of helplessness was the appropriate accompaniment to the vociferous sounds of her sister's labor upstairs. Isabelle walked around and around the large peach-colored living room with its big feather sofa and Oriental rugs as if she wanted to get away but could not break her boundary. She was almost grateful for the knock on the door.

Upstairs, Dr. Rose was being assisted by a midwife and a young German nurse who would later help with the baby. Helen's labor had come on quickly, but she was now having trouble delivering the large-headed child.

It was a hot September day, and Haven was perspiring with the effort, trying to turn the infant, for it was diving backward in a posterior position, which created intense back pain for Helen and a much more difficult descent. Helen was drenched. She had never felt so raw, so extreme, this close to her limit, both exhausted and then momentarily gripped. "Can't somebody open a window?" she pleaded. Two windows were already wide. She fell back upon the pillows, succumbing to that dream of relief for one minute before the next seizure took her. Then the nurse and assistant both pushed her from behind so that she could grab her knees and shove with all her might. She had been pushing for over two hours.

Finally the head turned and Haven said, "Terrific. Now we're getting somewhere." He stood up and wiped his forehead, went to wash his hands again. "One good push," he encouraged, "and I think you'll have your baby."

Helen could hardly imagine that there was another human being on the other side of this, but his encouragement gave her the necessary second wind, and she pushed with an unnatural force, until the veins on her forehead rose and throbbed, and her eyeballs burned behind her lids. Then she felt a heaviness descend. It was as if she had been shoving a gigantic boulder, and finally it was released from its firm, secure bed. The baby had made an inch of progress, *monumental*, then slid back into place as if nothing had been accomplished. At least, Helen sensed, the path had been loosened, and she simply had to muster an even greater strength.

After the next contraction, she felt a burning sensation, and then suddenly there was a flurry of excitement in the room, even the shades at the windows seemed to flutter with lake air and she was surrounded by cloths and helping hands. Someone was wiping her neck and then her forehead. She closed her eyes and put tremendous will behind the effort, holding her breath, pushing with more than her own might. She felt like she was calling on the force of God to make the impossible happen. There was a split of white pain, almost out of control now, tearing her in two and leaving her beyond it, but Haven was there, almost cheering her on, and finally when she looked, there were sounds of exaltation – the head was hanging out, like a growth between her legs.

With the spasm of the next push, the shoulders came slithering, followed by the body, all muscular and meaty – "My, isn't he *long?*" – as if it were a butcher's shop. It felt like a butcher's shop, slippery with whiteness and grainy with blood. The brutality of it. But then he started to cry, hanging upside down, as if he had come to life entirely on his own. With a mass of brown hair, slicked down with darkness. "Let me hold him," Helen said, for she couldn't get enough of him, but the nurse picked him up and walked him across the room.

"A handsome baby boy," Dr. Rose complimented Helen, sitting down for a moment as the nurse and assistant worked over the child, blocking Helen's sight.

"Don't cover him up," Helen raised herself up on an elbow. "I'm looking at him." She felt robbed of her most private possession. She wanted to hold him, skin against skin.

With the next after-shock the placenta was born and the cord was cut. Everything began to seem mechanical, the miracle receding with the angel's wings. "I want him," she said softly, but no one responded. She had never felt more like an animal. She felt a craving for her child, as if she could press his very essence back into her. She wanted him to attach, to suck, to hold on, but the nurse had already decided that it would be better if her breasts were bound. It would help keep her more youthful and shapely for her husband – certainly he deserved that much when he came home.

Helen wanted them all to go away now. She wanted to sleep with the baby in the curve of her arms, to feel him there, a part of her own sore body. She wanted to hear his steady breathing and to examine his tiny hands, to feel those fingers clutch and grip her own little finger. Everyone was being too helpful, and she was too exhausted to put up much resistance. All her strength had been drained, and she could barely move as they attempted to change the sheets beneath her, rolling her from side to side, wadding cloths between her legs to catch the blood. She felt limp, and yet in love with this small, unknown animal. "Alden," she called, as the nurse stole him away. "Alden Felton Faithorne."

"That's a lovely name. He'll be a regular playmate for Trumbull and William."

"I can't think of them being so big," Helen admitted. Constance Rose was still recovering from the birth of her twin sons.

"Will you be taking the baby in town soon?"

"I don't know," she answered, her eyes filling with tears, for what if something happened to Leonard. What if he died? She didn't even know where he was. All of a sudden life seemed so fragile. A human being was born, but another, just as easily, could be torn apart. She felt shocked by the brutality of nature. "Can't they bring me the baby?"

But Haven encouraged her to rest, and ordered Miss Goetsch to go down to the kitchen and have the cook brew up some fennel tea. Sensing her concern, Haven added, "Leonard will be home before this baby is walking." But that seemed an awfully long time. He stood up, but kept looking down at her with his warm, comforting eyes. "There is someone here to see you. But just for a moment, all right?"

"Oh," Helen cried, as Isabelle came to her. They both wept a little before they started to laugh. "You didn't hear all that commotion, did you?"

"You *were* fairly vocal," Isabelle had to admit. "Like some hideous opera. I can't believe you look so normal."

"I'm not," Helen grinned, for she had never felt so extraordinary before. "Did you see him? Did you see the baby? He's got beautiful auburn hair, and he's enormous, like Leonard."

"Mother's waiting next-door, with Lionel Hewitt in tow," Isabelle lifted her eyebrows. "But she said she'd come over by herself, once the worst was over. She didn't come sooner because of her nerves. Now I see what she meant. I'm a wreck."

"Well, it was brave of you to stick it out."

"I felt every single pain," Isabelle assured her. "Now what can I get to celebrate. White cherries?"

"Oh, yes!"

"And Max Farwell of all people is downstairs. He dropped by and I didn't know how to get rid of him."

"I just feel overwhelmed," Helen lapsed back into tears. "I don't want, I don't . . . " She couldn't finish her sentence.

Even Isabelle could see that Helen had been strained, that she needed total silence and no distractions.

"Will you tell them to bring me the baby?"

Isabelle nodded, but thought it best to leave her sister alone. Helen didn't realize how exhausted she was, and the nurse had been hired to help her.

Isabelle managed to dispose of Max Farwell by telling him he could return in a week or two.

"I had no intention of crashing the party," he said. "How is she? Could you give her these chocolates?" He offered Isabelle one from the open box before helping himself. Then he put the remainder on the front hall table, beneath the tapestry of the maiden with her hunting dogs. He seemed softened somehow, not so brash – like some old, battered cup that's been polished, still showing its familiar bumps and dents.

CHAPTER TWENTY

*A*licia discovered she was pregnant right after Joseph's departure for the infantry. She received five letters, and then no more. That wasn't like him, for he had promised to write every day. "This is just my luck," she complained to Lolly. "Take a look at me, will you? I can't even button this skirt, and it was loose last November. I can't believe he went off and left me to do this alone."

"You're not alone," Lolly reminded her. "I'll help you when the time comes."

"No one will be able to help me when I'm big and fat. I just don't know what got into him. He always put Germany first before." Alicia sat before the Venetian mirror that was hung above her vanity and shook out her hair, dissatisfied with herself. "Really, I think he was an imbecile, rushing off like that, as if he *were* guilty. If you're going to be an idiot, run along, but don't expect me to say prayers every night." She brushed back her hair, and clipped on two onyx earrings that dangled from her lobes like long black teardrops. "You know, I would have been a much better wife with a more difficult man. I suppose it's human nature. But even Walter's been getting on my nerves. All he can think of is sausages – knockwurst, knackwurst, bockwurst, bratwurst. You know what I'd like – a glass of champagne. Everything's such a gloom!"

Her main concern was that Walter might not like her change of figure. Alicia pictured herself left to ripen like a nasty, bulbous squash, growing bigger and bigger, bulging outward in distortion. "I hope it's a girl. That's all I can say. At least we might have some fun with a girl."

"Mrs. Faithorne had a baby boy I just heard."

"I'm sure that suits her." Alicia straightened up, closing the little flower-shaped buttons to her cream-colored blouse. "She'd ruin a girl child."

Alicia put her elbows up on the dressing table and talked into the mirror, where she could see Lolly hanging up clothes in the background. "I just wish I still had that rolling bear," she reminisced. "You could sit on it, and push it, and pull out this cord – *grrrr*," she growled. Alicia had never felt so trapped inside her body. She almost felt like one of Walter's big sausages, stuffed into a skin. "I suppose now I'll have to suffer a million baby showers and christenings. It's a damn good thing I'm an excellent actress. If it weren't for those stupid Germans I'd say, let's go to France. They know how to take care of pregnant women. They feed you like a queen and treat you like the Holy Mother Mary."

Lolly looked up at her, shocked.

"What's the matter," she asked, turning back to her mirror. "Don't I still look like a virgin?"

The sight of Lionel Hewitt driving Sarah Wells up to the front circle of Broadoaks in a topless automobile the color of a candy apple put Angeline into a tizzy. She refused to say anything to the gentleman when he came into the house, and she took her own sweet time when tea was requested in the living room. Sarah had to ring the bell more than twice. "I'm afraid she's losing her wits."

"What can you do?" Lionel shook his head. "It would probably be worse breaking in a new one. Mrs. Knutson's the only one who stands by me. Sometimes I think she's more in charge than I am." Lionel wanted Sarah to marry him, he could use a real woman in the house, but she felt it was not right to abandon Isabelle.

Angeline believed the friendship was a scandal. "Exactly two years and then a harlot-colored chariot." She banged down the tea tray. Lionel looked chagrined. Angeline's mind might have been off kilter, but it was an exacting clock.

Last autumn, Angeline's grief had become so acute that Dr. Rose had to give her a remedy, and prescribed chamomile tea before bedtime, but still her nights were often disturbed, and recently she had taken to sleep-walking. Twice Isabelle had had to lead her back to bed while she recited some fabulous fiction or horrible truth – "She set the fire. He was just the match" – Isabelle never quite knew.

And then one day Angeline informed Mrs. Wells that she had not been paid. Sarah knew this was utter nonsense, for she got paid every month, quite handsomely too. But Angeline insisted that she never had any money. When Sarah went up to Angeline's room and went through the drawers, she found hundreds of bank notes that had never been cashed. Angeline had thought they were receipts, not money. "When we get into town, we'll put this in the bank. You have quite a bit of savings. You can share it with your family."

"Just give it to them," Angeline said without feeling.

"But you can buy anything you want now."

"All I want is that picture of Mr. Wells." She was thinking of the photograph in the master bedroom. It was a very good likeness, just his face, turned to look at the camera, with his neat starched collar, and eyeglasses on.

"But I can't give you that."

"Then what good is money."

"Isn't there anything else? Anything else you might want?"

Angeline thought for a moment, and then said, decidedly, "I guess I'll have a bicycle and one green acre."

Sarah thought this was odd, but she was used to odd requests coming from Angeline. "I know you were very loyal."

"Hmpf," Angeline said, folding her arms, for as far as she was concerned, married people thought only of themselves, while she had thought solely of him.

Dear Aunt Clickey,

Little Alden wants to become acquainted with the fairy godmother who has launched him forth with such a fortune. I was perfectly overcome when we received your generous gift. You have heaped so many lovely things upon us.

Alden grows more precious every day, and of course I think he's very handsome. The first few days he had an elongated head and a red eye, but now he's the sweetest little bundle in the entire world. My one worry is that he sleeps eternally, and mother thinks we should wake him every four hours.

So, Auntie dear. How on earth do you like being a Great Auntie now? Won't it make you feel terribly ancient? And to think of Mother, a grandmother. It's just too funny, for both of you could still be taken for our sisters.

Lovingly,
Helen

When Max Farwell returned to Springwood Lee, he brought a silver baby rattle for Alden and twelve long-stemmed white roses for Helen. He knew how much she loved to fill the house with flowers, and summer was coming to a close.

"Aren't you lonely out here now that the season's over?" he inquired. She assured him that she relished the peace and quiet, hoping he wouldn't stay long. They were sitting on the lake-side porch, and she wore a blue cotton dress with a large white collar. He had never seen her looking so lovely.

"For some reason," she admitted, "I'm very glad to see you. I've been deprived of my husband's company for so long, he's beginning to seem like a figment of my imagination. Were we really married and living in Paris? It seems like ages ago."

"Birth can be a shock to the system," he explained, as if he knew anything about it. "You see, the baby is born with a perfectly clean slate. Sometimes that wipes out the mother's memory as well."

"Well, I can still remember some things. I hope you'll get to see Alden. He sleeps night and day. Mother can't figure out why he doesn't have nerves. Thank goodness some things aren't hereditary."

Max smiled, but he seemed rather sad. Usually he was such a clown, and now he appeared almost despondent. He took her hand and looked into her eyes, as if to say — I miss him too, and for a moment they seemed to share a sense of communion. She had never known this man to be the least bit thoughtful or sensitive, but now he was being rather tender. Oddly, certain features, which she had once thought repugnant, seemed attractive to her. He was overweight, but she suddenly found his excess physicality appealing. His lips were rather bulbous, but she was startled by their sensuality. He was a broad man with strong arms, and she imagined if he wanted, he could break her in two. It made her feel strangely feminine.

He too seemed disturbed by her presence and yet drawn to her.

Since the birth she had felt so many longings. She craved melons from the garden and lusted after fresh gusts of lake air. She wanted to hold baby Alden in her arms all the time, but Miss Goetsch was much too efficient. She felt the absence of her husband's form beside her in the bed, and she found she had too much energy. She wanted to be held and stroked — as if she needed to be reminded that her body had limits. She also missed her father, and her heart yearned for him. It was as if she couldn't get enough of life down into her. She had this craving for life because it could be damaged or over at any moment in time, and that was unthinkable. She conveyed this longing to Max Farwell with a sigh, and he seemed to register her mood and understand it. In fact, he seemed so unlike himself that she began to worry. For a moment she feared he had come with some horrible news. He knew something dreadful about Leonard that they had kept from her, and only now would he reveal the truth about his injury or illness, now that the baby had been born and she had recovered. "Is everything all right?" she asked. "Please, you must tell me."

"Strange," he admitted. "I came to brighten your day, and I feel like I'm having the opposite effect. What can I do?"

"What would you like to do?"

"I'd like to take you in my arms and crush you," he said.

Helen Faithorne straightened up with a look of alarm. Certainly this must be the old Farwell with his ridiculous jests. But now he looked so dejected, she realized he must be serious. The silver rattle he had brought rested in its box like some newborn thing. She looked down at the wrappings and felt stunned.

He took her silence to mean that he had the liberty to go on. "I know it must seem foolish, but I just can't help it – I'm in love with you. I've loved you even longer," he hesitated to say, longer than Leonard, while she tried to calculate if this could possibly be true, and suddenly little moments seemed to add up to something. How truly embarrassing. But she also felt vulnerable to the weight of his confession, as if it swirled around her like some living cloak. She feared that it would wrap around her and draw her in, that she would be fastened inside it somehow.

"But I'm married," she whispered, as if that were the only truth, and everything else were irrelevant. He must hang up his feelings, not stir such things up. "You will always be a part of our family," she added, hoping to appease him. "I was even thinking you'd be Alden's godfather. Leonard would want that, and you were here, right downstairs, waiting with Isabelle."

He nodded, but did not respond. When he looked up he was clearly suffering. "I've written you a note," he confessed, placing the sealed envelope on the glass-topped table. The roses were in a bundle there, and when the nurse came in, holding the tiny infant, wrapped securely in layers of flannel, she traded the little form for the loose bouquet.

"I'd better get these flowers in water," Miss Goetsch announced, walking back to the kitchen. "I've never seen such beautiful roses."

"Nor have I," Helen answered, gazing down at the rosebud lips of her baby.

"You'll probably want to burn it," Max said.

~ **PART FOUR** ~

CHAPTER TWENTY-ONE

$\mathcal{H}$ elen's springy brown hair could not be entirely concealed beneath the blue knit cap she pulled over her ears. Max Farwell wanted to nestle down into it, sitting behind her as he was, last man in the woven line of eight to interlock arms and legs. He didn't have much room and had to pull himself closer. "Just don't tip us," Helen begged, for she knew he liked to make things more exciting, and was apt to lean to the side, sending the toboggan and its passengers swirling out into an arc.

Alicia Ulrich, hostess for this Valentine's Day party, had placed herself at the very front, for she liked to feel the speed of the wind cutting into her, almost slapping her awake. Colin sat behind her to control the ropes, and Walter Schraeger made a big to-do, trying to unnerve the group. He stood at the rear and alerted them for take off. The toboggan shot out like a weighted arrow and Alicia screamed – strange to feel themselves linked together like one fated organism, gaining speed as they dropped from the lawn down over the bluff. Helen leaned back, allowing herself to be held by the padded layers that surrounded her. The curved wooden hull slammed onto the ice, gliding far out, until it finally came to a crunching halt.

After one more run the wind-blown group went up to the house to warm their hands and feet, but Alicia didn't want them to get too cozy and relaxed. She insisted on keeping the momentum of the party going, serving an afternoon brew of hot chocolate mixed with strong French coffee, and a dollop of fresh whipped cream from the farm. This proved to be the perfect stimulant. "Everybody fetch your skates!" Alicia called, as if driven to complete some sporting scenario. It was only five-thirty but already dark. Looking out through the leaded-glass panes of the living room, they could see the bonfire being lit down below. "I love to skate in the dark," Alicia announced, leading the way.

Down at the lake, Colin kept going on about the afternoon ice boating. "I swear, when the surface is this smooth, you feel like you're going to take right off. I wish you'd try it, just once." He wanted to share the thrill of the winter wind with his wife. It was such a beautiful sight, seeing the sails streaking across the frozen lake, but Dana could only think of her toes growing numb.

"*Please!*" she begged Colin, who was tucking a buffalo rug around her. "Next you'll be saying I should enjoy the cold. I feel like I've swallowed an ice cube." She felt the freeze, not only in her extremities, but at the center of her being.

"You married into the cold, might as well buy into it," Max goaded her while handing her his flask. The brandy helped to warm her up though she still looked humorless, shivering on one of the bales of hay that had been strewn about the ice for spectators.

Colin rubbed her shoulders and kissed her cheek, but then he was off, swatting a puck back and forth.

Dana didn't care for winter sports. She thought perhaps she could get Max to go back up to the house for a rubber of bridge. She watched as he circled round to Helen Faithorne, who was perfecting her figure eights, repeating the pattern over and over, gracefully swinging her arms and legs using the slowest of motions.

"If you keep that up, you're going to cut right through," Max circled Helen. "Where's Leonard tonight? I thought he was going to be here."

"Something must be keeping him at the store," she answered. She didn't mind spending time alone out at the lake, for she rarely felt lonely, and she wasn't one of those people with few inner resources. The Faithornes had winterized Springwood Lee so they could spend long weekends in the country. Soon Alden, her eldest, would enter Country Day and she wanted to take advantage of this freedom. Most of the lake mansions were unsuitable for winter. The pipes were not buried deep enough and if the water was not drained, the pipes would burst, releasing a flood come spring. But the Faithornes had buried their pipes far underground and installed a new oil furnace. "I think Leonard's working on a renovation in Winnetka. It was one of the old Liebenau stores."

"You know Joshua Liebenau's become a fairly well-known painter. Alicia's going to sponsor a show of his. Do you want to skate across the lake?"

Helen remembered how Leonard had once offered to row her halfway, but now she was eager to take up the challenge, even with the haunting boom of ice cracking beneath their weight.

"Hold my scarf so you don't get lost," he said. For some reason Max always made her feel as if she needed protecting. He watched over her in a special way that was peculiar, but it softened her. She allowed him this one familiarity, thinking it was simply the quirk of a bachelor who needed to provide security for someone. She grasped the end of his brown cashmere scarf and he gave a little tug, skating up beside her. As they zipped away from the glow of the bonfire, illuminated by the cooler light of the moon, the far edge of the shore became a darkened strip, and their breath came in short white puffs of exhilaration.

"Can you push me?" Helen asked, turning to skate backward. He slung his scarf around his neck and took both of her gloved hands in his, pushing gently backward so that the blades of her skates made curving undulations, swerving back and forth beneath his steady marks. Max Farwell was their closest family friend, but Helen's convictions about love and marriage had remained constant, and this very stance allowed his fantasies to run a bit wild, more so than if she had participated and given them any actuality.

Once in a great while Max joked about somebody else's situation. "You know Olga wants to divorce Hans Jansen," he told her, aiming for levity. "When the judge asked her if she had any grounds, she told him – Ay, sure, 'bout three and a quarter acres. But do you have a grudge? Oh yah, a double grudge, two cars you know." Max laughed, but Helen remained silent as they skated onward side by side.

It was Helen's steadfast belief that society would crumble if the institution of marriage was not honored. It made her think of her own moment of embarrassment earlier that week. "You know, Leonard found your letter, the one you wrote to me when Alden was born."

Farwell stopped on the ice, while she kept gliding. She had to stop herself by dragging one serrated tip. Max could remember that letter, word for word, as if he had written it yesterday.

Dearest Helen,

I fear it is not safe to write you this, but I must say what's been burning within me. I doubt if anything will come of my confession, but I am hoping that the strength of my love will win out, or that you will at least have compassion for a man who is and ever will be completely devoted to you.

You are in my thoughts constantly. When I see a woman's hands, I can only think of how yours felt when I last touched them, saying good-bye. When I see a generous mouth, I imagine the curves of yours and that remarkably perfect line of teeth as you smile. I want to know all parts of you, to devour you. If you were to let me out of this cage, I would fear for us both, for I have been famished for too long, and I would make you far too happy.

Ultimately, I feel that whatever it costs to know you more deeply will be worth it, despite the sacrifice. You are my one and only life's true love. Of course I will respect your decision and whatever contact is comfortable for you. Forgive me if I offend, for I remain, as always –

Yours truly,
Maximilian Farwell

Seeing his look of concern, Helen took his arm and tried to reassure him. "Don't worry, Leonard didn't read it."

"How can you be sure?"

"The wax was still sealed," she explained, for she had never read it either. And yet she had saved it all these years, hidden away in a little secret drawer in her desk, disguised as a sliding column. The desk had belonged to Leonard's mother, and he had been looking for his passport when he discovered the envelope. His mother had always kept their passports in there.

Helen had colored when Leonard presented her with the envelope, but just at that moment, Alden came into the big house dressed up in his snowsuit, and he was walking in such an awkward manner, it was clear she had to rush him off to change clothes, tucking the letter beneath her arm while escorting out the shamed child.

"I tossed it down the incinerator," she confessed. "Anyway, I'm glad that's behind us now. Come, we're just a little ways from shore." She raced ahead and he followed more slowly, as if the torch he'd been carrying had finally been doused, down some augured hole.

By the time they returned to the party, servants were arranging platters of food on a makeshift table – haunch of venison, breast of partridge, chafing dishes filled with roasted red potatoes and horse chestnuts, slices of winter squash sweetened with maple syrup, braised leeks, hot cider steaming from a thermos. The men had to slip off to the boathouse to get their clandestine drinks. Prohibition had made alcohol all the more enticing now that it was more difficult to obtain.

Alicia skated about the group in her fox-trimmed coat. She had bells laced into her skates, and her cap had a single curving horn that tipped to the side of her face. She tossed the tassel from side to side, but then stopped to announce some unpleasant news. She really felt she needed advice. A couple of months before she had rented the Hop House to some very peculiar men. "I thought they were interested in land investment, but sometimes ten cars line up all at once and I can barely get down the drive." She went on to tell how Morvan had knocked on the door the other day to mention something about the party, so they wouldn't create a traffic jam, and how he thought he had seen a machine gun.

"Good lord, they're probably gangsters." Dana looked about the crowd, as if expecting they might all want to take cover in the nice warm house now.

Alicia didn't go on to say that Morvan had overheard one of them saying, "I pay thirty million a year to those cops, now I want you to go get Zuta." She didn't know anyone by that odd name, and then her tenant, Mr. Camponeli, had brought out a case of gin and handed it to her caretaker – "For the party," he had said.

"What has she gotten herself into?" Lucy whispered to Lindsay Esser Allis, for these were hard times, and Alicia had obviously rented out the gate house for financial reasons. Prohibition was ruining the breweries, and Alicia hadn't changed her standard of living. Kreuser Beer was making malt syrup and brewing a nonalcoholic near-beer that had little popularity. Ulrich Farms had been doing fairly well, making a new kind of processed cheese, but Frederick Ulrich had sold the farm to a group outside the family years before.

"It's a good thing Joseph isn't around to see this mess," Colin muttered. His best friend had died in the Battle of the Meuse-Argonne, leaving Alicia to raise Joey Junior.

She had so desperately wanted a girl child that for the first few years of Joey's life she had dressed him up like one, letting his hair grow into long golden curls, for that was the custom in Europe. But now that he was five he had a short haircut and long woolen pants. Slowly he descended the wooden steps to the lakefront in his navy snowsuit and helmet cap. He wore a mohair scarf knotted around his neck, which seemed to restrict his movements.

"Let him take a couple turns around the fire," Alicia instructed the nanny as the boy slipped a bit on his double-runner skates. "Joey, come kiss me," she added, "and say hello to Mummy's friends." He hobbled over to Alicia, who was sitting on a bale heaped with woolen blankets. She slipped off her glove and he kissed her outstretched hand.

"Isn't he adorable," Lindsay exclaimed. Dana took another swig from Farwell's flask and refused to applaud the display.

"Here's to the youngest of the Ulrichs," Colin raised his cup to make a toast. "May he uphold the great tradition of his father and grandfather before him!"

The conservative nanny whisked the child away from the rowdy group, shuddering at the inappropriate attention, which could only damage such a sensitive child.

Helen Faithorne was also a bit mortified for the boy. She believed he needed to cultivate some playmates, and she took it upon herself to approach Alicia as the party began ascending the sanded steps back up to the main house. They had pulled on their boots, and the blades of their skates clicked as they mounted each plank. "You know Joey's just a little bit younger than Alden. We should get them together sometime."

"Yes?" Alicia answered, as if questioning the validity of such a plan.

"I took both my boys skating the other day. Carl Merrick always does so much better than Alden. Of course I would never let Alden know that's what I think. I don't want him to feel inferior, but it's true. He doesn't care to play much with other children. All he really wants are his paints and his crayons, then he's happy for hours." Helen believed if you put two introverts in the same playroom, they were bound to get bored and find a way to have fun. She knew Alden could amuse himself – he had such a good imagination – but she wanted him to socialize with other children his age, and she thought it her duty to press on. "I'm going to start Alden riding with Miss Molina soon."

"Really? So are we. I just found the sweetest little pony named Home Brew," Alicia laughed. "But I want Joey to have private lessons. You can concentrate so much better."

Intent on using the powder room, Alicia extricated herself from Helen's grasp. Constance, who had arrived a bit late, came rushing up. "How is your mother? We've been so worried about her." Sarah Wells had been suffering from a liver condition ever since Lionel Hewitt had married a Chicago railroad heiress. Sarah had hesitated about a second marriage and had lost her chance for companionship. Now it appeared she would live out her life in the company of her spinster daughter, who was getting more eccentric every year.

Overhearing the conversation, Walter Schraeger turned to Max Farwell. "Being friends isn't enough for most men. Even the second time around."

"Everybody's got a complaint these days," Farwell answered to silence him. "Women are getting so uppity, they don't even like playing second fiddle anymore."

Walter knew what he meant, for just that afternoon, Alicia and he had gotten away for a quick dash over to the farm under the pretense of having to collect some cream. She had announced to him in her most decisive manner, "I think this has gone on far too long. Nothing ever changes, nothing ever will. Our arrangement is apparently set in your mind. I've been a fool to think things would ever be different."

"You get the best part of me," he answered, his pat response.

"Part," she repeated. "There's the perfect word. A part. Sometimes I think you believe I'm an imbecile. I know who you love! Those children and their mother, that ridiculous creature."

"You love Joey every bit as much as I love mine. Don't you think he would find it strange if I just up and abandoned my family and moved in with you? Do you think he'd be comfortable with that?" It was true that Walter doted on his girls, and he took little Wally everywhere. Whenever he sat down in his big living-room chair, the children would climb all over him. He was teaching the older girls tennis, and Wally was going to be a pilot like his father, a great sausage maker too. He idealized Lucy because she was their mother. He had no intention of leaving her.

"I'm so tired of this – this same old thing, these same dull people and parties. This whole charade. I'm tired of pretending we're such great friends, always so *terribly* loyal." Her feelings suddenly rushed to the surface, spurted up like some hot, startling geyser in a snow field. She drove herself to overstate her case in search of a new response.

"We will be together some day," he promised. "That's the best I can do right now."

"Well maybe we should wait until *some day* then." He was never there when she needed him, ever. When the holidays came, she had to sit home alone, and she always had to include little Lucy, unless she was nursing another baby. Lucy persisted in simply turning her head, making it easy for him to lead this double life. Walter was the one who had suggested she rent the Hop House and now he was telling her not to bother those men, that she had better let the lease run its course.

"You'll get into more trouble with people like that if you cross them, I'm afraid."

"How would you know?" She turned her back on him, tired of his sham concern. He always seemed slightly amused by their arguments, as if they simply served to bring his passions to the simmering point. Inevitably now he would take off his glove and slip his hand between the folds of her fox-trimmed coat, nuzzling her neck for a moment.

"I'm going to leave you, Walter."

"And where are you going to go, my love?" He lifted her hair and kissed the back of her neck, his favorite spot.

"I haven't decided," she continued to speak, as if his kisses had no effect on her, "but I can tell you one thing – I'm not staying on Nogowogotoc Lake for the rest of my life. Go ahead and have another ten babies. See what I care."

Walter pulled the horses up to a stop and dropped the reins in her lap. Springing to the ground, silver bucket in hand, he said, "Hold them. I'm going to get the cream."

Alicia could not help thinking – You've already had it. Right off the top.

When she came out of the downstairs powder room, her auburn hair brushed back, her face was rosy with windburn. She looked as if she was at the height of her powers, invigorated by exercise and relaxed by the warmth. But then she turned her head and sniffed the air, "What is that horrible odor?"

"Something must have died in the walls," Constance suggested.

"Oh, these big old homes are so nasty," Alicia stalked off in search of help. This could ruin her party. "I'd like to tear it all down and start over. Mildred!" she called. "Morvan? Can't you do something about that smell?"

"I don't know where it's coming from, Ma'am," Morvan nearly whispered, as the stench seemed to grow stronger and stronger. "We could put out some baking soda, or a honeysuckle candle."

"Heavens! That won't help."

Finally, little Joey, on his way up to bed, came over and tugged at his mother's skirt. He led her over to a standing lamp at the edge of the living room. There was something burning against the electric bulb. She peered beneath the ruffled silken shade and saw the dusty corpse of an old dried bat. "Oh," she gasped. "How disgusting! Get it out of here, *now*."

The lamp had been brought down from the third floor and plugged in for extra light. No one had noticed the tiny, wizened creature, but the sight of the crisp, dead animal made Alicia hysterical. Walter had to take her into the library to try and calm her down. He called for a shot glass of brandy, then held her in his arms, looking up at the portrait of Joey in his little white dress, holding a beribboned bonnet.

Some of the ladies turned their heads and pretended not to notice as Morvan rushed off to the secluded library with a crystal decanter on a silver tray. They thought Alicia could not bear the sight of anything morbid because of the death of her husband, but it was the sickening smell of the smoke that had turned her stomach, how the heat of the bulb had toasted the remnants of that little black figure.

"Come come, it's going to be all right," Walter soothed her. "We're going to have something now to calm you down, and then we'll dance, and tomorrow we'll make love. Would you like that? I'll spend the entire day with you."

"I hate my life. I *hate* it," she sobbed against his shoulder.

In the hubbub of the living room, Max turned to Colin. "It might be a crime to imbibe, but this bootlegging seems a hell of a lot worse. Shipments are coming right straight through here, right down from Canada."

"Somebody's getting rich off of this," Colin shook his head, and it was no longer the beer barons of Wisconsin. "Everything's upside down. Women can vote and men can't drink."

"We should write the president," Max suggested. "Tell him in Milwaukee, we consider beer a food."

"Let's dance," Dana Hewitt surprised the two men by tugging on the sleeve of the stalwart bachelor. Colin gave her a look that said – Why not me? But Dana had put up with an entire day of freezing cold sports, and now she wanted *him* to have to sit there. She slipped her arm through Farwell's and wiggled her shoulders, inviting him to shimmy.

Alicia had hired a new group from Chicago, King Oliver's Creole Jazz Band, and there was a young coronetist who was quite a sensation. All the furniture had been cleared out of the paneled salon so that the guests could dance there. The band began to cook while fires blazed at both ends of the large, dark room.

CHAPTER TWENTY-TWO

I sabelle ducked into the Latham Art Gallery, refusing the service of the cloak room, for she had no intention of staying at the opening for very long. She only wanted to see the paintings, then go. But when she spied Joshua Liebenau standing across the room, talking with Dana Ash Hewitt, her heart began pumping like a machine in her stomach. His dark, intense eyes glanced in her direction, but he did not take her in. Isabelle quickly turned and walked to the corner of the room, where she felt a bit protected.

Alicia Ulrich was talking to an older, bearded gentleman, explaining how she wanted to present one show a season, except for summer, of course. She had supposedly *found* Mr. Liebenau on one of her expeditions to Paris. "Imagine having to go all that way just to unearth another Midwesterner."

"Chicago French," the man acknowledged. "I'd call these Chicago French." He did not mean to be insulting, but it was not what Alicia wanted to hear.

She took the man by the arm, escorting him over to another painting. She was going to give him one last chance to redeem his taste. "Now, what do you think of this?" she asked. "I think he let the blue here do all the talking. He wanted it to be very brief."

"It couldn't have been briefer," the gentleman agreed, making a small, apologetic bow.

Meanwhile, Dana Hewitt was telling the artist about a show she had seen back east, "But it wasn't as daring as this one. Your sense of color is outrageous."

"Do you think so?" He seemed pleased, turning his head a centimeter to the left, as if he could better compose the angles of her face. And then in a modulated, almost hypnotic tone, he continued, "I believe a painting is only interesting when there's tension. No two colors really clash – they react. You could call it a chemical response. It's not so different with people, do you think? Some colors do nothing together. Others explode."

Alicia came up and tapped his shoulder with her program. "Three paintings have already sold, and Miss Wells over there looks like a customer. Her mother is quite a collector, actually. Too bad she didn't come."

Dana took Alicia aside and whispered, "Don't be so *gauche*. It's not good form to even look at paintings on opening night. Really, you're not a shopkeeper. Next you'll be inspecting my shoes and my purse to see what I can afford."

"You might at least let him mingle." Alicia gave her a warning glare.

"He doesn't like crowds, never has. But don't worry, I'm going to buy something."

Isabelle was going slowly from one canvas to the next, trying to maintain her equilibrium. Each painting had a vibrant mood, but perhaps her own intensity of mind was exaggerating her impressions. The colors both drew her and put her off, dark purple, olive, a brazen yellow with a bland green, all in one crushed-looking arrangement. Another had planes of burnt sienna intersected by a turquoise sky. "Suddenness" came to mind, as if these were glimpses, both seductive and embarrassing, like flinging a door open on clandestine lovers. She wanted to own one of these, but felt like a voyeur.

Joshua Liebenau walked across the room and stood behind Isabelle, who proceeded to strangle the scroll of her program. She felt his presence behind her but she didn't turn until he cleared his throat. "And what do we have here?"

Scorched with a blush, she glanced over her shoulder. "I'm trying to see what you saw." She was struggling now to catch her breath. He was even more handsome than she had remembered.

"We know each other, yes?" He could not quite place this thin, dreary-looking woman, with her navy wool coat buttoned all the way up to the possum collar.

"Nogowogotoc Lake," she replied. "Don't you remember? Your father used to sell men's paper collars for twelve cents and dog-skin gloves for a dollar?"

"Ah, yes!" he had to laugh over this. "And now *your* father has the privilege. Merrick Wells," he remembered. "We climbed that tower, didn't we. My heart was beating rather wildly as I recall." Isabelle was alarmed by this recollection, until he added. "I'm terribly afraid of heights. You should never have taken me up there."

"I'm sorry," she apologized, unable to play along, for her eyes had landed on a painting of a lilac-faced woman dressed in a big black cape, arms raised before a sickening storm.

He tried to distract her, pointing to another portrait of a dramatic-looking man in a billowing white shirt. Large, ominous trees looked as though they might engulf him.

She didn't know what to say about it, for it was obviously a self-portrait, and she found it to be rather indulgent compared to the rest. "I'd like you to have it," he insisted. "Didn't I once promise you a painting?"

"I couldn't let you give me anything. I actually came here to select a painting for my mother. She's the one who usually picks out the art work. But I do rather like that one." She pointed to a junkyard composition that she felt reflected a certain remorse, while showing the beauty of decay. "My mother has a liver condition, or she'd be here herself. My father passed away several years ago."

"I'm sorry to hear that." It was the first moment he seemed genuine, though he couldn't maintain that for long. "I always thought he looked like he'd last forever."

"Only artists live forever." Isabelle blushed again, looking back to his portrait. "Is that the one you'd like me to have, then?"

"Only if it gives you pleasure." His dark eyes examined her as if she were the most curious object he'd ever seen. He could barely suppress his amusement, but suddenly his mood turned another corner. He made her feel panicked, humiliated, exposed. "Perhaps these aren't your style. Maybe you'd prefer a nice pastoral scene."

"No, no," Isabelle turned. "I trust your judgment. Just mark it sold for me, won't you? Mother would insist on that, but I've got to run along now. Another engagement," she added, nodding her head, hoping he might agree, but she could tell he knew she was lying, that her life had become one big pretense, a means of escape.

"It's the only self-portrait I've ever done," he said, before suddenly walking away. He appeared to have had enough of her. Perhaps she had not seemed grateful enough. It made her feel as if some cold front had just blown in and taken the warm, wide-eyed weather with it. She was sure he was lying anyway. He was probably his own favorite subject.

Before she had a chance to slip out, he reappeared at the door with one last word. "May I thank your mother in person? I'll be in town for another few days."

"Of course," Isabelle acknowledged, now truly desperate, for her mother knew nothing of this exhibit, and Isabelle thought it peculiar that he was acting like the attendant, grabbing open the door for her. "Good-bye, then," she said, making a dash for the cold evening air, such a relief after the overheated gallery with its dreadful mix of cigarette smoke and conflicting perfumes. She unfastened every button on her coat.

When Joshua Liebenau arrived at the front door of the orange stone Victorian, Isabelle had fallen back into her old amorous stupor, yet this time she recognized her foolishness. She knew she could survive this emotional state, for a broken heart, once mended, is not such a frightening thing, like a precious pot that has been broken – it is not such a crime to crack it again. She needed this image for composure in the face of her mother's enthusiasm.

There was nothing like a romantic "scoop" to rouse Sarah Wells from her sickbed. She rushed right out the following day and took in the show at the gallery, insisting that the Milwaukee Art Museum must have an example of Joshua's work. "We must do everything we can," she said to her daughter before putting on her best soft-gray wool suit with the pale pink blouse. "They say he's entirely eligible. I think it's wonderful to find someone who also has an artistic temperament."

"He isn't coming here to court me, Mother. We needn't pretend."

"You never know," Sarah said. "You look very nice," she added, without saying what was on her mind – nice, for a change.

As the three of them sat down together in the front parlor, it was clear that Mr. Liebenau was primarily concerned with what Mrs. Wells thought of the exhibition. She made it known that she intended to donate a painting, and she had selected a composition for herself, *Winter Gorge*. "I'm simply taken with my landscape. Look, it's already hung. The heat of light on that melting snow – well! It is simply breathtaking."

"Opposites have always attracted me," he explained, and Sarah glanced at her daughter, as if to say – See.

Isabelle gave her mother a responding look – Yes, Mother, now why don't *you* go and see about something. Sarah took the cue. "I think Angeline's trying to singe the soufflé just to annoy." She held up a finger. She would just be a moment.

The two young people were left to sit in silence. The formal parlor furniture was covered with a stiff, prickly material, and Joshua looked uncomfortable. Isabelle gazed intently toward the bay window as if looking for outside help.

"Do you still write poetry?" he finally asked.

"Not much," she lied, feeling no need to expose that part of herself. "I've been working on more practical things, mostly." She went on to describe the work she had been doing for Margaret Sanger, setting up a Planned Parenthood office in downtown Milwaukee. "It's amazing how little most women know," she continued, wanting to shock him. "Most of them don't even know how a baby is born. It's a terrible thing, really."

"*Terrible*," he repeated.

"We meet with a great deal of public resistance, but then that was true of suffrage as well."

"Now that you've gotten the vote, I suppose you have to create some issues."

"There are always plenty of issues," she assured him. She could tell his interest had waned now that the conversation had shifted away from him. "I jumped into the Milwaukee River last summer to protest the on-going pollution."

"You did?" he seemed slightly impressed, or amused.

"It earned me the title of River Rat. But don't get the wrong idea – I'm not an exhibitionist."

"I'd think not."

Isabelle sat very upright and waited for him to tell her something about his life, but he continued in a convivial vein. "And how's your younger sister? Still as pretty and popular as ever?" He had an excellent memory for details, as if he remembered everything just as it had been ten years ago – the color of the girls' summer dresses across the lawn at Broadoaks, the depths of the turbulent sky. "I've been in Europe, mostly, since I saw you last," he said, as if she needed some explanation.

She assured him that she had not been keeping track. "Most things can wait," she gave a dim smile as her mother fluttered back into the room.

"Certainly not a soufflé," Sarah came in on the conversation. "If you wait one second too long – *poof*." She whisked the couple into the dining room, where she sat down at the head of the table. She liked the fact that he pushed in her chair for her. "Finally," she said with a sigh, "*la nourriture*."

"*Je suis dans mon assiette*," he responded – I'm very much at home.

Isabelle bit into the surprising hot air of a popover. Her mother would take over the conversation now, which left Isabelle both deflated and relieved.

"I hope you like rack of lamb," Sarah said to her guest.

"My favorite," he assured her, and Isabelle thought – Of course it is. He can gnaw on the image of the innocent.

Dana Hewitt had been spending some time out in the country lately. Colin had been particularly annoying for some reason, always hovering about when she spoke to anyone at all, as if he meant to silence or correct her. His attentions made her uneasy, constricted, and she felt that she had to escape. But after a week at the lake, Dana was eager for diversion and planned a day trip into Milwaukee.

Dana asked Alicia's driver to drop her at Felton's, knowing it was right across from the Pfister Hotel, where Joshua Liebenau was staying. After some perfunctory shopping, she decided to cross Wisconsin Avenue and leave him a note at the desk – *Do come out and see me at Nogowogotoc. I'm staying at Topside with Alicia for a while, and we're bored to death.* But as she stood at the front desk copying out this missive, Joshua walked into the lobby.

Noticing the smart-looking lady with the large parcels and excellent legs, he walked over and discovered it was Dana. He did not ask her business there. He had been pursued by women before. "Come, let's sit over here, behind these palms. We'll pretend we're in Tunisia. *So,*" he sat down, clapping his hands to his thighs, "I was just wondering how I'd waste my afternoon, and now neither of us has to waste a thing." He offered her a cigarette, leaning to light it.

It did feel risqué, smoking in the lobby of the Pfister Hotel with a single man, but she found it easy to talk to him. "I had to come in town for a day to save my sanity."

He also was a city person, but nature had a special resonance for him – it reflected the inexplicably brutal aspect of the world. One could expect violence coming from Chicago, but Nogowogotoc Lake? Nature knew no boundaries – She was simply voracious when it came to suffering, human suffering.

"Do you enjoy that?" Dana asked. "I mean, being a witness?" He did not answer, but stared at her legs, from the well-formed calves to the leather straps of her navy shoes. His gaze made Dana slightly uncomfortable. "I can't tell you how lucky you are to have kept your independence. There's nothing more appealing than a man who's been able to create his own life. Have you always wanted to be a painter?"

"I've always wanted to take you to my room," he smiled, and then both of them laughed. She felt a little heady, as if she were in some foreign place with a different moral code, some casbah. "Really, why don't we talk upstairs. I have a sitting room, and I'll tell you all about my career – then you can write that article for the papers." He created this scenario with a single stroke, and she was impressed, ready to play along. But they had to remain discreet. He suggested that she lead the way to the room, slipping her the key beneath the palm of his hand. He would follow momentarily. He meant for her to wait, long enough for her to become slightly desperate, but not so long that she might change her mind.

She was hypnotized by his manner. She had never found a man more intriguing, disturbing, and at this point she didn't care what happened to her.

Sauntering into the bar, he ordered himself some seltzer, and then pushed a folded hundred-dollar bill across the counter. "We could use a bottle of champagne in four-forty-three."

The bartender glanced at the bill and took a little jolt. "See what we can do, sir."

Joshua sipped his seltzer, imagining how she was pacing back and forth, fiddling with her long string of glass beads. She was so cool-toned, so Anglican, with her stylish cropped hair and fine-boned body. She was obviously a snob, and that always appealed to him.

When he returned to the room, she was holding up the bottle. "You wild sweet duck! How did you know this was just what I wanted." She had not dared to open it. She had never cheated on Colin before and she didn't want to think about what was driving her on – it was simply a craving for something more in her life, something high and bubbly, dangerous fun. She held out her glass to catch the glorious foam, and then quaffed it down. He sat in an armchair across from her, pouring her another glass, then another, but then he put the bottle on the floor and said coldly, "Now tell me, why are you here."

She was stunned by his insulting tone, but recovering, she leaned back on the red velvet chaise and said, "I thought you knew, darling. I came up here to be immortalized. To pose."

"And what are you posing as?"

For a moment she thought perhaps she should leave, but he caught her hand and put the tips of her fingers to his mouth. "Most of my models take off their clothing."

She gave a little laugh, "Well, this time you'll have to use your imagination." She really thought that she would go now.

"Don't I get any?" he asked, meaning the champagne, and she begged his pardon, made a little pout, and babied his neglected thirst, getting down on the carpet to fill the glass. They ended up feeding each other the golden, fizzy liquid until she felt her insides loosen. He was unzipping something, while turning her about, lifting her up and laying her backward. He made her feel sparkly – "Smooth, so smooth," exposing the tops of her pale silk stockings. Coming closer – she turned, as if to get away, but it felt so good, and he was yanking the cloth down – the shock of contact on her exposed skin unfurled this luscious carpet of feeling. He started to get serious, struggling with something. His tongue in her mouth was large and insistent. She wanted to laugh, the way he ground himself onto her – holding her hands down above her head. He seemed full of hate, but she had to admit, she loved the way he was loathing her. Suddenly she found herself up, on top. Did he think she wanted to be a jockey? Making her ride him, back and forth, his hands on her hips, but she wanted some more, some more champagne. The glass was tipped and her heels were elsewhere. She leaned forward to kiss him, but he grabbed her throat and held her mouth just inches away from his. Flinging her down, he drove himself into her. She felt like a rag, ripped this way then that, her legs torn apart as he pushed himself into her, and she was still pulsing, unsatisfied, pulsing, left on some shelf where no one could reach her, as he came with a groan and crushed her down, there in a mess beneath him.

The feeling began to subside as the room grew darker. She didn't know what to do. He smoked, and both of them were silent. Perhaps she should try and call Alicia, but she didn't want to have to explain. Then she felt tired and drunk and rather comfortable. She didn't want to think about anything.

When she awoke, it was morning, and he was gone. The room smelled of liquor and ashes. She was ravenous, half-naked in the rumpled bed. The whole thing seemed a blur. Her clothes looked ruined. Luckily, she had bought a new outfit at Felton's. She would throw the torn stockings and skirt away. He could have at least left a note, she thought, but now the morning light made the whole scene sordid. The smell of his cigar permeated every fiber in the place. She would have taken a bath, but she wanted to get out of there before he returned. She wanted to get back to Topside.

Dana took a cab to the train station and hopped the midday connection to the country. Mildred answered her call and said she would send a driver on over, but the man did not arrive for over half an hour, and when Dana was finally delivered to the house it was four o'clock. She was not expecting to see her husband.

"What are you doing here?" she asked, as Colin opened the car door.

"What weren't you doing here, might be the question. We didn't know what had happened to you. I came out here last night when my meeting was canceled. We thought you'd been murdered or robbed!" He was incensed by his own wasted worry. "Oh, what the hell." They stood in the entrance and she looked at the octagonal stones with the gray slate keys, how they fit together so rationally with even, cement lines of grout. She was not very quick to compose an alibi – "I felt like I was coming down with something, so I checked into the Pfister to sleep it off."

"You look like you slept it off," he said, for she had a woozy, vague look about her and she smelled like a nightclub. "You were drinking," he accused.

"Yes, I was drinking! Is that the end of the world? Can't I ever have a little fun without you breathing down my neck?"

"I think it was rather rough of you not to call us, dear," Alicia came in on the scene, hoping to break it up. "We held dinner until nine-thirty. By the way, Mr. Liebenau just phoned – something about a frame for his picture?"

Colin had turned and was walking away, hand on chin, as if it were all becoming perfectly clear. Of course, that painter of the hodgepodge art.

Dana ran up the stairs after her husband, wanting to reassure him that everything was all right, nothing had really happened, but as soon as she closed the door to the guest room, he turned and struck her across the mouth. "You stink!" he said, and she fell to her knees. Clambering up beside the bed, Dana tried to get away but he pushed her so hard her head hit the bedpost. "You're nothing," he said. "Nothing but a whore. Thank God we never had children."

CHAPTER TWENTY-THREE

S even summers before, Constance Rose had given birth to identical twins with strikingly opposite natures. Both boys had light brown, curly hair, but one almost imagined William to have a golden glow about his head, while storm clouds darkened the countenance of the unruly, belligerent Trumbull.

"He's all boy," Constance liked to say, for she could not bring herself to chastise him. Even when he struck out at his brother or baby sister, she would only reprimand him mildly – "Trumbull, darling, don't do that," and there would be no consequence.

He had been a colicky baby, given to raging tantrums, and he was even more difficult to manage now, since he had begun to lose his teeth. William, on the other hand, gave the impression of having a premature self-confidence, an inner serenity that no one could wholly penetrate. He quietly amused himself, and was so good, he seemed to come from another world. He had slept so much as an infant, his father thought there might be some mental deficiency, and he was so easy to be around, it was hard to give him the equal attention he deserved, especially when he did not even seem to desire it.

Trumbull sensed that people found his brother more appealing. When he was mistaken for William, friends of the family, or even relatives, might try to give him a kiss or a hug, but feeling his resistance, they knew they had Trumbull in their arms instead.

Despite William's seemingly passive nature, he would surprise a guest with a fierce embrace, as if giving his entire heart to it – "Oh, Aunt Mitzi, I missed you!"

Trumbull often tried to torment his brother by pinching his leg or giving him a snakebite, twisting the flesh both ways on his wrist, but William resisted with the mind set of a catatonic, refusing his brother even this satisfaction. He would not demean himself by being a tattle-tale, and this additional reticence infuriated Trumbull further. His screams brought their mother rushing to the scene, whereupon he accused his twin of tripping him, and when William said nothing in his own defense, she had to believe he was to blame. "Go to your room," she told him, and so he went, without a word.

Constance should have known that William had a highly developed sense of right and wrong, for even as a tiny child he always knew when he had done something naughty. He would take his little wicker chair into the closet and sit there, punishing himself before his mother or nanny could reprimand him.

William Rose was Alden Faithorne's best friend. But of course, if they invited William to Alden's seventh birthday party, they had to include his twin. "But I hate Trum," Alden told his mother. She was tucking him in, as she did every night, for it was difficult for Alden to fall asleep on the screened-in porch without their bedtime ritual.

"You shouldn't hate anyone, Alden," she told him, though she knew Trumbull Rose was a difficult child. The summer evening remained so bright, and the June bugs hummed against the screen, Alden kept wanting to sit up in bed to see what boat was gliding by, making waves lap all along the shoreline. "If you're kind to him, he might learn kindness in return," she suggested, realizing that it was probably too late for imitation of that sort.

Alden only knew that Trumbull was mean, and would probably, somehow, ruin his party. They were going to have an Indian campfire and cookout down by the lake. Alden had been planning it for weeks.

The party of seven boys included Joey Ulrich, Wally Schraeger, and Rudy Kirchner from over at the farm. "Seven is a very special number," his mother told him, kissing his round, warm cheek, and smoothing down the thin cotton flannel blanket with the frayed satin trim. "Seven colors in the rainbow, seven notes in the scale."

"Seven days in the week," Alden added.

"It was always my favorite number. I received a pony when I was seven years old. Shadow," she said, "from Mr. Ulrich. Some people say we rejuvenate our cells every seven years."

"So I'll be a completely different person?"

"Not exactly," she laughed, kissing him once more. "It's a very gradual thing." As she stood, the seven tables kept rolling through his mind – fourteen, twenty-one, twenty-eight, thirty – but here he stalled.

"The sooner you fall asleep . . . " his mother whispered, but Alden Felton Faithorne had already drifted away.

When he awoke, the light was playing in the high oak leaves, and he smelled the dampness of the night-soaked canvas awning. Then he could not believe his eyes – for there at the foot of his bed was a drum, with two padded mallets stuck down through the criss-crossed gut that secured the top and bottom. He yelped, "Hooray!" and jumped onto the foot of his horsehair mattress, turning the Indian drum over and over.

Alden's sleeping porch was right off his parents' bedroom, and his father was already up, dressing for work. Leonard stuck his head in to see the birthday boy, "Rise and shine! Are you ready for your seven spanks? Come on, get dressed and have some breakfast with me." Leonard felt badly that he was going to miss the celebration that evening, but he made up for it by hiding a brand new silver dollar beneath Alden's cereal bowl, and he did have one more big surprise, which he related over breakfast. "I'm going to take you on a trip. You've had an invitation from Mr. Terhune!"

Alden had been in correspondence with the famous author, and the cranky old man had invited the Faithornes to come back east and see his special breed of collie dogs. Alden had read every one of Terhune's books many times over and knew the stories by heart.

Just as they were finishing breakfast, Aunt Isabelle appeared, carrying a small pot of African violets. She had purchased the plant as a thank-you for Winnie, the cook, but when she discovered it was Alden's birthday – the date had entirely slipped her mind – she presented the flowers to him instead.

Alden held the potted plant thoughtfully before saying, "This isn't a gift. A gift is a toy."

"Alden, thank your Aunt Isabelle for the beautiful flowers," Helen instructed, coming in on the scene. She had gotten up early to practice her forehand against the backboard. "Such a lovely, thoughtful present."

But Alden put the flowers down and ran off to join his brother, who was already over at the farm. They were going to look for chicken feathers to make Indian headdresses. Then, in anticipation of that evening's activities, they raced back down to the lakefront and gathered stones to make a fire ring, placing small select twigs in a teepee. That would serve as kindling for the bonfire. It was a special treat to be able to have an evening party, but Alden had convinced his mother, and she had invited the other mothers to stay and have dessert.

Alden's little sister, Carol, got to stay up long enough to see the big boys arrive. Wally Schraeger sported a simple headband with a single turkey feather sticking up behind. He had smeared streaks of bootblack on his face. With his thick dark hair and tanned complexion, he almost looked like a Potowatomi. William and Trumbull had made war vests by crayoning brown paper bags, while Joey Ulrich, blond and beautiful, was completely decked out in an authentic costume with beads stitched on soft, butterscotch deerskin. All the children fondled the suppleness of his sleeve, and his mother was surprised at how quickly he joined the group, dropping her hand to follow them down to the lakefront.

The sun was setting, and the path of orange light led straight across the water to their circle of stones and flaming twigs. As soon as they were assembled around the fire, Kirchner, the gardener, gave a little speech. "I hope there's going to be no scalping tonight, cause I'm in charge of you Indians. Anyway, I heard you was a peaceful tribe." There were whoops of protest in response to this, before the seven boys ran to grab their sharpened sticks, impaling the Schraeger bockwurst, squatting down to feel the presence of heat pushing against their faces.

As the sun was extinguished, the campfire took on greater glory – popping sparks into the darkness above their heads. Kirchner threw a handful of magic powder onto the blaze and it made wonderful flames of blue and green. The fire mesmerized them all, until the old farmer passed around the bag of marshmallows. They stuck these on their sticks as well, igniting each white hunk of sweetness. Trumbull held his flaming marshmallow up like a torch, *"Your house is on fire, your father will burn,"* while William tried to carefully toast his.

"You can eat it twice," Rudy told the group, slipping the ashen jacket off into his mouth and holding the silken white remainder back up before puffing it to a golden brown. The others tried to imitate this method, getting sticky fingers and gray rings around their mouths. Such sweetness following the salty flavor of the spicy, blackened meat made them all suddenly thirsty. Alden remembered he had left a jug of lemonade in the shallows. He led the band of boys down the embankment, while Kirchner sat back away from the fire beneath a shagbark hickory, smoking his pipe, pleased with the sound of the boys all together. He was glad that Rudy had been included. He had helped his son fashion a tommiehawk for a present, using a chipped piece of slate and a notched stick.

Now the boys each took a turn lifting the lemonade jug to their lips. When they rinsed the stickiness from their hands, the lake water felt even warmer than the night air. "Look at this!" Joey cried, plucking a magnificent bullfrog from the stones along the shore. All the boys crowded round to examine it. Trumbull wanted to hold it, but Joey said it was his.

"It's probably hungry," Trumbull insisted. "Why don't we feed it bugs."

Kirchner had picked up the drum and was slowly beating it from behind the tree. The steady, solemn rhythm entered the boys' blood as they climbed back up the embankment, and ran to throw their cooking sticks onto the fire. The flames blazed up above their heads. Merrick dumped out the remaining lemonade to use the jar, and the others began dashing out into the darkness after the pulsing fireflies.

"Rudy, you guard the fire," Alden told the farm boy. "Don't let it go out." It was a dark, moonless night, and the huge, dark oaks blotted out most of the starlight, making the fireflies all the more obvious as they gave off their pale-green phosphorescence.

Quietly Rudy gathered twigs, feeling on the outside of the birthday group now. He wanted to run with the others and catch lightning bugs too. He wanted to see one blinking within the cave of his hands, making his flesh appear ghostly. William came over and joined him, in part because he didn't feel like running around. "I think those marshmallows made me sick." The other boys were scattered about the lawn – William and Rudy caught glimpses of their costumes flickering amongst the trees.

After the boys had filled the bottle with fireflies, they brought it back to the fire. Joey held onto the frog, while Wally forced the creature's mouth open and Trumbull stuffed fireflies down its throat. Soon they could see the lights blinking on and off through the smooth, pale skin of its belly.

Up on the porch of the big house, all the mothers, except Rudy Kirchner's, sat together on the white wicker furniture, sipping fresh mint tea. The porcelain tea cups had golden rims, and just as Alicia held the cup to her lips and waited for the tea to cool, she gasped – for she saw, quite distinctly in the reflective rim, a gray, gaunt apparition. She turned and looked over her shoulder, but there was nothing there. She felt chilled as the other women went on with their chatter, for she was sure that she had seen something.

"Did you hear Pat Valenschein bought the cutest little buffalo?" Constance announced. "It was the one they used to model for the nickel."

"Maybe she was saving it from extinction," Isabelle added, arriving a bit late with a more appropriate present, a toy dump truck, for her godson.

"She insisted that they rush right out and buy a female bison so the old thing wouldn't be lonely."

"They'll probably end up with a herd," Alicia added. She wished that she had let Joey come over with Morvan, then she would have had a free evening with Walter. Missing that chance made her impatient with the small talk.

"Did you see that silly newspaper article?" Lucy asked Isabelle, who thought she was referring to the latest attack on her clinic. "It said there were one hundred and twenty-five rooms in Danport Lodge," the Valenschein estate, "that you could play tennis in their living room."

"How convenient," Helen responded.

But Sarah Wells thought it a terrible exaggeration. "I've never counted them, but I'm sure half that number would be closer to the truth."

"Who can count on the truth these days?" Isabelle put in. "They sensationalize everything they print in the papers."

"But these *are* sensational times," Lucy countered. Just the other day federal agents had raided Ulrich Farms with pickaxes, demolishing vats of whiskey. The police had been tipped off by a field of pigs drunk on refuse corn.

"And then they had the nerve to question *me*," Alicia spoke up. "Frederick sold that farm years ago, and from what I gather, at least half the police force is probably involved. I should have been questioning *them*."

"Walter wants to install an alarm system, with a panel in every bedroom," Lucy announced. And Helen added that *her* husband planned on taking the children to Washington to get their fingerprints taken. Leonard had also been practicing his aim with a handgun down at the family dump, but it was common knowledge amongst the boys that their father couldn't hit a thing.

Everyone was thinking about gangsters these days, especially since that shoot-out on Upper Nemahbin. Five men had walked into the dance hall there, carrying golf bags over their shoulders. The *Nogowogotoc Free Press* had described in detail how the gunfire had demolished the player piano as well as Jack Zuta's lavender suit.

Right after the shoot-out, the Hop House had been abandoned. The men had left piles of bottles and the carcasses of animals, which they'd apparently cooked like savages in the hearth. Cigars had been heeled out directly on the floor and urine sprayed all over the bathroom. "What good is a gangster who can't even aim?" Alicia had commented before Morvan and Mildred came in to clean up.

But all of this talk made Alicia nervous. Looking out into the dark toward the sound of the boys, she thought it was getting late.

Helen went to the top of the porch steps and called, "*Allez allez oxen free-ho.*" The seven little Indians raced up the hill, whooping and hollering. But then she saw Joey Ulrich guarding something in his hands. "What do you have there?" she asked him, getting a better look at the blinking lights inside the frog.

Alden didn't want his mother to see the poor creature. Just as he'd thought, she was aghast, and her shock squelched the wildness and fun of the party.

"Do you know why fireflies blink like that?" she asked the group. They were all solemn now, though Trumbull gave a spontaneous belch within the protective darkness, and a few of them giggled.

Rudy answered first, "For protection?"

"So they can see at night," Wally responded.

"Not exactly," she explained. "They blink like that in order to find a partner. They're seeking love out there in the dark. I think you should let the frog go."

No one had ever told Joey Ulrich to give up something dear to him, and he wanted to keep his frog. He had found it. But he responded to the firmness in Mrs. Faithorne's voice, and put it on the ground. He didn't feel he could contradict her, as he did his own mother.

Soon the frog was forgotten. The party of boys raced back inside to watch the present opening. Wally Schraeger gave Alden a bowie knife in a leather sheath. They wanted to play mumblety-peg with it until Helen stopped them and said that knives were for cutting. She then presented Alden with a treasured stopwatch that had been her father's, but he didn't linger, and went eagerly on – Joey gave him a big glass marble with a silver horse inside. It was the most beautiful thing Alden had ever seen. The twins had put together a doctor's kit in a black shoe box. There was a real syringe, without the needle, a wooden tongue depressor, some candy pills, and cotton gauze with adhesive bandage. Alden's brother surprised him with a chieftain's necklace he had made himself, using beads and acorn caps, special feathers he had collected, bluebird and finch, and even the claw of a bantie rooster. Alden put it over his head, saying, "This is the best thing!"

William went and stood beside his mother. He rarely complained, but she could see that he had a headache. She touched his forehead, and he seemed to have a slight temperature. "So much excitement," she said, but he claimed that he was only tired. He put his hand in his pocket to pinch himself, for he felt like he might cry. Instead he gripped the arrowhead he was going to give Alden. It was a beautiful black one, his very best, from Grampa Lionel's collection.

Constance told the boys about her father, how he used to see real live Indians on the lake. "Sometimes he saw smoke from their campfires, right along the banks of this bay." The boys all liked to picture Indians paddling their birch-bark canoes, but tiredness seemed to descend upon them, as if the hazy smoke of some distant campfire had settled over them as well.

The next morning William stayed in bed. His eyes ached and he was content to just lie there. It was an effort to even eat the simplest meal. He wasn't hungry, and he didn't like the tea his father had prescribed, though his mother kept urging him to drink his fluids. She changed the comfry compress on the back of his neck every hour, and offered him crackers, which he only licked.

Haven couldn't stay home to care for William, for he had his rounds to make. There were many people in much worse shape than his own small son. Constance was there to comfort him, but he even seemed to tire from her reading. After ten pages or so, he just held up his hand and said, "I think I'll try to sleep now."

The symptoms seemed like mild influenza, but it was not the season for flu. What concerned them both was that the condition seemed chronic rather than acute. Haven and Constance were both at a loss. Constance felt particularly helpless, and did not want to insult her husband by asking for a second opinion. She hand-squeezed lemonade and sweetened it with honey, brought him pieces of homemade zwieback and sassafras root, but nothing seemed to interest him.

Trumbull did not help the situation, for whenever William was being nursed, he would do anything in his power to draw attention to himself. Just that morning, the chauffeur had to tell the gardener, who came to inform the cook, who spoke to the hired girl who was supposed to be helping with the children, that Trumbull was pelting cherry tomatoes at the greenhouse, and he had already broken several panes.

When Constance heard this, she left William's side and ran down the stairs to the kitchen garden. She thought to offer Trumbull a snack if he would come inside, but when she saw him throwing good tomatoes, she was swept up by an unusual anger. "Trumbull Rose! You stop that right now. Do you hear me?" To her astonishment, he kept right on tossing tomatoes, in complete defiance of her, and when she tried to catch him by the sleeve, he raced around and around, laughing outright at her exertions. She was frantic to catch him, but he continued to run, changing directions, grabbing fresh tomatoes, launching them into the sky and adding his own booming sound effects. Exasperated, she burst into tears and walked away from him.

That morning Alden received one more present, from his godfather, Uncle Max. They had actually ordered it together from Montgomery Ward's Gift Catalogue. It was a microscope with little rectangles of glass, where you could smear samples of blood or look at the composition of a drop of water. There were supposedly tiny creatures swimming around in the most minuscule amount of fresh lake water, and Alden thought they should go down to the pier and collect a cup.

Racing down the porch steps, onto the curving walkway, Alden stopped. Not three leaps from where they had left it, Alden saw the frog. He picked it up, and turned it over. There were hard, lifeless lumps in its extended belly. No light came from within.

CHAPTER TWENTY-FOUR

A licia said she simply preferred to have her independence, but actually she could no longer afford a chauffeur. As she drove herself up the curving gravel driveway to Topside, the house looked particularly oppressive. There was only one light left on deep within, and the leaded panes looked even darker than the cement walls smothered with ivy. Morvan and Mildred had apparently retired to their garage apartment, and Lolly had gone to bed. Joey was staying with his cousins in town, and no one had bothered to turn on the lantern beneath the porte-cochère.

Ever since that birthday party over at the Faithornes', Alicia could not shake the feeling she had had when she bent to sip her hot mint tea and had seen the features of that apparition. At the time, she had sloughed it off, as if it were merely a bit of steam from her cup, but now, ascending the stairs to the house with its dark wood paneling and somber walls, the vision seemed a certainty. She knew who she had seen – for in that instant she had recognized him, as if he were appealing, or offering her something. It was her father, the bastard.

The light rain, which had begun on the road, now increased to a steady downpour. Normally the sound of rain would have been a comfort to her, but tonight it made her feel even more isolate, as if the pounding on the roof might mask her cry if she needed help. She felt tense, too frightened to sleep, for she was sure she could feel his presence, right outside in the hallway. She could sense him as surely as she had as a girl, when he approached her bedroom at night.

As a child, Alicia had had a terrible crush on her father. He was so elegant, handsome and thin. He always came with the pretense of telling her a story, but the plot would often ramble and grow. Using that low, melodic voice of his, he told her that she would grow up to be tall and beautiful – "No man will ever be able to resist you." But then one night he came into her bedroom, and she sensed that he was inebriated. He slurred his words and rubbed her bare arm with the golden knob of his cane. She complained that the brass was cold, and he said that he'd warm it up beneath the covers, and slowly, very lightly, he moved it over her body until she felt a sharp excitement running through her.

Alicia sensed that their closeness was wrong, but she had never known another form of parental comfort, and his smooth, lulling voice helped put her to sleep. He would say, "Now I'm a gentle wind," and blow from her ear down over her neck, or, "Now I'm cleaning Aunt Polly's washtub." He sometimes claimed he was a grazing horse, and he would tease her with his munching. Often she would lie in the crook of his arm and try to match her inhalations to his, wanting nothing to come between them.

But then her father had begun to date. She recalled one lady in a long mauve dress, who held out her hand with its white kid glove. Alicia had stared at it, as if it were the skinned corpse of some ferret she wasn't about to touch. Then there was that nervous woman with the irritating laugh – she liked to speak French, ignoring the fact that Alicia also knew the language and the idioms of love. She wondered why he had begun to parade these women when she had always taken care of him before.

Alicia's anger was transformed into violent demands. Whenever she saw a dress or a fan that she fancied, he purchased it for her, as if to say – See, I'm a good provider. She developed a passion for snuff boxes, and began her collection with a blue cloisonné. Another was round and made out of tortoiseshell, and one was a little pewter house, but her favorite was the ebony snuff box from Morocco with the mother-of-pearl moon on the lid.

Alicia had lost her first collection in the fire, but now she had thirty or so others arranged on a mirrored shelf in her boudoir. Suddenly she wanted to sweep them away, as those horrid feelings of closeness came back to haunt her. She remembered how she had been in a fury when her father had fallen for that little blonde tart, not much older than Alicia herself. When he said that he meant to marry her, she had locked her door and wouldn't let him in. She accused him of being disgusting, attracted to cheap bordello frills. "Bon Pres is my home!" she had yelled at him. "I'd rather see it in ashes."

Breaking her promise to Walter, she rang him up. Lucy answered. Alicia was almost tempted to ask for him, saying that it was an emergency. She did not know who else to turn to. But she remained silent, and then hung up, furious with Walter for not being there for her. She did not want to have to wait for the weekend. She decided to call again. Surely he would realize that she was trying to get in touch with him and would make some excuse to leave early, but Lucy answered once more, and she did not sound frightened or even annoyed. Of course she wasn't afraid in her bright cheery mansion with her five healthy children. Alicia lay the phone down on the bedside table and listened to her say, "Hello, *hello?*"

Still Alicia couldn't sleep. The slightest noise disturbed her, and she worried that she would look like a wreck for their three-day vacation. She wanted to take a relaxing tub, but was too uneasy to disrobe. She felt that she needed someone with her, to protect her, and she decided to go wake Lolly.

Taking the flashlight from her bedside table, she cautiously unbolted the door. The long dark Oriental runner gave the stretch of hallway a gloomy look. Why hadn't she painted this wood? How she detested the darkness of walnut. Walking step by step down to the end of the corridor, she tried to focus on the family photographs that were cluttered along the walls – there was Heinrich Ulrich, sitting with his knees spread, a riding crop across his thighs, looking like he might swat someone. Then there were the three boys standing in a row all dressed up in sailor suits, photos of horses and prize bulls, a family scene at the *gemütlichkeit* picnic. It was about time she took these down and put up some cheerful paper.

At the end of the hall, she opened a door that led to the maids' wing. In the old days, this part of the house had been used to capacity, but now there were six small bedrooms left empty, and Lolly complained that she heard things moving in the middle of the night. Morvan insisted it was only raccoon, but she said it sounded like a chest of drawers being shoved, inch by inch, across the floor.

Now a shot of chills raced up Alicia's spine. The storm was pushing the unpruned branches of an elm up against the house. The hallway was dark and narrow, and it felt as if the hot, humid air was trapped within the corridor. She rapped on Lolly's door but heard nothing in response, other than a moan that sounded like a soft, half-buried *no*, but Alicia kept on pounding.

Finally, Lolly got up. She looked groggy and irritated.

"I was frightened," Alicia said. "I think I saw a ghost."

Lolly shrugged and made a move to return to her own warm bed. "What time is it?"

"I couldn't sleep, and I have to get to sleep."

Lolly gave a little laugh, realizing that now her sleep would be sacrificed, as if that were a fair exchange. She saw Alicia as a demanding, spoiled child who pointed at whatever she wanted, and now she wanted comfort, companionship, a back rub perhaps or maybe a song. "I'll walk you back to your room," Lolly offered.

But once they were there, Alicia seemed wide awake and cheerful. She insisted that Lolly climb into bed and talk for a while. "Can't you stay with me for a minute? I'll brush your hair."

Lolly knew it would soon be her turn, and she would have to brush five times as long. They had been through all this before, and tonight she didn't want to stay in Alicia's soft bed where their two bodies fell together. "Tomorrow's Thursday, my day off. I want to get up early – I'm going in town."

"And what do you need now?" Alicia scoffed, as if all Lolly needed was a roll in the hay and an hour at confession.

"I want an education."

Alicia burst out with a rude laugh. "You're *getting* an education."

"Miss Wells said her college back east is offering scholarships to women who can't afford to pay. She said she would give me an interview."

"That woman has some nerve. Didn't you know that she's a lesbian? She hasn't had a date in her entire life. You never even went to high school, and now you want to go to Bryn Mawr? Don't you see what she's trying to do? Filling you up with false hopes so she can steal you away from me."

"Why shouldn't I have a chance?"

"Why?" Alicia repeated. "Because I took you in when everyone thought you were a piece of filth, that's why. No one else would have even had you. You would have been shipped right back to your uncle in Chicago, or have you forgotten about him? I dressed you up decently and taught you myself, gave you these rooms and an excellent salary. I've taken you into my confidence. I trained you and gave you a nice home, that's why!"

"I've also worked hard, and you know that I'm grateful."

"You know nothing about Isabella Wells. Did you know she believes in abortion? That's what her clinic is about downtown. She'll probably have you burying dead babies, her helpmate. You have no idea of what is out there in the world. What men are like, and what they want to do to you. You think they'd like to help you along? They'd like to help you right down to the boathouse, that's all. Or have you forgotten about that?"

"No, I haven't forgotten," Lolly answered, getting up from the bed. "And I won't forget you, either."

She walked quickly to the door and left the room. Alicia ran after her and slammed the door, locking the dead bolt, so that Lolly had to grope her way back in the darkness.

CHAPTER TWENTY-FIVE

*A*fter work on the following Friday, Walter came to pick up Alicia. As he pulled out onto the main road in his cream-colored MG with the dark green leather interior, Alicia leaned back and stripped off her hat and let her hair stream out in the wind. The joyful levity she felt seemed to confirm that this was the right thing, for them to be off together. She could not worry about Lolly now, though she voiced her grudge against Isabella Wells for selfishly encouraging the girl.

Walter likened Isabelle to the all-white deer he'd been spotting lately. "It's the saddest thing, really. None of the others will go anywhere near it." He figured it was because white was a warning color for the species – when a tail goes up, they run – so of course an all-white deer spelled danger. "Someone should probably put it out of its misery, but I suppose it's charmed."

"I would hardly compare her to a deer. She's more like a little brown muskrat, with whiskers." Alicia put her hand on his wide, braced knee as they flew down the primitive highway, tall dense pine trees on either side. The air was filled with their cool green perfume – invigorating to her. Soon nothing existed but Walter's physical presence sitting beside her, the sound of the engine as it purred.

When they got to the airplane hangar, the sun was going down. They sat together in silence and watched it, until he asked her if she'd like to see the sun set twice. Tossing their bags in the back of the plane, he gave the propeller a single turn. How quickly they were up, flying over familiar territory, yet how different everything looked. The entire lake could be taken in as a whole – there was the roof of Topside, tiled in red. The pier looked tiny, and a single boat looked like a miniature plaything. As the plane rose still higher, they could see the globe of the setting sun as it reappeared on the horizon line, and then as they flew on, they watched it sink for a second time. Alicia leaned over and kissed him as the plane was lifted by a current of air – what a thrill to go floating into dreamy heaps of cumulous cloud then to soar up above into the blue.

The Dells Hotel was both charming and seedy with its weathered clapboards and gabled rooms. The curtains were made of a faded material, which normally Alicia would have found a bit shabby, but now she wanted to memorize every detail, the bed in the corner, the old china pitcher and bowl on the washstand, the print of *Blueboy* over the bed. Walter pulled her into his arms and wanted to make love immediately.

More than anything, she longed for that hour after consummation, when he would hold her in his arms. She loved the dark hair that ran all over his chest and she liked to call him her big bear. She thought him the most masculine man in the world, that they were made for each other, but while she could have spent the entire weekend curled up with him, he wanted to get up and seek out activity.

The next morning they decided to take a boat ride through the natural waterways, and though they could have rented a private boat, it seemed more entertaining to sit with the locals. The guide went on and on, explaining how the current had carved out miles of channel through the ancient sandstone, creating strange formations like "Devil's Elbow" and "The Grand Piano." Alicia likened "Fat Man's Misery" to their friend Max Farwell in profile.

"Won't it be wonderful when we don't have to hide?" She believed something horrible happened to love when you forced it into a nasty little box, as if it were dirty and shameful, but Walter rather liked their secret life. He filled his lungs and drew her closer, keeping his arm almost constantly about her to make up for those times when they couldn't touch.

On the second night Walter insisted they go to the Indian dances. The spectators were set back on stone benches carved into a natural amphitheater. The drumming could be heard long before the Indians themselves came out to form a serpentine shape. They shook their bells so violently, they seemed to stir up the spirits of the night itself. They were hardly wearing anything but some dangling feathers and rabbit pelts, their firm bare bodies glistening in the light of the raging bonfire. Alicia swayed with the rhythm, and Walter too felt aroused. These savages made him feel a natural, primitive urge – he wanted to thrust his hands right into her clothes, to drag her off into the darkness. There was something about Alicia that made him want to spread her out, to pin her down and soil her.

Alicia marveled at the limber bodies of the Indians, how truly athletic they were. But then gazing up, the crowd focused on a solitary man – he was preparing to take a running leap from a mountainous ledge to a standing rock that rose like the stem of an enormous mushroom, at least fifty feet high. The drums grew louder and more urgent, while the dancers down below crouched and bowed their heads as if their concentration might help him in his flight. Then the man up above suddenly ran and jumped – landing on the other side. A cheer was released from the audience, accompanied by the rising whoops of the warriors, who circled and stomped before filing out, chanting and turning as they went. Alicia was left in a state, energy and excitement on the surface of her skin. The crowd began to make its noisy exit, pushing together like water through an outlet. Doc Oliver, self-proclaimed medicine man, had positioned himself at the opening. He held up a bottle – "Kickapoo Joy Juice, one dollar a bottle! This is miracle stuff, can cure anything at all! Anything save wife trouble." He winked at Alicia.

"But that's the only trouble we have," she complained, hanging on to Walter's arm.

By the time they had reached the hotel bedroom, Alicia was obsessed with the Indian on the rock. How would he manage to jump back again? Was he going to be left there in total darkness? Walter didn't even seem to care.

When he dropped Alicia back at Topside the following day, it was as if the expansiveness of their love closed its covers like a slapped-together album – *shut*. He didn't even bother to call, and she became more and more incensed. Nothing had really changed. She was back in her own life, and he was back in his. How could he be so duplicitous.

"You probably blame me for introducing you to him in the first place," Alicia said to Dana, who had been drinking port all evening, smoking one cigarette after another.

"To Joshua you mean?"

"No, *Colin*," Alicia answered, exasperated. Usually she and Dana could read each other like the Wish Book, but now Dana seemed completely absorbed. "Your husband, remember? The source of all misery?"

"Are you miserable too?"

"*I'm* not miserable. I'm in love."

"You're not *really* in love unless you're miserable," Dana responded, pouring herself more port. "*I'm* miserable." Dana could not figure out what she was doing at Alicia's, other than waiting for something to happen. Nothing ever seemed to happen. She kept thinking that the phone would ring.

"I always wondered if your marriage was my idea." Alicia held the corner of her eye and, looking deep into the mirror, applied a stroke of kohl. It was

Alicia who had suggested that she could get her friend married on Nogo-wogotoc Lake, and at the time they had both gotten so wrapped up in the details, the man himself didn't seem to matter very much.

"Of course we had our problems," Dana whimpered, gazing at Alicia's pale blue sapphire ring – the exact same color as Colin's eyes – "but when I think of our honeymoon . . . " So many days stood between that happy month and the present moment. She and Colin both seemed like different people – they knew each other now, and he hated her.

"Scotland would never have been my choice," Alicia said.

"I would have been happy anywhere. You don't know how lucky you are."

"Lucky?" Alicia had to laugh. She hardly considered herself lucky.

"To have Joey, I mean. You're never lonely."

"Yes, I'm *never* lonely." Alicia put her kohl pencil back down on the table, dissatisfied with her efforts. "But children are overrated." She picked up the ivory-handled mirror and turned to look at the back of her hair. "Maybe you should take a lover. Someone more discreet."

"I suppose that's made *you* happy."

"At times, yes, happier than you can imagine. I'd give anything to be with Walter right now."

"And how much do you think *he*'d give? " Dana asked. "I hate to disillusion you . . . " She hadn't meant to disclose this, but Alicia's attitude drove her on, as if she and Walter Schraeger were the only ones to ever know True Love.

Alicia turned on the silk-covered stool, listening, but not wanting to hear. A sinking feeling went through her, and her heart began to beat faster.

"Walter was over at Lindsay Allis's a couple weeks ago, and he propositioned one of her house guests. Actually, I met her myself, a pretty, innocuous little thing. She complained to Lindsay, who was obviously shocked. She wondered if she should say something to Lucy, but I said no, what good would that do. The woman lives in St. Louis. Doesn't he go there all the time?"

Alicia looked as if her eyes were made of metamorphic rock, changing from a molten material into something solid, hard. "Walter likes women, that's all. It's his charm. It's misunderstood."

"He's never going to leave his wife," Dana interrupted. "Everybody knows that." Dana seemed almost delirious in her delivery now, leaning toward Alicia for emphasis, as if she wanted to hurt her friend for knowing reciprocal, passionate love, while she was shut out, alone. She wanted to puncture that heart so full on itself, to watch her friend's face fall. Alicia walked across the room to get away from this news, collapsing on the overstuffed armchair with its pretty slipcover – yellow ribbons caught forever in a constant wind.

Alicia put a hand over her eyes, not sure who she should hate, but right now she hated Dana for telling her this.

"You probably didn't know he was a Catholic, did you. Colin discovered that. They don't believe in divorce."

"You're thinking of Lucy," Alicia said, standing up. "Walter is a Lutheran or something."

"Buying that bed from the King of Romania for eighty thousand dollars! They say it's not stuffed with horse hair, either, *crunch crunch* – but pubic hair."

"That's enough."

"Oh, yes." Dana emptied her glass. "Everybody's had enough – you, me, Colin, Walter." She dropped the glass on the covers, rolling over on the bed, and then gripped the pillow to herself.

Alicia tried to assure herself that people were always exaggerating sordid details in order to brighten their own dull lives. But beneath this explanation, she felt a deeper dread – that it was true – Walter was not only cheating on Lucy, but on her as well.

Dana wondered if it were possible, in some unseen, mystical sense, for her and Colin to be "one flesh" as their ceremony had claimed, for she yearned for him now as she realized how much pleasure and pain were wrapped up together. When he had struck her and walked out the door, she had felt a violent need to hang on to him. He had always tried so hard to please her, filling her cup, filling all the empty spaces, not giving her a chance, but now she was discovering what it was like to ache for a man. She confused her longing for liquor with this other hunger – just as the pleasing liquid going down left her with a raging headache, so the pain he had caused her lent her the pleasure of feeling, as horrible as that was.

"Of course," Alicia exclaimed, as if she had just figured it out. "Everybody knows Lindsay Allis was crazy about Colin. She's just getting back at me for introducing you two."

"I'm sure that's it," Dana answered, rolling over to pour herself another glass of port. Her hair looked as if it needed a wash, and there were smudges beneath her eyes. "Do you know what Grampa Hewitt offered me?" She lay back and gazed at the golden Venetian material of the canopy. Alicia was not in the mood to guess. "He heard about Colin hitting me, and Mitzi too. You can't keep anything from that old goat. I don't think he ever got along with any of his children, and Mitzi's married to a real misogynist. He's worse than Colin ever was."

"So what did he want?" Alicia asked.

"Want?" Dana repeated, her mind momentarily a blur. "He wanted to give me a million dollars." She sat up on the bed and stared at her friend, as if she were just remembering. "He wanted to give me a million dollars if I'd stick it out with Colin. But then I *also* heard, from the horse's mouth, mind you, that he offered another million to Mitzi's husband, to disappear."

"And?"

"We both accepted." Dana began to laugh. It was a sloppy, irritating, drunken laugh.

Alicia was certain she would never sell her freedom to stay with a man who hated her, but maybe she was wrong about Colin and Dana. Maybe they would get back together. A million dollars was a lot of money.

"We could move to Milano, or Paris," Alicia suggested, "begin a whole new life. To hell with this place and all of these families."

"That, unfortunately, was part of the deal. I have to stay right here. We're stuck, Alicia." She eyed the mirror on the far side of the room. It was made out of a hundred tiny octagonal mirrors, all pieced together, which threw one's reflection back a hundred times – every smile just the same as every other, every turn of the head – "Neither of us is going anywhere."

CHAPTER TWENTY-SIX

*H*aven Rose was not a regular at Margaret Elliot's speakeasy in Okauchee, but that night he needed some relief. Going directly to the bar, he put a coin on the counter. Everything here cost a quarter – shot of whiskey, book of matches, a pack of cigarettes. When her dresser drawer was full of coins, she'd yell, "The spree's on me!" and everyone was treated to a round of drinks.

Applause from the boisterous crowd went up as soon as Marg sashayed out from the back, wearing a low-cut black lace top, holding a ukulele. Haven realized that almost everybody in the room knew who he was, but no one knew what was happening to him. How could they understand what it was to be a doctor, to name a condition, and not be able to do a thing for your own child. William had developed "brain fever." He had been delirious now for over two days. Constance would not leave the room, but Haven could not stay there any longer. He drank his whiskey and then ordered another. The men began to sing as Marg struck up a tune:

In the church on the organ she'd practice and play
While the preacher would walk up and down
But his wife caught him pumping the organ one day
That's why dear old Aunt Dora left town

We don't speak of Aunt Dora
Her picture is turned to the wall
She lives on the French Riviera
But she is now dead to us all

They told her the wages of sinners was death
But she said since she had to be dead
She'd much rather die with champagne on her breath
And pink satin sheets on her bed

Haven turned to scan the room and saw Colin, his brother-in-law, uncle to little William. Even Colin didn't know about the severity of the illness. Colin was talking to Max Farwell. Neither of them had children, so how could they understand. Haven didn't want to talk to either one of them. He just wanted to drive off by himself.

Colin Hewitt had been spending regular hours at the speakeasy, in part because Lolly Jones was working there. Since his fight with Dana, he had started seeing Lolly. He often took her for a walk or drove her home after hours. Making love with Lolly was like sinking into blissful forgetfulness, but all too soon images of Dana returned to plague him.

"You know what you had," Max thought he could sum up their entire relationship – "Passionate incompatibility. You see, you were drawn together, but you couldn't stand each other. I mean, you loved each other – I'm sure you *loved* each other."

"Dana Ash never loved anyone in her life."

"Passionate incompatibility," Max persisted. "Being a bachelor, I see these things."

Colin gave a little snort, looking over at Lolly. He threw back the rest of his whiskey. It was true, he had been madly in love with his wife, but now he pictured her scrawny, frigid little frame and could not bear the thought of her – that selfish, aloof, impenetrable spirit.

"Only once in a great great while do you get real friendship *and* a feeling of passion mixed together in a marriage. I could have had it if I'd been a little quicker."

Colin ignored this idle bit of boasting and tried to catch Lolly's eye. Lolly, familiar with rough, drinking men, knew that certain familiarities had to be tolerated, but she kept an emotional distance. She pretended not to notice Colin, which gave him the freedom to stare. Max indulged in a few lewd comments, while Colin was torn between his precious anger and his base desires. He thought about how responsive Lolly was, how easily a shudder ran through her, but at the same time, he could not rid himself of Dana's image, her chiseled face, eyes closed.

Whenever Max had been drinking to excess he got into a rhyming mood. Now he thought to recite his latest ditty – *"No tits to pull, no hay to pitch, just punch a hole in the son-of-a bitch.* Do you know what I mean? *Carnation.* Canned milk!"* He was slurring his words, as if they were coated with a thick cream. The smoke-filled tavern seemed to expand and contract as Max took in the scene. He tried to focus on Lolly, as she stood waiting by the bar, and he thought how he'd like to thrust both hands right up her skirt. She had such nice, round, matching parts. Without warning, he stood, ready to move in her direction, but then he said, "Shit," swaying where he stood.

"Better watch your tongue, old boy," Colin warned. "Marg won't have any four-letter words in here. She'll have you thrown out on your ear. It's a privilege, you know, to be a guest in this establishment."

"She must be a real," he slurred out the rest – "a real, god, damn, lady!"

Lolly glanced up in their direction, and suddenly stopped. She recognized Max. Her face dropped to a rigid expression. She glared at Colin before swinging around, pushing through the double doors to the back. How dare he bring that guy in here, as if he meant to share her. She felt a sudden rage, a fury she hadn't felt since that night by the lakefront, when Colin had disappeared and the other two boys had held her down and gagged her with a towel.

"You know what I'd like to do," Max said, still swaying above the table, unable to move, but he pointed to the door where Lolly had gone. "I'd like to slop that girl in the mud."

Colin chuckled, and encouraged his friend. "I'm sure she's back there just waiting for you."

"Let's have another drink," Max decided, as if he needed more ammunition.

"You're looking at an almost free man. And I don't mean a nigger gone fishin' in Wisconsin. Think of all the pleasures awaiting us." He nodded again in the direction of the back room, but his mind was yanked back to Dana and more complaints. "You don't know what it's like, living with a woman – all that crap all over the bathroom. Taking an hour to get ready. Waiting and waiting, and when she comes home – she smells like a pig."

Farwell seemed to gain courage from this handsome speech. He quaffed down the last of his drink and rose again, turning in a circle before wandering in the direction of the back room.

The door swung open, and he saw Lolly sitting there with her elbows on the desk, both fists pressed against her mouth. There was only one dim light burning above her. "What do you want," she demanded.

Max was surprised, unprepared for this cold reception. He sauntered over and put a hand on her shoulder.

"Get away from me," she jerked back in her chair, but her fierceness only kindled his original intentions. He reached for the elasticized material of her blouse, muttering something about her being so pretty, mammiferous wench, but she yanked herself free and snatched open the desk drawer, pulling out a revolver. Max held up his hands and backed out of the room into the parking lot, but Colin swang in at that moment and saw Lolly aiming the small black gun – "What the hell!" He paused and then lunged, trying to get control of it – "You stupid sow, what do you think you're doing?"

The first bullet made a small, clean hole in the roof and kept on traveling, but the second hit Colin in the middle of the stomach.

By the time Margaret Elliot had gotten off the stage, called to her men, and pushed her way to the back, Lolly had disappeared, and Colin was lying on the floor, bleeding and groaning.

"That doctor just left," one of the men said, and the others suggested she get this bloody swell out of her back room unless she wanted to be shut down. "This isn't your mess, Marg."

So they dragged Colin out to his black-and-red Mercedes and flung him into the backseat before towing the car to nearby Okauchee Lake.

Leaving the tavern, Max Farwell was driving so wildly, he forced a black Ford sedan off the road, killing a couple instantly and leaving their five-and-a-half-year-old daughter unharmed in the backseat. Max had been too drunk or unnerved to stop and didn't know what had happened until he read the headlines the following morning: ACCIDENT, MURDER, DEATH.

When William Douglas Rose passed out of this world, his mother was standing by the window of his bedroom. She had been praying without cease for several days, and her words of supplication had become a throbbing chant, going on and on in her head – begging and pleading, promising, asking, offering to do more good works, if only, more generous to the poor, she would

187 ↩

work in His name – but she had finally worn herself out, changing the compresses, trying to get William to drink a little something, lifting him into the tin tub they had placed by his bed to give him cooling baths. She had not eaten a thing in over twenty-four hours, and she felt lightheaded when he finally murmured, "Sleep, Ma," as if he were thinking of her welfare, or perhaps asking for a little rest now.

It was then that she had kissed his brow and left his side to stand by the window. Looking out at the night, she heard the big bell from across the bay. It struck one, for twelve-thirty, or perhaps it was one A.M., or possibly even one-thirty, she didn't know, but she felt the relief of just being there, without any more words, at peace with the night and herself. She trusted God's will at that moment, for she knew she had no control over this. But when she turned back to the bed, the child's face looked so still it frightened her. She didn't know how long she had been standing there, gazing out at the black expanse where the water and woodlands merged. Haven was not at home and Trumbull was staying with her sister. Everybody else was asleep, all the servants. She could not believe that anything had happened because she had been right there, and the beeswax candle was still burning on the dresser.

"Sweetheart?" she whispered, but he did not move. His face looked rubbery. Overwhelmed with dread, she thrust her hand beneath the covers. The bed was still warm, damp from his fever, but his arm felt strangely still. She lifted him up by the shoulders, and his head tumbled back. At that moment she knew he was gone, but she took him in her arms, dragged him onto her lap, and rocked, staring at the faded rose wallpaper as if it had come to life on the walls and was beginning to climb and grow, brightening this old, gabled room with its two identical windows. She sat there with her beautiful, small son in her arms until she heard her own voice singing a lullaby he had once loved – "*Hush little birdie, croon, croon, hush little birdie, croon. The sheep have all gone to the silver rye, and the cows have all gone to the broom. . . .*" She held him and rocked him and imagined the vines of the roses wrapping them together, faded red flowers with terrible thorns, the most fragrant and painful of flowers, wrapping them tighter and tighter, until his absent life seemed no different than her own, and they were one in the rhythm of her rocking, in time with the ticking of the universe, whether sleeping or awake, singing or listening, holding or being held. Her rocking seemed to encompass it all, and yet she felt above it, above the pain of the living, the dullness of the dead, like some mechanical instrument merely set in motion.

This numbness continued even after Haven returned. Seeing them both there locked together, mother and child, he knew he was too late, that it was over. He fell down on his knees beside her and stopped her chair from moving, stilled it with the weight of his body, and wept. She looked at him oddly, as if he were not her husband, and yet she did not resist when Haven unclenched her hands and took the body of their child away. She did not struggle, for she knew that both his life and his death were deep inside her now, embedded in her, and no one, not even her husband, the doctor, could take that away from her, ever.

The following morning she walked about the house as if she were looking for something. She felt like a newly sheared lamb who could not get used to the feeling of lightness. She felt naked with the air so close to her skin, exposed, as if someone might see her. The only moment that brought her back to her grief was when Trumbull raced in the front door with Mitzi. Seeing the twin, the identical living shape, made Constance cry out. She turned to her sister – had she told him? Did he know? For he was demanding milk and a ginger cookie, hungry and thirsty as always.

Constance did not realize that Trumbull felt responsible, for he had often wished his brother would die. Everyone had always preferred William. And the only way he could protect himself now was to act even more impossible, so that no one would ever mistake him again. He feared his mother only loved his matching half, and he wished he too could sleep forever.

Grampa Lionel walked in after the others, looking thinner, more frail, suddenly older. His new wife was trying to act busy and cheerful, bustling about with Mitzi. Constance was almost grateful for the woman's inappropriate manner, though it did not remove the glaze of grief that seemed to stiffen each object in the house, making each chair appear unique, separate, not part of a living whole.

The new Mrs. Hewitt wanted to work on the preparations for the funeral reception. She was a good woman, and she wanted to be useful. Constance needed to be distracted, and yet she did not want anyone becoming overly familiar, too close to her. She didn't mind the plans – they were not her concern – she simply didn't want to be drawn into them. She was looking for something else, a sign. When Lionel saw his daughter's reaction, he told his wife to be silent. "Enough now. This isn't the time to plan a party." And then, turning to his girl, he said, "Come here, doll." Constance walked into her father's arms and began to weep until she feared she would never be able to see what she was looking for.

CHAPTER TWENTY-SEVEN

O ver the years, Alden and his brother, Carl Merrick, had buried animals in the ferny grove between their grandmother's and the big house, a place they called "the animal graveyard." They felt an unsentimental reverence for the shady spot, where mossy flagstones made a path through the undergrowth. They were always careful to stay on the stones, observing the different markers.

Since the death of their beagle, Leonard had been promising to buy the boys a collie, but right now Alden didn't want a thing. A gift would have been received as the keenest of insults, for it could not assuage his grief. He had lost his closest childhood friend, and in his innocent sorrow, he was sure he would always feel empty and alone.

"Couldn't you take him outside, for a walk," Helen pleaded with Leonard. "I think a little movement might do him good. It's too heart-breaking. I can't listen anymore."

Alden's eyes were red and smudged from crying, and his sobs seemed to catch upon each other, each sob linking and drawing out the next. It was beyond his power to stop the spasms, even when his father said, "Come. I want to show you something." Leonard had no idea of where they were going, but he knew he had to alter the perspective in order to stop this spasmodic weeping.

Alden stood, willing to take his father's hand. "I would have," the boy sniffed, then suddenly angry. "Nobody even told me!"

"Nobody knew," his father responded, and that seemed even more terrible, that something like this could happen, and nobody knew.

They headed down the drive, and the overhanging elms looked particularly vivid where they formed an arch of greenness above them. Walking across the gravel road into the bright fields beyond the cottage, Leonard decided to take the boy up to the old shooting range. The pitted cement wall gave a fortress-like sense of protection there. Leonard wanted to sit up at the top of the field and look down the gradual slope toward the pastures, with the farmhouse, barn, and greenhouse beyond, a certain stability in the familiar layout, though the day itself seemed freshly skinned, hung up for examination.

As they reached the top of the rise, Alden gave one final, delayed sob before asking. "Why did *he* have to die. Why not Trumbull."

Leonard was taken aback. He shook his head and Alden instantly knew it was wrong to have such thoughts. But at the same time, Leonard could sympathize with the bluntness of the question, for death had no orderly system of justice, and the random choice was difficult for even him to understand.

Leonard had once considered himself a religious man. He still read from the Bible daily and continued to pray, but without the security or companionship of fellow parishioners. His grandfather had been a Presbyterian minister, and Leonard too had considered taking up the cloth before he became disillusioned. He believed in God and the spiritual world, but not in the workings of the Church. Man was human and therefore corrupt, and the Church seemed more of an extension of that corruption than a manifestation of the Unseen Truth. And yet Leonard often felt the lack of depth in his work at the store. It did not challenge his deeper instincts, and he had to continually remind himself that there was something more important than net gain and annual profits. It would certainly be easier to worship the Almighty Dollar. Max Farwell was always bothering him to invest in stock, which seemed to be doing better and better each year, though Leonard in his conservative way thought it an inflated market. He preferred a more tangible investment, and believed it was enough to run his business well and to manage his family's affairs.

Leonard had a superior education, and all the good manners and breeding that went with it, but he felt rather inadequate when it came to responding to his son's simple question. "We don't know why people die when they do. I know it seems wrong that William was taken. He didn't do anything bad, and he wasn't being punished. You mustn't think that. I don't understand why this happened when it did, but I can say this – I do believe that William is alive right now, in a world we can't see, but which is right here, beside us, as close as the air to our skin. It's a part of the mystery of living, really. There is so much we can't conceive of, but sometimes you can feel it, if you remain very still."

Alden thought there was some truth in what his father said. They both were silent for a moment as they sat pressing down a nest of oat stalks before the pitted stone wall. Alden closed his eyes and listened, tried to feel the heat of the air pushing against his forearms as if to reassure him. A murmuring hum of warmth seemed to rise from the golden grain, the buzzing sound of fertile growth, and he took a fistful of earth in his hand, crumbled it, and looked at the particles sticking to his sweaty palm. A tiny bug was crawling up a nearby stalk, and Alden felt that he too could be just that small on some other scale, perhaps to God. He could be nothing but a tiny speck, and he wondered where heaven was and why he couldn't see over to the other side. For the briefest moment he released his questions and felt still and somewhat comforted.

191

"You have to imagine William very light, without his body to weigh him down, but with the same happy laugh, the same spirit."

Alden could almost hear his friend, and he thought he felt William somewhere nearby, saying sweetly, wordlessly – Don't be sad. Everything's fine, *really*. But immediately following that brief communion, Alden felt his sadness catching in his throat, and another stray sob came wandering out to surprise him. If his friend could die so suddenly, anybody could, his father, his mother, himself.

"When God calls for a child, the angels come to help him," Leonard said. "The angels help him so he won't be so lonely."

"But *I'm* lonely," Alden responded. "Why don't the angels help me?"

There were three funerals in the village of Nogowogotoc that week, and the Faithornes attended all of them. They didn't know the couple who had been killed in that terrible automobile accident, but they felt they should attend their memorial service.

Colin Hewitt had suffered a gruesome death that was still a mystery. He had been found in the backseat of his Mercedes, half-submerged in the swampy end of Okauchee Lake. The local police were claiming it a suicide, though no gun was found, and no one who knew him could believe he would have inflicted such a slow and painful death upon himself, even if he were despondent.

Max Farwell was too distraught to come forward. He could hardly trust his own intoxicated recollections, and he had left the speakeasy before the crime had been committed, so he didn't know anything for sure. He felt too guilty about the road accident to accuse another person, and he believed if he pointed a finger at Lolly Jones, she could easily be vindictive. No matter what he did now, it wouldn't bring Colin back, and the community at large was preoccupied with its grief over the wasted life of William Rose.

William's funeral was held at the Wahcheetah Mission. Constance wanted the service to begin exactly at noon, for she had a superstition that spiritual beings came closer to earth at that hour, when everything was intensely bright. Indeed, the day was so glorious, the mourners had to shield their eyes from objects catching the sun. No one could look at anything directly.

She did not listen as the minister spoke, closing herself off from the literal, waiting, as if for some sign, for a flash of light or meaning. After the service, she realized that she didn't want to be near so many people, or to receive their common condolences. She shrank from friends and acquaintances alike, wincing when they approached her.

Lucy Schraeger was heavily veiled with black netting pulled over a wide-brimmed hat. Lucy had lost her own first child in infancy, but she seemed to accept the course of events as if they were not so tragic. Heaven, after all, was a better place. Constance looked with misery at Wally Schraeger. It hurt her to see William's small friends, but it was worse when Lucy put a hand on her shoulder and said, "Death loves a shining mark. There never was a child more radiant." The image struck Constance like a blow to the forehead, blinding her momentarily.

She turned from Lucy and staggered across the lawn. Why did she have to hear such words! What did any other mother know? God had given her the most precious child, then taken away everything that mattered. Death had cut down her son and what good would come of it? What would little Wally Schraeger learn? That it was a pitiful thing to be a human being? She felt her wonderful, dear boy had been *slain* like wheat, felled, then rained upon. Left ungathered in the wasteful field.

But then Alden Faithorne came up to her. It was clear that the child had been suffering. She wanted to take him in her arms and bless him, for she was sure no one else understood, not even her husband, who blamed himself, who insisted that *he* should have saved the child. This made Haven seem stupid, ridiculous. As if he had anything to do with it.

Alden clutched the arrowhead that William had given him until it cut into his hand. The sharpness of the obsidian helped to keep him from crying. He wanted to say he was sorry, but he could not speak a word. He bit the insides of his cheeks, and on impulse, he thrust the arrowhead on Mrs. Rose, then turned and ran back to his mother. Helen too struggled to find something to say, but only shook her head. How could anyone bear this.

The group followed the small wooden coffin to the family plot, and a woman in black moved through the group, offering every mourner a single red rose so that each person could drop a flower on the coffin. It was the most melancholy thing, "Pathetic," Helen thought, the sound of each flower hitting the bottom. Only Alden looked down the hole.

When he returned home that afternoon with his parents, he asked his mother why his rose had changed, "when it touched the box." She asked him what he meant, and he said, "Nothing," though his flower on landing had turned white.

When the county wondered what to do with the girl child that had been orphaned the same night as Colin Hewitt's death, Dana Hewitt took it as a sign, for she was a childless mother, just as this was a motherless child. The girl was almost six years old, decidedly beautiful, with curly red hair and sparkly eyes that apparently did not see the magnitude of her loss. She had a spray of freckles running across her nose and the unusual name of Siobhan. She told Mrs. Hewitt politely, three times, that her name was pronounced "Shavon." Her parents had been first-generation Irish Americans, and there were no other relatives in the country, as far as anyone knew. Dana offered to adopt her, and the girl returned home with her that very evening as if it were the most natural thing in the world.

CHAPTER TWENTY-EIGHT

*I*sabelle had been working late and was just closing up when Lolly Jones arrived at the downtown Family Planning Clinic. The summer heat had been oppressive that day, as if the brown brick building were some gigantic oven meant to slowly cook its inhabitants, no relief, no cooling stretches of wide green lawn or lake breezes, no fluttering, leafy trees.

Isabelle was ready to get going. She always liked the evening warmth once she was out of the office, walking home. In the summer people came out onto the street, and were more jocular, lively, like Europeans. Restaurants and eating halls opened their doors and you could peer back into the darkened rooms, hear clapping and laughing, accordion music, smells of sauerkraut and knockwurst. Pots of mustard stood on the counters near flickering candles in their votive cups. The only thing that was missing from the tables to complete the ethnic scene were big pitchers of ale, for here in Milwaukee, beer was considered a necessity, almost more important than water. Isabelle didn't miss the sour scent of beer. She felt abstinence helped to keep male impulses in check.

That evening she and her friend Potter were going to get something light to eat at the Knickerbocker, and then walk in the park and talk about literature. Potter read all of Isabelle's poems, and gave her perceptive critiques, but all this was forgotten when Lolly Jones turned up at the door. Isabelle put down her briefcase and drew the girl inside. "So you heard – I've been meaning to congratulate you. Why do you look so worried? You've been taken off the waiting list! Now the only contingency lies with scholarship funds, but I've already spoken to my sister – we've been wanting to set up an annual fund anyway, and we're hoping that *you* will be our first candidate."

Lolly looked even more despondent, for she hadn't realized that her chances were so close, and now she would have to lose everything. "I can't go," she confessed, sitting down heavily in the one wooden armchair provided.

"What do you mean, you can't go? That's impossible. Everything's set. I know you'll do wonderfully. You're probably worried about what you'll need, but Helen said she'd put a trunk together – she knows all about trunks, and packing and whatnot. We'll get you out there if we have to send Krone in the Packard."

Lolly looked up at her benefactress as if Isabella Wells were speaking some inscrutable language only the privileged could understand. They were obviously worlds apart, and she had been a fool to imagine it – trunks, chauffeurs, professors, books, enough leisure time to sit down in one place and actually read a whole novel. "I can't," Lolly said. "I'm pregnant."

"Oh," Isabelle responded, as if the air had been let rather fast from her sails, as if her own hands had suddenly released the rope, her desire to help just blown away like so much of everything she did, her attempts. "Are you sure?"

Lolly nodded. Her large breasts had become even more swollen, and she had been vomiting before breakfast, though she hardly ate a thing.

Isabelle knew it was not her business, but she felt she had to ask. "What will the father do?" Hopefully the man would be honorable.

"The father's a dead man," Lolly said with the same blank expression. She seemed to be looking nowhere, thinking of nothing. "He never knew anything about this. Just as well. He had no respect, no feelings. I don't know what I'm going to do now." All the while she spoke she kept her head down and her eyes nearly closed. She was ashamed, trapped, terrified, but finally she looked up at Miss Wells and asked, "Isn't there any way?"

The girl looked like she wished she were dead, and it alarmed Isabelle, who had never been confronted with this situation in the short history of the downtown clinic. She had anticipated the problem, and had always wondered how she would react. Would she take the necessary risks? She had received the name of a man in Fond du Lac, but he was not a doctor and he charged a very high fee. Isabelle feared he was simply a mercenary, not on their side, and if there were complications, if Lolly were hurt or if the authorities found out, it might jeopardize their whole operation.

Then she thought of Haven Rose. Surely he would understand what it meant to try and change one's life for the better and make something of oneself.

Lolly had already told Isabelle that she was interested in nursing. If she went to Bryn Mawr, she would have a chance to make a difference in the world. If she remained unmarried and pregnant, what kind of life would she enjoy?

"We'll certainly do what we can," Isabelle said slowly, assessing the possibilities. Isabelle noticed the marks of perspiration that stained the girl's brown print dress. No matter how hot it was, Isabelle never perspired. She gathered her things together, and noticed that her own hands were shaking. "There are limits as to what I can do," she confessed, for she didn't want to get Lolly's hopes too high. "But come, why don't you spend the night in town. You can bathe, and have a good night's sleep, and I'll drive us out to the country in the morning. There's someone I want to speak to out there."

Haven Rose had been aware of what happened to Lolly Jones during the summer she worked for the Hewitt family. At the time he had not spoken up in the girl's defense, and he still felt badly about it, especially when the men continued to joke about her. Haven felt he could not condemn his brother-in-law and the friends he associated with on the lake. He had no actual proof, so he would only have been making a sentimental display, showing his true colors – that he was more aligned with the lower classes, with women instead of men. Through his practice, he had come to have a great deal of empathy for women. He had seen their suffering firsthand. He had noticed the anger and aloofness of husbands when complications occurred. He had also seen how repeated, unwanted pregnancies wore women down, ruined marriages, and brought no happiness to the resulting children.

But now he was being called upon to make a life-and-death decision. He did not believe that he could have anything to do with the termination of a pregnancy, though for a moment he thought that if the girl went ahead and kept the baby, he and Constance might offer to raise it. But wouldn't that only be a selfish response to her situation? The loss he and Constance felt was still so great that it was hard to conceive of denying life to any unborn being, and yet, from a personal point of view, he believed that the spirit came into the body at the moment of birth, not at conception. It was at the moment of descent, when the head crowned – he had seen this power of God-given grace too many times in the birthing room to doubt the reality of it. With miscarriages he never sensed the same thing. It was just flesh, wasted flesh, then hormonal readjustment.

Meditating alone in his study that night with his open notebook before him, he turned all the details around and around, the globe of the desk lamp illuminating an oval, bisected by the spine. It looked like a blank piece of anatomy, a tabula rasa, and he wondered how it would feel to draw an embryo, an umbilical cord, the beginnings of placenta, and then to shut the volume, to wipe that image out.

He had always thought Lolly an attractive, bright young woman, and he believed the sanctuary of a woman's college would be the best place for her right now. It was not too late for her to develop her mind. He pictured her studying very hard. He believed she would be an excellent nurse, as Isabelle had suggested. But then an image of William floated up before him, that fresh and lovely countenance. It seemed as if his translucent skin were drenched, illuminated by water. But then the light vanished, and he was left with his doubts. What if his boy wanted to return somehow, to begin a new life, close by? But no, he could not believe that was happening. Lolly needed his help, like any other patient, and though he would not go so far as to perform an operation, to dilate her cervix and deposit some foreign substance, he believed in the power of suggestion, and if gestation were in the early stages, he thought he could help her to spontaneously abort.

When Haven drove up the gravel drive to Broadoaks, he could see Sarah Wells bending over in her garden. The circular garden was embraced by the arc of a vine-covered pergola, laden with purple-green grapes. Sarah stood and waved, busy gathering flowers. She snipped off a rose for his lapel.

"*Gather ye rosebuds,*" she chortled, coming over to greet him. "My friend Emily Groom is coming out to paint these." She lifted a basket of pale blue delphinium, lavender phlox, and *Alchemilla mollis*. "Isn't it wonderful to think I can pick my own flowers and go on enjoying them forever?"

"They're lovely," he exclaimed, "just like you." It seemed to Haven that Mrs. Wells was growing littler every year, more compact, but she also appeared even more cheerful, more her own person, if that were possible, for Sarah Wells was one of the most pleasant people he knew. Isabelle, in contrast, seemed taller and thinner every time he saw her, urgent and dissatisfied and driven. Haven had tried to point out to Isabelle that most changes were gradual, and that if their work could make a small dent, then perhaps in their lifetimes, they might begin to see a new curve forming, not a radical shift, but a movement toward change. Isabelle was not convinced.

"The creation of a single law can make a huge difference for millions of people, overnight," she reminded him. She saw the condition of humanity in sweeping strokes, while Haven worked slowly with particular people.

Lolly was waiting for the doctor upstairs. Isabelle didn't want her mother intruding, and she had to keep the inquisitive Angeline at bay. Angeline still believed that she could cure most common ailments with some herbal tea, mustard plaster, or odd scrapings of root. Her scattered brain held a jumble of old wives' remedies that bordered on useful witchcraft, and though every family member had benefited countless times from her uncanny knowledge, Isabelle could not involve Angeline now, for the old woman spoke about everybody's business without ever censoring herself.

Lolly sat up on the bed when the doctor appeared, and Isabelle thought it best if she left the two of them together. Lolly had spent the entire morning in a dull, depressed mood, for she feared no real doctor would help her. She would be stuck, and she did not know what she was going to do.

"I hear you're in a pretty bad fix," the doctor said frankly, trying to put her at ease. His warm brown eyes were sympathetic and his manner very gentle.

Isabelle had already told her that Dr. Rose was prepared to help, but Lolly's lament came forth on its own – "I don't know where I'd live or who'd take care of the baby. I have to work, and what would I do? They'd probably send me back to Chicago. I want to go to school – I'd like to be a nurse." This sudden admission made her feel ridiculous, shy, embarrassed by her own wild dreams, but Dr. Rose didn't seem to think it too far fetched.

He assured her that everything would be all right, though he needed to examine her, briefly – not internally, for that wouldn't be necessary. He could estimate the month of gestation by feeling her expanding uterus through her thin cotton dress. No need to be alarmed. He did not look at her as his hands probed the insignificant swell of her abdomen – even his touch was gentle, reassuring. "You're probably in your third month, not too far along."

Then Haven asked her about the paternity. Her face turned white. She realized at that moment that the father of the baby was related to Dr. Rose, and that this child would be a blood relation, not that her offspring would have ever received any of the benefits associated with the Hewitt family name. She was afraid that if he knew, he might change his mind. "I don't know who the father is. It could have been one of several people. You know how rough that speakeasy gets."

Haven looked sorrowful recalling the evening he'd come into that establishment, and Lolly registered the present tense of his tragedy, and felt badly for having brought it up. "I'm real sorry about your boy," she said. "I always thought he was the nicest little boy I ever met. How is Mrs. Rose managing?"

"Not well, I'm afraid. It's been an awful time." Looking into her eyes he added, "I have to warn you, feelings of loss will accompany this, if it works. You don't know this child, but your body does, and your soul will grieve."

He was thinking of Constance, how the other evening she had come into dinner as if she had great news. She told him with such enthusiasm that she had had one hour that day, one whole hour when she had not thought about it, a single, blessed hour of peace, and how grateful she was, so grateful.

He looked into Lolly's eyes, searching for the affirmation he needed.

She was sure, yes, absolutely sure. There was no other possible way out for her.

When he saw that her mind was made up, he spoke – "These pillules," he rattled the small brown paper package, "are often successful in inducing labor. It might take a day before anything happens, but then again, it might start tonight, and you'll have to be prepared for a great deal of cramping and bleeding. You should drink at least a gallon of raspberry leaf tea. I brought you a bag of that as well, and then of course you should rest until the bleeding subsides. Do you have someone to take care of you? Can you stay here?"

"I think so." She looked eager to take the medicine as soon as possible, and when he handed it to her, she tore the envelope open and swallowed all the little sugar-coated pillules down.

He got up then, and she was surprised that their meeting was over. She followed him to the door, wanting to say thank you, for she felt he had given her back her life. He knew he had done very little. Walking out, they were startled by Angeline's presence – coming up the stairs with a sloshing bucket of ammonia.

Isabelle's spine did not touch the back of her ladderback chair as she sat before the black manual Underwood, tapping out confidential information, the names and addresses of the women who had used the Milwaukee Family Planning Clinic, an offshoot of Margaret Sanger's center in New York.

Some of the young women who came to the clinic appeared only to want advice. They were usually too shy to ask for a fitting on the first visit. Normally, after a woman began to feel secure and comfortable, she would admit that she did need contraception, and then her personal story would come out. For Isabelle it was an education, one she never could have received at Bryn Mawr College. There was always a sense of desperation about these women, as if they feared not only insemination, but pain, disease, and death.

One teenaged girl tried to convince Isabelle that she was engaged, even though she didn't wear a ring. But Isabelle assured her that as far as she was concerned, she didn't have to be married in order to protect her own body. The girl seemed immensely relieved, more terrified of a condemning look than of an unwanted pregnancy.

Another young woman broke into tears when she discovered she didn't have enough money to pay for a diaphragm. Isabelle assured her that no one would be denied birth control because of her financial status. "We have funds to cover such cases," she explained, not mentioning that most of those funds came from a trust set up by her grandfather William Felton. He had always believed that a woman's accessories were essential to her sense of self, and

Isabelle justified her use of the money by considering the diaphragm the most intimate of personal accoutrements.

One Monday morning before opening hours, Isabelle had come into the office early, leaving the shades drawn. It was a modest office, with only one extra room for examinations, an armchair up front, and her desk. She felt she had to accomplish this particular task in privacy, locking up the files before opening to the public. She was on edge because the day before she had received a message – "*Satan Plans. God Bestows.*" This had rattled Isabelle, who had sensitive nerves to begin with, but it also made her more determined, for she had every legal right to be where she was, providing advice and some basic contraception. There was no law that said she was breaking the law.

Margaret Sanger had written her recently, saying that Isabelle must be on guard, for there was a great deal of opposition. "*We must protect the women we are helping, otherwise we undermine our efforts from our very foundation.*" The clandestine atmosphere added to Isabelle's anxiety. Just as she was rolling a fresh sheet of paper into the machine, she heard a collection of footsteps, men's boots, outside the door. She stopped typing and listened. A spasm of fear shot through her. The men were being careful not to speak too loudly, but she could sense their gathering presence and felt trapped. Her breathing began to tighten. Suddenly there was a harsh banging on the door that shook the panes of glass. "Open up," they yelled, "or we'll shut you down!" She scraped back her chair, clutched at the recently typed stack of papers, and desperately looked for a place to hide them. Quickly, she tucked them up beneath her dress and held them between her knees. She stood back against the wall, as the doors were forced open and three men pushed in, shoulder to shoulder, as if they were animals released from a pen. Isabelle could do nothing but stand there as they swept toward the back, grabbing whatever they wanted – tossing a box of thin rubber gloves in the air.

"Who are you," Isabelle demanded. "What do you want?" It was odd seeing decently dressed men acting like vandals. One of them stopped and tried to open the cabinet, then toppled it over, kicked it, while another grabbed the ink pot and threw it against the wall. The largest of the men swept diaphragms and prophylactics into a brown paper bag, as if he had every right to them. Isabelle stood there with her knees clutched together and her arms crossed over her chest, but as the men started out, she said, "You can't do this."

The largest of the men stepped back inside, and walked up close to her. She could smell the coffee on his breakfast breath, and it made her turn her head. "You're nothing but a traitor to your race," he spat on the floor.

"What race," she responded, baffled, though she assumed he meant the white, male-dominated, Caucasian race.

"The female race," he snarled.

CHAPTER TWENTY-NINE

*L*ionel Hewitt kept his promise, and gave his daughter-in-law, Dana, the sum they had agreed upon, one million dollars in cash. The tannery remained in his name, both in title and management, and that gave him some satisfaction. Everyone had always said that the secret to Hewitt's success was that he had never let an outside force control the family business. Admittedly, he was getting older, and now with Colin gone, and Mitzi's husband strangely absent – that man had always been an incompetent anyway – Lionel undertook the painful project of finding a new director, someone with conservative good sense and innovative ideas. The man had to be brilliant and yet accommodating, a combination that rarely went hand-in-hand. So far, he had only found one suitable candidate, Herman Knobloch, and the man was a German Jew.

Walter Schraeger was not sure that such a selection was a very good idea, but Hewitt assured him, "He's a most decent fellow, very cultured, very bright. I think it's good to surprise folks once in a while."

Walter was all for surprises, but he thought Lionel might be in for a surprise himself when it came time to deal with the public. People were not so advanced in their thinking, Walter thought, but Lionel wouldn't accept that.

"This has nothing to do with the public. Business should be above such pettiness. We've got to lead the way." He slapped the younger man on the back, as Walter lit a fresh cigar and took the first, most satisfying puffs. "Even Dana thinks the man is superior, and you know how particular she is." The two men were standing on the Lake Club pier, waiting for some chap who had just run off in search of gunpowder, for they would be judging the E boat race that day, and they always fired a small cannon to begin the race.

"I suppose we can't count on things continuing the way they have," Walter admitted. "Boys today are pursuing any number of careers. Look at the Raifstangers – their lot's living all over the place. It's going to be more and more difficult for children to stick around Milwaukee and run the show."

"That batch of Raifstangers didn't have the brains to begin with. Just as well they're moving to Tucson and Naples and God knows where. But Colin," Lionel said, "now he had the brains and the will *and* the stomach. You only get that combination handed down."

"I always thought Wally would take over the factory, but I wonder about that now. He might very well choose some other course."

"Why give him the choice? Our business was always a family business as long as I had a damn family to run it." Lionel was not in much of a mood that day. It would do him good to get out on the water and watch the race. He walked up and down the planks of the wide gray pier, muttering something Walter couldn't quite make out – "Rotten, filthy corpses. Fifty years and all I've got."

Tired of the Hewitt family tantrums, Dana took her money and bought a large white Victorian on the west end of the lake. At first Dana tried to indulge her adopted daughter, but Siobhan preferred simple boys' clothing and uncomplicated food. Her one passion in life was animals. Every time they passed Ulrich Farms, Siobhan begged her mother to stop so that they could pat the calves. Dana felt a little awkward, walking up to the pens in her high-heeled shoes, but Siobhan showed her mother how to let the little black-and-white heifer suck a finger. The child did it so naturally, Dana had to try. "Goodness, it feels so strange," she laughed.

"But he likes you, see." Siobhan insisted. "He thinks you taste good."

Dana withdrew her finger and watched as Siobhan kissed the flat broad forehead. Each calf was as dear as the next, and sometimes the farmer let Siobhan pour a little extra milk into their empty pails. It seemed sad to take the babies away from their mothers. Siobhan wanted a calf of her own, but Dana convinced her she might prefer a dog. When they found the twin spaniels Siobhan was convinced. She named them Happy and Lucky.

Witnessing her daughter's delight, Dana overcame her squeamishness and decided they would build a petting zoo. They collected an odd assortment of ducks and sheep, chickens, and rabbits, even a miniature goat. The smallest baby black lamb had hooves no bigger than quarters. Dana let Siobhan bring the lamb into the house, where the girl fed him from an old beer bottle with a nipple pulled over the rim. Siobhan was filled with so much vitality it overflowed onto Dana as well.

Because it bothered Siobhan, Dana gave up cigarettes, and subsequently found she didn't need to drink. Only now did she realize that she had been living in a kind of blur. Sobriety was like the lifting of a veil, and now everything looked clear, in focus.

When Alicia first visited Dana's new house, she was surprised by a pet turkey sitting on the dining room table and an angora rabbit hopping about the foyer. "Dear Lord," she exclaimed. "Nature's encroaching. Now I see why you call this place Yelping Hill."

But Joey found the freedom of the house irresistible, and became fast friends with the domineering girl. He was always eager to see what new animals she had, and together they named them – Sofa the kitten, Pal the goat, and Creator the huge Chester pig.

"I just had to come see for myself," Alicia told Dana. "Everybody says you're getting younger every day instead of older like the rest of us. Do you think that's fair? You do look wonderful," Alicia had to admit, "but widowhood shouldn't become one." Dana no longer appeared so drawn and thin. Her face had filled out and her complexion had gone from a sallow color to a sun-warmed brightness. Alicia feared her own powers of attraction were waning. She had to freshen her bouquet every chance she got.

Dana, on the other hand, had not been worrying about men during this phase of her life. She was enjoying her independence, and perhaps that's why she soon discovered she had a suitor, Herman Knobloch.

"Knobloch?" Alicia repeated, as if getting a whiff of the name in translation. But when Alicia finally met Mr. Knobloch, she had to admit she found him very attractive. He was both elegant and swarthy. He seemed to embody certain male as well as female qualities, and he vaguely reminded Alicia of their Liebenau friend. She assumed that was part of the attraction, though in Joshua's case, the opposing elements were decidedly unbalanced.

Dana believed Herman to be the most remarkable, confident, modest man. He was both intelligent and kind, and wonderful with Siobhan. He had a marvelous understated sense of humor, never cutting or cold like Colin's had been. Colin had always used a human target, and his jokes were like well-thrown knives, consistently at someone else's expense, undercutting the bargain of laughter. With Herman, the most trivial divertissements seemed to amuse them. Within months he and Dana were engaged.

Herman Knobloch had moved from Cincinnati to take over the management of the Hewitt Tannery. That in itself seemed an odd coincidence, but their alliance could only make it easier for him, both socially and in business, though there was already some question as to whether he would be welcome as a member of the Lake Club, even with Hewitt and Schraeger backing him up.

He insisted that Dana keep her membership. Siobhan might want to learn to sail someday. But Dana had never been a water person, and she didn't want her daughter to sail. She had an irrational fear of drowning. Though she appreciated their lovely lake view, there was something about the expanse of water that made her shudder. Dana felt that the surface of the lake was only there to fool them, that it was really a treacherous, dark hole – concealed by reflected sunlight.

Together, the three of them took long walks around the property, discovering all sorts of things along the way – a dangling oriole's nest, a funny puffed woodcock, pussy willows, cattails, loosestrife, until they ended up in the chicken yard, and there was the most unusual sight – a pair of wild mallards had invaded this bit of domesticity, and they were creating quite a ruckus. Siobhan put her fingers through the chicken wire fence and screamed at the small male mallard who was chasing their blue Cayuga around. The male Cayuga in return took off after the little brown mallard, who jumped into the pond after a buff Orpington. Such a screeching and honking, feathers were flying, but Herman made light of the whole thing. "Duck dynamics," he laughed at their concern, hoisting Siobhan up onto his shoulders "Don't worry, they'll figure it out."

"Mr. Knobloch," Siobhan asked, "do you like sloppy-joes?"

"Indeed, I do, the sloppier the better."

"Can we go to the Kiltie tonight?"

"*May* we," Dana corrected, glancing at Herman.

"Yes we can, and yes we may, and yes she *shall*," he answered. The girl was heavier than she looked, and by the time they got back to the main house, he was afraid he had pulled a muscle.

Dana was not madly in love with Herman, but quietly stunned by the layers of their compatibility. It was hard for them to be apart for long. She loved him in a new and different way, one that was not dizzying, but deeply secure. She could count on him. She could trust his opinion. He was as steady and comforting as the shoreline wave lap, and she believed this consistency of rhythm and emotion suited her middle years.

Two years passed, and the three of them settled into family life as if they had always belonged to one another. It was now early autumn, and together after dinner, they sat in the living room before the warming fire and listened to a recording of *La Traviata*, which was playing on the gramophone. Herman loved all things Italian, and he hummed along with the libretto – *universo intero . . . misterioso . . . crocee delizia . . . delizia al cor.*

Soon the family would move back in town, abandoning the large lake house with its wide verandahs and porch swings. Dana liked the red brick mansion that Herman had selected on a fashionable stretch of Lake Drive in Milwaukee, but Yelping Hill was her true home. She always tried to extend the season for as long as possible, saying that she liked the change of temperature, the lifting of the humidity that had blanketed every move all summer and slowed her blood to a crawl. Now there were few deer flies and no mosquitoes, and the crisp air quickened her. She liked the way they all had to pull together in the evenings, snuggling up, so comfortable and cozy.

With Herman sitting by the fireplace reading the *Wall Street Journal* and smoking a cherry-scented pipe tobacco, the softened lamp light made the large space more intimate. Dana stroked the hair of her daughter, who had nestled under a pink mohair blanket and placed her head in Dana's lap. "Just one more story, *please* Mama? Pretty please with sugar on top?"

Dana was tempted to give in, just to draw out their lovely, peaceful evening, but she did think it best to hold the images of a single story in mind, not to dilute that with another one. "We already had a good, long story. Just close your eyes and think about the prince, how he felt when he had to climb that glass mountain."

Siobhan intuitively understood how a strength of will and wit could overcome most obstacles, even seemingly impossible ones. She had a lively mind, and had taught herself to read, to spell and count. She seemed to remember everything. Dana worried that the child tried too hard. It was as if she couldn't allow herself any weakness, and so presented this strong personality to the world. She tended to be rather bossy, and liked to have her own way. But she also had a great imagination, and could easily amuse herself.

"Fairies don't really die," she informed her mother. "They never die from being sick. When they're old and the queen thinks they shouldn't be living, she takes them to her palace to stay, and while they're up there, they sleep. When they come back down, they're very small."

Herman put down his paper and looking over his glasses asked, "What's this?"

"I've got six fairy friends, and they all have names – Silver Lily, Love Purple, Sky Wing, Singing Dawn, Dew Rainbow, and Rose Bud Love. Papa could read me another story, upstairs," she added, climbing onto her father's lap and giving him one of her fierce hugs – *a bushel and a peck, and a hug around the neck.* "Fairies teach me lessons," she told her father in all seriousness. "Be kind to all. Forgiving each other. Believe in fairies, always. And don't hit."

"Very good," Herman responded. "Would you like me to carry you up?"

"I think the fairies want to go to sleep now," Dana agreed. "They must be very tired, from watching over *you* all day." Dana leaned forward for a kiss goodnight, assuring Siobhan that she would come tuck her in before retiring.

Dana sat back, gazing at the subdued dance of the fire. She had thought nothing of borrowing one of Alicia's old fairy-tale books, though it had been a special one. Dana knew that Joey had outgrown such stories, while Siobhan had a mind for fantasy, and still loved to listen to her read. Herman's pipe smoke lingered in the room. She found that it soothed her at this time of night. Unlike Alicia, she was content within the confines of domesticity. She no longer found it limiting, but expansive. No bravado, no histrionics of mood – it was more like floating on a buoyant sea. She knew that the tides would bring a different wash of surprises, and she was prepared to receive both the good and the bad, though so far it seemed as if too much happiness had filled their lives, so it didn't surprise her to find something horrible in the back of Alicia's book.

She had just been paging through, almost absentmindedly, looking at the fine ink sketches of little underworld people crawling about on stumpy trees amidst spider webs and crow claws. The illustrated pages were each covered with a soft filament paper protecting the image from the ink of the text. Paging onward, Dana flipped to the very back of the book. There was a piece of ordinary black paper pasted down over the inside cover, just common child's cutting paper, nothing fancy. It was pasted down at all four corners, and for a moment she thought perhaps she shouldn't remove it. Perhaps it was covering something she was not meant to see, and yet this thought drove Dana onward. She sensed something ugly might be revealed, but she was not prepared to witness what she saw when she peeled back the paper and saw the simple pencil drawing. It was obviously done by a child. It pictured a cano-pied bed with a little girl inside it, her head propped up on several pillows. The drawing was primitive, not well sketched, but there was clearly a man be-side the bed. She dropped the book to her lap. The picture showed the man's penis sticking out, erect as a stick, the girl's hand reaching to touch it.

Dana felt thrilled with a sensation of horror she had never experienced be-fore. She was confused, and thought her own daughter might have drawn this and covered it up. Maybe something like this was happening right now, while she was sitting in her dream world downstairs. She ran up the risers only to find Herman walking down the corridor. He lifted a finger for her to be quiet. Siobhan had fallen asleep as he carried her up, and he had left her robe on for fear of disturbing her. He had rested for a moment on the edge of her bed, holding her helpless little hand. When she slept all the vitality that pumped through her small, extreme being, drained entirely away. It was like holding the hand of a baby.

Dana began to cry, ashamed of her suspicions. But she could not help pic-turing the perfect, untainted parts of the child, the lithesome figure dancing so openly, unashamed, with her smooth and swollen little rump, the fruit-like pubis. She could even imagine how that perfect flesh might tempt a man, though she could conceive of nothing more heinous.

As Dana and Alicia were walking down the drive toward the flower garden, Dana confessed that she had borrowed a book, but Alicia didn't mind. "The one thing I like about you, my dear, is that you always return the things you steal. Mr. Liebenau's been begging for another show, incidentally. Do you think I should keep him dangling?"

"His paintings have gotten rather ugly."

"I don't think his intentions were ever to *please* anyone," Alicia countered. "What book is this?"

Dana drew the book from her basket, and Alicia stopped and turned it over in her hands. "Oh, yes," she said. "What's the matter? Why shouldn't you borrow it. Did one of the pictures frighten Siobhan?"

"One of the pictures frightened *me*," Dana answered, turning to the back.

Alicia saw the black paper and her mouth dropped open, as if she too now sensed something dangerous, but could not quite remember what. She felt a tension springing through her limbs as she lifted the paper and saw her long-forgotten pencil drawing. Then she sank to the ground, and Dana sat down beside her on the dusty drive, putting her arm around Alicia's shoulder. "Did this happen to you?"

She could feel Alicia pull back as if she meant to throw Dana off, but then Alicia seemed to choke, gripping the striped material that covered her knees. Leaning forward, her tears mixed with laughter, spasms. Dana had never seen her so undone, as if a flood of memories had been released, as if she were still eight years old. She cried as if to cleanse her system, and it was draining through her mouth and eyes and nose, trying to wash her clean again. She wiped her face with her dusty fingers and looked at Dana as if she were a million miles away. "How could I have forgotten? How could I not know? I *have* been remembering some of it." She sounded like a little girl. "But I thought he only – you see, I thought there was something special there, much more than, just my heart – but *no*," she cried. "I remember now – I thought it was alive, like an animal. *Pat the puppy*, he said – his little dog. As if it had nothing to do with him, as if it were a bulb, and the flower was coming up – he said I was making it grow, all it needed was a magic kiss and then this cream. I'm going to be sick."

Alicia leaned over and vomited on the driveway. She put her hand in the puddle and stirred it around, mixing it like some disgusting brew. All of a sudden her life was nothing but a cesspool, a place for vomit and defecation. It all came flooding back, like pieces of furniture in a moving stream. She had to duck her memories as if they would collide with her, wincing as if she would be struck.

She wiped her nose on her sleeve, a stunned child. "He strangled my kitten, Bijou. He said she was a talker, that she had to be quiet – then he squeezed her neck, right there in front of me. Her eyes bulged out, and she clawed the air – then he dropped her in the basket with the trash." Alicia's body appeared to go limp. "Is it possible? He called *me* Bijou after that. Oh Dana, he's been trying to haunt me, I swear. He's going to make me go crazy."

Alicia made Dana promise total secrecy, but when Dana asked her why the book hadn't burned, Alicia drew back, coldly. "Is that all you care about? Why the book didn't *burn?* Everybody always says that, now you. Well, if you have to know," she now sounded haughty, familiar, herself, "I kept it in my playhouse, that's why! And my fans were on exhibit, and my jewels were in the safe, and *this* and *that*. I *should* have burned that house down. I should have done it myself!"

That fall the stock market fell. Several businessmen on the lake were ruined. Max Farwell, in particular, was on the brink of disaster, and even though the Faithornes offered him a room in their home and assured him of their unconditional friendship, he had pulled too many investors down along with him, and that involvement, beyond his own personal loss, was such an additional blow that he could no longer sustain the anguish. He waited until the *Cannonball* was thirty feet from the crossing, and then drove his Cadillac cabriolet out into the path of the engine.

⤜ PART FIVE ⤛

CHAPTER THIRTY

*T*here were rumors that Leonard Faithorne was taking unsold merchandise from the store and stuffing the material into the hollow walls of
Springwood Lee to insulate against the cold. "Nonsense," Leonard responded. "We use the *New York Times* for that."

It was true that Felton's was not doing well, and that several of the branch
stores had been shut down. Wood was no longer burned in the great triple
fireplace in the center of the store, which gave a somewhat depressing impression, and yet it made Christmas Eve even more joyful when Leonard gave
the order to light the fire. It boosted the morale of the shivering shoppers, and
rekindled the salesladies' pride.

Gazing at the antique elegance of the fireplace, surrounded by the green
tiled hearth, one could easily imagine oneself transported back to the ban-
quet hall of some English baron. The four-foot fire tongs and shovel stood
smartly in a niche beside the high brass holder for the massive logs. Dry
maple had been the preferred fuel in William Felton's day, but now they
burned whatever they could find. Iron pug dogs grimaced on either side of
the central fireplace, and two Ming vases stood on the mantel. In a special
recess there was a three-sided French clock, placed so that the time could be
seen from almost any part of the store. William Felton's favorite portrait of
himself hung above the middle fireplace – he was a bearded, distinguished-
looking gentleman.

Leonard knew that Felton's strength as a store had always been its ability
to provide the right ambiance of elegance along with top-quality merchandise. The salesladies were trained to help make the customers feel at home. It
was store policy to keep these employees on for as long as they were cheerful
and competent. Quite a few of the older clerks knew their regular customers
by name. They might even sense what Miss Harnischfaeger was looking for as
the perfect gift for Miss Van Aleyea's bridal shower, or know what kind of
soap Mrs. Puelicher would prefer. These often stout, helpful women felt that
they were a part of a large, happy family, and they were all fond of Leonard

Faithorne. He was their idea of an aristocrat, and indeed, as far as America could produce such a thing, he had all the qualities of the breed.

Leonard didn't mind setting an example by going without, since these were hard times, but even his slightly worn shoes, polished up, had a certain fineness about them. One of the things he promoted at the store was the idea of lasting quality. At their weekly store meetings he emphasized this. "It's very important that our customers realize, and not in a heavy-handed way, mind you, but for the thought to dawn upon his or her mind, that if one purchases a piece of clothing that is made exceptionally well, as ours are made, using the very finest materials available, it is bound to wear longer and look even better as it softens up. I know my own wife prefers her well-worn clothes – she claims she feels more comfortable in them."

"But if their clothes last forever," one younger woman questioned her employer, "we might never see our customers again."

"If a lady is pleased, she'll return. For as you must know, Miss Heffinger, women are still strongly influenced by fashion, and styles do continue to change. We not only furnish the classic wardrobe, but also the best of the current mode. Of course, at Christmastime, people are going to be as generous as their pocketbooks allow, but it isn't an easy time for any of us, so I'll count on you to be particularly understanding. The small, thoughtful present of today may become the grand gift of tomorrow. I'm optimistic. Things will get better. We simply don't ever want to get pushy or loud, jingle-jangle, like some of our competitors. Don't forget that our store is on the *east* side of the river."

On Christmas Eve, as closing hour approached, the atmosphere of the store was charged with energy and excitement, like the spirited weather before a storm. Everyone was wishing each other a merry Christmas. When the women closed their registers and fastened their woolen overcoats, slipping their stubby-heeled shoes into rubber boots with fur-lined tops, pulling on gloves and scarves, they were more than ready to meet the cold coming off Lake Michigan as it swept down Wisconsin Avenue.

The Salvation Army singers were right outside the main doors, ringing for any nickels or dimes that could be spared. A flurry of thick, white flakes caught on the dark-colored coats – it all lent a feeling of urgency. Everyone was in a rush to buy that last present, or to purchase a roast or splurge on a special toy before catching the electric trolley for home.

As Felton's emptied out that evening, Leonard was there to wish his employees goodnight, shaking hands with each one of them and handing out Christmas checks. It was already dark outside, and the street lamps were glowing. The supervisor bolted the doors and went with Faithorne down to the loading dock, where a truck had pulled up to receive its annual Christmas donation. Even Helen didn't know that her husband donated clothing and toys for the needy. The Good Will distributors made sure that these presents got to the right families, and it gave him even greater satisfaction to make the donation anonymously, to know that certain children all across the city would not be disappointed.

Leonard's own three children understood that they couldn't expect much that Christmas. Their mother kept speaking of "our family Christmas," so little Carol had begun to think that they were only getting relatives. She had not even submitted a list to Santa, though Alden and Carl Merrick had both written out theirs, with personal notes assuring Saint Nicholas that *they* at least were still true believers. They thought for sure he would hear their requests, and select at least one item to save the day.

This year Aunt Clickey was joining them, along with Aunt Isabelle and Little Gram. Angeline was also coming out to the country to help cook the Christmas goose, and Winnie would make cranberry cake with a delicious hard sauce. She had already prepared a great variety of Christmas cookies, which could be seen in all their glory through two towering glass jars. Each child had a favorite – the one with the apricot center, the pfeffernus, the one half dipped in chocolate, another rolled in powdered sugar and almond crumbs. As Alden ate a coconut log he mused out loud, "Isn't it funny how you think about swimming and going barefoot in the middle of the winter, and in the summer you dream about snow?" He sat looking out at the white stretch of lawn that descended to the frozen lake, while his mind wandered on thinking about tall leafy branches, making mottled light sway over the feathery grass, the warmth of the shallows in August.

That night before dinner, Aunt Clickey suggested that she and Sarah challenge the boys to a game of canasta. Alden and Merrick weren't fond of the game, but there was no polite way to decline. As Leonard tried to string a wire for stockings over the fireplace, Aunt Clickey dealt the cards. Little Gram was becoming somewhat hard of hearing, which made playing with her even more difficult. When Aunt Clickey's stomach began to grumble, Little Gram stopped the game and insisted that she'd heard a cat. The boys had to suppress their laughter, but then came more gurgling and violent growling. Little Gram put her cards down and said, "I'm sure I heard an animal. Shouldn't someone go outside and check?" With this the boys burst out laughing, and their grandmother wondered what was wrong with them.

After dinner, before the fire Aunt Clickey passed around a bowl of marzipan, little miniature fruits and vegetables. The children were more interested in examining them, but Aunt Clickey could not get enough of that sweet almond candy – she insisted it was the taste of Christmas.

Carol hopped up onto Aunt Clickey's lap and let her silly Auntie feed her a marzipan banana. The little curly-haired girl was wearing a felt holly ring on her head, with red felt berries and two-colored leaves. She nestled down next to her aunt and lifted the long strand of pearls, liking the feel of them as they fell through her fingers.

"You know, these are my lucky pearls," she told the child. "I wear them whenever I can, especially when it's a holiday, but particularly if I'm going to be traveling."

"Why are they lucky?" Carol wanted to know.

"These pearls saved my life," Aunt Clickey exclaimed.

"They save her life every year," Sarah told them all. "Haven't you heard that old story?"

"Go ahead and tell it," Isabelle asserted.

"Well, I had booked a passage on the *Lusitania*. You see, I'd just been visiting Sarah in Milwaukee, and she came to New York to see me off. But the day before departure I broke this clasp, and I decided I wanted to have my pearls restrung. There was a jeweler right around the corner from our hotel and he did very fine work."

"Very fine," Sarah confirmed.

"He promised he would have them ready, but when I arrived at his shop to pick them up, I had to wait for an hour."

"He hadn't even *begun*."

"Aunt Clickey can tell it," Isabelle warned.

"So finally, I paid, and made a dash for a taxi, which took me to the harbor, but the boat was just pulling out. I had missed the final call by five minutes. These pearls saved my life."

"How?" Carol looked confused.

"Why, the *Lusitania* was torpedoed! By those terrible Germans."

Leonard gave her a stern look. Most of his neighbors and employees were German, and he didn't like generalized statements of that sort.

But Caroline Felton was like a southern belle when it came to harboring bad memories. She didn't consider Miss Goetsch, or Angeline or the Ulrichs to be German. They were Americans, and that was something different.

Carol nestled down next to her aunt and said simply, "I'm glad the pearls were late, otherwise we wouldn't know you."

Caroline gave a snort of pleasure. "More importantly, I wouldn't know *you!*"

Helen tried to convince the children that the sooner they went to bed, the sooner morning would arrive. That didn't make sense to Carl Merrick with his astute calculations, but he was not about to argue and risk receiving a hunk of coal and a switch in his stocking.

The children made their round of kisses, one for every cheek, and then up they went. It was chilly in the bedrooms, and the boys had to sleep in their flannel robes, imagining that they would be well-prepared as soon as light dawned the next morning.

Carol was the first awake. After she had roused everyone, the children had to wait at the top of the steps – such a terrible lesson in patience – while their parents lit the candles on the tree and got the gramophone to play "Joy to the World." Then the whole family joined in the singing and the children marched, youngest first, down the steps. They squealed and ran when they saw the plump, odd-shaped stockings filled with striped and wavy candy, a tinfoil-wrapped potato (symbolizing food for the coming year), a box of pencils with their names engraved on each one. Merrick got a drawing compass and Alden secretly wanted it. He had to keep himself from offering an exchange, for he had received a glass ball on a stand, and you could shake the snow and see Saint Nicholas trudging through the blizzard, but you couldn't really do much with it.

Carol pulled an enameled barrette and a tiny rubber baby doll from her stocking, and there was a real cotton diaper with little pins. She also got a pale-blue-backed mirror – flowers engraved around the beveled glass.

Glancing at it, Merrick said, "You better not break it, or you'll have bad luck."

"She better not look at herself then," Alden added, and his mother gave him a look that said – Be nice on Christmas.

At the very bottom of the stocking, each child found a silver dollar. "I'll never spend mine," Carol assured her father, giving him a hug. Merrick was busy working his new wooden yo-yo, which gave Alden a chance to try out the compass. Each child was receiving a single wrapped present that year, and though they usually waited until after breakfast, that morning they were all too eager.

"The largest box for the littlest girl." Leonard set Carol's present down before her. She was so slow at unwrapping it that the boys loomed over her, threatening to help, but Helen told them to sit down, their turns would come. Then Carol very carefully opened the lid of her box and discovered an entire tea set. "It's just what I wanted, and I didn't even tell him!" There were four little cups with saucers, each hand painted with a bird. The teapot itself had a tree branch with a nest. Carol rushed to the kitchen to get a pot of water and promptly started pouring everyone a clear cup of tea.

But now it was Merrick's turn, and he received the most fascinating tool –

it was a prong you could plug in the wall and burn wood or leather and make pictures. A few pieces of balsa wood were provided, and Merrick immediately set up shop, before Alden even had a chance to open his present.

Alden felt a little heavy-hearted, for he was sure he would not get anything that he liked as much as Merrick's wood burning set. He dreaded the sound of the light muffled thudding when he shook his rather modest box, but his parents looked particularly interested, so perhaps it was something. He could not imagine what. But when he opened the box his face fell. It was a pair of wool-lined slippers. He was stunned, and a stream of memories washed over him. One time he had received an Indian drum, and he had loved that drum, but Merrick had put both sticks through the top of it, and once he had gotten a great big velvety horse – you could sit on it and rock, and it went forward – and he remembered the time when Carol was given a hand-carved box from Little Gram, and she had handed it back saying, "You can keep it," and how Merrick had once started crying when he realized he didn't have any more presents, and how badly Aunt Isabelle had felt for him – she was about to go into her wallet when Helen scolded him, "Aren't you ashamed."

Alden was ashamed right now, for he knew they had this lovely house, with everybody healthy, and they had enough food and clothes and all, and when he thought of the starving people out in the cold – he was getting too old for toys anyway, and the slippers were very handsome. He leaned over and kissed his mother saying, "Thank you. I needed these."

"Did you need this?" His father asked, wheeling out a bright blue Schwinn. Alden could not believe his eyes. He staggered toward the bicycle, a thick two-wheeler, then took hold of the rubber handlebars and eased himself onto the saddle. He wanted to ride it around the room, but his mother said he would have to wait, and ride it on the porch after breakfast.

"I'm going to keep it in my room," he insisted. It was the most beautiful thing in the world, he was sure. He remembered his happiness receiving that whole set of Oz books, and last year's erector set, but they were nothing compared to this.

Their mother always insisted that she liked a hand-made present best. Carol had pressed her hand into a slab of clay and painted it bright blue. Merrick had created a garden picture using rice and seeds and beans, and Alden had made a hollow string ball in art class by stretching starched string around a small balloon, popping the balloon after the string had dried. "How ingenious!" Helen held up the sparkly ball. "We can hang mistletoe inside it."

Over Christmas breakfast the family was very jolly indeed. Winnie passed around whipped cream for the hot chocolate. The children had gone to collect it with their father at Ulrich Farms just the day before. They always enjoyed that adventure, for the air inside the big barn had the warm, sweet aroma of slightly fermenting silage. Carol was mesmerized by the steady spurt of the milk hitting the stainless can. She became very quiet in the presence of the farmers – they seemed connected to the animals somehow, as if they all were in some working dream and their movements continued in a steady percussion, punctuated by the occasional *moo*. The farm had turned cooperative, and it was very clean. Even the tails of the cows were held up by small ropes to keep them out of their dung.

Alden and Merrick ran off to see the bulls – Big Roland almost filled his giant stall, and his bars were ten inches around. He crashed against the bars and the boys both screamed, pressing back against the white-washed plaster. They ran to catch up to their father in the cheese-making building, though the smell of the place disgusted them. "Why does it make me want to vomit?" Merrick asked.

Leonard tried to steer Merrick's perceptions toward scientific fact, away from bodily functions. He described how it took three thousand pounds of milk to make a single two-hundred-pound cartwheel. "And it takes a full eight weeks to ripen."

"You mean it gets juicier?" Alden asked.

"No, it gets stinkier," Merrick put in.

One of the workers tried to explain how a culture of bacteria was pressed into the curd, and how it worked on the cheese in the curing room, causing bubbles to rise until the wheel expanded like a rubber tire about to burst. But the worker didn't think it was stinky. He thought the baby Swiss had a nice hazelnut aroma. They took a small wheel home for Christmas week. Leonard loved to have grilled cheese sandwiches with homemade ketchup and sugar pickles. It was one family luncheon where they all agreed it was all right to use your fingers, and to express great gluttonous satisfaction over the strings that stretched from mouth to hands.

It seemed to Leonard that the running of a household was almost entirely based upon the purchasing or harvesting of food, its preparation, serving, consumption, and clean up. He could not blame his wife for wanting to avoid it. "If we didn't need to eat, we'd have so much free time," he often told Winnie, and she would laugh and poke him – "Too *much* time. Time to get into trouble!"

Even though there was less meat to eat during the depression days, Winnie made small miracles happen in the form of cheese and eggs. She put up jars and jars of stewed tomatoes and string beans, and they had a good supply of winter vegetables in the cellar, but Christmas dinner was something special – at no other time would they have such a bird.

After sledding down the hill for an hour, the children's faces were rosy and their appetites whetted. They had all dressed up in their holiday best, and as they waited for the food to be served, Leonard asked the children questions. "Carol," he began, "what is ten times ten times ten times nine?"

She hesitated for a moment, and Carl Merrick piped up, "Don't ask her, ask me. I'm the smart one."

Just at that moment the covered tray was set down on the table hiding the Christmas goose, and Leonard stood to carve. Winnie lifted the lid, and there it sat, in all its glory, completely raw, uncooked.

Sarah's mouth dropped open. Caroline Felton folded her napkin, as if she had seen this coming. Isabelle turned to her sister and said, "We can always eat the *légumes*," for there was a steaming pile of peas and a casserole of sweet potatoes with broiled marshmallows on top.

"We eat vegetables every day!" Merrick protested.

"Angeline put this in the oven at a quarter past ten. I saw her myself," Winnie insisted. The goose was stuffed with apples and sausage, all sewn up. Leonard assured the cook that Angeline probably *had* put it in the oven, she just forgot to turn it on.

Helen decided that they should all bundle up and go out caroling. She was not going to let this get them down. Everybody was allowed to eat a popover to tide them over. Alden grabbed two – he was suddenly starving.

"Ring up Kirchner and we can pile in the sleigh." Leonard thought that was the only way to travel on Christmas.

"I can't pile into anything at my age," Aunt Clickey protested. "I'll just sit here and wind my yarn."

"I'll help you," Sarah offered, for she didn't want to go outside either, and she liked feeling indispensable. But the rest of them agreed it was the thing to do – they should sing for the Vintrys, certainly, and then on to the Hawks-hurst caretaker's cottage, and finally, the Ulrichs.

It was wonderful singing outside in the cold, feeling your own warm breath rising out of your body, whitening into notes. When they finally pulled up at the Ulrichs', Alicia and Joey came to the library window and peered out while the family sang "Silent Night, Holy Night." Alden thought their house looked particularly warm and inviting. He thought he could smell gravy and corn bread stuffing. He could see the tree glowing in the corner of the room, strung with strands of yellow and orange lights, almost matching the flames of the fire. Alden waved to his friend, and then Joey disappeared from his mother's side. When the big front door opened, Helen saw Walter Schraeger walking across the hall with a glass of something in his hand. Imagine, on Christmas Day. Alicia finally came to the door and asked them to come in, but Helen gave her husband a warning look, and he insisted that they had to return to their feast before their goose was cooked – *ho ho*.

Piling out at home, the boys pelted snowballs to rid the eaves of icicles – they were dangerously long, six feet at least. But then Winnie called out that dinner was on the table. It was the most excellent meal the boys could remember. The goose was crisp and moist and tender, and no one had to eat the Brussels sprouts. It was late by the time they were done, and they all sat around the fire telling stories, while each child had a piece of candy to suck on, and they felt wonderfully sleepy and content, watching the embers crumble.

Before going to sleep that night, Helen sat on the edge of Alden's bed, pulling the camel-hair blanket up to his chin, and stroking the side of his face.

"I wish every child in the world had everything I have. I get to do so many things, toboggan and music and now my bike. I wish no one had to starve."

"My dear, dear boy," Helen said to him, grateful that her children were all kind hearted.

He lay awake for some time, thinking about the story Aunt Clickey had told them about the angels who sang on the very first Christmas and how the star of Bethlehem had lit up the sky. Alden listened, but he only heard the oak boughs creaking, rubbing like failed matches against the roof of the house.

Only a few summer families spent Christmas week out in the country, getting in some winter sports and having a quiet family time before the New Year's onslaught of parties and cotillions began.

Just before the train was about to pull out from the Nogowogotoc station, Walter Schraeger's limousine rolled across the tracks to keep the train from departing. His chauffeur sat there until Walter had boarded, though the whistle had already sounded. Walter bounded on board looking extremely pleased with himself. He claimed to love the Christmas season more than anything. His family observed all the German traditions, with a big feast and present opening on Christmas Eve. Leonard was sitting in "his chair" by the north window. He always carried a ritzy pigskin briefcase with him on the train, and it was his policy never to open it *en route*. In his boisterous mood, Walter could not help kidding him, "Whether you open it when you get to the office is what interests me."

The three other gentlemen in the club car chuckled, but Leonard only smiled. He was not about to lower himself and say anything concerning the present state of Schraeger Sausage. Milwaukeans did not have the same passion for bratwurst when they were not allowed to simmer it in beer all day.

But it was beneath Leonard Faithorne to make fun of another man's business or to comment upon his personal life.

CHAPTER THIRTY-ONE

*B*ecause of her children, Helen Faithorne was disturbed that the local brewmeisters had gone to Washington to put pressure on the president in an effort to end prohibition. "You'd think they'd have more conscience," she said to her husband. "Alcohol ruins so many people's lives." She didn't think it ethical to make a beverage that paralyzed a young person's mind, made him unsafe to drive, unable to support his own family.

Leonard had mixed feelings. He certainly enjoyed a good bottle of wine as much as anyone – he even considered it a necessary luxury – and it seemed a shame to have to go abroad in order to enjoy that privilege openly, but he could sympathize with Helen's position, because he knew that the average man didn't so much take pleasure in fine drink as cheap drink took possession of him. Ultimately, Leonard tended to see it as a political issue that related to personal rights. "I think it's a question, at least in part, as to whether we can put into law our own personal concerns for another's welfare. Can you regulate that? It depends on whether freedom is more important than the general health, but even the common man must make his own decisions, his own mistakes, if you will. And, frankly, prohibition never stopped alcohol consumption anyway. It certainly hasn't helped the local crime rate. Maybe education is the proper route."

"In this town? Alcohol is like a religion around here – people practically bow down to the breweries. At least Isabelle and I agree. I wish you saw it in the same light."

Leonard consented, even encouraged Helen to voice her opinion on the night of April sixth, though her small band in favor of temperance was hardly prepared for the power of celebration they were to meet on the streets of Milwaukee. Raifstanger Beer had thirty-five boxcars and two hundred trucks loaded for shipment, while Kreuser was planning to focus on the local market, knowing that Milwaukee's beer-drinking population turned the nation's notion of number one. Alicia's board of directors had announced that they would be giving away free beer that night, as much as anyone could drink,

and there were thousands of people milling outside the brewery an hour before the midnight signal. Alicia handled the mob scene brilliantly, telling the
crowd that there would now be jobs for all the people, as if she had the Midas
touch, turning common water into liquid gold. "The poor man must have his
beer!"

Alicia had not heard a word from Walter in the past few weeks, and she
thought it rude, if not strangely hostile, to keep a distance from her at such a
time. He hadn't even called to congratulate her for the brewers' success with
Roosevelt. She had gone out and bought herself a yellow Packard Country
Club coupe, and she'd hired a new man to handle it. That night she asked the
driver to take her down to the Schraeger factory where Walter had his office.
The new driver had to maneuver the long creamy-yellow car slowly through
the downtown streets with Alicia warning him every foot of the way. She was
repulsed by the crowds that pushed up against the windows, peering in with
their sanguine and grotesque faces, pressing their dirty hands against the
glass. She lifted a gloved hand in a shooing gesture, as if to wave them off.

Alicia planned on surprising Walter with a fourteen-carat golden keg
filled with beer, but when they pulled into the courtyard to Schraeger's, she
was alarmed to see kegs of Raifstanger beer on each long wooden table. There
were grills set up to cook bratwursts and the coals were already smoking.
Alicia pressed the button that lowered the glass panel between the front seat
and back and told the driver, "Park the car over there, close to that wall. I've
never seen so many people." She was anxious to reach Walter before the cel-
ebrations began. Surely he would have some excuse. Pushing her way through
the crowd, she recognized the doorman guarding the entry. She held up the
keg and insisted on entering, though he shook his finger, warning her that no
one was allowed to come in. Once he'd cracked the door to speak, she pushed
past him saying, "I have a gift for Mr. Schraeger. He's expecting me. Make
sure those ruffians don't dent my automobile." Before the man could say what
he was supposed to say, she had brushed by, and was ascending the back spiral
staircase that led directly to Walter's office.

Through the slit window in the stone stairwell, she could see the clock
tower – it was just minutes before midnight. She began to run up the cement
stairs, but it was difficult with the keg in her arms, and then the hour began to
gong and tugboats started honking in the Milwaukee harbor. Sirens were
wailing all across the city and a cheer went up from the waiting crowd. Every
factory in town was blowing its whistle. Working-class men and women alike
would cavort and drink free beer until morning, while society watched from
the windows above.

Alicia ascended the last curve of steps, prepared to forgive him, to kiss and make up, for it was a night made for excess and she longed to be back in his arms. The city was high on the festive feeling, all but one small band of protesters, who marched outside the Raifstanger brewery. They had chosen this location because it was across from the *Milwaukee Sentinel*, and they hoped to get some coverage. But their presence practically went unnoticed, and the deafening crowd only dealt them repeated insults – "Go home little missy. We're not going to drink mother's milk anymore." One man grabbed Lindsay's poster and broke it over his knee. "So much for your damn teetotalling."

The keg had become heavy in Alicia's arms. Walter had not thought to latch the back door to his office, and so when Alicia burst in on him – just as he was embracing Albertine Raifstanger – she was probably only twenty-five years old – he looked not only shocked, but defenseless.

Alicia assessed Albertine's outfit, expensive but tasteless, and thin blonde hair almost before it sank in that Walter had been kissing another woman. The girl was actually Joseph Ulrich's second cousin, and she was fine-boned, peevish looking. Breathless, Alicia set the dead weight of the golden beer keg down on his desk. "This thing weighs as much as a baby." Her eye glanced over the platter of meats, summer sausage, veal roll, Konigswurst, set out with slices of pumpernickel rye.

Walter didn't know what to say, so he resorted to formality, and began, "Alicia Bosquet Ulrich, this is . . ."

But she held up her hand. "I don't need an introduction. I'm sure you were just trading old family recipes handed down for generations. Or maybe you were playing our favorite – *Hide-the-Salami* – is that it?" She glared at the girl. "How wise of you to choose an older man, *so* experienced. I'm sure he can teach you everything you'll ever want to know, at least about pig snout, belly fat, and fat back. *Very* interesting." She paused, turning on the spigot and the beer began to spray all over the green inlaid leather of Walter's desk, running onto some important documents, which he leapt to rescue, but as he lurched toward the papers, she slapped him across the face, and the sudsy beer continued to spill, onto the round discs of meat, over the edge of the desk and onto the carpet, making a little yellow pool at their feet.

Glancing at the girl, Alicia said, "Good luck," before turning to march back down the stairs, without bothering to close the door. He did not call after, or try to stop her. He didn't attempt to explain. So, it was over, absolute. She couldn't even divorce the bastard.

On her way out of the building, she slammed the door so hard the panes of glass burst and splashed upon the cobblestones of the courtyard outside. The doorman shook his head, but he didn't bother to run after her – she was already engulfed by the surrounding mob. As she made her way through, some-one grabbed her elbow, and she tried to pull loose, but then saw who it was, Joshua Liebenau. "What on earth are you doing here? Looking for subject matter?"

"You're all lit up. I don't think I've ever seen you looking so beautiful."

She refused to respond to this comment, though the compliment was not entirely lost on her. "Have you had a free beer and bockwurst?" she asked him. "You should give up painting and go into business. You could make a killing."

"Are you offering me a partnership?"

"Ha," she scoffed, "a partnership is a sinking ship. Believe me, that man – " she jerked her head toward the building, "knows how to cheat just about everyone."

She looked around with scorn at the men who were glugging cups of free lager, swaying in unison as they sang an old German drinking song – "*Hoch so sie leben, hoch so sie leben, dreimal hoch.*"

Alicia pulled away from Joshua, who put his hand over his heart as if she had broken it, playfully mournful. When she turned to get into the car, she glanced back and he blew her a kiss. Climbing into the back she slammed herself against the seat, digging her nails into the velvet upholstery. "Let's go," she growled with such intensity that the driver didn't dare glance into the rearview mirror. "I gave that man my life!" She had to open her mouth to catch her breath. "I never got anything. Nothing!" She had waited and waited, been passionate, patient, year after year, devouring crumbs – she re-membered their little excursions, how important they'd been, three days a season, a pittance! If only Wally Schraeger knew that his big smart father was a lousy cheat. Walter had compartmentalized his life so well that he could walk into one room and play the part of lover, walk into another and be the good generous husband and doting father, and then, further on, he was also a ruthless businessman. How could she have ever trusted him? Or believed in him and their love.

Pony barrels of beer were being rolled down the sidewalk. Revelers linked arms and caroused down the center of Wisconsin Avenue. Alicia was tempted to tell the driver to take her straight to the Schraeger mansion. She would tell little Lucy everything. But she could not tolerate the possible re-sponse – Lucy saying, "I know. I've been through this before with him."

Lucy had been his real sustenance. She was the constant, warm slice of bread he relished every morning, without even thinking about it. And now he had simply selected a new brand of *confiture*, apricot instead of plum. Lucy was probably sitting at home right now, comfortable, content, knitting up a bunting for the new baby who would be baptized with water from the River Jordan. What a laugh. Brought all the way from the Holy Land. Alicia didn't envy their deceitful lives. At least she knew in her heart and soul that she was killer honest.

She looked out the window of her car at the violent carousers, disgusting, wanton, drenching themselves with beer, smashing kegs open with sledge hammers, prying off lids. One man lifted a large, buxom woman and splashed her into the rich, dense brew. Another peered in at Alicia and bellowed like a field animal, while a man with a torn white shirt pressed an inebriated *fraulein* up against an alley wall – the girl was shrieking from fear or hilarity, Alicia didn't know. She drew back into the darkness of her own compartment, pressing herself against the corner of the seat. "Drive right through them if you have to," she told the driver. "I want to go straight home."

CHAPTER THIRTY-TWO

*B*y 1934 there were over twenty-four million cars in America. The horse-drawn vehicle was only an occasional sight. A poor farm boy might ride into town and dream of owning a Model A, which would cost him four hundred dollars, while hay was sold for twenty dollars a ton. The wealthy families of the lake still enjoyed a parade of fine horseflesh when it came to sport or show, but the horse had become a mere status symbol, not a useful or profitable tool.

Despite all this, Eddie Faithorne had been born with a passion for horses. He would point to his mother's sixteen-hand hunter, shouting – "Up, up!" until someone lifted him onto the saddle.

Eddie, now four years old, had been a difficult birth for Helen, and she would not be able to have any more children. But she dreamed of the day when she could take her youngest out for a ride across the fields the way old Mr. Ulrich had taken her.

Just that morning, Miss Goetsch, or "Goetschie," as the children called her, had dressed little Edward up in a clean white tunic – she liked to see him looking picture perfect, with his brown bobbed head and rosy cheeks. But he was all boy, with muscular calves and a strong little body. His favorite place was the farm, where he could watch Tully grooming the horses.

The stocky black groom unnerved the German governess, but Eddie thought Tully was tops. He loved to listen as Tully kept up his steady, easy-going monologue with anyone who was willing to listen. "You can't go riding in no costume like that – you look like an angel, that for sure – you look like an angel come down from heaven, but not like no master of the hunt. Give me that hand, that pretty little hand of yours." He let the boy step on the cup of his palm and then hoisted him onto the bare back of the bay. "Grab on to the mane, now. He ain't got no nerves in the neck you can speak of – you could pull and pull, and he wouldn't mind. Yank out some strands – I'll make you a bracelet. First you got to braid it, then we singe it with a cigarette – that works just like glue. Oracle, here, he don't like to hear *nuthin'* about the glue factory, do you boy. But don't you worry, big fella – you're a long ways away from *that* end of the road." Facing the rear of the horse, Tully would stand by the shoulder, and shove the horse with his weight while lifting a foreleg to pick up a hoof. He would take his time and pick all four feet while Miss Goetsch fretted about Eddie sitting up so high without either saddle or bridle.

"How come your hands are pink?" Eddie wanted to know. Goetschie tried to shush him – the boy had to learn not to ask such personal questions – but Tully hushed Goetsch in return.

"S'okay if the boy wants to know things. He's curious, that's all – a sign of intelligence. Don't ever want to shut a question-asker up. When God was makin' me," he said to the boy, "He must have taken my l'il baby hands in His and dipped me into some mighty fine chocolate – that's what *I* think. He set me down here with my own precious mama, and when she unwrapped me, my hands were pink! Right where He was holdin' onto me."

"So God was a pink man?"

Tully hooted over this. "God was no pinkie – He was a Jew!"

Miss Goetsch was thoroughly astonished. The child needn't hear talk of such things.

Eddie didn't ask more, apparently satisfied and ready to get down, so Tully took him by the hand and, in an effort not to dirty the little man's outfit, lifted him up by one arm. Goetschie flew to the child's assistance, for surely his arm would come out of the socket.

Tully suggested they go help with the milking, but the farm hand only needed someone to hold the calf while he milked the pet Guernsey. The man handed Eddie the rope and said – "Don't you let go, now." Halfway through the milking, a peahen let out a screech and the calf took off across the barn-yard. Eddie took the jolt and went flying – the calf dragged him for yards through the oozing manure, and Miss Goetsch lost a shoe in the squishy mess trying to rescue her charge.

Carl Merrick and Alden saw the entire show from the roof of the hay barn where they liked to sit, one leg on either side of the rough green tile. From that height they felt like the lords of the farm, for they had a full view of the pastures, animals, and out-buildings. Merrick pointed out a steer that had aimlessly mounted another steer. "They're making a baby," he announced to his older brother, and Alden, who knew nothing of such things, was momentarily shocked. Quickly he regained his composure and said, "*Everybody* knows *that*."

At supper Leonard liked to talk about current affairs with the boys. He was now taking them into the store two days a week so they could help out in the basement doing menial jobs, carrying boxes, sweeping up. He felt that it would build character, and if one of them wanted to run Felton's some day, they should know what it was like from the ground floor up. "Never ask a workman to do anything you wouldn't do yourself," was one bit of advice that he liked to repeat.

The boys wore common work clothes to town, and ate paper-bag lunches, but sometimes, if there was not much to do, or if their father had a business meeting after work, they were allowed to take the trolley down to the lakefront where they could feed the mallards.

Merrick announced to the table that he had saved a nickel the other day.

"That's good," Helen commended him. "Did you put it in your bank?"

"No, we spent it at the popcorn stand."

"How did you save it then?" Carol asked.

Merrick went on to tell how he and Alden had gotten on the trolley car, but how they hadn't dropped their nickels down the slot. "The driver didn't even notice."

As soon as Merrick had spoken there was silence in the room. Only then did he realize they had done something wrong.

Their father looked long and hard at each one of them before he spoke. "You'd sell your honor for a nickel?" Alden hung his head. "Tomorrow, I want each of you to put *two* nickels in that box, and you can explain yourself to the conductor. Do you understand?"

"Yes, sir," they answered.

"You can both be excused now, without dessert."

Together they headed upstairs to the attic where they were working on some projects for their parents' anniversary. The gray carpet was thin on the way to the third floor, and the narrow ascent smelled of hat box tissue. "Why'd you have to go and stick your big foot in it?" Alden growled at his brother. "Are you an idiot?"

Merrick didn't answer, but quickly turned his attention to the guillotine replica he was creating. The blade neatly chopped acorns in half, and he thought it might be good for freshening flowers. The blade was razor sharp, and it fell with a *clunk*. Carol had donated several dolls but had cried when she realized they couldn't be mended. Girls always got in the way.

Alden was practicing the Gettysburg Address so that he could recite it for his parents' anniversary. Their mother always insisted she didn't want a store-bought gift, and Alden knew his father would appreciate the effort. Mr. Hawkshurst next door was coaching him. He turned his back to the copy, pinned to the wall, and said – *"Four score and seven years ago our fathers brought forth on this continent, a new nation, conceived in Liberty, and dedicated to the proposition that all men are created equal."*

"That's all rubbish," Merrick said, not looking up.

Alden stopped, and crossed his arms. So his brother really was an ignoramus. "It's what our whole society is built on, dummy."

"You're a stupid," Merrick answered. "You think they're going to like *that* as a present?"

"I'm sure they'll like it more than that thing." Alden pointed at the guillotine. "Don't cut your finger off, Four Eyes."

Merrick looked up at his brother and glared through his glasses, while Alden leaned down, taunting him – "Four eyes, four eyes, can't tell the truth from lies. Stupid little tattletale idiot."

Merrick picked up the hammer in front of him and said, "Shut up," but Alden continued to taunt him.

"Baby bonnet, baby boy, stupid little baby buggy."

Hauling the hammer behind his head, Merrick flung it with all his might. It flew through the air, just missing Alden's head. The beaver-sharp teeth sank deep into the plaster. Neither of them said a word.

Downstairs, Leonard and Helen finished their dessert alone. The walls of the room were painted with a scene of pheasant and fern. A portrait of Sarah Felton Wells hung above the sideboard on the end wall, and Leonard always looked with a comparative eye from mother to daughter, assuring himself that the most beautiful of the two was his. He liked a demitasse of strong coffee after dinner, though Helen considered caffeine a drug and called it disparagingly "a stimulant," but she did not openly reprimand her husband for his preferences. She simply set an example by abstaining.

"Did you hear that Walter Schraeger bought the old Cistercian Monastery?" she asked. "He's giving it to some order of nuns, so that they can take care of the elderly. Isn't that wonderful? I've never thought of him as being so generous."

"I can just see it," Leonard responded, "skiffs filled with black-and-white habits all over the lake. It'll probably scare the perch away."

"They're going to turn it into a nursing home. If they ask, I think we should make a donation."

"Why don't they do their soliciting in town." He didn't feel the lake should open itself up to business of any sort, no matter how charitable.

But Helen looked at her husband in disbelief – how could he be so cold-hearted? "Walter asked that his gift remain anonymous."

"Well, word seems to have gotten out somehow." Leonard suspected Walter of showmanship. "I'm sure it's a very nice present for Lucy, something to take her mind off her pregnancies. Some day they might have to set a limit." He finished his coffee, wiped his mouth, folded his napkin, and stood up. He could not share what was actually bothering him – how New York competition was trying to enter the market and undersell everything just to squeeze him out.

Helen looked at her husband as if he were a stranger, thinking of Lucy's excitement, how she had confessed to Helen just the other day – how wonderful Walter was, how she thanked God every day for giving him to her as a husband. "He might have his faults, but any other man would seem small next to Walter." Then remembering herself, she had added, "But I'm sure you feel the same way about Leonard too."

Walter was spending a great deal of time at the new Raifstanger Biergarten in Milwaukee, a throwback to the old days, when the general public came to drink beer and listen to music. "When you work as hard as we do," Walter told a group of like-minded men as light opera played from the raised pavilion, "you're entitled to enjoy life on Sundays. Americans have to learn how to relax. All a man really needs," he repeated the words of Grandfather Schraeger, "is simplicity, independence, and a wife with a sweet disposition." He winked at a buxom *fraulein* in her colorful outfit. "A good stein of beer brings me more peace and happiness than almost anything." He raised his mug to the waitress.

Everyone was enjoying more prosperity now, though the effects of the depression would linger for years, affecting the spending habits of the average gentleman. Walter Schraeger was the exception to this tendency toward frugality, for he always wanted the best of everything. Lucy was happily occupied with her new project, and so she didn't seem to notice that her husband spent the entire month of June traveling about Germany with a young, blonde companion. Before returning to Nogowogotoc, he shipped two hundred Hungarian partridge, one hundred and twenty quail, and some rare water-fowl, as well as beautiful, iridescent, ring-necked pheasant to stock the local game area.

Alicia decided she wanted to learn how to shoot, and she soon began taking particular pleasure in serving her guests his delectable, freshly hung game birds.

CHAPTER THIRTY-THREE

*W*alter tried to win Alicia back by sending her a six-strand necklace of pink pearls, but she returned the gift immediately, saying to herself, I seem to have developed an aversion to pink. Everywhere I go – pink petals, pink punch, pink strawberry ice cream. But as far as she was concerned, pink was for pale people.

Alicia decided to have a crimson cotillion to celebrate her birthday, Bastille Day. She wasn't telling how old she was. We'll fill the house with American beauties, she thought, feeling the vengeance inherent in her own vision of redness. She would wear her most magnificent gown, imported from France by Mr. Holland of Chicago. The dress had a brilliant scarlet skirt with a tight golden bodice, and Alicia's ruby and yellow-diamond necklace set looked as if it had been created to embellish the costume. The red cape, lined with a matching gold, would cover her smooth bare shoulders. When they had been lovers, Walter had often caressed her shoulders and told her how delectable they were.

Now that the breweries were back in full swing Alicia didn't have to worry about money, and she enjoyed hosting a party where she could be lavish. She ordered hundreds of electric bulbs in the shape of red roses to cast a rosy glow over the dance floor. Electricians mounted them amongst the greenery stapled to the makeshift trellis walls. Alcohol was once more free-flowing, and there was a different mood in the village of Nogowogotoc. The desire to celebrate seemed to overflow from one evening gala to the next, but everybody knew that Alicia's birthday party would be *the* event of the season.

She had gotten the Kreuser beer wagon to drive out to Topside, pulled by eight huge Percherons from France. The enormous red wagon with its gigantic blue wheels added to the spirit of festivity. Alicia still preferred champagne and had it served, to the approval of her escort, Joshua Liebenau. He was still one of the wealthier bachelors in the area, though he had reportedly been burning through his inheritance, as well as the most desirable women in Chicago. He was intent on indulging his hostess that evening, or perhaps he realized – with her grand sense of style, always the center of attention – that swirling her out onto the dance floor brought the limelight to himself as well.

"I thought you didn't like to dance," Alicia chided him.

"Men always say that until they find the right woman."

"And I'm the right woman?"

"You make dancing easy."

"And everything else difficult," she had to laugh. "Oh, look!" She stopped, taking him by the arm as hundreds of small white butterflies were released to fly about the tent. They fluttered over the heads of the party, finding their way out into the engulfing night.

Alicia and Joshua made quite an alarming pair, and though they seemed somehow audacious, most of the women had to approve, for as Biddy Hawkshurst Braeger put it, "At least he's single." That was the general sentiment.

Dana looked at the two of them with a mixture of admiration and dread. She felt as if fate were having its way, that the two of them belonged together, but at the same time she loathed the fact that she had ever gotten involved with that man. She feared that Herman, in his innocence, would speak to Joshua, who might reveal their previous intimacy, perhaps by mentioning the wine-stain birthmark on her lower back that he had found so intriguing. Perfection marred, he had said.

Dana now drank seltzer instead of champagne, and it was hard to enjoy a social evening without the aid of intoxicants. She had to work up a smile for the typical fraternity-type humor when one of the guests stood up on his chair.

> The Phantoms have always the wisdom to say
> As we journey through life, let us live by the way
> And to help give life its particular zest
> We adhere to the rule of selecting the best
> There's rare entertainment, fine food, drink, and talk
> When the Phantoms invade Nogowogotoc.

Walter Schraeger was looking a little hangdog. He came over to Dana as if seeking condolences. Together they stood and watched the dancing couple.

Dana tried to make him feel better by saying, "A man who makes a good dancing partner rarely makes a good husband."

Walter only responded with a low grunt. He mainly wanted to find out if Alicia was set in her rejection of him. He wanted Dana to convince Alicia that his brief affair hadn't meant a thing – "It was like New Year's Eve! I don't care about that girl." He made it all sound like a case of poor timing. "Who is that fellow, anyway."

Just then Mr. Schultz came up and clapped him on the back. Walter turned to the group of beer-drinking gentlemen behind him, wanting to distract himself from the sight of Alicia. "You know, my great great grandfather drank beer every day of his life," Walter told the group. "In fact, he always said he'd never tasted water."

"Never tasted water!" old Mr. Schultz repeated.

"At ninety-two, they took him to the hospital, and when the nurse brought him a glass, he asked – *Vas ist wasser?* She didn't understand him, so he drank it and he *drowned.*"

All the men laughed, "Ha, that's a good one," and drank to the memory of such a man.

Mr. Schultz told the group that he had heard some local brewers were mixing cheap corn and rice with their barley.

"You can't tell me it doesn't make a difference," Walter said. "We haven't changed one of our recipes in over a hundred years. Time and tradition are ultimately what count."

Pausing between dances, Alicia overheard this and said to Dana, "Would you remind Mr. Schraeger that this is a party. I won't have him promoting himself. You'd think he'd at least ask his wife to dance. Lucy always looks so abandoned."

Joshua took Alicia by the arm and led her to the center of the dance floor. "You're jealous, aren't you." He pulled her up close to him, so that she had to lean back, and the muscles in her neck made her look suddenly older.

"Jealous of Lucy Schraeger? Would you choose to eat oatmeal if you were offered oysters? By the way, we're having littleneck clams tonight, flown in from Boston, and then veal chops with Castillian sauce. Did you taste the caviar?"

"Such a sensual menu. What will we have for dessert?"

"Fireworks, I hope." She smiled up at him, but she felt no love for this man. She felt a mixture of attraction and repugnance, a familiar, even comfortable combination for her.

Red-costumed chimps walked out on stilts while three white poodles rode tiny red bikes around the dance floor before dinner was announced. Jon

Bloodgood Junior stole a tricycle from an excited chimp, who screamed his complaint to the tent top. "There hasn't been a party like this since your wedding," Helen Faithorne told Alicia, though in truth, Helen abhorred excessive spending and show.

Joey was running about with Siobhan, without much supervision. The children took refuge under the front hall stairs, one of the few places in the house that was actually dirty. They agreed that they disliked company because it meant clean clothes, face washed, and hair combed. So many of their parents' friends seemed to dramatize themselves. "They make so much noise," Joey said.

"They want to advance themselves," she explained. "My father says they're a bunch of soft soapers and chislers. He likes a man who doesn't put on a parade."

"I like parades," Joey contradicted, for the big red beer wagon always impressed him. "Don't you like fireworks?"

"Sure," she said. "Do you have some?"

"They're going to shoot them off from the dock. Let's go." They knew the terrain better than anyone, and skidding down the well-worn path that dropped over the bluff, they made their way through the bushes to the dirt road that led to the water's edge.

Sitting down by the old cement boathouse, Joey put his arm around Siobhan's shoulder, so she had to lean her head forward a little. It was not as comfortable as he must have imagined, but they were best friends, and she liked being close to him, running around like this in the dark. It gave her a strange feeling of freedom and security. She liked the hollow sound of water lapping inside the boathouse where the Chris Craft was stored. It was a gentle, rocking sound.

Siobhan looked over at Joey and smiled. Then he leaned forward and kissed her very gently, but he didn't smack at the end. He merely touched her lips with his and said, "That's how I kiss my mother." She wanted to laugh, but didn't say anything. She never kissed her mother on the lips, and she had never kissed a boy before, but she had always heard a crisp little smack at the end when her parents kissed, and his had felt soft and unfinished.

They just sat there in silence for a moment, looking up at the stars. Joey found relief in Siobhan's company, for he had grown up distressed by too much attention, and when he was with her, he was always at ease. Just that week she had given him a Golden Polish bantam rooster. It had the amusing habit of flying up onto his shoulder and knocking his hat off. Alicia thought the creature dangerous, that it could peck out one of his eyes, but he was fierce in his defense of the rooster, and his mother hated to deny him anything.

Perversely, Alicia placed Joshua next to Dana at dinner, while she sat down beside Herman. Twice Joshua moved his leg so that it rubbed against Dana's stocking, and she had to pull away. From another table, Walter stood up and made a toast to Alicia's unchanged beauty, and then finished his birthday wishes with a toast to F.D.R., true friend of King Gambrinus, the legendary monarch of brewing. "I'd rather drink beer than the best bottle of champagne. It's was the only true American beverage, the only drink appropriate to accompany a Schraeger sausage."

"I knew he'd work his way around to that." Alicia glittered with malevolence. "Nothing like throwing bouquets at yourself." Her ruby and yellow-diamond necklace seemed ablaze about her throat.

Alicia's mood was a mixture of excitement and anger, which translated to Joshua as pure physical lust. He was familiar with the female symptoms, and sensed that they were headed for an evening of Eros. He wanted to do new, shocking things to her, and her eyes across the table seemed to read his inclinations.

She wondered why she was attracted to him. He was not exactly handsome or even well-built, but he did have this magnetic energy.

As soon as the cake was brought out, and the band began to play "Happy Birthday," she stood to make her wish – which was to snuff out all remaining feelings for Walter – then Joshua made a big display, pulling her out into the dark before the watchful party. He hustled her off toward the boathouse, for he wanted to see the fireworks from the water. Even though she protested that she shouldn't leave her guests, she was eager to be off alone with him, to let Walter spend the rest of the night wondering where she was and what she was doing.

The two children went unnoticed as the grown-ups approached from the other side of the boathouse. Joey and Siobhan held their breath and leaned back against the building as soon as they heard voices. The couple seemed to rustle up against each other, collapsing with laughter. The man seemed to have hold of some part of his mother's dress, for Joey could hear the crushing noise of stiff silk, his mother's hilarity echoing in the boathouse. He heard the familiar whir of the crank being released, the plunge of the Chris Craft into the water.

Siobhan felt Joey's hand break into a sweat. She wiped her own hand on her dress and said, "Come on." Both of them ran up the access road that led back to the main-house garage. As they took off, Joey could hear the boat's engine turning over, as if devouring water and spitting it back out. Then it roared away, out toward the center of the lake.

By the time the children had reached Joey's room, he had put his mother out of his mind. They each lay down on a separate bed and talked about their favorite chickens, and a trip he was going to take with Wally Schraeger. "We're going to the Brule, to fish," he explained. "Why don't you like to fish?"

"I don't like to kill things." And then she wondered out loud, playing with the pump to his bedside table lamp, turning it on and off, "Does your mother always bark like a dog?"

Alicia had surprised the girl that afternoon. She and Joey had been playing jungle animals – she was a leopard, and he was an elephant – when his mother walked into the room, a large white bath towel wrapped around her, her long dark hair sopping wet. Seeing the children, she put down her glass of champagne and dropped the towel, falling to her knees. Laughing hysterically, she started barking, throwing her long, wet hair about. Siobhan was astonished by the look of her breasts. They were plump and soft. She almost wanted to touch one, but then Alicia rolled onto her back and her chest flattened out. Siobhan couldn't help staring.

Finally Alicia said, "Give me my towel," as if the children were to blame. Then she suggested that the two of them hop into her tub, it was still nice and hot. "You've got to get ready for the party. Your mother sent over your party dress. They'll be here by seven-thirty."

"I don't need a bath," Siobhan replied. She disliked the air of permissive encouragement, and she could tell that Joey was embarrassed. The two of them were always better off alone, without interference or pushing.

"What kind of dog would you like to be?" Joey asked her now.

"What kind of a dog do you think?" She imagined herself a bit like Mrs. Hawkshurst's curly-haired terrier. He was so quick and responsive.

But Joey thought for a moment and said, "How about a dachshund?" With that insult, Siobhan jumped onto his bed, intending to pin him, to wrestle him down. The two of them were squealing and struggling when the new maid walked in – she stood there in the doorway with her hands on her hips. "You little tramp! You get yourself out of here. Cheap trash orphan, go downstairs, and you," she yelled at Joey, "just you wait till your mother hears about this. Go brush your teeth!" she demanded, as if only that act would cleanse him.

Joey had never felt so small or humiliated or alone after Siobhan had fled the room. What right did that maid have to tell him what to do? His mother was not around to stand up for him, and he couldn't help thinking about her now, out in the Chris Craft with that ugly man.

Drifting in the Chris Craft alone with Joshua Liebenau, Alicia had kicked off her high-heeled shoes, dyed to match the crimson of her dress, and he had tortured her with the slowest of caresses, stroking her slender, shapely legs as the star-bursts of color opened above them. She lay back on the dark green leather of the cushions, lifting one leg slightly in the air so that his hand slid down the back of her thigh over the silk of her stocking. He was driving her wild, teasing her like that. Each stroke brought her closer and closer, until she was mad to be pinned down and taken, but he seemed to want to make her writhe. "Why don't you loosen that bodice, *Madame*. I'd like to study your form in this unnatural light."

What a strange way he had of proceeding, she thought, but she obeyed, loosening the strapless top of her dress, while he remained passive, watching. The more calm he became, the more aggravated she felt, until suddenly he took a handful of hair and yanked her toward him, pulling her into the most urgent, violent kissing – it was as if he were a crazy person. Then he stopped himself, held her against his chest, and slowly eased her down his body, stroking her cheek, coaxing her to do what he wanted her to do – it all seemed to braid together in her mind now – and she was surprised that he hadn't made love to her in the normal way, but it was more his style to take his own pleasure and give nothing in return. It was a triumph for him, a display of power, and strangely enough, his calculated withholding made her wildly passionate.

When she was done, she lay her head in his lap, covering herself with the loosened cape. He relit the cigar that he had stuck in the ashtray, the fireworks bursting like open chrysanthemums above them. He seemed to know that she wanted more, and it amused him. Just then the *feu d'artifice* began picking up for the grand finale – a series of quaking booms rocked the sky and star-bursts were blooming everywhere. The final *tour de force* was the spelling out of Alicia's initials – A.B.U. – sizzling in red, white, and blue.

He asked her if the middle letter stood for Bijou, and she gave a little start. Her hand went up to her throat and touched the cluster of gems there. In one movement she undid the clasp and tossed the necklace into the water. "What are you doing – are you drunk?" But she was pleased with herself. She didn't need her father's jewels anymore, now that she had Joshua Liebenau.

She flattered him by saying that he was the most wonderful lover. She wanted to stay with him all night, and she tried to interest him with kisses, but he turned his head. "Why don't you take off that dress – there's so much material." She gave a little laugh in response to this. If he was daring her, she was not afraid. She stripped and stood naked before him, pausing for a second on the edge of the boat before making a clean dive into the water.

Surfacing, she called out, "Come join me! It's delicious."

"I don't swim," he answered. Then, standing up on the opposite side of the boat, swaying with slight inebriation, he unzipped his trousers and relieved himself right into the water. She swam farther out, voicing her disgust. He sat down on the top of the seat and fiddled with the motor, getting it to start – pushing the lever that jerked the boat forward. She yelled, afraid that the propeller might cut her. Suddenly the water seemed ominous. She was afraid he might actually leave her out there, and swimming frantically to the boat, she managed to clamber up.

"You better dry yourself off," he said. "You'll get a chill."

"Fancy you taking care of anybody. Give me your jacket." She made this request in her usual demanding tone, and it struck him as the necessary thing to do, so he complied, without realizing all that he was handing over.

CHAPTER THIRTY-FOUR

*I*sabelle was not too keen on joining Helen's book club, for as she told her astonished sister, "I'd never be interested in that kind of thing. You'd just end up talking about your children, anyway, and I take literature seriously." Isabelle considered such a group akin to a *kaffeeklatsch*. "You should probably ask Mother. She'd enjoy it."

"We were planning on keeping it to the younger set," Helen responded. "We might not be your intellectuals, but we're not a bunch of ninnies either." Helen didn't like herself in reaction – it was as if she were tossing back some idea of Isabelle's before it stuck – and she didn't approve of her sister's attitude. Couldn't art be a regular thing, integrated into every aspect of one's life? Not just guarded in a leather folder, in some locked-up bureau drawer. She thought to say as much, but then checked herself. Family harmony was more important.

Isabelle probably only hated to be considered a burden. She did not want Helen including her out of pity or a sense of duty – at least this was how Helen explained away the incident.

"The Readers" was composed of Helen's regular lake friends – Lindsay, Teensie, Constance, Dana, Lucy, and Biddy. Helen and Constance were the only members who had finished the book in its entirety. When Dana arrived, it looked as if she had come straight from the barnyard. She admitted that they had just received a new chicken brooder, and how exciting it was. The other ladies took this monthly gathering as a chance to get dressed up. Lindsay thought they should all make an effort. "Some women only make a fuss when gentlemen are present."

Just then Teensie arrived, decked out for their scrutiny. White daisies were splashed across her dusty pink dress, and her pancake hat looked like a large, white flower. Everybody found it *too* fetching. Helen wore a pale green linen dress that was unremarkable and yet becoming. She had an understated elegance that all of them admired. That summer day, the majority of the group had to admit that they simply had not found the time to read the assigned novel. "Why does everything have to happen in August?" Teensie complained. "Life gets so hurried, it makes me feel terribly slow."

Lucy arrived a little late with a bowl of sweet peas. Their translucent lavender was just the thing to decorate the glass-topped table. "Couldn't Lindsay read aloud?" Teensie suggested, for Lindsay Allis had the most soothing voice.

"We should try to keep up with our assignment," Helen chastised the group, but she didn't really want to take on that role, for the afternoon was so mild and breezy. It was the kind of balmy summer afternoon that felt as if it had reached the still point, where the large oak leaves were at their fullest, neither growing broader nor withering back. The bare backs of the children glistened with water as they stood at the end of the pier. The younger ones were locked into the screened-in sandbox, which was shaped like a little house. Here the toddlers could play contentedly, digging, spooning, and patting the moist sand, protected from insects and the dangers of drowning while entertained by the older, more boisterous swimmers. The light on the water was beautiful, the hum in the air – Helen's eyes kept returning to the arrangement of sweet peas on the long, low table, her friends all about her, chatty and harmonious.

Lucy was doing a bit of knitting with some pink cashmere yarn. "I keep having all these girls." Lindsay had taken up her needlepoint and was explaining how she meant to stretch it over a brick to use as a doorstop, while Teensie bemoaned the fact that she could do nothing with her hands. How envious she was of Helen's place mats, for Helen was weaving a complicated pattern through the open work with her needle, using a thick, cotton, cream-colored yarn. She wanted fourteen place mats in all.

"I think we should each read a different children's book some month," Dana suggested. "Something unusual, then we could compare."

"I don't know about you," Teensie put in, "but half the time I'm reading some child to sleep, and I end up falling asleep myself."

"You know Alden just met Mr. Terhune," Helen told the group.

"Albert Paysen Terhune?" Dana asked, for his dog stories were Siobhan's favorites.

"The man's a terrible misanthrope. He thinks his dogs are far superior to human beings," Helen went on. "He told Leonard that he never meets anybody, but that he'd talk to Alden for an hour. Can you imagine going all that way? He lives in some impossible place in New Jersey. It was no small feat even finding it."

Sitting together in the musty front room (even the sink was piled high with books), author and child were discussing one of Terhune's novels, when the old man made a reference to a particular scene, and Alden had to correct him, saying – "That didn't happen in *Treve*, that was in the eighth chapter of *Bruce*." Terhune was not used to anyone contradicting him, but when he looked it up, he saw that Alden was right – there it was, exactly. He was very impressed. Normally, he never sold puppies – people weren't worthy to own 'em – but he wanted to give Alden an exceptional one-year-old, a gold-and-white, kingly dog, with a large, noble head. Terhune mixed his collies with the heftier sheep dog, creating a breed that had a more solid look.

"They had to tip the porter rather handsomely, so that Rex could sleep in their Pullman, rather than in the baggage compartment – Mr. Terhune wouldn't allow for that – but Leonard always manages those things so well. Rex *is* the most gentlemanly dog. When you open the door for him, he wipes his feet on the mat three times."

"You know, I wouldn't be surprised if Alden wrote stories himself some day," Constance put in, but Helen laughed, for Alden had recently informed his mother that he knew exactly what he wanted to be. Carl Merrick would be a scientist, Eddie a farrier, while he wanted to run a shoe shine shop.

Lindsay mentioned that Alicia had postponed her engagement a second time. Joshua Liebenau's financial status had become the subject of gossip, and most of them assumed he was pursuing Alicia for more than one reason.

"She could make him president of Kreuser Beer if she wanted to," Biddy said, but they all knew that Alicia would never bestow power on a man in a weakened position.

Helen, seeing Lucy's discomfort, pointed out that there was no sailboat race on the lake that day because the sailors were all over on Lac Le Beau. Nogowogotoc Lake appeared strangely vacant from the Faithornes' screened porch, which had one of the nicer views that stretched all the way to the Lake Club, with its big square front and colorful flags, alert to the wind, rippling above the blue-and-white awnings.

Just as Lindsay took it upon herself to pick up her book and clear her throat, taking one last sip of iced tea, they all heard the whine of an airplane doing barrel rolls up above the lake. Lucy apologized, saying it must be Walter. He was practicing for some contest in northern Wisconsin. But then the plane seemed to sputter, and the others looked worried as the seaplane skimmed the trees just above them in the most unnerving manner. Even the children on the dock ducked as if a wing might graze them. Instead of landing smoothly on the calm surface of the lake, the right pontoon struck at an angle and the plane was thrown over, smacking the water – a terrible explosion and then a burst of flame. In a state of shock, Lucy didn't turn, but kept on knitting, as the other women lurched in every direction – Dana yelled, "Get down!" There were flames spreading over the surface of the lake as the petrol leaked, and a spiral of black smoke rose from the aircraft. Big hunks of the hydroplane floated in the water and then slowly began to sink out of sight.

Lucy looked quietly down at her handwork. Constance was there on her knees beside her friend, as if pleading with her to respond. Finally Lucy looked up and said, "I smell something burning." Then she turned to gaze out at the collection of boats that had come as close in as they dared.

Alicia was discussing the dinner menu when she heard the roar and then the impact of the plane. It was as if someone had struck her in the stomach and she staggered back against the kitchen table, one hand held out. Running to the flagstone patio, she knew it was Walter. She screamed. She flew toward the boathouse, but by the time she got there she could see it was too late – there were several other boats already hovering about, waiting to be of assistance. Her body crumpled in half, as she sank to the planks.

Looking up, Alicia saw Joshua trotting down the hill. How she loathed him at that moment. He was dressed all in white, but he still wore his slippers, black velvet slippers, and he seemed intrigued, rather than concerned, interested in the ravaged expression on her face. "Don't look at me!" she yelled at him. She knew in that instant that Joshua Liebenau would never take Walter's place. The man before her had that peculiar spinelessness only tall, thin gentlemen seem to have, as if they can't adequately support themselves. She let out a groan as it all came back to her – how this man had obstructed their reconciliation. If Walter and she had still been together, he never would have been driven to perform such reckless feats. If Joshua Liebenau had not stumbled back into her life, she might have tempered her pride and accepted that necklace, forgiven him his indiscretions, for she knew that Albertine Raifstanger meant little or nothing to him. She thought of the golden keg spurting liquid on the floor, the way he had looked in another direction when he made that toast on her birthday. She felt the wind in her loosened hair, and thought of the chintz material in that funny little inn, where they had made love with most of their clothes on. She saw his hands on the bone-colored steering wheel, and felt him turning to look at her – how *he* should have been her husband. But now he was gone, and she couldn't stand to look at the man who stood before her, asking unctuously, "What can I do?"

"What can you *do?*" she repeated with a bitter laugh. "You can take off those slippers, for starters, and get out of my sight."

"Is that what you want?" he responded, as if he were not affected by her words. "Is that how you get rid of people? Don't forget, I know what you're capable of, darling."

"If you know so much you better run for your life." Then, as if wanting to beat him to it, she ran up the hill. By the time she had reached the house, all of her energy was gone. She climbed the stairs as if desperately tired, and drew herself a deep, hot tub, pouring in a large portion of orange-blossom oil. She did not know if she were capable of unbuttoning her clothes, and she sat on the edge of the marble bath for the longest time, until the water threatened to run over.

Only later did her maid report that little Wally Schraeger had been with his father in the airplane, and then for the first time, Alicia thought of Lucy, left with all those girls. Both Walter and his son had been strapped into their seats, and no one knew if they had died on impact, from the gasoline explosion, or if they had drowned, but Alicia believed that Walter went in flames, that he had been thinking of her at the moment of impact.

After the funeral, all day, and into the evening, cars crawled up to the sad house on the hill, in a stream that seemed virtually endless. Hundreds of friends and acquaintances called to pay their final respects, filling the porch with flowers – trucks kept bringing load after load. The Kreuser brewery sent a large wreath of purple orchids, but when Alicia turned up at the entrance to the house, dressed entirely in black, carrying a damp, black handkerchief, Lucy stepped forward from her line of girls – she came over to the door as if guarding the threshold. "I'm sorry," she said, "but you're not welcome here."

Alicia looked at her in disbelief. She attempted to speak, to say something in her own defense, but her eyes met a stony firmness. Lucy knew. She had always known, and she was claiming Walter now for her very own, and yet she did not seem grieved, only pale and steady. Her faith gave her this unearthly serenity, and Alicia was not prepared to deliver her usual amount of animosity. Turning to walk back to the car, Alicia only muttered, "She didn't even know the man."

CHAPTER THIRTY-FIVE

Constance Rose had eased into middle age with a little more weight than she would have liked to carry. Her full brown hair, pulled back, was neither flattering nor unbecoming, but simply her way, which was pleasant. There was a lethargic kindness emanating from her physicality. Children felt comfortable in her lap, and the old men and women at the nursing home, Our Lady of Goldenbank, looked to her if they wanted encouragement. Some of the old people had taken to calling her Rosie, "Miss Rosie." One man in particular had it in his mind that he was attached to her in some way. When she entered his room, he would reach out to her, clutch the material of her sleeve, and make some odd entreaty – "You have to let them know I'm here. No one knows where to find me."

It broke her heart, his desperation, but all she could do was try and console him. "You're here with us now, and we're looking after you. How do you like your flowers? Mrs. Valenschein brought them." The old man had been her butler for sixteen years.

"Oh my, she shouldn't worry about me. I'll be fine when I get home. I'm just so tired. May I go to sleep now?"

"It's good to sleep," she encouraged him, drawing the filmy curtain so that it cut the sharpness of the light. Lucy Schraeger wheeled by with her cart, and Constance held a finger to her mouth, tiptoeing out of the room.

"Last week," Lucy whispered, nodding toward the man, "he insisted that I was the chambermaid, and for a moment, I thought I *was* the chambermaid." Lucy always looked so cheerful and efficient. She had a considerable presence despite her small stature. Constance wondered if Lucy's inner strength came from living with Walter, and all she'd had to put up with there, or if it came from some higher source, which endowed her with this endless capacity to give. Lucy never indulged in overzealous energy. Her inner life of prayer and morning worship seemed to balance her outward motions, and perhaps the evenness of her temper was the secret to her vitality. She never seemed to tire of her work, as if she carried some heroic image in her mind, while Constance often felt weary, burdened. The weight of the summer humidity pressed down on her mood and made her feel sodden. She was often exhausted by the end of the day.

Lucy, on the other hand, was charmed by the strange lucidity of her patients, as if their aberrant talk was akin to prophecy. The more terrible her patients' statements, the more sure she was that they were drawing close to God, that it was a privilege to care for them as they prepared to leave their worn out earthly bodies. Soon, one by one, they would be released, like butterflies, finding their way out into the engulfing night. It was important to help them prepare for that journey, a transition that Constance could only dread.

Both women believed in their work at the nursing home, though Constance was more concerned with relieving her patients' physical discomforts. She hated to see anyone suffer. Constance felt that she and Lucy were on a trek together, but that Lucy always managed to get far ahead, halfway up the mountain, and it was difficult to communicate when you were trying to catch up.

As they left the old converted monastery that afternoon, heading for the launch that would take the two of them home, Lucy bent to pull a weed from the gravel walk. "People can be so cruel. And I don't mean only to each other. But to themselves." Lucy was not talking about the aged, the dying – she was thinking of Alicia Ulrich, and a tendency people had to seek out painful situations. "We all have such a great need to feel – we go to such extremes." Perhaps she had even chosen Walter in order to experience some emotional struggle that was wholly contrary to her temperament. Certainly her married life had been one of humiliation and self-sacrifice, but how he had made her feel things! Surely no one could ever take Walter's place. Her life would simply be tranquil now, like the calmness of the water at the end of the day, and for that, at least, she was grateful.

Lucy did seem a curious mixture of humbleness, denial, and resilience, which most would label feminine virtue. And yet beneath that surface, she was fiercely particular, but in such a hidden way that more outright personalities found her profoundly irritating.

"If someone really wants to hurt himself," Constance responded, "what can you do? People are human, they're going to have to stumble sometimes. You can't feel responsible for everybody all the time."

"That's where we differ," Lucy admitted, carefully stepping from the pier onto the platform of the bobbing boat. As she settled herself down, her face looked serene above the blue cloth of her blouse. She didn't give the impression of having worked hard all day, changing bedpans and hospital linen. Constance thought she looked like a queen, with a modest yet assured sense of her own regality. She knew she could govern, and govern well.

"You see, I do believe I'm my brother's keeper," Lucy went on, "that we have to be responsible, or no one will care – eventually everyone will simply be out for himself. Can you imagine such a world? Ruled only by the baser instincts, by selfishness and greed?" And then Lucy had another idea that seemed to illuminate her. "Why don't we get the girls to help us, perhaps one day a week? I'm sure they'd cheer up the patients, and it's so important for them to learn how to be giving and useful. Sometimes I think they receive too much."

Constance knew that her daughter would resist the idea of spending a summer day at the home, for she complained of the nauseating smell. The child had an abhorrence of anything sickly, and Constance wondered if that came from a general, unspoken familial attitude toward death.

Prudy Schraeger, on the other hand, would probably respond to her mother's proposal with interest. It would make her feel more grown-up. Constance wondered if she were failing as a mother, maybe as a wife as well. Perhaps it was the late afternoon light playing across the water, but she felt like revealing one of her most secret thoughts. "You know, sometimes," she began, "I imagine Haven is in love. With someone else, I mean. Someone very young and beautiful. I can see how happy they are, and it makes me feel better. Isn't that strange?"

Lucy seemed disturbed by this confession, though she only showed it in the blanching firmness of her lips.

"What I don't understand," Constance continued, "is why I *like* to picture it. I do wish he were happier. He deserves it."

"You must feel your imaginings are generous," Lucy said, "but they free you to do nothing, don't they. You don't have to give a thing."

"But I want to do nothing. That's just it. I'd like to shut myself away in some room and just sit there. Doesn't that sound heavenly?"

"I doubt if it's Heaven's idea for you. How long do you think you'd be happy doing that? I don't mean to burden you," Lucy added, but her slight, immaculate presence, her clear-as-glass complexion, everything about her suddenly *was* a burden. "Family life is far more precious than anything else. You realize that once you don't have it anymore."

That was true with almost everything, Constance thought, everything that mattered. But not much mattered to her right now. Life itself seemed to shrink from the edges. Everything seemed a little duller than it need be. Her perceptions were made through a mental transparency that dimmed the light to a subtle gray. Perhaps it was a matter of sleep. She was not getting enough of it. Constance often woke from a terrible dream – she was dragging an extra limb around, like some dead bird hung about the neck of a dog that won't give up its killing. She had let her own son die, and too often the question plagued her, what had God wanted with William? What were His intentions there? And yet here was Lucy, who obviously believed He was on her side, and He had taken both husband *and* son.

Constance knew if she expressed her fears, Lucy would only say that God's spirit could heal all ills, that our bodies were no more than expressions of His goodness. If we allowed Him to completely enter in, there was nothing He couldn't transform.

Why hadn't He saved William then? A child who was utterly blameless.

They sat together in the middle of the launch, which slowly cruised toward Hewitt's Point. The low baritone of the inboard motor rumbled behind them as the mild lake air beat gently against their faces. "I saw the most gruesome thing the other day," Lucy began. "I was walking down the path near the lawnmower, and I saw a snake – it was very large, yellow and black, and it was moving straight for the mower as if attracted to the sound – but before I could call out, the thing was picked up, sliced, and thrown across the path."

"How horrible," Constance responded.

"What's strange is I *felt* like that snake at that moment." Lucy paused, as if to calm her breathing. "Ever since Walter's accident – it's been like an amputation."

"Yes," Constance said, for she had also felt this way. She often wondered if God wanted no part of her. "Do you think a shepherd would spurn any member of his flock?" Constance looked straight ahead, the churn of the electric motor vibrating behind them. "I mean, possibly the maimed or sick ones?"

"Those are just the ones He loves best. Suffering makes us more vulnerable to Him."

"Then why not let people hurt themselves?" Constance responded, bringing them back to the beginning of their conversation. But Lucy's train of thought was moving forward, circumnavigating this unnecessary obstacle.

"He knows I am all the more His because of my loss. The hardest part is not taking personal blame. I've never told anybody else this," she went on, reaching over to take Constance's hand in hers while looking straight ahead, as if put into a mild trance by the hypnotic dance of light upon water, "but that day when Walter took little Wally up, I thought, very strangely, but clearly – Please God, leave me the girls. It made no sense, but it was as if I knew it was coming. Maybe I should have stopped them from going up that day. I could have said – Walter, no more flying. But I couldn't prevent God's will."

Constance was stunned. So Lucy believed that God had willed it? That it was all part of some plan? That alone was horrifying, that the story was already written – they were simply characters reading their lines aloud, actors playing out some predestined part. That made her feel even more helpless.

CHAPTER THIRTY-SIX

*P*eople often said that Emerson Rose had been sent to Constance as a blessing, for he resembled his brother William in many ways. They had both been fair and beautiful as babies, and Emerson was also a light-hearted child. Still, in Constance's mind William would always stand apart, as if he had a special talent or gift. Who knows what he might have accomplished.

Trumbull sensed his mother's preference, even now, as if he knew, deep down, that he would never measure up, that he was simply tolerated. The more mistakes he made, the more it seemed bad behavior was expected of him. At least Emerson was also somewhat mischievous, so Trumbull no longer had to carry all of the family darkness.

Though Emerson was several years younger, Trumbull took him along when he went over to the Faithornes' in his five-and-a-half-horsepower putt-putt. Tuesdays and Thursdays when Constance worked at the nursing home, Helen kept an eye on the boys. Helen was usually very busy, but there were plenty of people at Springwood Lee to help watch over the children. Miss Goetsch generally had her hands full with Edward, but there was also the housekeeper and Winnie, the cook, Kirchner, the head gardener, and his assistants, as well Little Gram and Isabelle next door. Lolly Jones was also in residence at Broadoaks. She had completed her nursing program and was working with Haven at the Nogowogotoc Hospital. But as far as the older boys were concerned, they didn't need supervision, and they liked to be left to their own devices.

For weeks now they had been building a tower in the horse field. Alden had designed the three-level structure, and Merrick had engineered it with fence posts, laid log-cabin style. Trumbull claimed the role of president, and Joey Ulrich tagged along giving orders to Emerson, who was considered the club mascot. They all enjoyed spying on the girls, who were planning a circus over at the farm. The boys took along their hand-carved guns and packed wads of dirt for hand grenades. Watching from the hayloft, they made fun of the girls' activities, while planning the next devastating raid. "I think we should tie up Siobhan in the tack room. Then maybe we can take Carol hostage," Trumbull said.

"We should get Eddie to join us," Merrick added, for he thought it despicable that his younger brother had joined the girls' group just because he liked to ride. Tully was teaching him how to jump.

Rex, the Terhune collie, was such a quick learner that he was being featured in the main ring of the circus. He let Merrick's pet monkey ride around on his back, and Tully howled when the monkey made a prune face, clinging to the dog's white ruff. "I never seen such a petrification!" the groom laughed, slapping his meaty thighs. This had the big boys rolling in the hay. "You better buy him some silks or something."

"She's not a boy, she's a lady," Carol corrected the groom. They were trying to get Rex to run around the paddock, hopping over a series of low hurdles.

"Looks like a little old man to me," Tully hooted. "What kinda lady's gonna ride sterk neked?" This was too much for the boys. They tumbled down the ladder from the hayloft howling. Running for the fort, they fell together and collapsed as if laughter had rubberized their limbs.

But the girls decided the monkey should be dressed up as Lady Godiva. They made her a wig out of corn silk, cut out a crown and stuck it on her head. Now it really looked like a circus act.

There was something endearing about the spider monkey, her utter ugliness and pathetic, groping hand that always wanted to be held. She clung to Carol's neck like a baby, blinking her beady eyes and chopping her jaw. Even the boys wanted the monkey to come up for a visit when the girls drove by in their pony cart. They were on their way back to the big house to find supplies, wanting to braid ribbon into the pony's tail, but hearing the voices from the fort, the scrawny little spider monkey shaded her eyes like a mariner's widow and began screeching up at the boys.

"Wait," Merrick yelled, and Carol pulled the pony to a stop. "What are you doing with my monkey?"

"Can I see?" Siobhan called out. She wanted to know what it was like up there on the highest platform. "I've got string licorice!" The boys had just finished tacking on birch board siding, above the darker pine, which gave the tower a two-tone effect. They'd nailed slats up the side for a ladder.

The boys had a quick conference and decided that Siobhan could be a guest, "But only for a minute, and Carol can't come."

Siobhan jumped from the cart, and the spider monkey screamed at the deserter. Carol felt betrayed. Tears sprang up in her eyes as she snapped the double reins, making the pony jerk forward and the monkey plop down on the seat.

Siobhan squatted on the top floor of the fort and handed the licorice over to Trumbull. He was the oldest, and she wanted to stay on his good side, but when he kept an entire string for himself and gave everybody else just a bite, she couldn't keep from saying, "That's not fair."

"Who says I have to be fair?" he answered, screwing a finger to the side of his head and looking around for approval. She choose to ignore the mockery and crossed her legs like one of the boys. Her freckled nose was red-brown from the sun and there were grass stains on her knees. Emerson stood behind her and played with her curly strawberry-blonde hair, while Alden checked their homemade sun dial and announced that it was getting close to noon. "We need you to go get provisions. Emerson can help."

Merrick took a basket from the wall – it had a string-like yoke that made it useful for hauling supplies up and down. Emerson slung it around his neck as they took turns sliding down the pole that went through the center of the fort and ended up in an underground hole. Beneath the tower there was a network of trenches that the boys had dug before building upward. These curving tunnels had been covered with boards and then sod so they could crawl out in various directions, mystifying the enemy. Siobhan took the shortest, brightest exit, while Emerson wormed out in another direction. When he finally appeared, he seemed stunned by the light.

They tromped off to find stones and pebbles for soup, flower seeds that could be sprinkled on pine shavings, handfuls of green stripped oats, tiny bird berries. This would make a good mash. But just as they were climbing back up the slats to the upper deck, the older boys decided to run and hide. Whooping and screaming, they fled down the exit pole, scrambling out the maze of trenches at the bottom, zig-zagging across the pasture. Joey hit the dirt as if he had been grazed by a bullet, then, crawling on all fours through the high grass, he was soon out of sight.

Siobhan looked grim, for the game was over, and she knew that they had been ditched. Even her best friend, Joey, had taken sides against her. It was then that she saw Alden's stopwatch on the wall. Emerson was getting hungry, and not for stone soup either. "I'm going with my brother," he announced, just as Mrs. Faithorne's motor car pulled up the drive. She tooted her horn, but Siobhan pulled Emerson down – Mrs. Faithorne was considered the enemy. Peeking back up, they saw Joey riding his bike toward the garden, and Emerson called out for him to wait up.

Before departing, Siobhan kicked over the pitcher, stored in the corner for water balloons. She ripped the Air Force calendar off the wall, tearing it into little pieces, and then littered the foodstuff all over the floor, grinding it in with her foot. Finally, she slipped the stopwatch from its bent nail hook and dropped it down the front pocket of her overalls.

Inside the big house, Helen reminded the children about the plans for the rest of the day. She had just returned from a Service Club meeting, and she was eager to get going after lunch. She had a tennis match at one. "You've all had free time this morning," she reminded them, but the way she spoke seemed to trivialize that day's adventures. "After lunch, you'll need to do your reading, but then both boys have a tennis lesson, and I want you to practice the clarinet," she said to Carl Merrick. "We'll be going to the Lake Club for buffet tonight, so you can soap up in the lake after you help Tully with the hay bales. Now," she said, surveying the various dishes, "what do we have here," as if luncheon were one more activity on the schedule. "Where's Emerson today?"

"He's sick," Trumbull answered.

"Siobhan was being mean," Carol told her mother, but Helen hardly listened to that complaint, for people were always being mean to Carol.

Winnie was passing a heaping platter of baby bantam corn. There were beets vinaigrette, a platter of sliced tomatoes from the garden, and a piping hot cheese soufflé, which the Faithorne children were used to, but Trumbull spread it about his plate with his fork.

Trumbull knew how to make trouble and skirt the repercussions, often curiously courteous to adults, a trait Helen Faithorne found unnerving in a child. She knew from her own boys that when they were too polite, they were usually brewing some plan. So when Trumbull said how delicious "the cheese stuff" was, she assumed he was trying to hide something.

Helen thought the tower project a trifle dangerous, but she had decided it was good to encourage Alden. She felt he needed to be more active. Too often he was content to stay in the house on the nicest day, slumping down in an armchair to read. Recently he had completed a model house, cutting cardboard and balsa wood for walls and furniture, meticulously coloring and gluing the parts. When Alden presented this creation to his parents, he pointed out the tinsel stream that ran over a rock garden and became a cooling river beneath the structure. You could see it through a glass pathway set into the floor, and the refrigerator was sunk into the water for cooling. He had even thought of a connected arboretum – the flower beds would have the tiniest little holes, so that you'd never have to water them. Swinging beds were all hung from the ceiling on ropes. Alden insisted you'd need half as much sleep if you had a bed that was motorized and that gently rocked you back and forth over the sound of moving water.

His father looked it over and said, "That's very nice, but where's the study? Every man needs a place where he can shut the door," and his mother reminded him that the most important feature in any house was storage space – basement, closets, attic. So when Helen asked him how the new construction was going, he sprinkled a generous helping of sugar on a juicy round slab of ripe tomato and answered with a shrug.

The boys were in competition to see who could eat the most ears of baby bantam corn, but Carol spoke for all of them when she said, "Beets make me sick."

"Just give them a taste, that's all I ask." Helen was certain they would come to appreciate certain foods, like watercress and eggplant, if they only gave them a try. It was then that they all heard the collie barking. Rex kept up a steady, loud, authoritative bark as if calling for help. Alden asked if he and Trumbull could investigate, for Rex never barked mindlessly like some dogs.

Excused from the table, they ran down the hill and found Rex blocking Emerson at the foot of the pier. The children were not allowed on the pier unless supervised, and Rex seemed to be enforcing this rule. Emerson was hungry and snotty and his face was streaked with muddy tears. "Why did you leave me?" he cried.

"What are you trying to do, get us into trouble? We can't help it if you went off with a girl."

"I didn't go," he wailed. "You made me."

Trumbull tried to clean his face with a handful of lake water, and Alden promised him a double dessert if he'd wait it out in the boathouse, but he refused, following the big boys at a distance. When they returned to the kitchen, Helen was surprised to see Emerson standing by the door. "Oh, are you ill? Carol, you can read to the little boys. Then they have to take a nap. Carl Merrick, I want you to read alone today. I'll be home by three-thirty. Don't forget," she reminded Alden, "Tully's expecting your help." Then off she went to get changed. She was ranked number one in the ladies' singles at the Lake Club, and this was the semi-finals. If she won, she would go on to the state tournament.

Walking up the wide, carpeted steps, Alden told Trumbull, "Terhune's dogs are just like his stories. All the males are wanderers. It's probably in their blood."

Trumbull didn't like to have to lie down after luncheon. He thought the two of them should sneak out, but Alden actually looked forward to reading his book and dozing a little. He was eager to get back to his novel, but felt self-conscious reading in front of his friend. He needed privacy to read, just as he liked to shut the door to the bathroom when he was brushing his teeth. He didn't want anyone to witness it.

"When we went to Chicago," Alden continued, "Rex ran off and got all the way to Wahcheetah, but the man at the pound was crazy about him. He had him all combed out by the time we picked him up. Rex doesn't think jail's so bad, do you boy." The majestic dog liked to take his nap on the landing, halfway up. Leonard had trained him to lie there. He thought the unexpected placement might surprise an intruder. There was an unused dog house littered with straw attached to the house, but somehow that dwelling seemed beneath Rex.

Alden led the way up to his screened-in porch bedroom, and Trumbull suggested that they lock both doors, so the others wouldn't invade them. As always, Alden lowered the dark green canvas awnings, which gave the room a cozy, protected feeling, especially when it was warm and dry like today. The bed, a small double, big enough for both boys, was covered with a vanilla-colored flannel blanket, comforting to the touch. They were both happily tired from all the activity, but when Alden lay down and picked up his book, offering another to Trumbull, his friend flopped down on his belly and said, "I don't feel like reading. Why don't we trade back rubs. I'll do you first, if you want."

Alden thought they might as well, for he was not used to sharing his room, and he doubted he could enjoy his book with Trumbull making small talk. Unbuttoning his shirt, he lay it neatly on the wicker armchair in the corner and then carefully lay down, his arms at his sides. Closing his eyes, he thought for a moment of William. He wondered if William would still resemble Trumbull. Trumbull's hair was now dark, yet Alden remembered William as golden.

Trumbull did not like to talk about his twin. Once Alden had said how fun it would be – and Trumbull had shut him up with a stare. Climbing onto Alden, a knee on either side, he sat lightly on his buttocks, leaning forward to press down with both hands. Alden groaned, a physical response to the pressure. He was not used to being touched, and it was hard not to be ticklish. "Relax," Trumbull said. "If you go to sleep, you can do me next time." He then sank into a mindless motion of rubbing, moving back and forth with his own body, up and down the untanned, skinny back.

The previous summer, the Hewitts' chauffeur had given Trumbull money to help him polish the family car. Mr. Hewitt liked it to be cleaned every weekend before he was driven back to Chicago. After the waxing was done, the chauffeur and the boy sat together in the front seat, and the man often gave him candy from Okauchee. After a while, he offered sips of gin. He made Trumbull feel older, important. He took his time, winning the boy's friendship and trust. No one had ever been so kind and generous to Trumbull before. He complimented Trumbull on his developing body, saying he would grow up to be big and strong, probably a movie star. He also invited the boy up into the garage apartment and offered to give him back rubs, since he was probably sore from working so hard. Nothing happened the first couple of times.

Upstairs, in the chauffeur's apartment, the dark-haired man walked around naked when it was hot – there was little ventilation. "They used to store hay up here, I guess, till they needed a place to put me." It was hot enough to warrant a cold bottle of Kreuser, one for each of them. The man was casual about his body, but Trumbull was amazed by the size of his organ. He told the boy he could make his grow longer too. "All you have to do is stretch it out." He sat back and showed him, talking about girls, even telling Trumbull what he could do to his sister. No one in the Rose family ever spoke about sex, and everyone was careful to be modest. This man said that sex was a secret adults liked to keep to themselves – but that anyone could enjoy it.

When Trumbull rolled off of Alden, he had an erection. It pressed up at the khaki material of his shorts, but Trumbull didn't seem embarrassed. Once when this had happened to Alden, he was mortified, but Trumbull acted as if it were completely natural. "Did you ever ejaculate?"

"I think so," Alden hesitated, nervous about showing his ignorance. He had woken up on several occasions and found a disturbing pool on the clean white linen, and he had rubbed it into the sheet with a sock, hoping no one would notice. He had been disturbed by the workings of his own anatomy, as if he had mistakenly wet the bed.

"You move it up and down, like this," Trumbull demonstrated. He apparently didn't mind Alden's ignorance. "I'll show you," he offered, lying down next to his friend.

Alden was not comfortable with the suggestion, but he didn't want to do it himself, either. He lay on his back and closed his eyes, as if bracing himself for initiation. The doors were locked – nothing to be afraid of – and it did feel good, almost painfully so. The room was darkened, and the canvas shades smelled warm. Parts of him felt lazy, while this sexual part felt sublimely shocked, as if it were something separate.

Trumbull sensed Alden wasn't used to this, so he talked as he touched him, and moved his hand in a casual, mechanical fashion. "Remember when we turned the sprinklers on that christening party? And all the old ladies started screaming? Mrs. Hawkshurst got it right up the dress. That was so funny."

Alden remembered the thin material clinging to her legs, and how one of the servants had slipped – they had been able to look up her uniform. It was Trumbull's idea, but they had gotten Emerson to turn on the water. Alden gave the go-ahead by removing his cap, and they had been thrilled by the chaos they'd created. He remembered the wet shape of one woman's breasts, the way she plucked at the material so it wouldn't cling, and now he let the memory of that event cloud over him – he was almost holding his breath, sensitive to the rhythmic contact. He felt absent from his body, far away, enjoying this on some other plane, as if it were not actually happening to him, but to another boy in some exquisite dream he was watching, reaching out to caress a large bosom, when suddenly there was an explosion of melting carnations – creaming from the center of his brain out his groin – opening, blooming, dissolving in an instant. He lay there, very still, back in his body, where he had to waken to his senses and witness the splattered mess.

Again, Trumbull made nothing of it. He leaned over and took a handful of tissues from the bedside container. "Your mother won't notice. They don't know anything about this." Alden was certain Trum was right on that score, for his mother would never suspect such activity, and yet now he felt guilty and awkward. He was quick to agree with Trumbull that they should keep this to themselves. "Merrick's too young to understand," Trumbull added.

Then the two boys heard muffled footsteps on the thin green carpet of the guest room next door. It was Miss Goetsch, going into the bathroom to hang fresh towels. She stopped and listened, and then asked the boys, "Are you two still reading?"

Simultaneously they answered, "Yes," suppressing bursts of laughter with their pillows. Alden's confusion was absorbed by the giddy act of covering up.

"You better put on your tennis whites. You've got the first lesson, and your mother wants you waiting down by the court."

CHAPTER THIRTY-SEVEN

*I*t was the feeling one gets in early spring – wanting to get outside and do things, a quickening in the blood, a desire to snap a wand of pussy willow buds, to whoop across the field, whipping it overhead, glad of heart and grateful to be released from the dingy confines of the classroom. Joey Ulrich was certain of one thing – that he would always love Siobhan.

Alicia had another opinion. Approaching the breakfast room, ready for her morning coffee, she was still in her peach satin bathrobe with the matching slippers. She had not slept well, and she was irritated that the morning had begun before she felt ready for it. Her slippers had white puffs of feathers on the fronts, and from the distance of the kitchen, Joey could hear the *clop clop* sound they made as she walked across the bluestone flags. Taking the breakfast tray from Mildred's hands, he backed through the swinging doors into the breakfast room with high hopes of starting the day off right. He set the tray down carefully on the oval table.

Alicia surveyed her breakfast without first looking up, as if it were perfectly normal for her son, as much as anyone, to serve her. The single poached egg looked rather overdone, and the white napkin not properly folded. She turned the rosebud in its silver satchel vase, and then, picking up a piece of dry toast, she asked her son with a touch of condescension, "So what are you going to do with your day?"

"I thought I'd row over to Hewitt's Point and go fishing," he said, but it was as if his mother could read his mind, and knew he was thinking about Siobhan.

"I hope you're making real plans for this summer. I don't want you just playing around with that girl. She's not a good influence. I can just read the headlines – *Mother raises chickens while daughter raises hell*. I don't know how Dana can let her run around so. Last summer people were saying terrible things, if you want to know the truth. They even say she steals."

Joey knew that that was ridiculous.

"She took a pacifier from Steven's Drugstore," Alicia insisted. "She hadn't any money and no intention of buying it – they call that theft where I come from. She probably can't help it, but that's no excuse. Her parents were very common people. No one knows anything about them, and I, for one, have to think of your future. You should have a summer job at the brewery by now." She blew at the top of her coffee, and glanced up at her son. "Your father was working at your age."

But the only thing Joey liked about the brewery was the smell of warm peaches from the yeast-making factory, and the twelve-foot copper kettles. *Hopfen and Malz. Gott erhalts.*

"And fishing," she added with disgust. "I don't even like the taste of lake fish."

"If no one knew anything about them, they might have been very decent people."

"Why don't you call up Emerson Rose. He's a nice boy, and it's good to have a large group of friends, then you don't have to rely on any one person. I just thought you should know what people say. It'll reflect on you."

"Since when did you care about what people say?" he answered defiantly, standing squarely in the middle of the large doorway with its dark carved wood. He looked so alive in his worn khaki pants and white Oxford cloth shirt, rolled up to the elbows. She could see he was beginning to have veins in his forearms, though he was only fourteen. "Do you know what people say about you?"

"I'm sure most people have nothing better to talk about, but I'll have you know, men used to walk smack into buildings because of me. And if people ever said anything, it was usually with envy. I had the smartest clothes, the most lavish parties, and the greatest love. Your mother was a very happy woman."

He could see she was off into her own world now where he couldn't really follow, for his memories were very different from hers. He remembered her always in a frenzy, elated, sweeping off into the night, and leaving him alone. She had been fiercely merry, frantic, all aglitter, but not "happy," as she recalled.

Funny, that she should care so much about his social life when she had completely given up her own. People continued to invite her, but she always refused, saying that she never met anyone interesting. She had even had a falling out with Dana, and that probably influenced her feelings about Siobhan.

Morvan, the old caretaker, posted Joey's love letters. Whenever an envelope arrived with that sunflower scrawl, he would tease the boy, holding it above his head, and Joey would have to leap for it.

Dear Joseph Ernest Ulrich Junior,

I got your letter last Friday and I will pester my Mom to come out to the country as soon as possible then I can ride over to see you or we can meet at our special spot. I won't say wear. Funny that someone things I'm the bad influance when you taught me how to — and — ! As Mrs. Bolton (P.U.)

likes to say – Pot call the kettle black much? She really thinks shes funny but shes not. I can't stay in my seat at boring old Downer Seminary. My teacher is so mean. She took all my trading cards yesterday and I really hate her with a purple passion! I also hate math and can't wait to get out to Nogowogotoc. I WANT TO BE FREE! We'll have tons of fun this summer. We can ride double in our bathing suits, and maybe you'll beat me at tennis for once. Ha ha. What do you do out there all winter? Freeze? See you soon balloon.

Your Pen Pal,

Siobhan

p.s. Don't do anything without me! S.W.A.K.

By the time Siobhan arrived in the country, Joey was already hard at work on a gypsy caravan, using every old wheel he could find, a great assortment in various sizes, bolting them on so that the caravan would roll. Unfortunately, it could only roll straight ahead, though he had installed a steering wheel for looks. The hard part was getting all the wheels lined up so that the base was even, but finally it looked as if it would go. They painted each hubcap a different color and Siobhan put up curtains and paintings inside. Joey found an old single mattress in the abandoned apartment above the stable, and together they dragged it down and stuck it in the back along with two chairs, which they nailed to the wall. There was also a board they could lower for a table, or swing outside to sell produce.

Alicia gave up trying to keep track of her son. She had no idea that he was involved in such a project. She just assumed that he had things to do. She had immersed herself in a strange new hobby, cutting bits and pieces from magazines and pasting them onto her bedroom walls, creating a strange mosaic. Every picture had some special meaning for her, even if she had only found it in Life or Vogue – a picture of a trellis covered with morning glories, a red leather saddle or an Indian chief. She included a strange hodgepodge of telegrams, Christmas and birthday cards, anything she received in the mail, including old bills, calendar art, postcards of some truly uplifting vistas from a world that seemed to have slipped entirely away from her.

Siobhan stayed clear of the main house, and no one bothered the two of them. That summer they were in their own private world, working and playing and picnicking. When they heard the bell tower chime twelve, Joey headed for the house while she spread out an old plaid blanket in their secret place, a nest in the tall dry grass back behind the garage. He would tromp off to the kitchen to collect their lunch, and when he asked Mildred what they were having, she would tease and say, "Hot tongue and cold shoulder." Then she would wink and hand him the basket. "Hope it's enough for you. Such an appetite!"

Siobhan and Joey had a feeding game that had become a kind of ritual. She lay back on the soft warm blanket and pretended to doze. When he returned he would gently shake her shoulder, and say something like – "Don't worry, we'll survive." She would pretend to be slightly unconscious, only the smell of food could revive her. He would wave a morsel beneath her nose, till she took a sniff or stuck out her tongue to sample the thin slice of cabbage-smelling kohlrabi, or the wet-tasting cucumber stick. She would have to guess what it was before opening her eyes. Then the two of them sat up and ate.

Just that day Joey sat down beside her without saying anything, and she heard the crinkle of tinfoil. Then she caught a whiff of chocolate and when she leaned up to taste it, he kissed her on the mouth. She opened her eyes and said, "Cheater."

"I don't have to share with you."

"Who wants any, pig."

She was already up, ready to run, but he didn't want her to go. He caught her by the ankle and convinced her to stay. "Come on. I was just kidding. We've got liverwurst sandwiches and lots of stuff." Mildred seemed to take pleasure in packing elaborate lunches for the two of them – long celery sticks with farmer's cheese wedged down the middle, sprinkled with Hungarian paprika, a carton filled with miniature tomatoes, a bunch of crunchy string beans, two garden carrots well scrubbed, retaining their feathery tops, and a double slice of Black Forest cake wrapped up in a piece of wax paper. She even included grapes – they liked to try and see how many they could stuff into their mouths at one time. The record was seventeen.

Afterward, no longer miffed, she let him lie down behind her, like two silver spoons in a set. They made up fantastic stories, alternating line by line: "There once was a brother and sister."

"Their parents had left them on a desert island and they'd just eaten the last of their provisions."

"We'll have to sleep for a very long time," he told her.

"There are vultures above us." Siobhan liked the scarier details.

"Do you think we'll ever get married?" Joey asked, breaking the story line.

"I don't know about you, but I'm going to be a steeple chaser."

"You have to marry someone or you'll never have children."

"Maybe I'll just have dogs. Let's be quiet." She was irritated that day. She felt like kicking him when he tickled the back of her neck with his breath. Suddenly she sat up and said, "I need some medicine." This was their code way of saying liquor. When she wanted medicine, he fed it to her with a teaspoon.

"I could use an entertainment. You?" This meant he wanted a puff of smoke. Crawling under the bushes that circled their secret spot, he uncovered a box that was hidden in a hole, buried under branches and leaves. He'd made the pine box in wood shop, and it had leather hinges and a stick lock. They kept all of their booty inside – partially smoked Pall Malls, lifted from the cork-lined humidor in the living room, wax lips, a candy necklace, a spoon with the name "Ash" written in cursive, a sewing needle, which they used to prick their fingers, NLC matches, a brown rubber horse, and a tiny clear bottle with a red airplane and cotton balls stuffed inside. When Siobhan had asked Joey what it was, he said that his father had crashed during the war, as if the bottle contained that moment somehow. She had also included an old smelly chestnut from her horse's leg. She had picked it off, thinking it was kind of repulsive, but that it had magical properties. There were also a couple of pictures from a magazine showing half-naked ladies. Siobhan had a hard time believing she would ever look like that.

The two of them wrote things on the inside lid of the Dare Box, names of enemies pierced by daggers dripping with blood, dirty words he had heard rough boys using at school. She wrote *Grumpy Forever*, and he wrote *S.A.K. & J.E.U.* Sometimes they dared each other to climb to the top of certain trees or out-buildings. She dreaded that he would someday dare her to swim across the mucky canals. If you were dared, you had to do it.

Siobhan dared him to get the glass ashtray from the library. It had an etching of a boy blowing bubbles from a pipe. "You can dare me back if you get it."

Unfortunately, Alicia happened to see Joey walking stiffly toward the front door, and she called him over to her. "How do I look?" she asked, and even in his terror he thought she looked amazingly well, for she wore a fresh linen suit with a silky white blouse, and high heels that matched the creamy white color. "I'm going to play bridge at the Hawkshursts'," she informed him. "They needed a fourth, so I'm going. I might even stay for dinner. You can eat with Morvan and Mildred, can't you?"

He did not answer right away. He could tell she was nervous and he felt sorry for her. She didn't even notice the hard rectangular ashtray stuffed in his pocket. "I don't know what you do with yourself. Why are you standing there like a dummy? Don't I look all right?"

"You look fine," he assured her. "Really excellent."

She planted a crimson lip mark on his cheek, but instead of going out to the waiting car, she turned and went back upstairs. Joey could hear her turn the dead bolt to her door and figured it was safe to leave.

"You took long enough," Siobhan chided him. "Let's see." She grabbed the glass ashtray, examining both sides. "It's pretty. We'll keep it in the box."

This reminded Joey that he had a dare coming – he wanted to "see" Siobhan.

Usually she was the leader and this new approach made her uncomfortable, but she didn't want to lose the dare. She lay back on the blanket and pulled the elastic waistband of her shorts down, exposing her pink flowered underpants. "More," he insisted. So she pulled those down too, and he took a long, curious look. "You're funny," he said, wanting to pinch the thing together, but quickly she pulled herself up. Leaping on top of him, she dangled her hair across his face. He had always considered that torture, but now he took a strand of her hair in his mouth and sucked on it like candy.

When the caravan was ready to roll, Siobhan sat at the steering wheel and Joey gave it a push, jumping in the back as it rolled down the drive and barreled into the bushes. They had to shove it back out, push it over one of the bridges. Then there was another straight stretch toward the road, where they set up their vegetable stand. They had two big baskets of produce, ripe beefsteak tomatoes, beets, summer squash, fresh limas in brown paper bags, ears of corn. If they made enough money, Joey said he would take her to the carnival in Okauchee. Siobhan had gone to great lengths to make signs for the road, and now while she got everything arranged, he pounded them in with a hammer – GOOD FOOD / Lowest Prices / Delicious / Ripe & Nicest / STOP TODAY! But even after they hung the bargain price signs all over the caravan, car after car sped by, setting up clouds of dust.

Siobhan held up an enormous zucchini when she saw a truck rolling their way, but the farmer only laughed and whistled.

"I guess they have gardens of their own." Joey tried to understand it. Then Miss Wells pulled up in her motor car, and both of them were optimistic.

"What a nice enterprise," she told them. "We do need green beans, and the price looks right." She was even to the point of opening her pocketbook when she realized she didn't have her change purse. She had left it on her dresser that morning. She promised that she would return the following day, but after that near success, they were despondent.

About every twenty minutes another car would roll by, and some of the drivers ignored them completely. This was especially insulting. Whenever they heard a car in the distance, they jumped up in readiness. Siobhan had decided that it was not enough to simply wave. This time she took two large tomatoes and stood beside the road, but the car just honked to keep her out of the way. In frustration, she heaved one of the tomatoes at the trunk of the car. It struck and splattered, and the black Ford screeched to a complete halt. Joey yelled, "Run!" And they took off down the driveway while the car backed up the gravel road.

They were about to duck into a side path that went to a little dock and rowboat, tied up in the canals, but the car was now pulling in after them, and the man could see where they were. He honked his horn and yelled out the window, "If you don't come out, I'll be calling your mother."

Joey decided they had better talk to the man. He was the owner of the hardware store in Nogowogotoc. Getting out of his car, in his steel-gray overalls, he looked imposing. "Don't you two know anything? You think you can throw rotten apples at a car? That dent'll cost you, and who's gonna pay for it?"

"We'll pay for it," Joey said, hanging his head. "We've got $4.53 in our cash box."

"I don't want your small change, you little whipper-snapper. I knew your father and your grandfather before him. They never acted like this, I'll tell you. Those men were gentlemen, not little ruffians who want to get away with something. Your mother ought to hear about this if she wasn't plain daffy." That was the end of their vegetable stand.

Word got back to Alicia somehow, and Joey was punished. He had to stay in his room for an entire day. It was the end of summer, and he didn't want to go back to school. No one really cared about him but Siobhan. He didn't have a real family, and he didn't want to own a big famous brewery. He thought perhaps that the man was right – maybe his mother was crazy. He wanted to get away from her.

When Mildred caught him taking cans of food from the pantry, stuffing them in a satchel he had tied to a stick, she asked, "Now where are you going?"

"To Rome," he said, for he had learned in school that all roads led to Rome. He gave her a look that said – Please don't tell. Hesitating by the screen door, he came back and gave the old cook a kiss on the cheek.

"We're having Swiss steak for dinner, sour cream and horseradish. Mashed potatoes and peas, somebody's favorite."

He didn't care. He thought he didn't care, but by the time he got to the end of the driveway and the chauffeur stopped to offer him a ride – he was just standing there with his satchel not knowing which way to go, and he had less than five dollars to his name – he decided to take the ride back up to the house, for his stomach was growling and the short, lonely walk had sobered him. Siobhan had moved back in town, and soon he would return to school. Joey's grandfather had built the little country school house that stood five miles away on the edge of their property. His mother had always insisted that the drive in town to Country Day was much too far and that public school would be the best thing for him. It would make him like all the other boys. But he knew he would never be like the other children in his class. He was in a class set apart. When he was not with Siobhan, he felt alone in every way.

CHAPTER THIRTY-EIGHT

*D*rawn to the urgency in the announcer's voice, Dana crossed the room and turned up the radio. The man was trying to make sense of some awesome disaster – "Terrible news here from Lakehurst, New Jersey . . . the Hindenburg dirigible just burst into flame . . . apparently a spark from its mooring mast . . . ignited the hydrogen . . . no one on board could possibly survive this . . . "

On the evening of May 6, 1937, picturing the massive aircraft fluttering to the ground, Dana first remarked on her symptoms – fever, headache, nausea. She believed she had the flu, but the achiness in her back and neck persisted, and the muscles of her chest became tender to the touch. She groaned when she tried to turn over in bed. Soon that became impossible.

Often she thought of that collapsing dirigible, because she felt as if she were losing air from her lungs – she could not support her own breathing. "The worst part," she confessed to Herman, "is that we had no time to get used to this. There were so many things I wanted to do with Siobhan."

"You'll do those things when you get better. We'll take a trip to Sicily, anywhere you want. Where would you like to go?" Herman's face looked thin and angular. He had begun to grow slightly bald, and it made his eyes seem deeper, filled with caring and sensitivity.

"We were just going to fix up the bunny hutch and get some angoras," Dana murmured. She closed her eyes and imagined Siobhan combing out their fur, rubbing a ball of it against her cheek.

Dr. Rose had diagnosed her condition as "bulbar poliomyelitis," explaining to Herman how the tiny virus entered through the nose or mouth and attacked the brain and spinal column. "But I'm sure this won't be permanent. I have great faith in Dana, and I know you have too. It's important, of course, to keep her well rested – heat packs can do something to relieve the pain, but she will need constant care, and it would be my advice to move her over to the hospital as soon as possible." He didn't go on to tell Herman that this was the worst kind of polio. When the chest lost its muscle action, the patient was in danger of suffocation. Most likely she would need an iron lung.

"I've heard one's mental condition can have miraculous effects, isn't that right, Doctor? Dana's always loved her lake home, and I know she'd be happiest here. Believe me, we'll take all the necessary precautions. We'll hire a nurse, three nurses if we have to, and we can wear masks or whatever you say. We've got to make the best of it, Doctor."

"Of course," Haven agreed. "I can come by and see her easily."

But as soon as word got out that polio was on the place, delivery men started dropping parcels off at the gate rather than venturing down the driveway. Even the milkman left bottles in the mailbox out by the road, and the cook had to waddle down to collect them, muttering all the way. She did not like venturing out in such heat, but Siobhan didn't mind the weather or isolation. She spent most of her time with Grumpy, her horse, creating an entire course for him through the woods with ditches and jumps and obstacles. Sometimes Joey came over and timed her, but he was not allowed inside.

Everyone in the household was supposed to wear a mask when entering Dana's room, but Herman usually just walked in, kissed his wife, and started talking. He was preoccupied with the tannery. There had been a sit-down strike, and he was not sure how to handle it. "It's not as if we haven't been making improvements. I've already given them scheduled pay raises, and we've been working on a retirement plan." Usually Herman was even-tempered, ready to negotiate, wanting to work things out for everybody, but the mid-June heat seemed to aggravate him, and he was particularly irritated with Isabella Wells. "You should have seen her, right up at the front, egging them on – her family's always been against the tannery. As if they didn't sell shoes. Why doesn't she acknowledge what we've done? Cleaning up the river, for instance. We even treat the animals more humanely now."

"Can't you sit down and find out what they want?" Dana asked.

"Frankly, I don't think they want to talk to me. I'm just another Jew, trying to gyp them."

"I'm sure that's not it," she responded, taking his hand. "You've always been so good at this before."

"It's greed, I tell you, spreading greed. That's all anybody cares about, money." He gave a deep sigh. "But now here I am burdening you with all of this. I did bring you a little present, though." He went into his briefcase and pulled out a leather-bound copy of *Gone with the Wind*.

She felt a small thrill as she touched it, for everyone was reading this book. Siobhan had promised to read it out loud, one chapter each afternoon, and

Dana had been looking forward to that. She didn't have the strength to hold a heavy book, and making conversation tired her out. She and Siobhan had had an upset earlier that week and they both were trying to smooth things out. It had set Dana back and Herman was worried.

Years before, Siobhan had been struck by something the Ulrichs' maid had yelled at her, calling her an ugly name. Siobhan had fled the bedroom and the party forgetting the hateful appellation, but recently in school they had been reading Charles Dickens, and the same word caught her attention. Something stopped her as she read about the pitiful helpings of oatmeal – was it possible she was like one of those children?

When Siobhan came into her mother's room, she lay down on the bed and tried to cuddle up, though there was hardly enough space. Finally she asked, "Am I an orphan?"

"Of course you're not," Dana answered. "I love you more than any mother possibly could."

"Yes," Siobhan answered, "but are you my *real* mother?"

Finally Dana had to say, "I see." She had never realized that a secret could be a burden, or that the truth would feel so heavy pressing down on her chest. She had to admit that she had adopted Siobhan. "You were very young, very beautiful. You seemed to want to forget your past. I don't know why I never told you. We don't usually keep secrets, do we."

"Sometimes," the girl said, looking off at an angle with a blank expression on her face, as if she had not really let this information enter.

"You were just so happy to be with me, with all of our animals – that was even before I met your father. It would hurt him if he thought . . . He loves you so much. But I'm sure your first parents loved you wonderfully too, or you wouldn't have been such a terrific girl."

Siobhan seemed distant, cool. She didn't like to find out that she had been living in ignorance, especially when other people knew. "Where are my first parents?"

Dana could see that her daughter felt cheated somehow, cheated out of the truth by someone she had always trusted. "They were killed in an automobile accident. They didn't suffer. It was instant. You were in the back. You were left all alone, with no one." She turned her head then and closed her eyes, pinching the bridge of her nose. She was afraid of crying, because she knew if she began it would hurt too much. "It was the same night," she continued, willing herself to say it, firmly, clearly, calmly, "the same night, you see, my husband died, Colin. He was my first husband."

"Did you love him?" Siobhan asked. She seemed to have no pity for her mother now. She simply wanted to know things. She had always pictured her parents together, as if they had always been married, and now even that image was rent in two.

"Yes," Dana said. "I loved him very much. But I wasn't kind to him. I wasn't a nice person."

Siobhan could hardly believe that, but maybe she didn't know her mother very well.

"You made such a big difference in my life. I was like a bum, really, a nothing. I didn't care about anything. And you made me care about everything. You're more precious to me . . . "

Dana started to cough. Siobhan wanted to hug her but she was afraid. She wanted to say, "It doesn't matter. I love you too." But instead, she got up and ran from the room.

Haven Rose was just coming up the stairs. He dropped by the house at least once a day. Alarmed by the girl's tears, he almost stepped on a small box turtle at the top of the landing. Siobhan didn't stop to chat like she usually did, but ran quickly down the stairs, slamming out the screen door. The little turtle peered from its shell. He picked it up and carried it to Dana's door. His patient seemed exhausted, yet relieved to see him.

"I was having the most dreadful sensation," she said. "I felt like I was drowning in my own body, as if I had one body inside another. Is that possible, Doctor?"

He got out his stethoscope and listened to her lungs. The metal felt cool, and his touch was always soothing. Dr. Rose was the only one who consistently wore his mask, but it was not unattractive on him. It focused her attention on his warm brown eyes, which always seemed filled with assurance, compassion – not pity, but a love that went way beyond the human. Placing the turtle on the palm of his hand, he showed it to her. "See how this hard case protects him? Well, your body could use some help right now too. Your husband has been very generous, as usual – he's offered to buy the hospital an iron lung. We can get one from Massachusetts, and it would help you breathe. It would do all the work for you, a bit like taking a vacation."

"They look so horrible, though, don't they? It might frighten Siobhan."

"I don't think so. We all want to see you get better. But that might mean a move to the hospital for a while where we can really keep an eye on you."

Dana turned her head away. She was afraid he would next remind her of the president. That's what everybody said – look at F.D.R., how he survived this. He went on to do great things. Imagine a polio victim, leading the nation. Well, why not. But she did not want to think about him or his accomplishments. She just wanted to look out her window. She did not want to move. If she lay very still, she believed she might pass through this – that the pain might drift away. The long white curtains luffed and sucked back against the screen – like Colin's sails, she thought, his full, white sails, and large brown hands – how he had loved to hold that weathered line, as his sailboat keeled out over the water. She had seen how it filled him with happiness, and now she too had a similar happiness, and that was her home, being safe inside it. She was happy whenever she heard familiar sounds, Siobhan running up the stairs, the creek of the porch swing, the slam of a door. She loved the smells from her kitchen, currant jelly being made, corn boiling. "Couldn't we bring the dirigible in here?" she asked. "I'd agree to that. But really, Doctor, you're keeping me in the dark about so many things. Can't you tell me what's happening in the major leagues? I'm from Pittsburgh, you know. How's Red Lucas pitching?"

"The Pirates aren't in the running, I'm afraid. New York is ahead. Lou Gehrig's been killing the ball."

Dana's face fell. They sat there in awkward silence for a moment. Then the songbird in the living room seemed to awaken. "Listen," Dana said, and they listened together. "I wonder what makes him sing like that." It was strangely heart-rending, almost melancholic. "Is it love, or pain, or just loneliness. Maybe he doesn't like being trapped in that nasty old cage."

Haven believed that the bird had been blessed with song. Song was its gift, just like the miracle of scent from an open rose, or the ripeness of peaches – it could be no accident. It was not simply science. He had seen too much beauty and mystery at the bottom of fact. He was a strange doctor, who didn't like to give a scientific explanation for everything. He knew Dana's stubbornness and love might also make her well, and he did not want to disrupt that. He believed her happiness was of the utmost importance, just as he knew the bird's song was not simply a response to some change of light, but a form of yearning for life – God given.

August 28, 1937

Dear Siobhan,

I wanted to write you because there are a few things I have to say and it's not always easy to say them in person. You have been the shining light of my life, and you've made me happy in so many ways. What a wonderful, special girl you are.

Though it's hard to conjure death, even when you are this sick, I wanted you to know that I believe in God. Perhaps when you're out in nature you will feel my love surrounding you. Remember our walks together? They brought me so much joy.

It would hurt me to think of you grieving endlessly over this. It is a rotten thing, and I know you will cry, but then try to let it go. Try to be open to what lies ahead. Take care of the animals, and keep anything of mine that you might treasure. You are going to have an exceptional life. I'm just sorry I won't be around to witness it.

I don't ever want you to think that I just gave up. I have done my best, and put up a good fight. If I'd had any say in the matter, I would have wished to remain here on this good earth a good while longer as your loving mother. Know with all your heart that I love you completely, and that it was my greatest and happiest privilege to have known you at all.

Mother

When Joey asked his mother if he could drive a car, she answered carelessly, "Why not." She didn't seem concerned about his safety, or who might teach him, or how fast he went. He was a boy and he would do as he wanted.

Joey had acquired a second-hand Aston Martin, and after cleaning and tuning it, he spray-painted it red. The mechanics in town thought it hilarious when Joey Ulrich turned up with grease on his hands, but Joey wanted more than anything to be an ordinary person. He didn't like it when people hopped to when they found out he was an Ulrich. He liked getting down on his back, wheeling under a car, tightening, adjusting, making the engine run right. He liked to feel the response, as if man and machine were in dialogue. He liked the smell of rubber tires and the neat slam of the hood.

The bang of metal startled Siobhan as she rode up. She had come around the lake to visit, and it always surprised her how quickly she could make the trip, cantering along the roadside where the fields opened to a sweep of ripening grain. It made her feel unattached to anything, as loose and fluid as the shifting clouds.

Joey was always glad to see Siobhan. Every time they got together, each summer, something was rekindled in him, some small dormant fire, and each year it grew bigger, brighter. "I was thinking of opening her up, out on the new highway toward Madison. You could put Grumpy in the barn." The old Ulrich stable was still halfway down the drive, though the stalls were now all broom clean. It always amazed her to see how many stalls there were, each marked with a golden plate – Tyack, Double Dawn, Amity, Frisky. The old tack room still had dusty red and blue ribbons on display, only an occasional yellow. There were not any saddles, but a faint residue of leather still permeated the place. Grumpy didn't like the sound of the bare board floor beneath his hooves without the customary shavings. He trampled around in a circle, wickering, when Siobhan latched the door and told him to be good.

Jumping into the low red car, Siobhan felt strange to be sitting so far back, feet out. Her head lolled back against the seat as Joey accelerated down the driveway, scattering gravel. They both leaned in the same direction as he took the curves over the canals, and went sailing over the bridge, as if they could take off into the air.

Of course she wasn't afraid, but once they were out on the new, straight highway, he pushed the pedal all the way down and brought the speedometer up to sixty, sixty-five, pushing seventy. She had never gone so fast, and she was grateful when he slowed down and turned the car toward home, driving a reasonable thirty miles an hour.

"Do you have to cool it down?" she asked.

"This isn't a horse. You only feed it when it runs out of gas. And you don't have to muck out the garage, either."

"Did you ever know I was an orphan?"

"No," he lied. "Are you worried about your mother?"

"She's not going to die, if that's what you mean. I can always tell when something's going to die. Animals get real quiet, and she wants us with her all the time."

"She's not an animal," Joey responded.

"We're *all* mammals."

"You might be," he said, and then added, as if to match her boast. "I think my mother's going crazy. She never wants to go anywhere."

"That makes two of them, then."

"And two of us," he added. "Two only children. My mother always said that only children are more apt to be gifted."

"Ha," Siobhan responded. "She probably said that 'cause she was an only child. My mother came from a very large family."

"But that's not your real mother."

Siobhan didn't answer. Her mother had always felt real before. "I don't remember the other one."

"It's pretty common," he explained, down-shifting as they turned back into the drive. "I never knew my real father, and he never knew his mother."

"Maybe we should get your mother to come over to my house, tell her my mom wants to see her. They used to be best friends. Don't you think it would cheer them up?"

"My mother just misses Mr. Schraeger. Did you know about that?"

"What, that he crashed?"

"No, that they were lovers. She loved him ever since my father died."

Siobhan looked pensive as they came to a stop before the garage. "But Mr. Schraeger was married."

At the end of July, Joey convinced his mother that Mrs. Knobloch wanted her to come for a visit. Dana had taken a turn for the worse, and Alicia believed that possibly Dana had something weighing on her conscience, that she wanted to make peace. Heaven only knows, Alicia thought, I don't need any more ghosts in my closet.

But as soon as Alicia stepped into the sick room, she could not help saying, "Uh oh." She had refused the cotton mask, fearing it would mar her lipstick, and she didn't believe in catching things. Sitting in the wicker armchair with its well-molded cushion, she crossed her legs and surveyed the collection of cards Dana had received. "You should have invited me sooner," she announced, opening and closing the gold clasp of her purse. "You probably forgot I'm all alone over there in that big, horrible house, with no one to entertain me, and here you are with visitors and flowers, family coming and going."

Alicia's tone put Dana at ease. It was nice to hear someone complain. Everyone had become so accommodating, polite, and this was just like old times. Thank goodness Alicia had not brought soap beads or a stiff bouquet. Dana couldn't even remember why they had argued.

"You don't know how tiresome it's been," Alicia continued. "Half the time, I don't even want to eat. What's the point of getting up and getting dressed? But anyway, I didn't come here to complain. I came to forgive you. So there."

Dana could only smile, for Siobhan had said something about Mrs. *Ulrich* wanting forgiveness, but it didn't really matter who was right or wrong. "I'm glad you're here," Dana whispered.

Alicia went on in her own vein. "Life is just too dull. I can't find anything to interest me. Joey's always off, and I gave up the gallery – I'm sure you heard that much. There hasn't been any decent art for ages. Joshua Liebenau's disgustingly popular, if you can believe it. He's painting W.P.A. murals all over the place, wherever he can find a surface – farm scenes, industry, even post offices. That man is such a rogue."

Dana always marveled at how Alicia could take someone's name in her mouth and shake it like a rag – she had a real talent for perceiving and naming anybody's weakness, summing Joshua up as a scoundrel and a snake. But Dana also sensed that Alicia was crying out, wanting to find some direction in her life.

"I was thinking of opening a dress store. What do you think, a special little store, very exclusive."

"Why don't you help build a music hall," Dana suggested, and Alicia's eyes lit up. She liked the idea of being the focal point of some artistic endeavor.

"But we'd only have top-rate performances. Who knows, we might even attract New York. What made you think of such a thing? Milwaukee could certainly use a little culture."

"It's what we all need," Dana said very quietly, closing her eyes as if she were unable to continue. "People long for it, like love."

"I suppose you're right. I'd give anything to feel something strong again. Even if it's just an aria."

"I miss my husband," Dana barely spoke.

Alicia leaned forward, concerned now. She got up and stood by the bed, for she could see that her friend was having trouble breathing. When Dana opened her eyes, she looked so far away, as if she were slowly sinking, and she couldn't get back.

"Herman's right downstairs," Alicia assured her. "He was building something out of matchsticks."

"I want my husband," Dana repeated, gasping, and Alicia went to the bedroom door and called out to Herman, but when Alicia came back to her bedside, Dana grabbed her hand and squeezed it so hard, Alicia thought that she might be bruised.

"Not him," Dana said. And before Herman Knobloch could make it to the door, Dana Hewitt had slipped beneath the surface of the lake.

⤳ **PART SIX** ⤳

CHAPTER THIRTY-NINE

*T*he giant shoes of the four great Percherons cut into the ice as the horses heaved, straining forward, pulling the wagon onto the paved road. Their massive forms and steaming nostrils, heavy yokes with fist-sized bells, only added to the monumental effect of rolling out into the darkness beneath the winter moonlight. The old German driver sat hunched on his seat, bundled high with blankets, not much of a chaperone. His whip cut back and forth across the cloudless sky as he got the team to move on out – they jangled off into a stomping trot that shook the grinding wagon.

The group of eleven young men and women settled down into the straw and began to sing "Listen to the Merry Bells," lowering their protective woolen scarves and letting the cold race down their throats, shocking to the lungs. The air seemed to pinch their nostrils. Carol Faithorne, who had chosen the rear corner, was secretly thrilled when Trumbull Rose grabbed the one place open beside her. The mere closeness of Trumbull's hulking form made her feel tiny ecstasies like pinpricks of frostbite heated under running water. She was all in a swirl as he nestled down into the loose hay, encouraging her to snuggle down too. When he sang, he bellowed in her direction, as if he meant his breath to warm her face. She felt something akin to the electrical stabs of a holiday sparkler on the surface of her skin.

If only her brothers hadn't been included, for they were both gawky and unromantic. Even now that they were both at Yale, neither of them had a serious girlfriend. They stood together on the footboard of the hay wagon, taking turns leaping off, hollering, and running to catch back up, like a couple of twelve-year-olds. And there was Prudy Schraeger, with no one beside her at all, poor thing.

Alden had warned his sister about Trumbull Rose, insinuating that he was not a nice person, but she paid no mind to that. Trumbull did like to get vaguely lewd, and told silly jokes she didn't understand, though she sensed that whatever it was he was saying was meant to excite her, and her rabbit heart leapt when he put his big paw under the covers and took off her glove, rubbing her hand between his, insisting that she must be cold.

"I got these gloves for Christmas," she told him, showing him how the insides were lined with fur. He smiled and recited:

Ma in her kerchief held toys in her lap –
with her nightie pulled high and their son said – Vats dat?
Oh, your soldier is wearing a little fur hat.
Second thought, here's another.
I give this fur one tonight to yer fadder.

She laughed, though she didn't know what he was talking about. It sounded naughty, but it made her feel closer to him somehow, as if they could merge amidst all their clothes and the heavy covers that surrounded them.

Their flirtation had begun earlier that month at a cotillion held at Dapper Hall, over in the village of Nogowogotoc, where many college students were staying during the holidays as they awaited the 1939 Great Lakes Open Speed Skating Championships, and the U.S. Olympic Trials. The winter sports events were drawing a national crowd, and all the hotels were filled to capacity. It made the little town seem quite cosmopolitan. They'd had a roller skating masquerade earlier that week, where the young guests in colorful costumes had skated about the ballroom floor. Carol had come dressed as Little Bo Peep and she'd had a wonderful time, mainly because skating came naturally to her, and she liked being partially disguised. Many of the debutantes were having their parties out in the country that winter, though Carol Faithorne would have hers at the Woman's Club in downtown Milwaukee.

On the night of the Dapper Hall cotillion she managed to put a difficult question to Trumbull Rose. "Mother thought that Alden would do," Carol confessed to him, as he turned her about the dance floor. He was a proficient dancer, considering his heft. He had the agility of a football player, meaty but quick, and she liked the force with which he guided her. "But don't you think it would be embarrassing, to have your brother walk you into your own party?"

"Very," he agreed, smiling at the thought.

"Mother thinks it's perfectly proper – one's escort isn't the point. It's all the young men one is supposed to meet. But I never meet anyone new at these parties. Do you?"

"I thought the point was *not* to meet anyone."

"I don't understand the point of entering society when you've grown up in it all your life."

Trumbull put his face close to hers and hummed along with the Charles

Harris tune that was playing. "*Many a heart is aching, if you could read them all, many the hopes that have vanished, after the ball.*"

Trumbull moved her about, pulling her so quickly at one point that her head was thrust back, exposing her pale, freckled neck, and she laughed – "You're going to give me whiplash." Carol had always been a natural athlete, but it didn't make her much of a dancer. She was not fluid in her movements, too self-directed and firm. Still, she had never had such a good time, or felt so free in conversing with a boy. Though she had known the Roses for most of her life, Trumbull seemed like a different person. So maybe coming out did change things – you saw things in a new way. She noticed that his eyes kept returning to one of the girls in uniform, Annalise Jacobson, a tall, blonde Swede. Siobhan was apparently friendly with her, for Joey and she broke the unspoken rule that one did not socialize with the help in public. "So what do you think?" Carol asked him.

"About what?" he responded. Carol would become a lovely woman, though she was not especially pretty or flirtatious. She reminded him of a Brittany Spaniel, elegant, English, and well-behaved.

"Do you think you would mind?" It was hard for her to be explicit, and she wished that he had gotten the gist of her need without her having to ask directly. "I was just wondering, if you might relieve my brother of his duties, and be my escort? He'd be so grateful."

"So would I," Trumbull responded, knowingly applying a little extra pressure to her lower back.

Carol blushed to the roots of her hair, and lowered her eyes as if to hide her gratitude.

"Let's take a break. I could use a smoke."

She didn't approve of smoking, but she was eager to walk with him out to the foyer, where new arrivals were rushing in with their dates. The young men were all taking the girls' wraps and leaving them in a heap to be checked, while the young ladies whisked off to the powder room to comb and primp, applying strokes of rouge and lipstick. Carol decided that she should follow suit and freshen up, though once she was in the ladies' room, she felt particularly awkward. Her plain brown hair lay flat on her head, curling only at the bottom. She had a prim, erect posture, and a freckly nose that she never bothered to powder. Her mother didn't approve of makeup, though she had loaned her daughter a pair of simple earrings, and the screws were now irritating the lobes of her ears. She felt foolish standing there amidst the crowd of girls with their full, colorful evening gowns. When one girl bent forward toward the mirror to inspect her painted mouth, Carol noticed the plushness of her breasts packed into her bodice. Carol's gown was cut rather high as she had a trim, sporting figure, and her mother didn't think it appropriate for girls her age to expose too much of themselves.

She was grateful that Trumbull was still standing there, waiting for her, though he was also helping himself to a canapé from the tray of the pretty blonde waitress. He turned his full attention to Carol as she came bursting up. "I just love this big old inn," she exclaimed.

Trumbull pivoted slightly. "Did you know they keep a Dresden china bed-pot under every bed?"

Carol shrieked with hilarity. "Where do you pick up such things?" But Trumbull was especially pleased when he saw a glimmer of a smile pass over the face of the beautiful Scandinavian.

Carol took Trumbull's arm, meaning to walk with him back into the ball-room, but now he wanted to duck outside to take a swig from his flask. She pretended she didn't mind though she shivered a bit as she remarked, "They call these pillars the Seven Bridegrooms. Isn't that silly?"

"I can't imagine coming here for a honeymoon, can you?"

Carol didn't know how to respond to this. She wished she hadn't brought it up. Embracing her own upper arms, she enthused, "But don't you love Nogowogotoc in the winter? We get out here so seldom, and I adore winter sports."

"I actually prefer *inside* sports in the winter." He winked at her, but he was bored. Opening the door, he walked in ahead of her, a gesture of rudeness she was forced to ignore.

"Aren't you interested in skating, or the long distance jump?"

"That girl over there," he nodded to the pretty one with the platter of hors d'oeuvres, "is going to be in the women's speed skating race this Saturday. Do you want to go?"

"Oh, yes!" she answered, entirely pleased that he would make a plan with her.

"Looks like the ladies are losing a shoe. You better hurry up," he in-structed. This was one of the more unusual dances of the evening – the girls each took off a slipper and tossed it into a pile in the middle of the room, and then, at the signal, all the boys had to run and fetch a shoe and find the girl with the matching one.

Alden Faithorne was not comfortable during these social occasions, and he thought this dance the epitome of tastelessness, for he was not inclined to want to witness the powdered interior of any girl's ugly shoe, though the boys knew they had to participate, for if there were any shoes left in the middle, all eyes would fall on them, and he and Merrick did have a certain degree of em-pathy. All this must be horrible for the girls as well.

"Just don't pick a big, smelly one," Merrick said to his older brother. "Prudy Schraeger must wear size ten."

When the master of ceremonies dropped his hand, the band started playing a mazurka, and the boys raced to the pile and lunged for various shoes, pearl stitched and satin covered. Alden didn't scramble with the frenzy of the rest, and got stuck with a worn patent leather with a big gaudy buckle. Merrick, curiously enough, snatched up Carol's white pump, already marred by a streak of boot black. She frowned menacingly at him when he showed up with her slipper, but she didn't see Trumbull anywhere, so she benignly accepted him as her partner. "Just don't step on me. I already have a blister. Oh look, Alden's dancing with Edith. She makes him look so tall."

"You look nice tonight," Merrick told her. "I hardly recognized you."

"Did you pick my shoe on purpose?" Her shoes matched the white organdy top of her dress, with its long puffed sleeves. The skirt was black silk velvet – it felt good to her hands no matter which way she rubbed it. But then Carol noticed Trumbull sauntering out onto the dance floor to scoop up the remaining, solitary shoe.

"What luck," Merrick said as Trumbull made his way to where Prudy sat on the bench. He seemed quite cavalier as he knelt in front of her, and eased the shoe onto her foot.

Carol had to admire him for his gentlemanly spirit, though she thought, once the music commenced, that he held the broad girl uncomfortably close, so that she looked like she was pushing away from him, arching back in order to exchange a few pleasantries. Carol only wished he had been quicker and had searched for her pump – that would have completed this fairy-tale evening, but now she felt vaguely dismal, and it seemed intolerable, wrong, to have to dance even one whole dance with her brother when she wanted to be held by Trumbull. It didn't matter to her that he was slightly overweight, gruff and unpredictable. She had to drag her eyes away from him, and make herself look at the yellow silk fabric covering the cushions that ran all around the room. She gazed up at the magnificent chandelier, not knowing what her brothers knew – she would not have wanted to know such things – how Trumbull had gotten Joey Ulrich to help him convert his old sedan. With Joey's blow torch they had cut out the backseat, and slid in a mattress. You entered this bedroom on wheels through the trunk, and Trumbull apparently kept a list of all the local girls he had managed to pick up at bars in Okauchee. He kept a notebook in the glove compartment, and had code marks to indicate the kind of seduction – first try, forced, oral only, more than once in a night, no luck/try later. Some people said that Joey and Trumbull took girls on together, but most disagreed, saying that Joey was in love with Siobhan and would never consider such a thing. But worse than these rumors, Merrick had also heard that Trumbull was one of the Bundt Boys. "You shouldn't get involved with him," Merrick warned her. "He's a bad egg."

"Did Mother tell you to say that?" She was not about to listen to such nonsense. No one else had asked her to the Olympic Trials. None of the other boys knew how to dance the way he did, with such strength and direction. Carol didn't know that he had asked the pretty blonde, Annalise Jacobson, to drive home with him that night. He had insisted that it was too cold for her to walk, and that she should save her strength for the race.

Now the master of ceremonies announced a Ladies' Choice, and Carol left her brother without apology and nearly raced to the far end of the room in order to find Trumbull, who was helping himself to a glass of punch. Turning, he winced at the sweetness of the beverage. He lifted his glass to her. He could see that she was undone. Her sexual imagination was a tabula rasa, and all of the future possibilities excited him. Prudy Schraeger had been like soft dough in his hands, and the contrast between the two girls was amusing – one so slender, the other plump – while the blonde waitress was somewhere in between, both tall and full of figure. She would be the real challenge.

Alden came up then and said it was time to go home.

"You big boys don't still have a curfew, do you?" Trumbull asked.

"No, but my sister does."

"Just one more dance," Carol pleaded.

Alden gave Trumbull a warning look, for he knew Trumbull Rose had no limits to his appetite, nor did he have the moral restrictions that guided most of the boys when it came to the women they cared about. Trumbull didn't care about anyone. He only felt that he should take what he wanted, that somehow, something big was owed to him, and that women, in particular, deserved to pay the debt that his mother had unwittingly created.

Helen Faithorne had seen enough of Carol's infatuation to want to nip it in the bud. She hadn't heard explicit rumors, but she was a good judge of character. Helen had never thought Trumbull a young man to be trusted, and she had never seen Carol so blinded before.

The sun on the ice was intense that day – the air was crisp and cold and windless. In the distance one could see thoroughbreds pulling two-wheeled sulkies over the frozen lake. The horses were shod with special needle-point shoes that gripped the ice like crampons. But most of the spectators gathered that day were focused on the Olympic Trials. The ring had been measured into a half-mile oval, with a two-lane track where the contestants alternated inner and outer lanes to balance the advantage.

The Montgomery Wards had a special box seat, which their butler had constructed out of metal poles and canvas. It held four chairs, and the small group was all wrapped up in steamer rugs, the only warm spectators there. Many envious friends, including Lionel Hewitt on his black figure skates, came up to greet them and call them sissy, "What are you doing hiding out in there?" They looked comfortable and self-satisfied and not about to budge, but Lionel couldn't help shaking his finger at Montgomery – "You'd be a whole lot warmer if you got up and moved about. Just look at those girls," he exclaimed, nodding in the direction of the skaters who were warming up for the race. "Don't you love to see them exerting themselves?"

The committee had been working hard on preparations so that all would be in readiness. Loudspeaking equipment had been installed to announce the various skaters. Governor Julius Heil was present, and would make the presentations at the end of the events. The trials were set up in varying distances, 500 meters, 1500, 5000, and finally the 10,000-meter race. No admission had been charged, and it was one of the largest crowds that had ever gathered in the little town of Nogowogotoc.

Carol felt lucky to be there with Trumbull. Together they had managed a position close to the front. The winter had been perfect for ice, cold and snowless, and it was thrilling to be in close proximity to so many athletes. Carol's exuberance was only dampened when she saw her mother approaching.

Mrs. Faithorne came and stood beside the two of them, announcing that a local girl was racing another Wisconsin skater, Maddie Horn, who had skimmed more than sixteen seconds off the half-mile record when she breezed around the six-lap oval. "Our Nogowogotoc girl is apparently untrained, but she has good long legs. I think it'll be a contest."

Helen made no move to leave the young couple alone, and Carol felt humiliated. She wanted to get away, but felt trapped by the crowd. Trumbull was managing fairly well, applying a bit of forced cordiality.

"That was a terrific party the other night. You always have the best gatherings. I don't think I've been on a hay ride since I was ten years old, but everybody had a great time." He glanced at Carol, but she looked grim. Several small boys were throwing their caps up into the air – the sky was intensely blue, the kind of sunny winter weather that makes you want to rejoice – but Carol Faithorne was speechless.

"Once the holidays are over, do you have any plans?" Helen asked Trumbull, knowing that he had recently dropped out of Harvard.

"My future seems to be all carved out. I've been given a position at the tannery."

He would work his way up quickly to an unwarranted, high salary, Helen thought. The crowd pushed to the left and all of the spectators had to take a step to adjust their view. The racers were lining up in their sleek, tight-fitting outfits. They seemed nervous, swinging their arms around and around.

"It must be painful for them to wait," Carol said, eager to change the subject, but her mother continued.

"Does your grandfather approve of your joining the family business? I can imagine him wanting you to strike out on your own." Each new question seemed to scrape another layer of epidermis, as if she meant to expose the real Trumbull Rose. "I've always hoped that Merrick and Alden would find their own niche, explore their own interests, but your mother must be pleased that you've moved back in."

"It's nice to be home," he answered.

The final blow came when Helen brought up William, Trumbull's twin. She turned to her daughter and said, "Constance was always so attached to William. We were just thinking about him the other day, what a lovely, special boy he was."

Just as the starting gun was raised, Trumbull turned to Carol and said, "Excuse me," slipping off into the crowd. The two female finalists crouched close to the ice and with the bang of the gun they exploded forward, their backs nearly horizontal to the ice, arms flashing back and forth. Carol turned from the scissor-slicing cuts of the blades to glance at her mother, who was now entirely caught up in the performance. Carol bit her lip and kept herself from saying – How could you do that? You drove him away!

Helen knew she had done her daughter a favor, that he was not the man for her, but Carol stood there numb. All the joy and excitement had gone out of her. Rather than expose her feelings, she turned her back on her mother and watched Mattie Horn flash by, just ahead of End-the-World Jacobson, her long blonde braids tucked beneath her cap.

Annalise seemed to be gaining on the lead skater, who was greatly favored by the local press, but the crowd was rooting for the underdog. Suddenly Annalise seemed to have a spurt of energy and was about to pass, when the two skaters criss-crossed for the final turn, and the long swinging arms of the Beaver Dam Miss swang into the face of the local girl, throwing her off balance. She went skidding out across the ice on her belly, and when she came to a stop, she put her forehead down on the frozen track and just lay there for a moment. Finally, she gathered herself together and slowly stood, brushing herself off, disqualified. The crowd was clearly disappointed, but as she skated off to the sidelines, they gave her a round of applause. Carol's heart went out to the girl – and she clapped and cried and cheered.

CHAPTER FORTY

*W*hen Isabelle Wells returned from Venice with Lolly Jones as companion in tow, she was obsessed by one thing only, and it was infuriating to have to try and convey her findings to her mother, for Sarah Wells was becoming progressively deaf.

"But how can you say that he's dead!" Isabelle protested. Lolly too had been at the seance and had witnessed all that Isabelle had, which lent a certain credibility, but it did seem strange that they would have to go so far away to hear his voice through another's.

Perhaps Venice was a stopping-off point for spirits in migration. Isabelle felt such a strong stirring there, as if she had lived some past life in that maze-like city. They had walked for hours and hours, and she had always sensed their direction, as if it were vaguely familiar. Instead of tiring, Isabelle wanted to go on and on, pointing out statues, pronouncing the name of each canal as if it were a line of poetry – "Rio della Misericordia" – admiring the painterly color of the walls – yellow ochre, burnt sienna, pink, and tawny peach. Even the door knockers were amazing, especially the twin bronze devils with tongues sticking out to be pulled.

In the evening the two women wandered from one alley to another, until they stumbled upon some *trattoria* that appealed. One night they dined outside by candlelight. The table was set up against a wall overlooking a small canal, and they could gaze through the potted geraniums down to the water. Now and then one of the long black boats would stop, and the gondolier would order a bottle of wine for his passengers – they would hand out a bottle and two glasses from the kitchen with a great deal of chatter and good cheer.

The two women drank Chianti that night, and made the acquaintance of a strange little bearded man, who said his name was Hector. He told them he had grown up in North Africa, and that he was a scholar of the classics. After dinner he offered to show them more of the night life of Venice. They both thought he seemed safe enough, though he had walked so swiftly, it was hard to keep up. From the Teatro la Fenice toward the Ponte dell'Academia he

seemed to be taking them in circles. The Chiesa della Salute was regally illuminated at the end of the island, and he began to recall scenes from the time
of the plague as if he had personally been there. They went on and on, from
narrow, ill-lit corridors to open *piazzas*, walking for hours, it seemed, until
they finally ended up at the table of Madame Stefanova.

Now as Isabelle walked by the lakefront at Nogowogotoc she was reminded of the lapping waters of Venice, where she and Lolly had rested back,
drifting through the dark water alleyways. Her feelings had strained against
the limits of her heart, but she had never been so happy. Away from suspicious, condemning eyes, she had taken Lolly's small hand in hers and held it
protectively. They were both enwrapped by the soul of the city, the shadows,
the music, the ocean smell mixed with the scent of lagoon, the Italian families bantering above them in shuttered apartments – it all created a kind of
wrapper or cocoon, which kept them in a state of soft inebriation. But now,
when she thought of the hollow sound of the wooden oar maneuvering them
beneath those low, curved bridges, their private gondola appeared in her
mind like a hearse, gleaming and black, for she realized in this clamorous
American light that their trip abroad had been a journey toward death – in
Venice, she had not only opened herself to illicit love, but she had sought out
and found her father.

"How can you say that he's dead," she repeated, "when we heard from him.
We received a communication! He's only absent, unseen, not dead. He's not
in his physical body, that's all. We contacted him, Mother. Do you hear me?"

Sometimes Sarah took offense when her daughter challenged her ability
to hear, but now her face was powdered with a potential smile. "And how was
your father, standing on one foot or two?" She wondered if he were still wearing his steel-rimmed spectacles, his black dress jacket trimmed with satin, a
stick-pin through the tie. Was he still snipping nose hairs and bothered by in-
digestion? Was he anxious to see all the shoes set straight in the closet, or to
check the menu for the week ahead?

Sarah had felt remarkable relief in the years of her widowhood, eating
whatever she fancied, skipping breakfast and indulging herself at tea. She had
become more and more her own person, and she didn't want to summon up
the past.

"Don't you even want to know what he said? There were things this
woman couldn't have possibly known, names and places. She even said – *a
Helen goes by*, didn't she?" Isabelle turned to Lolly, who firmly agreed. "She
said she was contacting a man who looked like me. Everybody always said I
resembled father."

"Well, I wouldn't dwell on that."

"Listen," Isabelle continued, reading from her scribblings, *"He speaks of two daughters and Marjorie is with him* – that must be Marjorie Hewitt, I suppose. And then, *Woman that you're named after, a beautiful one, is it a grandmother?* How would she know I was named after father's mother? It's just too strange." Isabelle looked up to get her mother's reaction, but Sarah's face looked distant, blank.

Life had been so calm before Isabelle's return. Sarah had amused herself over the simplest things, writing bits of verse, arranging flowers, setting up the small table on the porch with her favorite English china. Lionel Hewitt was a widower for the second time, and although neither of them had serious intentions, they enjoyed each other's company. She liked to hear him play the harmonica, and they both played honeymoon bridge. After finishing a rubber, she would often ask him to tell her something about dear Heinrich Ulrich, and he would repeat some familiar story, about the million-dollar raindrop, or how Alicia had beaten him at lawn croquet and how he never played another game after that.

Lionel didn't mind her hearing problem, for he could keep up his own rambling monologue without any help, and she didn't mind the smell of his cigar, though Angeline claimed it was bad for the curtains. "Mister Wells never smoked in the house."

Often, Sarah sent Angeline off to town against her will, for Angeline resented holidays, not knowing how to amuse herself, but Sarah would pack her off anyway, instructing the chauffeur to pay her round-trip fare on the commuter train into Milwaukee. "Walk up Michigan Avenue," she suggested with a wave, "and look in all the windows," while the old woman growled and turned her head like an insulted, banished child.

How peaceful Broadoaks was on those days with no one around. The lake wind would breeze in through the tall French windows and gently wave the palm fronds. She would stand by the front door, looking out into the sunlit world of her garden embraced by the pergola, and smell the sweetness of viburnum warmed in the sun, see the cellophaned wings of a dragonfly catching the light above the borders of hosta with their variegated leaves and long slender stalks, dangling purple flowers. The statue of the waterboy, holding up his shell, half-filled with rainwater from the night before, provided a bath for a purple martin, who lit upon the lip of it, dipping his head to spray a flutter of droplets. She believed this place was as good as heaven, and that she, for one, didn't have to die in order to achieve salvation.

But summer seemed over now that Isabelle was back with her excitable ways. The month of August should never be intense, Sarah thought, but drowsy, well-fed and listless. She sat politely and tried to listen because

Isabelle, as usual, seemed to care so much. How tiresome to care about everything. It was her opinion that women should keep their cares to themselves, and spare their male companions.

Isabelle glanced over her shoulder and saw that Lionel Hewitt had just arrived. He sat down on the high-backed love seat in the hall and appeared to acknowledge that they were having a family conference. He was an old man now, with time on his hands. He seemed to doze off as he waited.

"Listen to this," Isabelle continued. "*Many figures in a market place, the sale of chiefly women's garments.* Felton's, of course! But then it did get a little creepy, didn't it?" she asked Lolly, who nodded, yes, for the psychic had given a definite jolt, as if she were going down onto some other level, and Isabelle imitated the deeper voice she had used – "*Remember me, remember me, my will persists I charge you – comfort her, comfort her, it can be through me when I say Thy Will Be Done ask not why Submit and know that I persist it is enough I leave YOU now I see for her I would say more Is all I say God Bless You.* And then it was over. She came out of the trance."

"She looked exhausted," Lolly added.

"No wonder," Sarah said, for it had always been so tiresome trying to keep his attention. "Now Lionel's here, and we mustn't be rude."

"But isn't it remarkable? Father wants us to comfort you."

"I *am* comfortable. He has no reason to fret."

"But he said – I persist!" Isabelle hadn't been so enthusiastic since women's suffrage, and she wanted to grab Lolly's hand and run down the drive in search of Helen to share her news. "Perhaps you'd like to study my notes," Isabelle suggested to her mother.

"I think I got the gist of it. I'm quite all right in the morning," she defended her hearing, "one-on-one. I only have trouble later in the day." She rose then and went to the door, waving as she walked. Isabelle raised her eyebrows, glancing at Lolly, whose face suddenly clouded over, for Mr. Hewitt reminded her of things best forgotten, and it made her strangely taciturn.

"Let's go find Helen," Isabelle urged. She felt her sister would be just as thrilled as she, and yet Nogowogotoc and all its inhabitants seemed so self-content, dulled by the humid air. It was enough to drain anyone's excitement over anything. Italy, Germany, and France had been so vital and alive, bustling with commerce and art. It was hard adjusting to this sedentary pace, and to conversations that amounted to nothing. She had nowhere to steer her nervousness, except into the daily poems she wrote. Lolly was her muse, her inspiration, and Isabelle dreaded to be apart from her. It even pained her when Lionel reached out to touch Lolly's elbow, as if the contact sullied her friend.

"So when are you going to give up this dreary hospital work with that tire-some son-in-law of mine, and come to work for me?"

"Dr. Rose is the most decent man we know," Isabelle interrupted. "Miss Jones and he have a common vision. I'm sure you don't mean to insult her."

"Now, now," Sarah put in. "We'll have no swearing."

Lionel was practically ogling Lolly. "Most men share a common vision," he chortled. Isabelle turned away in disgust. "So what does my son-in-law propose to believe in now?"

Lolly waited to see if Isabelle would answer. When she did not, Lolly said, "He thinks the general practitioner should continue to do bedside medicine first, and not let modern devices turn a physician into a machine."

"If it weren't for modern devices, some of us wouldn't be partaking in this conversation."

"People aren't just laboratory specimens," Isabelle inserted. "They're spiritual beings. Haven treats all aspects."

"Oh, malarkey! I make regular donations to physicians of the soul. If he wanted to operate in that way, why didn't he go into the priesthood?"

"If he had, you wouldn't have all those adorable grandchildren," Sarah put in, following the conversation perfectly. Isabelle wondered why her mother always seemed to hear everything Lionel Hewitt said. Perhaps it was the deepness of his voice, and his irritating, slow delivery.

"Well, Miss Jones." He winked at Lolly. "I will commend you to my son-in-law, and tell him he has a true believer in his midst. If he doesn't give you a raise promptly, I'll have to up my offer. I get terrible heart pains, you know." He put his old paw to his chest, and made a mock attempt at a mild angina at-tack. "I really shouldn't live alone," he said, turning to Sarah, "now that Mar-jorie's gone." He seemed to have forgotten his second wife. "Mrs. Knutson keeps threatening to retire. Don't forget, I also play whist," Lionel resumed his entreaty.

"Perhaps we could part with Angeline," Isabelle suggested. "She's still a fine cook, and she's always preferred serving gentlemen." But Lionel didn't think too much of that idea, seeing as Angeline always misplaced the rat poi-son whenever he came to visit. "I'm just part of that aging legion," he went on, as if they had nothing better to talk about, "progressively gray, increas-ingly bald, and perpetually cold. Circulation, I suppose." He looked about for acknowledgment of this neurotic recital of aching ailments, but Isabelle only grimaced.

"We're off to find Helen," she said, taking Lolly by the arm.

"Fine, fine," Sarah answered. "He's probably in his study, working on the Greeks."

Then, as the girls departed, Sarah whispered to Lionel in confidence, "I can assure you of one thing, my last trip to Europe cost three times what it cost Isabelle and her companion. I think she practices too much economy."

"But it gives some people particular pleasure to practice economy. Especially when it's unnecessary."

"Isabelle's been tipping stones," Sarah added, for all of this psychic phenomena reminded her of turning over the white-washed stones that were set at intervals along the driveway, how all sorts of bugs and beetles and worms scurried down into the dark, moist earth when they were exposed. Sarah felt that this seance business was just as repellent and unclean, a kind of violation, unearthing things that needn't see the light.

"That man talks so much rubbish. You don't need his money any more than he needs a nurse! I don't know why my mother puts up with him. You can't have a decent conversation without Lionel showing up." Isabelle felt valiant now, but actually she had keener fears – she dreaded what might happen to them now – now that they were back in Wisconsin. She was afraid that all of their happiness would disappear, like a precious scent released from a container, wafting away, soon gone. She realized with a kind of primitive knowledge that the love she felt for this woman was akin to the emotion she had experienced at her father's death, and it was odd that the two sensations, yearning and grief, could be so intertwined.

Isabelle pressed her latest poem, neatly folded, into Lolly's hand.

While still your name on passing strangers' lips
Is like a death knell tolled within my heart
While still the thought of life without you grips
In vise of torture my mind's every part

While still illusion's fleeting bloom can climb
That passion's tendril to such host should cling
While long days linger that alone in time
Are witness to its perfect flowering

On other planes, beyond this aberration
Old ties still bind which I would not betray
Deep in my soul I know there is salvation
When once this fevered dream has slipped away

But what if now with wounds still all unhealed
That ultimate hope should crash around my head

And part the present love, life but revealed
One lengthening vista of despair and dread

Often, when Isabelle finished scribbling, she hardly knew what it was about. She would have to decipher the meaning like the notes she had taken down from the psychic. She felt as if she too were a medium – sitting in a trance, letting her mood transport her until the words came pouring through.

"Oh, good." Isabelle released Lolly's arm, for there was her sister gathering wax beans with Winnie, the cook. Winnie, short of stature and round of shoulder, looked like a strange gnome hunched over the bean vines, plucking. Her odd appearance was startling in broad daylight, for her cheeks were smeared with rouge, and her fine white hair was dyed an Easter-chick yellow. Helen, in contrast, never wore makeup, but the two had a genuine understanding and fondness for one another.

"We're going to have some party!" Winnie winked at the new arrivals. She hunched up further and clapped her hands together. "The leaders of the nation."

Helen brought Winnie to the garden at lunch time, when the crew of men were taking their break – otherwise, Winnie would flirt with each one of them.

Isabelle couldn't resist sharing her findings again. She thought it rather inconsiderate of her sister to continue picking while she was imparting such awesome news, but Helen's reaction was even more astounding.

"That all seems like Pandora's box to me. You must know there are charlatans all over the world who make money off of people's suffering. Certainly the dead persist in spirit, but it's wrong, I'm afraid, to call them up. It's like waking a sleeping baby." It also disturbed Helen to see her sister so obviously enthralled with Lolly Jones, and she wondered if their peculiar friendship would influence the children. "Isn't it time we turned our attention to real work in the real world?"

"I think it's time for love, don't you?" Winnie chortled. "The minister over at the Presbyterian is crazy about me. Last Sunday when I came in he slammed shut the Good Book," she clapped her hands together for emphasis, "and said there would be no more sermons."

Lolly smiled, though Isabelle ignored the woman, too wounded by her sister's rebuff. In her own defense, she thought of the letter she had just received from Margaret Sanger in New York, saying that Isabelle was a great friend to the cause – she had helped them clean up their debt, and Sanger was optimistic for the future, believing that contraceptive service would soon be a

285 ↩

routine part of public health care. "I've always admired your efforts, Helen. You have no need to disparage mine."

"You can't forget the words of the Lord when he kisses you every night," Winnie added, flashing three fingers at Lolly, as if that were a sign.

Just as Isabelle had rescued Lolly Jones, so Helen had welcomed Winnie Wolfgram into her home, saving her from the detestable hands of a Swedish paperhanger, who had boxed her ears and made her work daily with no reward. Life in the Faithorne kitchen had seemed like a holiday ever since.

Leading the way down the grassy path, Helen mentioned that they were having important guests the following evening, but it had to be kept a secret. "We're trying to plan our menu," she thought out loud, more concerned with gastronomy than destiny, Isabelle thought.

"Mr. Kirchner brought me some corn and some nice tomatoes," Winnie suggested. "He thinks *I'm* a juicy tomato, ha ha!"

Helen had learned to ignore Winnie's prattle. It was hard to keep a good cook. The last one had been mean to little Edward, and the one before that had a running feud with Kirchner, who began to deliver daily bushels of vegetables to the kitchen door as soon as he discovered this annoyed her. Finally, she had thrown a squash at him and quit without notice. That's when they had stumbled upon Winnie.

"Perhaps we should start with a soup course," Helen said.

"Mr. Wolfgram always liked cream of mushroom. He said that it made him *hot*, if you know what I mean, ha ha!"

"And we must have one of your very special desserts."

"A sweet and happy ending to a long, hard day."

"I guess you have it all worked out, then." Helen relinquished her authority, knowing that Winnie would compose an extravagant meal.

As they left the garden together, Helen unconsciously offered her wicker basket, full of small zucchini and yellow wax beans, to Lolly to carry. She then turned to Isabelle, remembering something. "You left Mother with too much time on her hands. She's given her assent to a carnival of sorts, Felton's Day, with a free show out on the street, and everything on sale. She also hired that Liebenau fellow to paint a mural on the west side of the store, a lake scene, I believe."

"How could she hire that man?" Isabelle protested. "Popa would roll over in his grave."

"He seems to be up and about now, anyway," Helen responded, ducking beneath the staining berries of the mulberry whose bows hung laden over the garden gate.

"A high-grade painter of international reputation, Liebenau is the holder of many imposing and valuable trophies. When you pay his studio a visit, you will find a survey of portraits that are always on exhibition. They will give you cause to marvel at the refined beauty and finish that are the crowning achievements of artistry." Sarah Wells put down the advertisement as if to say – So there.

"And now he's taking his supposed artistry to the streets," Isabelle scoffed.

"I've always supported public art before. Can't you think of it like Italy, with all those nice statues and murals?"

"Felton's is not San Marco's, Mother, and this man's not Raphael. He's a schemer and a user! The masses won't be uplifted by some stupid painting of Lake Michigan done on brick when the real thing's right before them. How ridiculous. And what would it look like in winter? Did you ever think of that?"

Sarah Wells didn't think of everything as her daughter did, and she was set back by this outburst.

"You could put five thousand dollars into an orphanage fund and do more for the city of Milwaukee. Or donate your Turner to the art museum. That might be doing the masses a service. The whole event seems so tawdry, handing things out on the street, as if we didn't respect our own prices. Are you listening to me?"

Sarah leaned forward and said confusedly, "Produce?" When Isabelle became shrill, Sarah was less receptive. She hadn't heard every word, but she sensed her daughter's decisiveness, and it soured her on the mural plan. "I think I had better call Leonard. We'll tone it down, for you, dear. I'll have Leonard cancel the arrangements."

But Joshua Liebenau, renowned public muralist, about to set up his scaffolding, was so enraged by this affront that he insisted Felton's pay his entire fee, claiming that he had already put a significant amount of time into designing the art work – the mere execution was nothing – and that he'd turned down several other important offers to keep this space of time open for Felton's. After several nasty letters to his benefactress, he threatened Felton's with a lawsuit.

"If only Merrick were here," Sarah said wistfully, for her husband had always managed all of their problems so well, and provided them with an unperturbed world filled with all of the physical comforts. If only he could comfort them now.

CHAPTER FORTY-ONE

S arah Wells did not like to impose herself upon her daughter's family, for she felt discretion was even more important when family members were immediate neighbors. While she had always enjoyed her grandchildren, she waited until they sought her out. It was Edward, the youngest, who most often dropped by to see his Little Gram, bringing her the freakish nut he'd found or wanting to show her his shiny silver dollar. He had always known her to be hard of hearing, so he was not self-conscious when it came to shouting, "President Hoover is coming for dinner!"

"Come over?" she responded. It was a blustery end of August day, and the wind picked up their voices and carried them off, while turning the dark green oak leaves back to show their lustrous undersides. The surface of the lake was crisp with wind blow. "I'm not sure what Isabelle has planned."

"The ex-president!" Eddie repeated, feeling some regret at having spoken, for his mother had sworn him to secrecy. She wanted to keep the dinner party small and simple.

Still, Little Gram didn't get it. She assumed a look of befuddlement, gave a jolly laugh, and shrugged, oh well.

The Hoovers came and went that weekend, and no one discovered the fact until they were on their way back to Palo Alto. Sarah was chagrined, for she would have liked to have shaken hands with the president and shown Lou Henry about her garden, but Helen insisted that they had had so little time – it was barely a stopover. The Hoovers had been visiting relatives in the Midwest, and Helen had implored her friend Lou to make the jaunt to Nogowogotoc so they could discuss their mutual passion – the furthering of Girl Scout troops in America.

"You boys will have to keep an eye on Edward this evening," she had warned Alden and Merrick. "No hopping up from the table."

Alden assured his mother that they could keep Eddie in line, for Merrick had just invented the Mujiji Chair, which gave its victims a mild shock, and Eddie wouldn't want to sit in that hot seat again.

But it was not only Edward who concerned Helen Faithorne. Leonard seemed to be more and more self-absorbed of late, shutting himself away in his study to pore over his books. He had a passion for Greek mythology. He was also overly involved in a rather morbid hobby – burying dead animals and unearthing the corpses a year or so later so that he could study their skeletal structures. Just that morning she had come upon him handling the skull of some small rodent. "How can you stand that," she accused, "picking at a corpse."

"It's hardly a corpse any longer," he answered calmly, holding the assorted bones in the palm of his hand. "You can tell a great deal about an animal if you study the skull."

"What's that." She pointed to a particularly frightening visage.

"Oh, that's a badger. Isn't he marvelous? The state animal, you know. Very fierce. Kirchner cornered him by the tool shed with a shovel. Luckily, he didn't crush the bone. But look at the size of those teeth."

Alden and Merrick thought the skull collection terrific too, and they brought their father various finds, while Carol took after her mother and collected china dogs.

"Can't you clean up? The train will be coming in at five. I was hoping you'd go with me to the station." She found it remarkable that he could remain so undisturbed by the arrival of Herbert Hoover. Most men would be in a nervous state, fussing over every detail, but Leonard seemed strangely calm.

"I'll be finished with this in an hour." He stood his ground, checking his watch. She couldn't bully Leonard.

Minutes before the train came bellowing around the corner, pulling up beside the little fieldstone depot, Edward lay a penny on the tracks. The train screeched to a halt with an exhale of steam, smelling of iron and engine oil, and Eddie found the flattened piece of copper lying on the gravel. It was warm to the touch. Leonard had driven the Studebaker over, and Helen was proud of her husband now, how handsome he was in his white linen pants and navy blazer, his hair slightly gray at the temples. He had a youthful, unmarked face, taller and thinner than the stolid president. Lou Henry was warm and enthusiastic. "I can't wait to see Springwood Lee, after all you've told me. I'm sure it will seem like heaven on earth after all this traveling." Helen and Lou had been the guests of Lady Baden-Powell at the World Girl Scouts Conference in Switzerland, and they had much to catch up on.

Helen insisted that they have a tour of the lake, so Alden drove the wooden Chris Craft around the perimeter, perched on top of the red leather seat so that he could feel the evening air. Lou and Helen sat up front with him, while the men sat in back and discussed the future of the railroad. Edward pointed out the important homes for the Hoovers' interest. "That's Mrs. Ulrich's. They own Kreuser Beer. Her son is a speedboat racer, and that's Mrs. Schraeger's home over there. They make hotdogs. They even have a weiner mobile," Eddie added to Mr. Hoover's amusement.

"And what's that big white building?"

"The Lake Club, of course. Haven't you ever seen one?"

Inside the bay, the water was particularly quiet, and Helen pointed out the old monastery-turned-nursing-home – Goldenbank. Across the body of the main lake was a reproduction of Anne Boleyn's castle built on the site of Bon Pres.

At sunset the family gathered on the screened-in porch overlooking the water. "What a dream," Lou Henry exclaimed. "No wonder you never want to leave this place." She took up one of the cherry tomatoes stuffed with cheese that Winnie was passing, and sampling it she said, "These are delicious."

"They should be," Winnie replied. "I've been around the world three times."

Herbert laughed. He was in a fine mood, for Helen, who did not drink a drop and who didn't comprehend the power of the substance, had poured him a full glass of straight Scotch over a single ice cube.

Leonard was having a Faithorne Special, forty-year-old Irish whiskey with a squirt of soda, stirred with a spoonful of Wisconsin maple syrup. "Did you know when our local post office burned down," Leonard told the president, "the *Wall Street Journal* thought it could hardly make a difference – they didn't think letters addressed to such a place would ever get here anyway."

"It's easy to spell," Edward piped up – "n-O-g-O-w-O-g-O-t-O-c. Indians named it." He plopped down on the wicker divan by the president, leaning over to help himself to a cheese stick, while Miss Goetsch raised her eyebrows and sipped her glass of lemonade.

"*Nogowogotoc* supposedly means firewater," Merrick explained. "A great Indian hunter came here and thought the lake was on fire."

"Probably just this time of night." The president looked out at the glorious sunset, pleased by his own explanation.

"Most of the places around here are corruptions of Indian words," Alden added. "*Mukwonago* means fat bear. *Nogowogotoc* is the Indian word for whiskey."

"Whiskey!" Eddie shouted. "Drunk on whiskey."

"The white man unfortunately introduced the Indian to liquor," Helen put in.

"And you do all right here, Faithorne. Excellent Scotch."

"But I always thought *Nogowogotoc* meant Indians sleeping," Leonard added.

"Maybe they were sleeping it off." Merrick smiled.

"It refers to the whiskey-colored falls in the village," Helen asserted. "The water over the stones is brown, that's all."

"Isn't it amazing, how everything's open to interpretation?" Mrs. Hoover said as they headed into the dining room, but Eddie ended the discussion by saying, "We don't really know what it means."

There was a wonderful buffet of garden vegetables, hot and steaming on the sideboard. Lou Henry was entreated to help herself in the casual summer manner of the family. "You have to take at least four ears of corn," Helen urged. "It's baby bantam." Silver prongs were provided at each place setting. There were baked garden tomatoes with bread crumbs on top, creamed cabbage, and slices of their own farm lamb with a special homemade apple chutney. Steaming potatoes, salted and buttered, filled a casserole dish. A heap of wax beans and tiny glazed carrots stood on either side of the basket of biscuits that split open in the middle as if asking for a swipe of fresh butter. Winnie's currant jelly, ruby red, glistened at either end of the dining-room table. Edward had been warned not to take too much of it, for he was incorrigible when it came to butter and jelly. He even liked to eat butter straight, and would consume a whole stick if he was not stopped. "I hope you like vegetables," he said to the president, making a face.

Herbert Hoover winked at the boy, skirting the wax beans and taking a large helping of lamb. Once everyone was seated, Leonard said his standard evening grace, "Lord, we thank thee for this food which we are about to receive . . . " and then everyone dug in, conversation starting up all around.

"Tell President Hoover about your courses at Yale. Alden's very interested in philosophy, as well as Greek and Roman Art."

Leonard told Lou about the present problem on the lake, how they were having trouble with a man who'd built a saw mill just above the falls. Sometimes when the lake residents wanted to raise the water level they lowered the dam and cut off his supply. Lou questioned whether the alteration of the water level affected the wildlife in the area, an issue that had not been considered at all.

Edward, anxious to be part of the conversation, blurted out, "I have an all-black gelding with a pure white star, but he bucked me off last weekend badly."

"Were you hurt?" Lou Henry asked the child.

"Only his feelings," Leonard answered. "It was actually quite a stunt — Edward did a perfect somersault and landed on his feet."

"Father stopped and helped me, but Mother caught my horse and beat him."

Winnie had been instructed not to disturb the family during dinner time unless Helen rang the bell, so when Miss Goetsch heard the telephone, she quickly excused herself from the table and went to answer it. When she returned, she stood at the entrance to the dining room and announced, "A phone call for President Hoover."

"They always track you down." He shook his head, crumpling his napkin by the side of his plate. "I could be in Nogowogotoc and the phone would ring!" He followed Miss Goetsch to the telephone room, which was no larger than a broom closet. It had a tiny built-in, curved table and a booth-like chair, hardly big enough for him. They could all hear him exclaiming, "My word, I didn't expect to hear from you!" And then, "What do you mean? When did this come in? . . . I can hardly believe it. Terrible . . . terrible. Yes, you'll have to keep me informed. For the rest of the evening. We head back tomorrow. Of course, by all means. All right, then. Please, don't hesitate." And then finally – "Over and out."

When he returned to the table he looked grim. He didn't say a word for a moment, and no one dared ask. He picked up his napkin, and looking first to his wife, he informed the table that he had just received a call from F.D.R. – "Germany has invaded Poland." Lou Henry and Helen both gasped. Miss Goetsch was left frozen with her little finger lifted in the most delicate fashion as she raised her cup, for she considered this affectation to be one of great elegance, and Merrick, who had been imitating this gesture unmercifully, burst into inappropriate laughter just as their middle-aged nurse fled the room in tears.

Leonard shook his head, "Good Lord, after all you did for Germany."

"I'm afraid this is just the beginning, that's what troubles me now. To think of the flower of our youth, cut down again." Lou was up by his side, comforting him, her eyes filled with tears.

"Do you think we'll get involved?" Alden asked.

Merrick was now humbled into silence. Both boys were old enough to participate, if it came to that. An even darker mood fell over the room.

Before dessert was served, Roosevelt rang again, and by the time Herbert Hoover returned to the table, the blueberry pie had been served. Edward could not stand blueberries for some reason, and Miss Goetsch was no longer beside him to make him behave. His older brothers were in a heated discussion about whether this was really a new war, or simply a continuation of World War I. "I say it never really got resolved," Alden asserted, and his father gave him a silencing look, while Eddie took his large white dinner napkin and pressed it firmly down on top of his piece of pie. No one seemed to notice.

After coffee, the third phone call came, and as they sat there waiting, they all realized that soon this news would be moving out across the nation, and then on to the entire world, and here they were, at the heart of it. They felt connected to a greater network that was spreading outward in every direction, connecting all mankind.

No one spoke as Winnie began to clear the table. For once, she too remained silent, lifting her finger in the "*shhh*" sign to Merrick. When she came to Edward's plate, she reached over and lifted his napkin in the air, and Eddie's eyes followed the piece of blueberry pie as it clung to the napkin, ascending above him, and then his mouth opened as the piece of pie began to loosen its hold, and finally dropped – splattering all over the white linen tablecloth. Everyone burst into laughter, grateful that something had broken the mood. Helen had to forgive him, and said that he could be excused. "Why don't you run outside now, and play with the dogs," she said.

CHAPTER FORTY-TWO

*H*ard to share one's keenest joy when you fear your own child might take the news and turn it into her gravest sorrow. Herman Knobloch was afraid his daughter might do just that, for as Lucy had warned him, "She's bound to have a reaction," especially since the girl had been so close to her father and the only child. Lucy didn't think that was healthy.

She knew her girls would never let Herman replace their memories of their own adored father, and yet they liked Mr. Knobloch well enough. He was a kind and generous man who took a genuine interest in each one of them. Lucy was proud of her girls for not being selfish. They were mature enough to realize that Mr. Knobloch loved and respected their mother and made her very happy. It could only be the best thing for all of them.

But Siobhan, with her full red hair and animal eyes, with her long, lean limbs and determination, didn't give a hoot for the Schraeger girls. "Prudence, Thankful, Hope, and Grace," she rattled off their names. "Sounds like a bunch of dwarfs." She was not about to become chummy with any of them, least of all Prudy Schraeger. And she thought their mother, Lucy, acted like some sort of queen, having to have everything perfect. "She never has a hair out of place, that woman. She makes me feel like I smell."

Siobhan's best friend, Annalise Jacobson, was the daughter of the tennis pro over at the Lake Club. The Jacobsons were not members, and Annalise didn't live on the lake but in the village of Nogowogotoc, which was another world entirely, but Siobhan felt she had much more in common with Annalise than she did with Prudence Schraeger.

Siobhan still agreed to a formal Sunday lunch, for she liked having time with her father alone. She was a young woman now, but still his little girl, trapped between these two worlds, confused by her dual desires to control and escape her father's household. Herman had abandoned his large, carved chair at the head of the table and faced his daughter now in an attempt to be more casual. Siobhan had become somewhat sullen since he had started seeing Lucy Schraeger, and he wanted to reassure his daughter that their special love would never change.

From the dining room they could hear the steady whir of the push mower that was trimming along the path where the big riding mower wouldn't go. The sound of humming could be heard coming from the kitchen, a comforting clatter of pans on the stove, then water splashing in the soapstone sink, the smell of chicken broth mixed with celery. Siobhan was eager to ask her father something, but she was afraid he would be stodgy about it.

Herman had decided to tell Siobhan of his plans in full daylight, hoping the openness of the hour would make his revelation seem more normal. After they finished dessert, she was willing to walk with him down to the lakefront. He wanted to sit on the stone bench there beneath the giant maple. Siobhan hadn't been able to speak her mind during lunch, and the expanse of lake before them now opened a space for conversation.

The Schraeger home was not far from Yelping Hill, built on the same side of the bay, and Herman was sorry, momentarily, that he could not gaze toward Lucy's property, and imagine her sitting by a window. It was harder to long for someone who already lived by your side.

"I want to get my ears pierced, Papa," Siobhan informed him. "Like Annalise. I'll get them done professionally," she added, picturing the thin gold hoops she would select, how she would look like a gypsy.

Herman was somewhat relieved by this diversion of subject, though he worried that Lucy would not approve. He could almost hear her calling it "cheap." She would never let her own daughters pierce their ears. It was something that poor people did in undeveloped countries, or old women from the old country with their sagging lobes. Herman's own mother had had pierced ears, but he didn't know if it was proper for Siobhan. Instead of getting into a confrontation, he postponed the issue and said, "We'll see."

"I hate it when you say – We'll see."

He was almost afraid of his daughter, as if a comment were a match that could ignite the bonfire of her hair. She had become so headstrong and impulsive since her mother's death. When he looked at her now, tall as a woman, he could barely conjure up the little girl who kept field mice in her pocket. He was afraid of the intensity of feeling between them, which had turned from adoration to anger. He was unable to guide her now with his gentle coaxing and stories of example, for she no longer held him in the same regard. She was critical, sharp, to the point of cutting, and he was her most obvious victim, because he was all she had.

"I thought you wanted me to try and look more ladylike," she reminded him, "wearing skirts and all." She was not wearing a skirt now, just a baggy pair of blue-jean overalls, and yet she still looked startlingly feminine, with her developing figure and full mouth.

"I just want to talk it over with Lucy."

"Why her?"

"Because we've decided to get married. Not for a while," he added quickly, "but in the spring, nine months from now."

Herman was surprised when her initial response was one of easy enthusiasm. "Oh, that's nice. You shouldn't be alone."

Almost out of gratefulness he responded, "I haven't been alone since the day you were born."

She gave a little laugh, not bothering to correct him about the biological fact of her birth having little to do with him. She did resent being told in this way. Why hadn't he asked her opinion first? Or didn't he care what she thought. Certainly her father and Lucy Schraeger could have no intention of raising any more children, so why didn't they continue as they were, side-by-side, as neighbors. "Where are you going to live?"

He was hesitant to respond, for he realized how important Yelping Hill was to her. It was as if the big old house continued to mother her in her mother's absence, and yet perhaps it was time for a change. "Lucy thought we could renovate their playroom on the third floor, do over the bathroom up there, so you'd have your own suite. You could pick out the material and furniture, though you might want to bring your own bed."

"You're going to let her put me in the attic? Mother loved this house. Don't you even care?" She was standing now, flushed, and as he rose to face her, she seemed almost fearsome.

He didn't know how to speak of this. He wanted this new life with the woman he loved, and yet he still wanted to have his daughter, for things to go on as they always had. He didn't want to make a choice. He thought he could have it all, but even Siobhan knew that that was impossible. Everything would change and it was awful.

"How can you marry her," Siobhan said with disgust. "Everybody knows she's a Catholic."

This comment shocked him. The one thing he wouldn't tolerate was intolerance. Dana and he had not raised their daughter in any church, but they had always tried to impart a feeling of reverence for nature, and a respect for each individual's personal relationship to God. He had never been a particularly religious man, in fact he had often joked that he was a devout atheist, but now he announced, "I'm going to convert. I've already begun private instruction. It means a great deal to Lucy."

"Are you going to take her name on too?" Siobhan felt like she was being disowned, tossed out. She had played the part of little wife for so long, bearing the burden of his loneliness, that she felt she had certain rights. She had come to think of the house as her own. And it was not just the house, but the land, the barn, her animals, Grumpy. Where would they put the chickens and rabbits? She loved gathering flowers and berries from the gardens, and she didn't mind that the place was not so orderly – she rather liked the way they kept it now, without much help. She liked being in charge, the mistress of the manor. Their cook was all right because she stayed in the kitchen, and honored Siobhan's often strange requests – pink soup, which was a beet purée with Ulrich cream, or banana soufflé. Siobhan liked white radish sandwiches and homemade pickles, fresh pea pods, no lima beans, but she especially loved their fresh, home-baked bread. Their cook always let her pound her fist into the rising dough when it was time, and the comforting smell of the cooling loaves was another thing she would probably never have if they moved over to Lucy Schraeger's.

"I'm going to leave the house to you, but I thought we'd rent the place during the summer months, until you can use it for your own family."

"My *own* family? And who are they? What's my real name, anyway?" She wanted to break his heart at that moment, just as he apparently was willing to break hers.

"Your real name?" he repeated. "We never took it away from you, Siobhan Alair. Did you know your first parents were Irish? Irish Catholics?" Siobhan was silent as he went on. "If there's one thing I've noticed about the Irish, when they want to, they can go straight to the top. They've got the fire and determination, but that can misfire too – anger, belligerence, intemperance – it can ruin a person. You'll have to pick your path."

"You can send me away to boarding school, but I'm not going to live over there." She clasped this statement shut like a snap-lid purse.

"I want you to be with me. You're my only child."

Ha, she thought. Soon he'll have all sorts of daughters crawling all over him – little Grace had always charmed him – and there wouldn't be room for her anymore. "Go buy yourself a new family."

Herman caught her by the arm and held her, for he thought he could feel her whole world coming loose. She was nothing but flying parts. He loved her more than any other creature in the entire world. His eyes were pleading with her, but she could see his weakness – for his love was mixed with tenacious dread, as if she were standing on some high, dangerous precipice, and he could neither walk away nor let her jump. He could only try to bargain, and so he agreed that yes, she could probably pierce her ears, if there was a sanitary way to perform the operation.

She seemed cheerful for a moment, for she had gotten what she wanted, but she quickly realized it was not much of a trade. She pictured Lucy's well-lit home, each girl playing an instrument. She always thought it somewhat obscene, the way Prudy stuck the cello between her legs, displaying her thick German ankles. She only felt sorry for him in his poor utter ignorance, for despite his supposed brilliance, he was a stupid, stupid man. He had no idea of all he would have to give up if he became Lucy Schraeger's husband.

She yanked her arm away and ran up the hill. Flinging herself down on her beloved bed, she buried her face in the long, soft pillow. The nubs of the bedspread pressed into her skin. She sobbed, looking at the familiar wallpaper her mother had picked out so long ago, French blue lilacs with pale green leaves and yellow ribbons weaving through all of it. There was a worn hook rug by the side of her bed that pictured three kittens playing with a ball of yarn. Her sore, burning eyes looked over all the pictures of animals she had pinned to her walls, her horse show ribbons, the silver cups she'd won sailing and playing tennis, her scrapbook on the top of her bookshelf, the ivory-covered prayer book her mother had left her and the lamp with the porcelain figurines, the breezy dotted Swiss curtains and her collection of nests, the feathers she had stuck in the windowsill. Did her father really think he could pack all of this up and move it over to Lucy Schraeger's?

Trying to make up, Herman took Siobhan and Annalise to a Milwaukee Polo Club match the following Sunday. The sport was enjoying a bit of a revival, and Herman liked to tease Siobhan that it would be the perfect sport for her – with her naturally aggressive nature and equestrian ease, she would be a disarming contestant.

The Milwaukee team was playing a group from the north side of Chicago, including a newcomer, Joshua Liebenau. His sponsor, Elena Schultz, had purchased a string of the most agile thoroughbreds – their quickness and sensitivity certainly helped his game, though he also had a natural seat, and swung his mallet with precision as the players and horses began to warm up. Elena's geldings all had Italian names, Zucchero, Cavallo, Oggie Pommerigio, an affectation that Isabella Wells couldn't help but enjoy. "I wonder if they have any called Malo or Stupido."

Isabelle was in the bleachers with Lolly Jones, and she pointed out Elena's caramel-colored suit. The tall, stout woman was pacing back and forth alongside the boards, as if waiting to walk out one of her horses, which was actually the last thing on her mind, for she had several stable hands for that essential chore. The horses got terribly hot and lathered and had to be carefully cooled, their legs rubbed and wrapped, their tails meticulously tied. Everything about the game was sleek and precise, fast paced and very expensive.

The men changed horses every chukker. Most of the players had a good deal of heft, with the exception of the Argentinean, an eight-goal player for the Milwaukee team. The Raifstanger brothers had hired him, and he had kept their team in the lead for the past two seasons, though Leonard Faithorne was also a fairly high goaler, and the Raifstangers were an intimidating pair. The Milwaukee men wore dark brown jerseys, while Chicago sported a more visible red.

"Elena's eight years his senior," Isabelle told Lolly. "Apparently she doesn't let him out of her sight."

"That must be tiring on the eyes," Lolly commented, concentrating on the action as the ball was pitched between the two ranks of players. As soon as the ball had left the umpire's hand there was a whirling commotion until the ball was smacked and the horses went racing down field. How they kept from killing each other, Lolly didn't know. It was unnerving. Neither of them understood the rules of right of way, why the two mounted umpires kept blowing their whistles, but it was all very exciting, and Isabelle felt exuberant, especially when Miguel Moreno swung his mallet and sent the ball flying into the goal – the audience rose in unison.

Bells sounded from the timekeeper's table to begin and end each seven-minute period. Concessionaires were selling paper cups of iced lemonade and dusty peanuts in the shell. Lolly and Isabelle shared a bag. It was almost as exciting as a baseball game. Chicago scored, and then once again. A feeling of dismay spread over the audience, until Leonard rode in and made a terrific save, leaning over the left side of his horse and banging the ball backward.

"You'd think Helen would come and watch Leonard. He's wonderfully good, don't you think?" Isabelle spoke proudly of her brother-in-law, who was much slimmer than either of the Raifstanger brothers. "I wouldn't want to be carrying one of them on my back – look at that poor horse." It was running its heart out. Isabelle was almost grateful, for the horse's sake, when the bell was rung for half time.

All the young people got to run out onto the field to press back the divots, bits of turf that had been whacked by ill-aimed mallets. It was fun for Siobhan to be out on the large, flat expanse, to see it from that perspective. She and Annalise were too old to play horses, but she felt as if she could suddenly whinny, shake her mane, and gallop off. Instead, they walked back to the bleachers, awkwardly aware of their tall, thin bodies.

As the second half began, the Chicago team was a point ahead, an unexpected lead, especially since they had the disadvantage of being visitors. When the Wisconsin horses ran out from the south end of the field, Annalise stood and yelled. She had a crush on Miguel Moreno. The girls' golden earrings glistened in the sun, which was baking the horses and spectators alike. Siobhan liked the intensity of the summer heat. It made her feel safe, cozy and comfortable. She had pulled her long hair into a ponytail, and now it whipped back and forth across her shoulders as she followed the action. She loved the swoop of the mallet cracking into the ball, how far it flew on solid contact, the thundering race of the horses flying down field.

But then in the sixth chukker, galloping toward a cluster of action, Liebenau changed his course, cutting across the line, and a hard-hit ball from Faithorne's mallet struck Zucchero right on the forehead. Stunned, the horse staggered and fell to its knees while the rider went catapulting over its neck, dragging the set of double reins with him. The horse broke free and danced off to the side, while one of the boys rushed out to catch him. The rider lay still on his back, his mallet awkwardly twisted above him. Several men raced out from the sidelines while a hush fell over the audience. Only Elena Schultz could be heard, bossing several men. Apparently they needed a doctor on the field. Was there a doctor in the stands? A young gentleman ran up and down the bleachers, calling for professional help, and when no one else responded, Lolly ran down the planks and leapt onto the track.

The other riders had moved off and several had dismounted. Leonard was trying to remember exactly what had happened, how Liebenau could have ridden right into the path of the ball.

The stunned horse had apparently recovered, but Lolly was afraid the rider might not have fared as well. He was lying there moaning, but unconscious. She was afraid he might have damaged his spinal column. "Don't move him," she instructed. "Don't take off his helmet. You might make it worse. We've got to call for help – for an ambulance."

"Are you a doctor?" the man in charge asked.

"I just wouldn't want to be responsible . . . "

"*You're* not responsible. Do you know the rules of this game? If a player is injured, you give him fifteen minutes, and if he can't get up, well then the game goes on." Turning to several men behind him he said, "We'll have to use a substitute player."

"But his neck might be broken," Lolly persisted. "You could damage his spinal cord. Can't you at least wait until a doctor gets here?"

"And disappoint this crowd?"

"Would you move Mr. Raifstanger, if he were hurt?"

The man turned away from her, shaking his head. "Mr. Raifstanger wouldn't fall off his horse."

CHAPTER FORTY-THREE

*E*ver since the wedding, Lucy had been carrying around this dreamy quality – it seemed to soften her edges, loosening the knots of her usual industry. She accepted her present happiness as if it were beyond her, or trailing behind, like a train of exquisite memories – the scent of beeswax candles mixed in with gardenias, placed on every windowsill, how the candles grew brighter as it darkened outside, how the tones of the French horns had sounded, beginning that slow, heart-rending processional – little Grace stepping out with her basket of petals, all four of her daughters like white waterlily flowers floating on an evening pool, each wearing a circlet of rosebuds and fragrant stephanotis, sprigs of Daphne and creamy sweet peas. Lucy remembered the sparkling clean windows of the chapel, for she had cleaned them herself, inside and out, as a majestic gesture of Lenten penance – how the blue dusk had shone behind each simple candle, making the chapel glow. She remembered her daughters scattered about the steps of the church – like dogwood blossoms, reaching – beneath the soft, dark moistness of the evening hour and the sounding of the bell.

The only one who hadn't quite fit into the pretty picture was Siobhan. She had worn a long black dress to the wedding and high-heeled shoes. Joey Ulrich was her escort, and he looked particularly handsome in his crisp evening clothes, his straight blond hair slicked back. He had given Siobhan a yellow diamond brooch, and there was some concern that the glamorous young couple was trying to upstage the bridal pair. Lucy had felt some resentment.

Before moving out of Yelping Hill, Siobhan had gone through her mother's things and found a small square bottle of perfume – it smelled of tuberose. Siobhan treasured this little black bottle because it seemed to contain the essence of her mother, sweet smelling, yet natural, like climbing roses cascading down. Sometimes she would pull out the stopper to take a whiff, and sometimes she would dab a little on a handkerchief, close her eyes, and sleep with it, but that evening she put a streak of her mother's perfume behind each ear, and over the pulse points of her inner elbows as Annalise had told her. She even dabbed on a little lipstick and piled her hair on top of her head, feeling like a full-blown rose herself – rich, ripe, and deeply red.

When she walked into the living room that night in her high-heeled shoes, which made her almost as tall as her father, little Grace trailing in awe behind, Herman was standing over by the radio, adjusting the volume to a new Cole Porter recording. He had his back to Siobhan, but as she came up behind him, he stopped, lifted his head, transported back to some other realm. He smelled the essence of Dana, and as he swung around, eyes wide and smiling, he took in the vision of his daughter. She was indeed a part of the woman he'd loved. "I like your hair that way," he complimented Siobhan, though it made her look a bit too mature. Turning to face the rest of the room, Siobhan laced her arm through her father's.

"Why don't we have our sherry," Lucy suggested. Their ritual aperitif was set out on a silver tray, with the two exclusive glasses, amber filled, their evening sacrament, nearly defiled now by Siobhan's display. Siobhan sat down next to her father, as if she meant to help herself, but perceiving this impulse, Lucy pushed the tray out of reach. Imagine thinking of such a thing in front of little Gracie.

No matter how hard Herman tried, Siobhan felt outside the happy ring of Schraeger women, with their family discussions, singing in rounds before the open fire – "White coral bells, upon a slender stalk, lilies of the valley deck my garden walk. Oh, how I wish that I could hear them ring. That will happen only when the fairies sing." Siobhan liked to change that ending to – That will happen only when the Schraegers shut up.

"Were we at your and Daddy's wedding?" Hope asked her mother as the family sat together before dinner.

"We didn't exist," Thankful retorted, which was a strange thing for the two youngest to hear, for they could hardly imagine such a thing.

"You were in heaven," Lucy explained, "waiting to be born. But you girls will always be my littlest angels."

Siobhan peered into the fire and made a face.

Lucy saw her expression and wished she wouldn't scowl so. It was difficult to follow Herman's advice, which was simply to ignore Siobhan a little, not to make such an effort. Lucy didn't understand that Siobhan was used to feeling special, set apart, but Lucy was particularly sensitive to the slightest negative mood. She even felt that Herman shifted his personality whenever Siobhan appeared. He became oddly self-conscious, overly friendly, not his relaxed and normal self.

Prudence seemed heavier and more dour than ever, and Siobhan wondered why her mother didn't enforce a diet and make her wash her hair. Perhaps the Queen could not tolerate competition of any sort, not even from her own misshapen daughters. The girls were always eager to plop themselves down before dinner and pack their cheeks with the provided nuts. These days the family inevitably ended up talking about the war – Hitler invading Britain, and now the U.S.S.R., how difficult it was being German-American with this detestable war darkening Europe.

"Am I a Kraut?" Hope asked, and Thankful chimed in – "Hotsi Totsi, another Nazi."

Lucy had to hush her daughters up, for this was a serious subject. She and Herman believed that the Nazis were only a very small group who had managed to get control. The majority of the German people were being duped by men of the lowest instincts.

"Hate and fear are far more forceful than reason," he explained. "People are weak and they're easily swayed."

"You don't know how lucky we are in America," Lucy said. "But Germans still have much to be proud of – look at Goethe," she suggested. "Look at Mozart and Strauss."

"Beethoven and Bach," Prudy added.

"We must keep their spirit alive," Herman told them. "Music and beauty and the world of thought."

"I'm glad I'm not a German," Siobhan announced. She knew her stepmother had a temper, though Lucy never displayed it in front of her husband, keeping that steady, false composure for his sake alone. Siobhan wanted to rattle her, to get a real response, but Lucy's only response to this pronouncement was to pray for peace in the world. She asked the whole family to bow their heads, to pray against the forces of evil.

Even Siobhan had been dragged to Catholic Mass several times, and to her surprise, she found that she rather liked it. The smell of the incense, the priests in their robes, the dim light illuminating the stained-glass windows, it all seemed other-worldly. She even liked the way Father Gregory spoke in Latin so no one knew what he was saying – Pater noster, qui es in cælis sanctificetur nomen tuum.

The little girls squeezed their eyes shut tight while their mother prayed. Siobhan looked about from one to the next, until she met Prudy's stare.

Prudence Schraeger did not think the Germans were all that wrong. She knew her stepfather was not a real Catholic, and she liked to imagine the army taking him away. She thought of him as unclean, though she was always overly polite to him.

The four Schraeger girls were meticulously trained when it came to table manners, except perhaps for little Grace, who was still learning by example. The girls all knew to put their napkins in their laps at the beginning of the meal, and to ask, "May I pick the violets?" if they wanted to use their fingers. They all had the same evening prayers and the same Advent rituals, the same deeply instilled sense of order, which made them all comfortable in continuity, but Siobhan felt awkward at the large dining table, which showed even a thumbprint if you dared touch its sheen. Everyone sat so properly, no elbows, no singing, no talking with food in the mouth, no excessive laughter. No slurping, no real enjoyment. Lucy even warned her daughters not to chew too loudly, as if you could control the texture of your food. Once, Thankful spilled her glass of milk, and it ran straightaway for the crack between leaves. All the girls ducked under to watch it spill, and Siobhan was almost grateful, fascinated by the ghost-like mark the milk left on the dark mahogany wood.

Siobhan often found her stepmother's conversations rather limited. There were many things they were not allowed to discuss at the table. Whenever Siobhan was asked a specific question she felt she was being put on the spot. Thankful wanted to know about the pets Siobhan had left behind. Despite the painfulness of the subject, Siobhan was eager to recite the list of animals she had once loved and cared for – there had been seventeen chickens, three roosters, four rabbits, a goat, *and* a pig, and of course her Morgan, Grumpy, who now had to be boarded at a riding stable. They'd had two spaniels, Happy and Lucky, and a boxer pup who was hit by a car. The Schraegers had only a lame and cranky Alsatian who rarely got off his rug.

"I had a pet one time," little Grace whispered.

"Oh?" Siobhan answered. "What was that?"

She answered almost inaudibly, "I had a firefly." Even Lucy had to laugh.

The children were all supposed to eat everything on their plates, members of the Clean Plate Club, but Siobhan hated slimy foods, and refused to eat eggs of any sort. She did not like seafood, and eggplant was disgusting – she almost gagged when it was brought around. She had to fiddle-flip her portion into her napkin and then go excuse herself and flush it away. She detested tapioca pudding, with those snot-like clots, revolting. The Schraeger cook seemed to pride herself on British fare, boiled turnips, mashed rutabagas, while Lucy reminded them of all the poor starving people in Europe who had so little to eat. That seemed a gluttonous reason to stuff oneself. "Why don't we send them our food," Siobhan suggested. "Do we have to hog it all?"

"Don't say *hog*."

"But Siobhan's right, we really should send more packages." Herman reminded Lucy of how appreciative her relatives had been when they received that last box of provisions.

Lucy agreed, they should share as much as possible, but that shouldn't prevent them from eating well themselves. She liked to begin the evening meal with a soup course, and tonight it was Siobhan's favorite – cream of fresh pea.

Siobhan's hair began to collapse from its perch as she leaned over her soup plate and scooped spoonful after spoonful into her mouth.

Prudy looked over at Hope, lifting her eyebrows with a smirk.

"What's so funny?" Siobhan asked.

"Nothing's funny, exactly," Prudy answered, looking to her mother for help. "It's just that you're supposed to tip your bowl away from you."

"So you don't appear ravenous, my dear."

"But I'm hungry, for a change."

"I thought it was so you didn't spill on your clothes," Thankful piped up, and Gracie added, "I *can't* tip my soup!"

"Manners are like customs," Lucy admitted. "Often we don't know their origins. Like the Christmas tree or curtseying."

"In Ethiopia they eat with their hands," Herman put in. "The Russians belch at the end of a meal to show their appreciation."

"Can you imagine if they did that here?" Lucy said to her daughters, thinking it a rather vulgar choice to use for illustration.

"If it's not really right or wrong, what difference does it make?" Siobhan wanted to know.

Prudence turned to Hope and whispered loud enough for everyone to hear, "Didn't her mother teach her anything?"

Siobhan let her spoon clank into her bowl. She wanted to take her water glass and fling it at Prudy, but instead she knocked her chair aside and ran from the table. "At least I'm thin!" The rest of the family just sat there.

As soon as Siobhan had her back against her bedroom door, guarding her third-floor territory, all she could think was – I hate you, *I hate you!* All of them, including her father.

Downstairs, Lucy shuddered. What a display. Prudy had only wanted to show Siobhan how to do it properly. Someday it might matter. But Herman had a different opinion. "Kindness, you know, is much more important than table manners."

Lucy quickly chimed in, wanting to agree with her husband, "I think you all can be a bit more charitable with Siobhan," as if Herman's daughter were a house guest who had to be offered the last muffin.

But Siobhan, still listening to their stupid conversation, didn't want any part of them, their food, or their company. She slammed her fists into her thighs and bit the insides of her cheeks. It was then that she noticed her garter snake. Even in the safety of his glass terrarium he was disturbed by her upset, and began to wind himself around the piece of driftwood planted there in the sand. The snake had been a big concession for the Queen, who never allowed reptiles or rodents in her house. Perhaps she thought she would be safe with him upstairs in the attic, but now Siobhan thought to take her pet snake downstairs.

As she tiptoed down the carpeted steps, the small, black snake threading through her fingers, she could hear the girls chirping over their dessert. Thankful said that she wished Siobhan would come join them. Fat chance, Siobhan thought, creeping into Prudence's room. She rarely made a visit to this posh sanctuary, decked out in dusty rose. Siobhan tucked the snake down deep in the covers of Prudy's bed, pulling the top sheet tight so he wouldn't escape. Then she heard Lucy saying their end-of-meal grace, what a backward family. She replaced Prudy's book on the coverlet, then dashed back up to her room.

It was not long before she heard all four girls coming upstairs. Prudy had her own bathroom, and Siobhan had to grin as she listened to the water being run then turned off, Prudy humming, "*Oh my darlin', oh my darlin', oh my dar-lin' Clementine . . .*" With the mind of a nine year old, Siobhan thought. She could even hear the click of her bedside table lamp as she lay down, the fat girl moaning in comfort as she stretched herself out in the dark.

But then Prudy must have felt something move – something separate – and then it was as if she had been seized from a waking nightmare she couldn't get away from, for the snake slithered right along the inside of her leg. Prudy screamed, but she could hardly scream loud enough or sweep herself clean or get far enough away – Siobhan clapped her hands together, silently, Yes! But then she heard a crash and a gathering commotion. All because of her harmless little snake. Think of how frightened he must be. But then there were more emphatic tears, a great deal of sobbing, accusations that included Siobhan's name, and suddenly she worried about the repercussions. She lay perfectly still and pretended to be asleep when her father came into her room.

A family conference was called the next evening. Siobhan sat alone in the big leather armchair, while the four Schraeger girls sat together in silence on the couch, ankles crossed, heads down. Prudy alone felt Siobhan should be punished, for Prudy had smashed into her bedroom mirror and cut herself in three places. Dr. Rose had come and lifted a sliver from her thigh. He had bandaged her nose in such a way that she looked even more ridiculous than usual.

"If we're all going to get along," Lucy began, smoothing down her blue-gray skirt, and Siobhan quickly thought – *you would die*, "then we're all going to have to be a little more tolerant," *and less ugly and stupid*. "We've been thrown into a difficult situation. I'm not afraid to recognize that this is not easy for any of us, least of all Siobhan," *who would rather eat mud than chow with this troop*. "If she does things differently, it's not for us to judge. But I won't have," *my daughter taking any blame*, "open warfare in my home." *Note, she says my home, not ours, because it isn't mine and never will be*. "We must all keep our sense of humor," Lucy continued, and Siobhan had to pinch herself – *What a laugh. She's about as funny as swallowing an ice cube*. "What I want is for you girls to be friends," Lucy concluded. *Why doesn't the idiot say anything. Why does he always let her take charge*.

But Herman had been thinking things over at his own pace. He was not afraid to let Lucy have her say, reserving his own comments. He spoke calmly and yet firmly as he tried to make his stepdaughters understand what a big change this had been in Siobhan's life. "It wasn't easy for us to leave Yelping Hill," he began, looking first at Prudence, and then at each one of them. "Think if you had to give up your home and move. Look at that window seat, with its nice, soft pillows, and those leaded windows above there – think of all the games that you've played right here. Would another house suit you better?"

Thankful shook her head no, afraid they would all have to move and start over, just because Prudy had been mean.

"We've all had one big thing in common," he looked at Hope now, and then to little Grace. "We've all lost someone we dearly loved. You girls loved your father more than any other person in the entire world. I know that. And Siobhan loved her mother, and lost her too. Parents can't be replaced." Thankful started to sob, and Lucy also dabbed at her eyes. She was proud of her husband for speaking so frankly, for compassion was the only way to heal these hearts, compassion, understanding, and love.

"We're not two families against each other," Herman explained, "but a new family, all mixed up together. A little like the United States. We're a mish-mash of people, with different backgrounds and beliefs, but your mother and I do love each other and we want a peaceful home. Can you understand that? Can we try, despite our differences?"

Prudence frowned, for she wanted a formal apology, and no one was forcing that from Siobhan. Instead, Herman added, "There are going to be times when you have to fight, that's natural. We can't always be good. But let's try to get this out of our systems and put all hands on the table. What do you say. Why don't we go over to The Kiltie right now and get a hot fudge." A cheer went up from the three youngest girls, who were eager to drown their sad feelings with sweets. Thankful came over and took Siobhan's hand and said, "Sorry, Mister," pulling her up from her chair. Siobhan liked her best, and said, "Thanks," to her, though the girl didn't know if she were shortening her name or actually, truly grateful.

CHAPTER FORTY-FOUR

No matter how consistently Lucy Knobloch and countless others prayed, there was no peace in the world. There was only more aggression. The war continued like a roaring disease, striking new parts of the body, and then on December 7, 1941, the nation was jolted from its wary state of gloom and sprung, fully clothed, with arms and ammunition into active participation in the war.

Alden Faithorne had enough credits to finish his senior year at Yale after the first semester, and he decided that he would enlist. His parents were both reminded of a time when they too were filled with purpose. But Helen feared for her eldest son, for he had never been physically assertive. She knew Merrick could take care of himself – he was naturally alert – but Alden had a dreamy, artistic quality, and she believed he was too naive to understand the nature of the enemy. He was too trusting and good-humored, while this war was bringing out the very worst, the most hideous aspects of human nature.

But there was no stopping him now. He was pulling away from his family's protective circle, away from the privileges of Yale University and Nogowogotoc Lake. Perhaps for the first time in his life, Alden felt like he was one of the boys, stripped down like all the rest, inspected by the army doctors – one passing in front, the other behind – and he was pronounced fit for service, whole, a part of something immensely important. He was no longer his mother's dear child, or his father's *cum laude* student – he was simply a tall, thin, handsome nobody.

Perhaps because of this anonymity, he allowed himself a certain freedom now, ignoring the rules of his own good upbringing. He was traveling south to a base near Savannah, and when he saw two pretty women on the train, he felt like teasing them. The taller one, who sat on the aisle, struck him as very glamorous, with her dark, wavy hair and long, thin legs. She wore a silky-looking navy polka-dot dress, and the sight of it made him feel rather giddy, despite his discomfort on the prickly cushions and his dislike of the train's filth. He did not know what to say to these two, but he could tell they were aware of his staring, and their giggling encouraged him.

The blonde woman on the far side leaned forward and broke the ice. "You going overseas, soldier? What do you think of the South so far?"

Alden was shy when it came to women, but he bent forward and looked out their window, as if they might have a different view. "It's a pleasing climate," he admitted, "but look at those wretched hovels." A scattering of pickaninnies were waving up at the train. "Doesn't it depress you?"

"Even our mansions have an aura of decadence," the blonde responded with her heavy accent, and both girls laughed, for honestly, was that all this Yankee could perceive? It was one of those glorious winter days that only the South could bring forth in January. The sky was a perfect blue. The sun was shining and the winter grass was a brilliant green. Even the camellias were in bloom. Why didn't this Yankee notice that?

"How do you manage to get any studying done when it's so nice outside?" he tried again, for he could see they were both probably college students.

"You mean, how can we possibly work in such a sultry, debilitating climate?" she rephrased his question, and they giggled again.

"I've heard that most southern girls won't take a refreshing swim if it means getting their hair wet."

"I guess he'd rather cuddle up with some old, wet lap dog," the talkative one said. Alden wanted to hear the prettier girl speak, but she remained rather aloof. He could not help looking at the open toe of her stylish shoe as she swung it slowly up and down in rhythm with the Pullman's clacking.

Finally he remembered his manners and thought to introduce himself, holding out his hand. "Alden Faithorne, from Wisconsin," he said, and the dark-haired girl, Mona French, gave him a look that said – Is that so?

"Are you taking this train to Savannah?" he asked her.

She turned her big brown eyes his way and said, "This train only goes to Savannah."

When Alicia found out that her old friend Biddy Hawkshurst Braeger was having a brunch after the christening of her first granddaughter, she was deeply offended, for she had not been invited. It didn't matter that Alicia hadn't been anywhere for quite some time. Wasn't that all the more reason to include her? Alicia even went so far as to ring Biddy up, with the pretense of discussing cleaning help, and Biddy was all atwitter, trying to make up for the oversight.

"I simply must get you to come with us to Fish Fry at the club next week. We haven't seen you over there in ages, and everyone's always asking. It's really time we – "

"I never eat at the club anymore," Alicia interrupted. "I almost died of food poisoning over there. They leave their tartar sauce out all week. I'd get a taster if I were you."

That evening she told her housekeeper that she would be gone for a little while, and then she locked herself into her bedroom. She actually barricaded herself in with several drawers from her highboy because she didn't feel safe. She felt oddly anxious, jittery, strange. Perhaps it was the weather, for it was sickly gray outside. Walking over to the tall French windows, she drew back the brocade curtains and a ripple of chills passed through her, for there on the glass were her father's initials, GDB. It looked like an old person with a shaky hand had etched the glass with a diamond. George Dufault Bosquet.

It was not a planned or conscious decision, simply an impulse that had been half asleep, lurking just beneath the surface, and now her desire came fully awake – she knew that she wanted to die. She went directly to the bathroom and started unscrewing bottles, swallowing pills, washing them down with brandy. No one wanted her around. No one loved her or cared. This house was cursed and she was too. She just couldn't take it anymore. Something had always been wrong with her. People could see it. She was set apart. She didn't feel comfortable with anyone. The pills fell into her hand like candy, colorful, slippery, tasteless pills. "Give me some peace," she whispered.

But then, looking at her drowsy face in the mirror, she thought she saw her mother. The woman was laughing, a high, chortling laugh that astonished her with its lack of frugality, as if she meant to spend all of her mirth on Alicia, but it wasn't funny. It was horrid. Her mother had a mass of fiery red hair and pale, pale skin, but then suddenly her image changed, and she became this wrinkled hag, asking for money, demanding. "You're not my mother," Alicia spat at the mirror. "I've never seen you before."

The old woman bared her breast, and there was a birthmark in the shape of a kitten's paw. In her stupor she did remember something – it made her feel nauseous. Where was the bed? It was a black-and-white memory, with a sickening slant of light. She stumbled into the bedroom, and the covers came off, melting in her hand. She remembered that woman in the doorway, a feeling of heaviness weighing her down – it was dark and she could hardly breathe – a sensation of circles getting heavier and heavier, until she heard, "That's enough, George." Then the circles became light and very far away, farther and farther away.

> *Dearest Alden,*
>
> *Already I realize what a smile and understanding can mean to the sick. I wouldn't take anything in the world for being in the Red Cross. For the first time in my life, I find myself thinking of others before myself. I never knew how much satisfaction could be derived from that.*
>
> *Your mother wrote me the sweetest letter. She is very dear, Alden, and she loves you terribly. So do I! She said that she wanted to share all the news and worries. You can't believe how happy it makes me to have her write to me. I love you so much, I certainly want to feel close to the only woman in the world whom you love better than me.*
>
> *It's awfully hard not knowing when you'll come back. It seems that I'm the only one who believes you really love me. Even Sister wrote and said, "I do hope Alden is as wonderful as you say, for it seems odd that someone that in love with you, enough to be the real thing, didn't give you a diamond before he left." That hurts a little. I don't know why. I may not have a ring like a lot of other girls, but I know that I have you!*
>
> *Wiggle your toes for circulation. I'm afraid that you'll get trench foot. And don't forget to number your letters.*
>
> > *Always adoring,*
> > *Mona*

When Dr. Rose appeared at Topside, Joey and Morvan had broken down the door. Haven had to clear everyone away. He and Lolly rushed over to Alicia where she lay on the floor, wrapped up in the covers like some large cocoon. Lolly cradled Alicia's head, while Haven threaded a tube down her throat.

"She doesn't have much of a pulse," Lolly told him.

"Will she live?" Joey asked from the doorway. Siobhan was trying to hold him back. Alicia had taken bottles of codeine and sleeping pills, washing it all down with brandy. "Could she have swallowed all of that by accident?" Joey asked.

"Maybe she thought they were vitamins," the old housekeeper whispered, in an effort to protect Mrs. Ulrich's good name.

"She's been trying to drink herself out of a cold," Siobhan told her husband. They all knew that Alicia considered brandy a cure-all, but then so did half of Wisconsin.

"Lolly, have them wait downstairs. This might not be pretty." It looked like the patient was beginning to have abdominal contractions. Dr. Rose held her so she would not choke, and then everything she had swallowed in the past twenty-four hours came back up in a sour brew. Lolly rushed to moisten a washcloth.

"Don't worry," she said to Alicia. "You're going to be all right," quickly whisking away the soiled towels.

Alicia opened her eyes and Dr. Rose was there. "You're a very lucky woman," he said kindly. Coming from anyone else it would have had the tone of admonishment.

"People keep saying that, but they don't know." And yet seeing Lolly's soft form, her curly hair and the moisture that had pearled slightly on her upper lip, Alicia believed she might be lucky.

"I'll stay," Lolly offered, and Alicia nodded, grateful for once in her life. But she seemed to only have a very distant form of awareness, as if she were still in some clinging dream.

Haven touched Lolly's arm, and bent slightly to convey something to the nurse. He wanted to go reassure the family.

Joey Ulrich was extremely grateful that his mother was alive, but more importantly, would she want to live.

"She's a bit like a half-drowned kitten right now, that's clawed her way back," Dr. Rose explained, sipping the cup of black tea Mildred had brought him. "She'll have to have a lot of quiet. She may become manic, trying to compensate. She mentioned that her mother was here."

"Nobody was here," the housekeeper insisted. "She said she'd be gone for a little while, as if she had anywhere to go, poor thing. And then she locked herself into that bedroom. I don't like to snoop, but I heard her talking – talking to no one on this good earth. I thought she was getting scary. She *is* awful scary sometimes."

Lolly quickly changed the linens on the bed. She wanted to get her patient neatly tucked in, but then Alicia said, "He drowned himself. He was lying in the bathtub, and he was already stiff. I had to give him mouth-to-mouth."

"Hush," Lolly whispered, wiping her brow, but Alicia raised herself up on her elbows.

"There was a sign in the closet that read – FEAR. A closet of sheepskins."

"Your father died a long time ago," Lolly assured her. "No one's going to hurt you, not anymore."

"He was dead," she repeated, "but I brought him back to life."

"Why don't we take a nice warm bath," for that had always served to calm Alicia down. The small, heftier woman took Alicia under the arms while

Alicia went on in an excited vein – it was the nervous excitement of the extremely weary.

Everything seemed to have a greater tactile reality – Lolly's starched white shirt, the lip of the bathtub like a pearly shell, the oily enveloping water. Lolly eased her in, dampening her cuffs as Alicia groaned with a sigh of contentment but her mind kept racing on. "I always thought I had a beautiful mother," she shuddered as if trying to rid herself of some image, that rouged old lady with the burnt-orange hair, bright blue eye shadow and overdone lipstick melting into the cracks above her lips. "When I wouldn't give her money, she said terrible things, how she never wanted to be my mother anyway. She stood in the light and let him climb onto me. *Le Barbe Bleu*," Alicia said. "My father always read that, over and over. How I hated that story."

Mona dearest,

I am not going to propose by letter and have everybody feel that it was caused by the fact that I'm lonely over here. When I propose to pose the proposal, I propose to pose it in person. Oh, what prose.

Seriously, love is an intangible thing, and though it can outlast many material objects, it is of such a quality that it can never be forced. Let me draw an allegory: Take two young people and put them together under rather trying circumstances. During the brief time they know each other, they fall in love – the one completely, the other more so than he has ever been before. The two are admirably suited, everybody agrees, yet there is something hidden which keeps them apart. The man is not quite certain of himself. Perhaps he has an instinctive distrust of making decisions at a time when the obvious thing to do is so pressed upon him. But he begins to feel like a man who has been dealt a full house at poker and muffs the take because he was too cheap to put out the money to play the hand. He has not realized what happiness he held, perhaps because he did not have to fight to obtain it.

It's man's greatest desire to have a passionate and adoring wife, and this I will certainly have. Do you also dream of an easy-going half-hearted household handyman, building you a dream house to live in? I know I will be very proud of my energetic wife. Not all Southerners need to be prodded to do things, and I know you'll be a wonderful homemaker.

One thing does concern me. Won't your father be upset if you're not married in the Catholic Church? I don't mind that you were raised Catholic, as long as you are willing to convert. It is good that you and I are both open-minded, and won't let religion stand in the way of our union. Going to sleep now to dream about you.

Love from your lanky Yankee,
All-done

When Alicia woke the next morning, Lolly was still there, asleep on the chaise with the pink blanket pulled over her.

As soon as Lolly was fully awake, Alicia spoke in an excited vein – "I want to move out of here. I'm done with this place. Let Joey and Siobhan take over. I want to do so many things. Will you stay with me, can you? For just a little while?"

Lolly found herself agreeing, caught up in Alicia's exuberance. She could also see that Alicia truly needed her, and that was the only thing Lolly needed herself, not love so much, but necessity.

"I want to build a music theater, downtown," Alicia went on as if the idea had just occurred to her, and then, turning to the younger woman, she admitted, "You always took such good care of me. I was never very nice. Do you think I can change?"

"Lots of people change," Lolly said simply, running her hand over the soft bristles of Alicia's brush.

"I'm going to move down to the Hop House," Alicia decided. "It's really quite charming now that it's been cleaned up." It was a lovely little Tudor with leaded-glass panes and a window seat, old tiles and a very cozy kitchen. "With a few pieces of furniture, I think it could be perfect." Alicia was picturing the two of them there, how Lolly would make an evening fire in the hearth, and they would have a big soft rug, a couple of comfortable armchairs. They would sip hot cider while the snow fell outside and music played from the Magnavox.

Dear Alden,

Just to show you that I am true blue, ah is ritin to you on this blue stationery. You are my dream man, Alden. Please don't ever rub this star dust from my eyes.

Some of the men here call me "Georgia," and another lad calls me "Slim," strictly verboten, but we can act a little less professional when we have a party. Last night we made some punch and served it, trying to make everybody enjoy themselves. A few of the men seemed afraid of the women, big bullies too bashful to dance. But my Brazilian friends were there, and I danced a rumba with Pedro. He wants me to go back to Brazil with him, but I say I love America too much. He says – No, you love Alden! Very

*persistent. I wish you could know him, though he says he'd like to shoot
you, such a typical Latin.*

*Today a fellow walked up to my desk and started to pour his heart out.
He'd just arrived from Italy, and it seemed impossible to him that he was
still alive. He told me how they had just finished a terrific battle, when a letter came from his sweetheart, saying how she had married somebody else.
He was right pathetic, telling me about it.*

*When I think back to how wonderful Fate has been to us, putting us
both on that Savannah-bound train, don't things work out in a funny way?
Remember that night at the Cloister? You wanted to stop dating me, thought
it was unfair because you didn't love me enough to marry me? Sweetheart,
think if I'd agreed to that. It was there on that terrace I knew I loved you
more deeply and completely than I'd ever loved anyone.*

*My days are strung together by letters from you. I am living for that
leave. To my wonderful sweetheart,*

Mona

"How can you leave Dr. Rose?" Isabelle asked her. She was desperate to talk
Lolly out of this. But Lolly assured her it was a temporary situation, that there
were several other nurses who could step in to assist. "But that wouldn't be
the same," Isabelle argued. Suddenly she felt like an ugly, big-toothed horse,
turned out to a back pasture, not even a joy to behold.

Lolly knew the strength of Isabelle's desperation, and she wanted to free
herself from it.

"But I love you," Isabelle turned to her. The two of them stood between
the stone posts at the foot of the driveway, the name Broadoaks cut into the
square cement tops. Isabelle had thought that what they shared was permanent, but Lolly, despite her earthy appearance, was more of an illusive person.

The two women were both bundled up with hats and scarves. The temperature had dropped that week, and the winter woolens had just been taken out
of the cedar closet. Isabelle thought she could taste the medicinal camphor
smell of mothballs. She wanted to strip the leather gloves from her hands, to
lace her fingers together with Lolly's, to make some gesture of solidarity, but
Lolly turned away as she spoke.

"I love you too," she admitted, "but it's different for me. I'm different. I
love everything you stand for, all you've given me, your strength and firmness.
You've made me feel like I can do anything. You helped me become myself,
my best self, and now I have to keep on doing that. You can't just keep me
here."

"I'm not keeping you," Isabelle insisted, for that's exactly what she assumed Alicia would do.

"You're the finest person I know." Lolly turned back to face Isabelle, but looking up with her blue-gray eyes she had to admit, "I just can't love, like you do."

Isabelle turned toward the house and thought perhaps she would be sick. Her breathing was coming with difficulty, and she could smell something acrid in the crisp fall air. She felt as if she were inhaling some toxin – pains shot through the glands behind her ears and even her teeth began to ache. All her life wound down to this one realization, that no one wanted to be close to her.

"Neither of us can love men properly," Lolly followed the taller woman, "though of course I admire Dr. Rose."

"My writing will be nothing now," Isabelle said with downcast eyes, though Lolly wouldn't listen to such nonsense.

"You'll probably write more now with me gone."

Isabelle cast that comment off as if it were an insect with no right to land. This all seemed obvious, ludicrous, as simple as some nursery rhyme – *The maid was in the parlor eating bread and honey, along comes a neighbor and offers her more money.*

"You helped me," Lolly repeated. "And now I have to help her."

"Alicia always gets what she wants."

"Don't be jealous. It doesn't suit you. I won't do anything I don't want to do. Don't forget, you had a decent beginning, a good man for a father. Alicia and I had something else, and I have sympathy there. I can help her get over it. That's all I want to do. Besides, your sister was beginning to dislike me."

"My sister has her own life."

"And I have mine. You of all people should understand that."

Isabelle took one more glance at her friend – just a short, stubby woman in a brown overcoat. Then she turned toward the chestnut that stood by the carriage house near the hidden cistern, remembering how Kurtz used to open the lid for the sisters to gaze down into it, into that dungeon darkness – salamanders sprawled on the slimy surface of stone – how it sent the shudders up through her, even though she was stretched out on the warm, feathery grass, up in a world of brightness.

Chestnut burrs had recently fallen, their thorny shells split open. Isabelle stooped to pick one from the ground, and flicking off the shell, she rubbed the burnished nut across her mouth – cool, dark, oiled, smooth, the dry matte spot like a birthmark. How quickly little Helen had scampered around collecting them, gathering a shirt-front full, as if they made her wonderfully wealthy. The two sisters had raked a large dry pile of golden leaves to throne themselves, but Helen had always been sovereign.

Even now, Helen was organizing everyone, as if she were in charge of the war itself, getting women to do volunteer service work – canning, preserving, knitting mittens and socks, rolling bandages, collecting tinfoil, filling cheer packages for departing soldiers. Helen wore a star on either lapel for her two sons, Alden and Merrick. Yes, Helen was like a little general. "But she doesn't have to rule my life."

Lolly, who was walking down the gravel drive, thought she heard the word *ruin*.

CHAPTER FORTY-FIVE

*L*ucy Schraeger Knobloch rarely said a harsh word about anyone. When conversation tended toward gossip, she would set her mouth in such a way that said – Let's not lower ourselves. She knew it might limit one's conversation, but it was worth remaining charitable. "When you always see evil in others, you attract it to yourself." That was all she had to say on the subject.

But her daughter Prudence had a different attitude. "I think it's dishonest to act like everything's nice and everyone's fine, a *fine human being*," she repeated one of her mother's favorite phrases. What Lucy didn't realize was that Prudence was disturbed about many things, the worst of all being that she couldn't speak directly to her mother about anything real, anything that mattered.

Recently Trumbull had introduced her to "booze" and the other morning, when she was supposedly taking an overnight at Carol Faithorne's, Prudy woke up in the backseat of his two-tone Oldsmobile, and she couldn't remember what they had done, though she ached in this most unusual way and her clothes were in disorder. Prudence Schraeger was no longer an innocent little girl, and yet her mother refused to see her any other way, until something unusual happened. Both mother and daughter discovered they were pregnant at the same time. They both had morning sickness.

"Who are you to talk?" Prudy cried until the fluids ran from her nose. "It happened to you and Father!"

Lucy felt that she'd gotten nowhere. She had lived day in and day out, only to have life repeat itself. All of it, the architecture of her perfect reasoning, her entire moral structure, her personal code, the house of her future dreams and precious past remembrances, all of it was collapsing – nothing seemed to have any substance, not even the tiny embryo that had robbed her of her usual vitality. "What kind of life do you think you'd have," she asked her daughter quietly.

"What kind of a life did *you* have! Was it so horrible? Was it? Besides," the girl asserted, "I love him, and he loves me."

"Love," Lucy repeated the word, as if it were the name of some magical city she had visited once upon a time, but it had been ravaged, burned down. "You don't even know what love is."

It seemed as if the word itself had been soiled, smeared with meconium. But instead of getting out her polishing cloth to shine the edifice of her impeccable armor, she could only see her world crush like tinfoil in her hands. She cared very deeply for Herman, but she was no longer a young woman, and she felt as if her nourishing soil had been used and over used, that she could not sustain new life anymore, and then, as if she had willed it, Lucy began to bleed. She could feel that tiny being falling away, beyond her control, releasing itself in juicy clots, and she blamed herself for bringing it on, for not being a more courageous person.

Herman didn't want Lucy to go to Dr. Rose. He wanted her to see a specialist at Mt. Zion Hospital. The chief obstetrician there ordered a full hysterectomy, and the hormonal repercussions dropped Lucy into a sudden, jarring menopausal depression. She couldn't get out of bed.

Herman felt deeply saddened by their loss, but he had been working long hours at the tannery, and he had so many things on his mind. What was the meaning of one unborn child, when millions were being murdered.

Lucy had always been the perfect little wife, but now she was a perfect nothing. It was as if her body were stuck in mud, as if her limbs weighed a thousand pounds, instead of one hundred and seven. Herman kissed her dutifully every morning and evening, reassuring, kind. He believed she only needed to rest, but she could not think – she could not plan – she could barely stand a word.

She thought back over all of her efforts, and all of it seemed useless now. She had devoted her life to a man who had loved another woman, who had flaunted that love for everyone to see. She had allowed him to kill her son. She could have prevented their flying. He had been showing off for that vicious whore, but Lucy knew that she was no better – that she was also covered with sin. She imagined fouling her linens, too tired to rise – she imagined rubbing her hands in it, smearing herself with her own defecation, buttering her empty stomach and breasts.

When Constance came to visit, her buoyant mood was almost unbearable, like wincingly bright light. Lucy felt dull and unkempt in comparison, but she didn't care – she just wanted to protect herself from so much good cheer and vitality. Constance looked ten years younger, and Lucy doubted if she knew about Trumbull and Prudy, but her friend had not come to talk about that.

Settling herself down on the edge of the bed, Constance began, "Oh, *everything* has changed. Haven and I – " she beamed, but then she dared not finish, as if speaking of their love might scare the golden bird away. She played quietly with the lace work on Lucy's cuff, and then began again. "I just wanted you to know – I'm *so* happy. You can start over too. It's possible." Her eyes pleaded with her friend to get well, so that she too could partake in this new phase of life. "And you know, I have Lolly Jones to thank. Can you imagine, that fuzzy little girl? I always thought her somehow harmless. But he was mooning around so all winter, really heartsick, and then it all came out."

Lucy didn't have a response for this. Constance was happy because her husband had fallen for another woman? This supposedly made her glad? Lucy could not fathom such reasoning.

"Haven is so even tempered. The only time he ever raises his voice is to call in the dogs." Her husband was a lot like Lucy in that way, always on an even keel. He did not respond to the heaves of surf, but just kept gliding through. Now both of their lives had begun to leak, and yet it was not so bad, this shipwreck. It had brought her husband home.

Because of his present suffering, he had finally broken down and told Constance of his other more terrible grief when they had lost William, how he believed her love had died for him then, because he hadn't been able to save their child. He no longer felt like her husband. He had turned all his energy into his work, allowing himself this platonic relationship with a dedicated, pretty, lower-class girl. Lolly never expected anything. She only wanted to serve, to stand by his side. It had almost been better than marriage. But now she was gone, just like that, and many other feelings came back to overwhelm him, how he had always felt out of place here, as if he were some kind of impostor. "I'm lower class too," he had said to her. "Never good enough for your family. Such proper, fine, people – they wouldn't even give me a chance. If only you knew how I hated them."

"But isn't that wonderful?" Constance gaped. "He was able to admit that he hated them."

"How lovely," Lucy agreed.

"I was just so proud of him, don't you see? You have to let your feelings give you life. They can bring you back, I promise. Oh, everything has changed."

Constance could not describe the golden wash, the rush of emotions that had spread through her being when she realized her husband was the man she loved, not just the good, kind doctor who ran around helping and healing. Now that he had broken down, she saw him as a human being, as flesh and blood, so handsome, with his toasty skin and large, warm hands, a dusting of gray at the temples. "He doesn't want to live here anymore. He wants to move back to Chicago – we're going to open a clinic for poor children. We'll leave the house here for Trum and Pru. Isn't it amazing how life marches on?"

"So you know," Lucy said.

"I know." Constance smoothed out the top edge of the bed linens as if giving her personal blessing.

"Herman thinks he's part of that group," Lucy whispered, her eyes filled with dread, for she feared for her daughter and this sad, sordid union. She felt Trumbull Rose was the kind of man who could actually hate without feeling – there was no telling of what he was capable.

But Constance was not thinking of this. She had been floating on her own peach-colored stream when she had taken Haven's head in her arms, held him and wept over him. She was amazed at his manliness, even now, how smooth and yet virile he seemed. He had grazed over her, every inch of her skin, as if were a starving person.

When Constance rose from their conjugal bed, blessed by the oils of communion, it was as if each object her eyes touched upon had suddenly turned to love – the dressing table with its curved glass top, the wide window and the poplars beyond, the smooth silky ears of her little dog, Stuffy, even Cook, with her sagging and dough-like skin, powdered and plumped with love. Her hand skimmed over inanimate objects that were alive now with energy. Everything seemed part of some living whole – the banister, down to the dazzling carpet, the screen porch door with its endearing tear, the diving martins out over the lawn – even the water in the lake had turned to love.

"I think Trumbull will make a good husband." Constance had to remain optimistic. She felt Prudy would change him, fatherhood might – he could no longer remain so selfish.

But Lucy turned her head on the pillow and groaned, insisting that she had to sleep now. She couldn't tell her friend about the photos she'd found in Herman's desk, but ever since then she'd been having nightmarish thoughts, imagining terrible scenes – she kept seeing that terrified dark-haired boy, stripped and bound to a tree, another with his head bashed in, a Nazi insignia painted across his back.

Lucy feared for the health of her husband, for Herman had been losing weight, disturbed by his recent uncovering of at-home atrocities. The press only focused on the war crimes overseas, as if they didn't believe Americans were capable of prejudice. Herman had enough proof to expose several prominent Milwaukee businessmen, including two members of the Lake Club, and Herman himself was now being threatened. There had been talk of him losing his job. He was no longer able to concentrate.

And what if Prudence were involved somehow. What if Trumbull was merely using her. Lucy knew that her daughter was just as much in love as she had once been with Walter. But people did terrible terrible things, especially to the women who loved them. Lucy knew if you loved a man completely, if you turned your whole body and being over to him, he would have to degrade that attachment, as if love itself were a leeching force that could suck the life blood out of him. What was strange, even now, Lucy had to admit, was that she had found debasement empowering. It was as if her unholy self-righteousness had intuitively known that it had to be dragged by the sex and the soul through mud.

But now she believed that the Schraegers were doomed, that some curse had come over from the Old Country, sewn like counterfeit coin into the soiled underclothing of Great Great Grandfather Schraeger. He had bought his labor dirt cheap, and worked his men to the bone, squeezing the meat out of them to make sausage, the profits pumped back in, like a man his muscle, unsatisfied – but now that greed was corrupting her children and she was unable to lift her sword.

Prudence had been allowed to witness certain raids on the "Chosen People," as they called them, but Trumbull usually got Prudy drunk beforehand, so her memories were often vague. She remembered holding the greasy clothesline that bound a boy's hands – he was there on his back, lying on the floor while Trumbull shaved off his pubic hair. "Don't cut me," he pleaded.

But Trumbull only laughed – "Doesn't he know he's already been *cut?*" And then harshly to Prudy – "Get out your rosary, Mother." She had to get down on her hands and knees and wrap the beads around his wilted organ. "Now pray to your God," he instructed.

The next thing Prudence remembered was lying on the floorboards somewhere else, the raw scraped leather on the rounded toes of a man's brown boot tips visible. Bits of words or phrases washed back in her memory like dead fish floating in the foamy scum – "Let's feed her fat ass to that herb eater."

Trumbull Rose had no conscience or compassion. He simply needed to copulate, male or female, it didn't matter, the younger the victim the better. He simply needed to be encased, as if his member were his own small infant self, spurned by both father and mother, needing some physical, primal clutch to assure him that he was a man. He liked sticking Jews because they were so pathetically afraid. And they kept to themselves. They didn't seek publicity. After all, his bundt usually spared them death, unlike the masters in Germany, who went all the way with their sexual war games, shoving orifices full of explosives, gas. Trumbull only wanted to fill them with come, to stir their dead shit with his life-giving sperm.

"No," Lucy thought, writhing on her pillow, back and forth in a nightmare of thoughts. "No! Don't let this happen."

Four weeks later they found Herman Knobloch sitting in the driver's seat of his blue DeSoto, a bullet hole in the back of his neck. The car was parked on a deserted street in the industrial area of Milwaukee, and there was not a single clue that could help the investigation.

Trumbull and Prudy took over the main house on Hewitt's Point. Old Daddy Lionel now stayed in the guest house with his personal nurse. She told him, "That boy is dishonest. He lies right to my face." But Lionel didn't want to hear about it. He wanted to go out to the point and watch the sailboats racing. He liked to remember those times.

From the promontory, the nurse could see Trumbull in the family rowboat, how he did not bother maneuvering the boat so that Prudy could easily descend from the pier. She was holding a purse in one hand, a quart of raspberries in the other, and he told her, "Step in," refusing to put out a hand, though his wife was eight months pregnant. When she did step down, putting her weight in the flimsy boat, it bounced and rocked and she toppled backward, over the plank seating, twisting her ankle and bruising herself. "What a damn fool," he muttered. "Why didn't you grab on to the side?" Prudence didn't answer, but went limping up the hill to their unhappy home.

CHAPTER FORTY-SIX

*T*his isn't a criticism," Joey said to Siobhan as he snapped on his helmet and strapped himself into the low, sleek boat, "but couldn't you do something about those cats?"

Siobhan didn't give him a response, much less any encouragement for that day's race. It was early June, and "the itch" was in the lake, so no one was swimming. Besides, it was rather cool and windy – the water surface looked all scuffed up.

"Aren't you going to watch?" he asked.

She gazed out over the lake toward Yelping Hill. The auction would begin on the following day. "I think I'll go over to the house and say my last good-byes," she said. There was something about the smell of the water that morning that made her feel mildly nostalgic. It had a sweetness, this feeling of longing, as if some part of her childhood were just within reach, until Joey started his engine, and the roar of the motor made her step back.

"Your last good-byes?" he repeated, gripping the red glazed, cherry-colored wheel. Haven't you done that already?" He regretted his words as soon as he'd spoken, for he wanted to make peace with Siobhan. "Can I have a kiss, for good luck?"

She leaned down to kiss him, but as he strained upward, she bit him *hard* on the mouth.

"You rat!" he yelled after her, but she was already running away down the pier, quickly moving out of reach.

Joey's anger that morning entered his blood, and he knew he was going to win. When the judge dropped the flag for the trial race, the whine of the five long boats heaved up – the hulls seemed to rear before they smacked the water and went bucking across the lake. Flying over the surface, the boats screamed around the marker buoy before heading back toward the bay. And to think that Hans Jansen's invention had only been intended to push a poor man's rowboat against the wind. These engines had such power, they nearly tore the water like a ripping sheet. Speed, noise, danger, excitement, it all appealed to Joey Ulrich, though he'd already had several accidents. His first racing boat had exploded, and he had fractured his back. It had kept him out of the army.

Siobhan didn't like the noisy dare-devil boats, the oily smear on the surface of the lake, or the fumes of gasoline in the wind, but then *he* didn't like certain things either. He didn't like Topside, his family home, being turned into an animal shelter. It had all started when Siobhan made a pet out of a wee little chipmunk, feeding it seeds from their morning muskmelons. It would sit on the downspout and make a scolding noise until she came out to feed it – then it would chortle and scamper about the flags, flirting with her outrageously. She would coax him with her absolute stillness, and soon he was completely tame.

Next, she became fascinated with a golden raccoon, whose mask was white instead of black, the rings around her tail an orangey-brown. Her four little babies were always bounding about her as she hobbled along. The mother raccoon had only three legs, and Siobhan often wondered how she had lost one – fighting, probably, or maybe she had been shot, for the raccoon had learned how to lift the heavy lids on the sunken garbage cans.

"They're incorrigible," Joey complained. "I don't know why you want to turn them into pets. They're scavengers. They'll eat anything."

A buck and his doe and their twin fauns had also taken refuge at Topside. Siobhan scattered corn in the snow and then waited to see the wild pheasant land. They were so elegant, trailing their tails through the deep, fresh powder. She hung bird feeders everywhere, for they kept the air alive, and she needed something to distract her during the long winter months, when it became so easy to turn inward. Siobhan felt their marriage had almost ruined their friendship. She couldn't remember fighting so fiercely before, but now they always seemed to disagree.

Word got out that she was an animal lover, and soon people began dropping unwanted litters of kittens off at the foot of the drive. Joey said he was allergic and would not let them into the house, but the courtyard was often overrun, and he complained of the pungent male cat odor. Siobhan had Morvan build shelters in the woods, where they could take refuge in the cold, and each evening she would put out great butcher trays of milk with bread and hunks of raw ground beef. "As if they lived at the University Club. The day I see one of them inside, I'm gathering them up in a sack."

"Maybe you'd like me to go too. Everything would be a whole lot neater. You could have your old house back just the way you like it. Your mother could even move back in."

"But some of these animals carry diseases," he insisted. "It's not good for a pregnant woman to spend a lot of time around cats. I read that somewhere. Especially wild ones."

"But I'm not pregnant." She didn't need to remind him. They had had difficulty getting pregnant, and it had become a source of resentment for both of them. He felt she was trying to replace their potential family life with all these animals, that she would never get pregnant if her maternal instincts were being satisfied elsewhere. And she blamed him for never being around when it was the right time of month. He was working very hard at the brewery now, sometimes six days a week, but she felt work had become a form of avoidance.

Joey had made one major improvement at Kreuser by promoting an innovation that had clearly caught on, the metal can of beer – small, individual kegs, each kept completely fresh, six to a cardboard carton.

Alicia was incensed that her son drank beer right out of the container. To her, such an act was not only bad manners, it was almost obscene. But Joey had earned a reputation for leading the brewery into the modern age.

"Eight brews a day, at fifty barrels a brew, forty-one gallons to every barrel, makes how many cans of beer? Sixteen cans to a gallon."

Siobhan had no idea. She hated the mechanics of math. Her father had often quizzed her over the breakfast table, making her spell difficult words for the last sweet roll, Reykjavik and hippopotamus, but she had always gotten them wrong. How she would like to make it right for him now. Her father would never have hurt anybody. He was the kindest man in the world. They had even shown a picture of his car in the papers, with a vague dark shape slumped forward on the wheel. She wished that she hadn't seen that. It was then she decided to sell Yelping Hill.

Strangely enough, the first people who looked at the house offered the asking price. Joey thought that she had asked too little, but Siobhan was convinced that Mr. McKenna would have paid any sum to get a foothold on Nogowogotoc Lake. They were from the south side of Milwaukee, and he had made millions in the trucking business. Siobhan had offered the house "furnished," but Mrs. McKenna was not interested in "all those musty, tattered things," which were now to be auctioned on the following day.

The old gardener had remained on the property in his two-room cottage, and he had pointed his shotgun at the new arrivals when they had first pulled up to inspect the house. "*Oh, mein Gott,*" he told Siobhan, "dat new owner know nothing 'bout running dat place! Dey want for me to show dem, but dey won't do no good, no how." He wagged his finger in admonishment. "When I think of da lily beds, Miss Dana's favorite, from seed too, not just bulbs yet! Dat flower garden was tip top. Thank goodness she not see dat now." He went away worrying, shaking his head. "Such people."

This new family would come in and clean everything up, strip wallpaper, paint, remake the old house with brand-new tacky furniture. But that could no longer be her concern. She felt she had done something dishonorable by selling Yelping Hill – it was a bit like dishonoring a grave, selling sacred land to the highway commissioner, encouraging him to bring a new road right through. She only wished she had no past, for her personal history oppressed her. All the objects and heavy furniture weighed her down. She wanted to move forward, into the future. She didn't suspect that one step forward in the guise of progress could actually be a detrimental move, devoid of any deepening. She wanted to live for the present moment. She wanted to experience joy as fully as possible – the spreading colors of the morning sunrise filling her with warmth, or an evening ride, along the fields of fresh corn. She didn't want to think about harvest.

Walking into the old house, she felt like an intruder – two thousand five hundred thirty-six items – distanced from it all. She picked up the newspaper article, left on the kitchen table: AWESTRUCK BUYERS TO ATTEND LAST PARTY AT YELPING HILL. Then she thumbed through a copy of the catalogue. Odd to see certain precious objects displayed in a line-up of items. She didn't want any of it. She didn't even want the painted black lacquer sideboard, or her parents' Victorian sleigh bed, though the decorative wash set made her pause. She didn't want the boxes of fine linens or the ecru tablecloths, the heavy Flemish tapestry or the Steuben fan vase, not even the little silver bonbon basket. She ran her hand over her father's massive walnut library table, where he had once spread out his papers. She could almost see him looking up at her over his glasses, the soft feeling of affection that came over his face whenever she interrupted him.

Looking down the list of items, she saw that they were stupidly selling her old Kodak brownie camera. She wondered what on earth that would bring. She marveled at all the house contained – Oriental Temple Bells, clear glass liqueur set, the purple moon-and-star-covered bowl her mother had been so fond of, the tall and shapely blue Sèvres vase. But here was her mother's white bisque rabbit, with its pink neckband laden with forget-me-nots. She put the little rabbit in her pocket, along with a silver stopwatch. Some day she might have a daughter or a son, and it would be nice to have something to pass on.

Everything that used to have a meaning now had a number, and the numbers themselves reduced the value for her. They were just material items. The house felt chilly though it was hot outside. As Siobhan walked from room to room, her footsteps had the sound of emptiness. She walked carefully up the back stairs and entered her old bedroom. There on a side table she saw her patchwork quilt, and her worn flannelette blanket with its grungy fringe. She picked this little rag of a blanket up and buried her face in it, as if to capture some treasured smell. *Oh dear little fairy believe me, I love you I love you, I do.* She sat down in the mission oak rocking chair that had been brought down from the attic. It had a good cane back and leather seat, but the card attached read "In need of restoration." The whole house felt desperately empty, though with all these things, it was over full, like a party crammed with people you don't even want to talk to. She wished that she hadn't come.

Siobhan intended to donate the proceeds from the auction to an orphanage overseas. Surely small children were the greatest victims in a war, and they could use the profits more than she could. Rocking back and forth in the chair, she continued to scan the list, wondering how much it would bring – Sheraton Mahogany Desk, Complete Pool Table with Ivory Balls, Marble Garden Fountain, Electric Fixtures from Florence – her father, in particular, had liked fine things, while Dana was more simple in her tastes, though she had purchased the large bronze sculpture of horses and the Italian inlaid marble table.

During the house's disuse each winter, vandals had broken in. Once robbers had stolen the Oriental carpet from beneath that massive table. No one could figure out how, for usually the table had to be lifted on jacks in order to get the rug out for cleaning. The previous year the sheriff had caught two men going off with a davenport strapped to the top of their car, but Siobhan had not pressed charges. Usually it was just teenagers who broke into the house, smashing a pane in the French doors, letting themselves in to steal whiskey, or to use the freezing-cold beds upstairs.

There was an excess of silver, Siobhan noted. Why had nobody stolen that? Tray Lot: Pie Holder, Two-Piece Crumb Set, Oval Brush, Coin Dish, Silent Butler, Expandable Trivet. Siobhan was amused at how they had grouped certain items, as if they made up a family: Black Leather Opera Glass, Dutch Footed Bowl, Brass Pillbox, Cigarette Holder, German Alarm Clock, Matchbox Cover, Nut Picks, Indian Buffalo Buttons. All of her parents were gone.

It had been eerie enough listening to her own footsteps as she walked through the house, but now she heard a pickup truck pulling into the yard, the slam of a metal door. She stopped rocking in the chair and sat stock still as she heard a man coming into the house. She felt a sudden panic. Whoever it was walked into the kitchen, and he seemed to have a distinct shuffle, or limp. She knew it was not their old gardener, for he moved at a different pace and always hummed to himself as he went. She knew that she was off-limits, and she didn't want to be discovered. Then the man started up the front stairs, and she was filled with dread. Waves of fear were radiating from the seat where she sat as she heard the footsteps mounting. She wanted to call out – "Who's there?" But she could not say a word. The man stopped at the top of the stairs, as if to catch his breath, but then his shuffling resumed, and he came down the hallway, past the open bedrooms, one after another, stopping before he reached her door. Then, just as he poked his head around, she gave a happy snort of astonishment – "Damn!" It was only Emerson Rose.

"Good Lord, you scared the pants off of me," he gasped, standing in the middle of the doorway, hands on hips. "What are you trying to do, give your customers a heart attack? These things all for sale? Good Lord."

"Even my baby blanket," she held it up for him to inspect, and he limped over and sat down on the bed, sticking one leg straight out in front of him.

"They shot me on the rise," he explained his war wound. "I actually came to check on the rabbit hutch. Do you think I could buy it before the crowd comes tomorrow?"

"Did you think you'd find it up here?"

"Well, no." He grinned. "I was just being nosy. But I found *you*, so I'm glad." He paused and looked around the room. "I was just thinking how different the house seems. Remember how we all used to play under the porch?" They used to lie on their stomachs in the dirt and peer out through the latticework.

"I remember it being very smooth," she said. The earth itself was dry and hard, though they had rubbed little gullies with their bellies.

Emerson thought Siobhan looked pale and withdrawn, not the fiery, domineering girl from his childhood who ran barefoot over the gravel and had scabs on her toes and knees all summer long. He had heard about the horrible death of her father, and he knew selling the house must be hard on her, after everything else. "I'd hate it if they sold Hewitt's Point. It would be like losing an arm, or a leg." He nodded toward his injured limb, hoping to make her smile, but instead she surprised him and began to cry. She could not help sobbing into her blanket. She felt safe with Emerson there.

He had always been the best of the boys, but now he was surprisingly tall and manly. He had let his blond hair grow long in front, so that it hung down over his eyes, accentuating his cheekbones. He leaned forward, wanting to collect her, and his gesture said – Come here, I'll hold you. I'll take care of you now. He pulled her up from the rocking chair and encompassed her there on the twin-sized bed, as if they were brother and sister. She was grateful for his kindness, his warmth, and when she finally stopped crying, they just lay there together, neither asleep nor awake, though perhaps she did doze off for a moment, for she felt herself snap back, and when she opened her eyes, the room seemed different – everything looked clear. She looked down at his two hands locked together, holding her in, and they were golden, like toast, with long, elegant fingers. Carefully, she separated the interwoven fingers and they fell apart to her touch. She examined each section, each crease and line, the flexible thumb, the span of the surface. He didn't wear a wedding ring, and

327 ⟻

she couldn't help wondering if he had a sweetheart. She touched each finger pad with her own, pulsed on them like a spider on a mirror, and then crawled *eensie weensie* up his long, bare arm, till he laughed and pulled away. "I always hated tickling."

"And I hated getting dunked," she reminded him. Both of them sat up then, and readjusted their bodies, easing back into the pile of pillows, which would soon be scattered to various homes. She hugged the one with the jute trim. She used to suck on that soft string trim, like hair. Emerson put an arm around her shoulder, and she let herself lean back against him. She wanted him to keep her held in like that, as she recalled other incidents from their childhood. "Do you remember when we made stone soup?"

He remembered squishing bird berries, adding unripe milkweed. "I remember thinking you were the greatest girl. Because you were just as strong as the boys."

"Maybe stronger." She smiled.

"I wanted you to be my sister. I pretended you were."

"You did? I can be your sister now."

"I don't want a sister now," he said, lifting a strand of her tangled hair and looping it behind one ear.

Waves of pleasure radiated out from the same place that had previously been the focus of her fear. She turned to look at him, and caught her breath as he wiped a tear past her earlobe. She looked down, away from his hazel eyes, but then back up, and there in the sunlight of her childhood room, their lips closed lightly upon each others'. It was the most tender kiss, like melting chocolate, smoother than her old stuffed penguin, yet real and solid as her blue metal bank that still registered $3.25. Once she had thrown it out the upstairs window, making the money splash on the walkway below. And there was her favorite board game – Gypsy Fortune Teller. What would it say if they played? But no, this had nothing to do with the future – it was too late for fantasies now. This was only for one blissful moment, carrying them both back to the protective past where everything bobbed in the wide blue yonder of spray and sun and molded sand, the smell of metal screening, the lick of it, the imprint of grass blades on a pure white wrist, the taste of malted milk balls, yes, this one moment was sacred.

When Siobhan returned to Topside in a kind of daze, Joey was polishing silverware. "Why don't you let Mildred do that," she said. She didn't like his obsessive nature, but he enjoyed polishing anything – chrome, shoes, silverware. He liked watching the tarnish blacken the strips of torn cloths. The finished shine always gave him pleasure, but it was a pleasure that wouldn't last, for real people handled these objects. The sterling utensils could not always lie spoon-to-spoon in the velvet-lined box where no oxygen reached them.

Without looking up from his chore he said glumly, "What the hell took you so long?"

"I went through all my old things," she offered as a vague excuse. "But I don't know – what good is it."

He took this as a bad sign. Didn't she at least want to save her old red rocking horse? Surely a child of their own would be on the way fairly soon. "We had sixteen calls. I don't know why people think they can ring up here. Why can't they wait till tomorrow?" This auction business was getting on his nerves. He thought Good Will should have come and taken it all away.

"Emerson Rose couldn't wait," she mentioned, testing herself as she said his name. "He dropped by to get the rabbit hutch. I gave it to him for his new animal hospital. Maybe I'll help him," she added.

Joey's eyes narrowed. Though he knew his wife of all people had a reputation for handling animals – the worst growling dog would calm down and sniff when she crouched and cooed and held out her hand – he was a jealous man. "I found a cat in the pantry this afternoon. Maybe Emerson would like to have that."

"Maybe you should leave me alone."

"Why should I?" he answered. "Aren't you even going to ask about the race?"

"Did you win? Of course you won. I can't imagine you had any competition. Why don't you ever ask about *me?*"

"About what?"

"About how it felt?"

"How *what* felt?"

"Goodness!" she exclaimed. "You really are like some kind of salt shaker without any salt. If I have to watch you polishing silver one more night, I think I'll go out of my mind! Come on out to the patio, darling," she mocked him now. "Come look at the lovely view." Then she turned on him, snarling, "I've seen it a hundred *thousand* times! It doesn't mean a thing to me."

CHAPTER FORTY-SEVEN

*A*t seven o'clock that morning, Mona French was awakened by the blare of radios, and WACS screaming, "The war is over!" She jumped out of bed, wanting to write Alden, but could not find a pen, and why write now, when he was coming home? She decided to go straight to morning mass. Everyone would be going, all over the world – think of all the happy people. She could hear horns blowing as she began to dress. It was just too wonderful. She felt like crying. She wanted to rush outside but had to keep her ear glued to the radio. Just the night before, she had looked up into the sky and thought about how much she missed him, and how she would send him a message by the stars, telling him how much she loved him. But now he was safe and there was nothing to fear.

Music, fanfare, ticker-tape parades – it was hard to believe that the war was over, or what it had taken to end it. Most everyone was jubilant, as the machinery of war ground to a halt and the boys came marching home. Sweetheart married sweetheart, no time for prolonged decision making now, not even for Alden Faithorne.

Carol had just announced her engagement to an army man from Lake Forest, Illinois. He was a big, jolly fellow, a graduate of Brown University, and now, on returning from service, he planned on applying to business school at the University of Chicago. They had plenty of time to prepare for a late June wedding, which they hoped to have out in the country.

Helen Faithorne's mind was already full of details. Carol, after all, was her only daughter, and after the disappointment of Alden's elopement, she wanted this event to be especially fine. They had already decided on the orchestra, the caterer, and the florist. Felton's would order the dress. Carol would need something simple, but full – they would make her look like a princess.

By ten o'clock that evening, when Leonard crawled into bed and pressed himself against his wife, her mind was still active. He sensed that she was elsewhere, but he kept on giving the caresses he normally gave, until she moved his hand away. "Do you think it would be better to have the ceremony in town? We could put up guests at both houses, and it is so often cool in June. It might not be seasonable enough for a tent, and we could always use the Woman's Club."

"What does Carol say?" he responded. "It's her wedding."

"Oh, Carol doesn't have time to think about all this. She's turned the whole thing over to me."

"Well, I'm sure everything's taken care of then." Leonard liked to tease her about her tendency to take control, her masterful manner when it came to organization. Think of where they would be today if Helen had been running Felton's.

"But really," she persisted, cuddling up on his shoulder, begging him to ponder this seriously. "Do you think the bridesmaids should wear blue? Pale blue? Or yellow, perhaps. Yellow would be a nice complement for Carol's complexion. Fox's is going to do the flowers, white peonies, but I think we should use something more delicate going up the aisle."

Leonard turned Helen's face toward his and kissed his little general. He wanted to go to sleep. He wanted to tell her to surrender, to stop battling the future with her insufferable head. Finally, she did respond, kissing her husband in return, but by the time he got around to doing what he had had in mind, something had happened to disturb the process. This had never happened to them before.

When Helen reached down to touch him, to ease him in, she was baffled. It was like trying to stuff a marshmallow into a piggy bank slot. She had heard of this kind of thing happening, but now that it had, she was vaguely insulted. He was too young for this. She wanted to feel sympathetic, but her actual response was irritation, as if he had only been teasing her, tempting her and then turning away. Or perhaps he was making a statement about her femininity, as if she lacked the appropriate powers of arousal.

Helen was still a good-looking woman, though her face had begun to line and her hair was turning gray. She was considered unusually athletic, and had kept her youthful figure, but she never wore makeup of any kind, and she slept in simple flannel. "What's the matter?" she asked. He claimed that he was tired, wanting her to take it lightly, not to focus on this one incident, but she was disturbed, wide awake now, and it seemed she wanted to make an issue of it, to rouse him from his sleepiness in order to fulfill her demands, but he was having none of it. He simply rolled over and fell asleep. Now she felt doubly rejected.

When she woke the next morning, Leonard was already up, slurrying his toothbrush around in the basin, moistening the powder, then meticulously brushing each angle of his teeth. She lay there silently and watched him through the open door to the bathroom. She could see him lathering his chin in the round extension mirror. He flipped it around, so it became a magnifying glass, and clipped several hairs from the depths of his nostrils. She was repulsed by the exactness of his toilette. "Perhaps we're getting old," she said, hoping that he might contradict her, but splashing a little Lilac Vegetal on his smooth, clean face, he agreed – that was probably it.

She felt a physical form of anxiety that morning, until she decided to go for a ride. Her chestnut gelding stood a proud sixteen hands, and she always felt better when she took the time to curry him, burying her nose in his lustrous mane, getting the sweet animal essence, picking each hoof. She didn't even mind the smell of manure as it dropped in a steaming pile on the stable floor.

Unhooking his cross-ties, she led Civilian out. He was a young, eager seven-year-old, not hard to hold back but ready to run. Galloping across the farmland freed her mind from its irritable mood. The corn stalks in the Ulrich fields had been shorn to a crisp eight inches. The stubble looked like rows of privates standing at attention. Crows and grackles flew overhead, the leaves were down, the trees broom-clean. But then, walking her horse back into the woods behind the Wahcheetah Mission, Helen came upon Siobhan Ulrich. The girl was sitting on the ground, curled over, apparently crying her heart out. Her Morgan stood several yards away. "My dear, are you hurt? What's the matter, did you fall?" Helen quickly dismounted, kneeling down beside her.

Siobhan shook her head, "No," sniffing back the tears. "I'm just upset." She wiped her face with her fingers, leaving muddy streaks across her cheekbones. She looked around, stunned by her emotion, as if wondering where she was. "May I ride with you for awhile?" she asked, sounding like a little girl.

"Of course," Helen answered, going to catch their horses. Both women were agile and found it easy to remount. It was easier to speak once they were walking their horses side by side down the woodland path, looking straight ahead. "Is there anything wrong at home?"

Siobhan admitted that she was unhappy. "It was all a mistake. I never should have gotten married. I just wanted to get out of that house."

"Joey doesn't have trouble with alcohol, does he?"

"No, it's not that." It was a struggle for Siobhan to speak about it, in part, because it was difficult to name the thing that was bothering her.

"Is there someone else?" Helen asked, and Siobhan was surprised that Mrs. Faithorne could intuit such a possibility without a tone of accusation.

"There might be, I mean, not really – *he* doesn't know – I don't think he does, but I feel like I might be in love." A leaden mood of guilt fell over her when she imagined running off with Emerson. "Joey would be so *crushed*. He's always been my best, *best* friend. He depends on me for everything."

Helen thought how oppressive that must be. "You have a very strong heart. Strong hearts don't like to compromise, but at least they're capable of it. I once was in a similar fix, and I believe I made the right decision, but then your circumstances are somewhat different. You haven't any children."

Siobhan nodded, though that was part of the problem. She thought perhaps she might be pregnant now.

"Some day you'll see there are many kinds of love. The kind you're feeling is the most intense, but the shortest lived. The love you develop in a marriage is different – it's hard to describe, but it's built on the smallest, silliest things, like the way we eat our grapefruit. My husband always calls me the White Monkey when I pick up my grapefruit and squeeze it – I hate to waste a single drop. I call him the Perfect Gentleman, because he wouldn't dream of doing such a thing. We've come to enjoy our differences, to joke about them. Perhaps that's the only way. A woman's love for her children is the deepest. I know your own mother would have hoped for your happiness."

"I'm happiest when I'm alone."

Helen considered this surprising response, then added, "I am too. Or when riding with someone of a like disposition." They both saw the wooden fence at the same time. Helen urged her horse into a canter. Siobhan quickly followed over the crisp covering of the shed woods, feather-light leaves scattering. Helen went first and her athletic horse cleared the fence by several inches, while Siobhan just missed the top rail. On the other side, a large mown field opened up before them. They both felt exuberant and had to agree that some fences *asked* to be taken.

When they parted, Helen gave her standard warning, to be careful, for accidents often happened on the last few miles toward home.

Riding back past the horse field, Helen's eye looked with fondness down the small curving path that cut through the summer pasture. Over the years their horses had carved a little gully or depression, not a direct line, but a wavering one, and she wondered if her own life had made such a demarcation. How important it was to use the time one had, to make a significant mark.

When she walked in the door, Helen discovered a telegram on the front hall table – Alden was bringing his new bride home. The house was suddenly in upheaval. Two single beds were pushed together in the blue room to create accommodations for the newlyweds. Winnie was bent on making the most elaborate meal since the war began – roast beef, mashed potatoes, popovers, green beans, certainly cucumber salad, each peeled and dragged with a fork, and they would have to have tomato bouillon, Alden's favorite, and finish the meal with a *linzer torte*.

Winnie had not had many complaints about the meager food supplies during the war years, for she could make a meal out of a rutabaga. The only thing that peeved her about rationing was the scanty supply of hair nets, for, as she liked to point out – hair gets in the food.

Leonard didn't need to hear about that – it was enough to snuff an appetite. He was concerned about meeting Mona French, and wondered if she were an opportunist, taking advantage of Alden's lack of experience and the excitement of the times. Leonard had heard that she was glamorous, and that didn't sound like Alden's type, not to mention that they were from such different backgrounds. He wondered how a hothouse flower from Savannah would ever survive the Milwaukee winters.

When their cab pulled up beneath the porte-cochère, she was the first one out, throwing her arms around Leonard. "I knew it was you! The tallest, most dignified, handsome man. Next to my Alden of course, and Mama," she reached for Helen, who had come to the door with her two hands up to her lips, prayer fashion, holding back her extreme emotion. Mona felt that his family would be her family now, that Springwood Lee would become her home, but as they stood there – Alden finding change for the taxi cab – the November damp plunged through her stockings, down into her long, lean, beautiful bones.

Helen Faithorne felt like crying, for what terrible grief and senseless loss this war had brought upon the world – think of the mothers whose sons were not returning. "My darlings," she said. "Come in, come in. This is the happiest moment. And look who's here," for there was Edward, standing at attention in the foyer, and then Carol squealed and leapt into view, dragging Winkler Scott with her.

Carol's fiancé was eager to shake Alden's hand, congratulating him on his success in France. "We heard you were laid up for a bit."

"And the next thing we knew, you were married!" Carol exclaimed. "I can hardly believe it – we always thought he would never get married. That takes real courage," she turned to Mona, "marrying a wounded soldier. You look all right to me."

"It was only a severe case of athlete's foot," Alden admitted for their amusement. He stood somewhat apart from his bride, and she wished he would show more overt affection. She needed to be brought in, to feel included, and his standing apart made her feel unsure. It was a queasy moment for her, a strange mixture of dread and regret that made her speak out in a rather forward manner.

"Did you know Alden's plane almost went down over enemy territory?"

"Thank goodness we never knew that," Helen exclaimed.

"He had to dive bomb in order to get the engine started."

"Really?" Edward asked.

"Merrick's still out on the Pacific," Carol said. "We're hoping he'll be home for Christmas. Wouldn't that be wonderful, to all be together?"

Eddie wanted to hear more war stories and Carol wanted to hear about the honeymoon. "There's not that much to tell," Mona confessed. "Alden wanted to come straight home. He knew how much it would mean to everybody."

As they all settled down in the living room, Leonard brought over a decanter of sherry on a silver tray with small etched glasses, and Mona looked up at him with a grateful smile. He felt like taking her hand and kissing it. He knew this could not be easy. She had such a radiance, as dark as she was. "Here's to our beautiful bride," he said.

Mona didn't refuse a glass, and Helen wondered about that. Carol shook her head, no thank you, and both girls admired each other's rings. Carol's engagement ring was a Scott family diamond, and seeing the size of it, Alden insisted that they go through the vault and use one of Grandmother Felton's stones to make a proper ring for Mona.

She got up and walked across the living room, over to the large picture window. Mona knew that when summer came, Alden would be unmerciful about her keeping her head above water, always worrying about the ruination of her hair. He had claimed that his parents didn't care how she looked – they only wanted to get to know her. But now she wondered if they wanted to know the real Mona French, or did they only want her to gradually become someone different, or someone a little *less* different, a young lady who fit into the Faithorne clan, a little less dazzling, more prim and proper. She knew she was an outsider, and she felt she had to keep up her guard. Her own father was a postal officer, nothing to be ashamed of, but Alden had warned her not to talk too much about certain things until she was fully accepted.

Sitting down beside his new daughter-in-law, Leonard felt the sudden, excited energy of an ardent boy. He could tell Helen was making an effort – her heart was dragging rather low despite the joy of reunion. He put his hand on Mona's shoulder as she told him about her war work – she had been sent from a clinic in Savannah to an army hospital in New Orleans. "Those boys were mighty grateful. Sometimes it was downright pitiful though, they were so starved for a little kindness."

Winkler insisted that New Orleans was the dirtiest town he had ever seen. "It's ten feet under water. That's why they have to build their graves up top."

Mona felt defensive, for she had adored that colorful town with its spicy food and lively music. "It's not your typical southern city."

"Not like Charleston," Helen agreed. The Faithornes had always admired Charleston.

Mona didn't want to seem overly impressed by the country grandeur of Springwood Lee, but she made the mistake of saying, "What a lovely estate." And then over the midday meal, she leaned toward Leonard and asked him confidentially, "Aren't you afraid of spoiling your children?"

"Oh no," he chuckled, shaking his head. "They're already spoiled as far as I can tell." She thought he was the dearest man.

Edward shouted across the table, "You should see Father's skull collection. It's twice as big as it was."

His sister tried to hush him up, but Edward wanted to tell Alden about Mr. Pulling, his headmaster at Millbrook, and how he had gotten British naval officers to come up from the harbor in New York. "We followed the action every day, moving flags around on the map. Mr. Pulling said the Allied Forces won because we held together like a bundle of sticks."

"We won," Alden countered, "because we had the atom bomb."

"Two atomic bombs," said Winkler.

"Why didn't you drop one on Hitler then?"

"Goodness, Edward, on Europe?" Helen exclaimed.

Then Winnie marched in humming "The Caissons Song." She produced a small shrill whistle and blew it once, waving a miniature flag in the air, before plunging it into Alden's bread roll. He called her "my old girl," and Winnie hunched up and clapped him on the shoulder. It was a grand welcome home for their soldier.

Leonard struck a serious note then, wanting to make a toast. He clinked his water glass and rose. "Your mother and I remember well the Sunday of December seventh, 1941, when we heard over the radio out here at Springwood Lee the announcement of Pearl Harbor, and now the day has arrived that we feared might never come – unconditional surrender of countries dominated by ruthless tyrants and dictators. When a democracy is aroused, it can become a formidable force. I would like to propose a toast, to Alden and his lovely wife, and to the safe return of Carl Merrick."

The rest of the family rose solemnly to drink from their water glasses, but when everyone else sat down, Alden remained standing. "I just want you to know that you've been the very best parents anybody could ever have. Mother," he turned in her direction, "you might have worried about our spiritual education at times, but I think an example of right living is far more valuable than anything else. Though my sense of religion might be grounded in a kind of skepticism," Alden now faced his father, "I have to admit that love is the essence of divinity. That's one Christian truth I've come to believe in primarily because of you both." This speech was so moving that Helen found she needed to distract herself from her feelings. She asked Eddie to run back into the kitchen for milk.

As he opening the ice box, Winnie came up and started right in. "You are a big boy now, but you still like Winnie's sweet cookies!" She smacked her hands together and pulled him over to show him what she was doing, which involved flour and sugar, butter and vanilla. "You're all big and handsome and my honey boy, still are, but you're a thirsty one, aren't you?"

She laughed her gurgling laugh, puttering around the central work table, opening the bin that came slanting out, scooping out a cupful of flour. She didn't have to think about what she was doing – it was automatic, and her desserts always turned out exactly right, not like some cooks, who were always blaming the quality of the eggs or the excess of humidity. "You and me, Eddie, I've been waiting for you. Remember your promise to Winnie?"

No, he didn't remember, but he knew their cook liked to make things up, "Fabricate," as his mother would say.

Winnie handed him a stick of butter to eat. She knew he liked it raw, and she was the only one not disgusted by this unhealthy habit. "Well, I'm not holding you to it," she hunched up her tiny, fleshy shoulders. "I've got a boyfriend down the road, now that you're not home to keep me on the straight and narrow. But you've been up to things yourself. I can see it, just the way you stand there. I don't blame the girls, I don't." There were no girls at Millbrook School, none in the vicinity, though they did have a dance once or twice a year. "I've got one down on Mixter Road," Winnie continued, needing no encouragement. "He's real sweet to me too, takes me riding in his car, giving me kisses and everything. I know you boys, you've got to be watched."

With this, Eddie managed to slip out of the kitchen. His mother was ringing the buzzer, a device she pressed with her foot. Winnie didn't look up, but burst into song: *"Oh, I can make a sweet jam, and I can make a pie, but when it comes to my lover's time, well I won't ever go dry. No, I can call you mister and I can call you up, but darlin' darlin' sweetheart, I'll just call you mine, Oh, I'll just call you mine."* She was always singing these simple tunes, making them up with no recognizable melody – she simply loved to sing. Yes, she was an original. She wasn't fazed by the appearance of Mona, though Alden had been on the top of her list as a suitable marriage partner. Apparently, she was now reconsidering her options, for without looking up she continued – "You might not be tall and handsome, but at least you're good and sturdy."

CHAPTER FORTY-EIGHT

*W*hen Sarah Wells returned to Broadoaks that June, she felt she had come home for the last time. It was a welcome feeling. Isabelle seemed particularly calm, and read to her mother every afternoon, and the children came by regularly to visit. Even Caroline, Sarah's sister, had come to Nogowogotoc for a spell. She and Isabelle took regular motor tours, which kept them nicely occupied, and the big old house was in a restful mood.

Angeline had retired, leaving Mrs. Jetner to carry on with the housekeeping. And the new cook was a pleasant soul. She catered to Sarah's idiosyncrasies, peeling the skins from her hotdogs, avoiding raw celery and any spice that might upset her digestion. Her favorite fare was a fresh purée of garden vegetables, though Edward said it looked like baby food.

That evening, for Sarah's seventy-fifth birthday, they were having a cream of sorrel soup made with a reduced veal stock, followed by braised leg of baby lamb, fresh peas, and scalloped potatoes. All of her family was around her again, though Carol was off on her honeymoon. Merrick had become engaged to the daughter of Leonard's business school roommate, and everyone was thrilled, for this union seemed more than a random occurrence of romance, but a match that was practically predestined.

Edward insisted that he would always remain a bachelor, for as he described it, Goetschie had relentlessly hovered over him, and she and Aunt Isabelle, both spinsters, had repeatedly tried to influence his love life. Goetschie admonished him every time some precious prom date slipped away, and Auntie was sure he would marry a foreigner, possibly because the whole thing seemed so foreign to her sensibilities.

Little Gram didn't think he should worry about marriage, for why shouldn't a young man live on his own and explore all possibilities? She thought briefly of Heinrich Ulrich, and how he had loved tending sheep. "Did you know that they're geotropic?" she told the table, but they didn't know what she was talking about.

Lionel Hewitt and his nurse had joined the group. Jetner kept up a familiar complaint, muttering beneath her breath, "Two too many. I thought this was supposed to be a family gathering." But her fussing made Sarah feel even more at home, comfortable with her intimate entourage. The boys had picked their grandmother the most beautiful bouquet. Its fragrance seemed to spread beneath the warm light of the low-hung Tiffany – pink daylilies and pale blue delphinium, with fleshy, peach-colored roses. It made her feel deeply nostalgic, for what exactly she didn't know, but she found herself reaching for

Lionel's hand as if he might reassure her. The moment itself seemed to be so perfect, it almost receded from her consciousness, the haze of the light and the smell of the flowers, the general melt of their voices together, the laughter and ping of crystal on crystal, as if it all came from a great distance.

They took turns giving toasts to Little Gram, recalling some incident from the past – how she had once found Alden locked in the ice house.

"Eisenhower?" she asked.

"That was the time we had the baby-doll party," Edward put in. "Alden wore a bonnet and carried around a bottle, remember? And Merrick was Buster Brown?"

"And you," Merrick reminded the youngest brother, "dressed up as Miss Goetsch with a pillow for a hump."

"He ran around the party telling everyone what to do and not to do," Alden explained to Mona.

"That child," Sarah said of her daughter, as Helen came flying down the gravel road. "She drives just like she rides."

Helen came in with a kiss for her mother and a jar of green beans as a present. Lionel followed suit and presented Sarah with a most treasured possession – his NLC Commodore's pin. She even let him attach it to the collar of her dress where everyone could admire it. Having gained the attention of the table, Lionel spoke up. "I was over in the village just the other day having my Sunday breakfast, and I said to this young waitress they have over there – I bet a pretty high-school girl like you finds some rather good use for tips. High school nothing, she said – I've got four kids at home, so don't be generous! She was saucy, yes she was. I left her a ten-dollar bill."

Sarah nodded, though she was listening vaguely to some far-away trumpet, as if it came from the wide-mouthed flowers on the table, her eye following the lavender lines that plunged down into their golden throats.

"I saw Alicia Ulrich at Steven's Drugstore yesterday," Aunt Clickey informed the table. "She came in while I was having a soda, not that she noticed me. She bought the tiniest bottle of perfumed lotion, and then asked to have it delivered. Can you believe it? I guess it was beneath her to carry a package."

"At least she's up and around," Alden said. "She's still a terrific-looking woman." He gave Mona a reassuring squeeze, but she playfully pushed him away.

Hearing the sound of the piano, Isabelle suggested that they all take their coffee into the living room. Geoffrey Hollenbeck, the chauffeur's son, had been summoned to play. Little Gram was putting him through music school. As Leonard walked his mother-in-law from the table, she turned to him and said, "Are you really going to shoot deer in Central Park?" Leonard assured her he had no such plan.

Sitting down close to the keyboard, she was able to hear all her old favorites, Haydn, Schubert, Brahms, but best of all was the closing nocturne by Chopin – it was a perfect evening. She had never felt so wistful or happy, a most pleasant combination. It was almost like being in love. She thought, very briefly, of dear Heinrich Ulrich, of Merrick too, and how good he had been to her, how quickly the time had passed since they had both departed.

That night when she bade goodnight to each member of the family, each one got a special kiss and hug, but when it came to young Edward, she took him by the shoulders and looking him in the eye, she said, "I won't ever forget you."

There are lives so apart from the turmoil of the world that, like the hidden spring, they are chiefly to be traced by the verdure and freshness that has its source in them, quickened by the grateful refreshment of their living waters. Only those nearest them feel their tranquil influence, but the refreshment of soul is priceless, and once lost can not be regained.

One of these dear women has just left us, it is safe to say, without an enemy in the world, for no one lives who had aught from her but gentleness and kindness. Mrs. Wells, daughter of the pioneer merchant William Felton, was the founder of the Layton Art School, and some of the gallery's most valuable paintings were gifts from her, including the Abbott Thayer's oil, The Angel, exhibited at the Chicago World Fair.

Young at heart, and quick in appreciation for everything fine, she enjoyed life to the utmost, and won through her personal qualities not only gratitude, but deep admiration from people of all ages. Her will was dictated by her love of art and by the philanthropic impulses that have marked her life.

So quiet and self-effacing were her benefactions that even those who knew her intimately were often unaware of them. Mrs. Wells was as sweet and gentle a spirit as you could ever find, overflowing with generous impulses, a dove-like lady, always exquisite in her fineness and fragility.

Isabelle was not to be comforted, no matter what Aunt Clickey said. "We must think of it from her side. She didn't suffer pain. She had all of her faculties, and she lived a grand long time." But Isabelle had never dreamed of her mother passing away so soon. She had been such a healthy, carefree person. "She did so much good throughout her life. She was loved more than most people are privileged to be loved."

"More than most," Isabelle repeated, stifling a sob.

"She was in her own home, and we were all by her side. The flowers that night were so beautiful. And the musical program, the most lovely I think I've ever heard. She was here where she loved to be most, with all of us around her, thinking such tender thoughts of her."

"But it's so strange, on her birthday."

"Life would be odd indeed if it weren't very strange."

Everything so well-timed, down to the very last minute – then another feather falls in the universe and everything is changed.

Out of her fifteen-million-dollar estate, Sarah Wells bequeathed the city of Milwaukee three million toward the construction of a fine arts theater. Her forethought paralleled the wishes of two other leading ladies from Nogo-wogotoc, Lucy Knobloch and Alicia Ulrich.

After her recovery, Alicia had taken on the redecoration of the Lake Club. She bought new wicker furniture and woven grass rugs. She even had the ball-room painted with a handsome mural of sailboats, and she completely refur-bished the ladies' lounge. The barroom received bright red leather benchettes, nautical wallpaper, and a compass design made out of mosaic set into the floor.

Gaining confidence there, she decided to raise money for the proposed music center downtown. She began her fund drive by collecting an "Album of Artists," gathering personalized signatures and sketches, bits of musical scores, poetry, and quotations, even a kiss mark from Carol Lombard and the thumbprint of Joe DiMaggio. Believing that politicians were also performing artists, she included the signatures of well-known senators, as well as a sketch of President Truman, but mostly the album contained bold autographs of ac-tresses and movie stars, radio crooners and popular writers. She put together over a thousand selections, bound the book in leather, and mailed it off to Christie's in New York, where it was auctioned for forty-six thousand dollars. Joey Ulrich had promised to match whatever price it brought, and the coffers of Kreuser Beer would double that, so they were well on their way when Lucy Knobloch decided to join their forces. With the help of Helen Faithorne and Isabella Wells, who meant to carry out their mother's wishes, the women set up a committee. They all felt Lucy would be particularly good at approaching wealthy patrons and leaders of industry and getting them to contribute. Alicia spoke to the Raifstanger family, telling them they couldn't be outdone by their cousins and competitors. Mrs. Schultz followed suit with a very generous do-nation, and by November 11, 1949, the center was ready for dedication.

That evening, from the large curved stage, Helen looked out over the thousand faces that filled the auditorium. She spotted her sister, Isabelle, sit-ting on the aisle toward the back. And there was Siobhan next to Joey

Ulrich. Lolly Jones was engaged to an electrician from Wauwatosa and they were sitting in the middle, up front.

"We are gathered here together tonight in memory of three very special people," Helen began. "Because of Dana Ash, Herman Knobloch, and my own dear mother, Sarah Felton Wells, the city of Milwaukee and the state of Wisconsin will now benefit from this marvelous structure."

Once the thunderous applause had subsided, she continued. "I don't know if you read the *Sentinel* this morning, but we were described as the 'Mothers of Milwaukee.'" A murmur of amusement swept across the audience. "But I think we'd rather be dubbed the 'Grandmothers of Nogowogotoc Lake.' I prefer that appellation anyway. My oldest son is now expecting a child, and I can only join him and his wife with great anticipation. We have such high hopes for this new generation and for the second half of the century.

"Of course there's no telling what the future will hold, but it's my feeling that we cannot allow this newest communication, the television, to rob our social interests in the arts – if you can imagine such a world, where each individual is cut off from his fellow man by empty, lifeless entertainment. Our theater stands in contrast to that fate. We must participate in our culture.

"The country now has a ready surplus of funds to purchase what it has so long been denied during the difficult war years, but don't let this be a temptation for squandering. Let us be all the more cautious and thoughtful of those in the world who are still healing their wounds, who have far less than we do. We must continue to be vigilant in doing what's best.

"Our grandchildren, born into the second half of this century, will lead remarkable lives, free from the worries of war and depression. They may not understand the struggles and hardships that we have experienced, and though we may want to spare them these hardships, I think it will be important to share our stories with them. They will have such great advantages, more so perhaps than any other group of children ever born. How important it will be for them to use these advantages in the right way. May we raise them wisely, raise them to appreciate beauty, to feel reverence for nature and respect for their fellow man. We must teach them that their privileges should lead to a sense of duty and generosity, not just to themselves but to one and all. The gift of this theater, from each one of you here tonight, is symbolic of that impulse."

Instead of staying for the celebratory dinner and concert, Alicia drove herself home that night. Most of the traffic on the highway was going into Milwaukee, rather than back out to the country. Once the road opened up she felt a wave of relief. She no longer felt threatened or angry. She had this wonderful sensation of absence, of peacefulness, no longer inhabited by ghosts. Her father had finally left her, and she was in possession of herself.

As she continued west toward Nogowogotoc, a rain storm swept toward her car, until she was entirely engulfed by it. Through the light-filled rain, she could see the giant ball of the setting sun, all aglow, like a mysterious planet come close to earth, making a strange visitation. She drove on through, mesmerized by the uncanny juxtaposition of rain on the windshield and this burning sphere – it almost looked like the fiery ethers of eternity breaking through the mist of oceans. How odd and beautiful it was.

PART SEVEN

CHAPTER FORTY-NINE

*A*s children we were always dismissed from the midday dinner table early. There was no way to keep us from squirming as the adults went on with their restrained discontent and family matters were discussed, next-door neighbors joked about, table conversation, while we all just wanted to be excused to race out into the sunlight, or to swing the canvas bed on the screened-in porch, knocking the wall as we moved it higher, smelling the must of the old porch furniture as we lay down into the rocking, down into the thought that the whole house was made of wicker, and maybe even Auntie, her bones and her being, bound by that wicker.

She had always looked the same to me, her white and wispy hair. It had always been like that. Someone said it reached down to her waist when it was undone. That was hard to believe, as it didn't look thick enough to be other than it was, always pulled back into a bun with the help of an invisible hair net. Her movements were delicate and sure, a guarded sense about her that became all the more controlled when someone outside the family was around. At times, with just us, her humor came to the surface and played like light, though others saw her as eccentric with her loose, dark dresses, the flat black hat pinned onto her hair. But she didn't look so odd in her looks to me because she'd always been the same, like the interior of her house, which seemed to protect her because it too was untouched and unchanging, and that always pleased me and satisfied my eyes.

Her mother, my great grandmother, had decorated the house, and that's the way it stayed. Auntie was not proud of the fact, it was just that she had no sense of these things, and if she were to alter it, she feared something would be marred.

My grandmother's house had always been filled with complicated activity. Children and grandchildren had grown up here. There was a sense of generation and that things had progressed. The houses were actually about the same size, but Gramma's, painted a deep amber yellow, was a friendly place to enter, and when you came in there might be the smell of pumpkin, and no one seemed to notice the wear of the Oriental rugs. One had a feeling that the house had embraced a very large family. Graduating heights were penciled in and dated on the third floor door that led up to the widow's walk on the roof.

Auntie's house was shingled dark brown. "More architecturally perfect, balanced on either side," my father liked to say. Her house was always cooler than one might expect, perhaps because the doors and windows were left closed. The dark green rugs seemed to keep in the coolness, preserving it like a cave stores wine or a dense glade shades you from the heat, like a cellar keeps its tubers and winter squash from going bad, so the rooms seemed downstairs in Auntie's house.

There were plenty of windows, but they were all covered with curtains, cream-colored and green with an oak leaf pattern, that gave the illusion of a controlled yet excitable environment. We could hide on the other side of those long, lined drapes and watch the real oak leaves in their mass and maturity caught up in the vibration of air off the water. The drapes were usually kept drawn, because Auntie believed the light off the water wasn't good for her eyes.

Often in the evening the lake appeared calm, but that too was an illusion, not its true nature, like the feminine pose often given to the camera or to a man's admiration – it had nothing to do with what was down at the bottom, stirring in a woman, which was darker, and often a secret even to herself, something she feared, which was maybe slightly dangerous, even violent at times. It could not be known just by swimming on the surface. Perhaps Auntie felt that it was waiting there for her and so she avoided it.

But why hadn't she married. She seemed to be set apart from the life that had been held up for us to imitate. She was not part of the model we were to identify with and replicate in detail, certain habits, ways of speaking, manners and good taste, lives that would shine only in resemblance. And yet ours was a different generation, maybe the first to disrupt the original program. Now that we were older, we were sure that we would never take part in the kind of conversation that went on around the table, the pettiness that dominated the relations between our aunts and uncles, all smoothed over by a common name, Faithorne, that gave them a sense of determined importance.

But Isabella Wells didn't share this common name. It was Auntie and Gramma's father who had earned this place for us all, with enough left over to last for generations. We were all secure and didn't have to think about it. Auntie never had to think about it, though she was afraid it wouldn't last. My father thought this was a terrific joke, but his laughter betrayed he was slightly worried himself. It took so much money. The place ate it like food.

Auntie barely ate. She was never finished even after everyone else was through with dessert, and she would simply say for us to go on, that she was slow, but that that was her pace. She did as she wanted. She never felt obliged to replicate the pattern of children and family, maybe because it was all around her, provided without labor.

I too wanted to break the original pattern, but in a different way than she, who appeared to be constantly held like the changeless design of the drapery material, the twist of the oak leaves, little cluster of nuts. It all seemed to move if the eyes were unfocused, or if you gave yourself over to the pattern, letting go. It had a static and yet at once a moving vibration that relaxed the mind and yet smelled of resolution – that nothing really happens, that nothing ever would again.

I think she had this distance, she must have recognized this – sitting back by herself, perhaps as a young woman – when she realized that what had occurred to her heart was fastened, sealed and saved, just like that forever, for the man in the portrait my sister found in the attic looked like an actor, foreign and bold, his hair wild and windy, with a billowing white shirt, and he'd signed his portrait, *with affection, for Isabelle*.

This man must have touched her in some way that was invisible to everyone, even to him in his sensual bravado, and if she clung to that image and let it consume some vital part of her that would never be allowed the living movement other hearts demanded and sought outright, then she could just sit by herself on the overstuffed sofa, under the swaying indoor palms, and feel as if she must try to preserve what it was he had given her. Maybe it wasn't much, but it was hers just the same. So she sat pushing her finger into the puckers that were buttoned down into the sofa, upholstered with the same material that hung at the windows, which was meant to illustrate the name of the property, Broadoaks.

Sitting there, she probably didn't realize that her own life was now bound like the wicker porch furniture, smelling of yarrow, bent into performance, stayed, and only slightly stretched, giving out a creak, the sort of groan you might hear if you tried hard enough to disturb the no-longer living.

So this hope or flash of feeling had made its one appearance, and for her it was like the privilege of witnessing some natural phenomenon one might only have the chance to observe once in a lifetime, like the lightning that had struck and formed into a fiery ball and rolled across their lawn – she would never forget it, but she wouldn't ever see that again.

They say that Auntie resembled her father in looks, even in manner – his reserve and his brains. "She has the brain of a man," my father liked to say, "if she'd only use it like a man" – meaning that if she were a man, she would be working to help support this family, but she hardly spent a thing, living as she did.

And if this were all hers, there was no reason for us to question it, for hadn't the stairs always had those four-inch risers, so that you hardly felt any effort in ascending, the ease of her life a kind of compensation. Yes, everything had always been this way, that was my impression – the black china cat had always stood by the fireplace that was never burning anything, and certain quilted pillows lay forever on certain sofa beds. The thin glass lamps that had the shimmer of butterflies captured, the silver cow that poured cream into their coffee, and the painted xylophone that had a padded gong and that was only played to call everyone for dinner, the square telephones that hung on the walls, even though they no longer worked, they had been left there, like the plumbing for each extra bedroom – Auntie just locked the door to the room when the pipes broke or the faucet needed fixing.

I loved the details of her house because I'd always known them. They were odd enough to be beautiful, not timely, but continuity preserved. I knew when I entered the dining room I'd be able to gaze at the heavy conical shade that hung its green and blue glass grapes down over the table, and it would sway slightly as it hung from its chains when everyone pulled in their chairs and waited for the courses.

Auntie knew what we liked to eat and she always had it served. She still rang for the finger bowls at the end of the meal though it was an old-fashioned custom. We were always intrigued by the story of the man who'd come to visit, and how when the finger bowl was placed before him with a cut of lemon rind and several rose petals floating in the fluted glass bowl, he had lifted it up and sipped the lake water, and how her mother, our great grandmother, had been a perfect hostess and she had done the same thing.

When my sister, Casey, found the portrait of that man, the romantic-looking man who had signed with much affection, she had been infatuated with it, with him and his look, or maybe with the thrill that we now finally had a clue to the mystery we could never quite uncover. But when Casey took the picture in to show Auntie, she never got an answer, because she could see too quickly how Auntie had been struck by the shock of seeing it again, how the mere sight of it had filled her slight frame with another substance, such as helium or embarrassment, and how she had gotten up and pulled the curtains back, just to do something.

Casey didn't insist. She felt Auntie preferred not to press down too hard on such sensitive places. Her mind didn't want to upset her body with emotion. She had learned how to keep herself from dwelling on these things, which had already made too deep a mark, and which at one time had left her with a frantic sense of failure. There was nothing she could do, there was no way out of the heaviness of cloth, of tradition, history or family – call it what you will.

But what set of images, what was the rekindled memory that must have lit up her body. I see her as the girl in the photograph, something else my cousin Lee and I discovered in one of the closed-up rooms, in a drawer, wrapped with tissue and then a chamois cloth. It was a picture of Auntie as she was in her late teens, and how it had shocked us, because we saw her for the first time as someone looking strangely beautiful, and yet we recognized the face, full instead of sunken, her round lips and her hair pulled back with a ribbon – she hadn't been pretty, but she'd had a special elegance, even at that age.

Perhaps it was at this time she met the man in the picture. He might have come to Nogowogotoc and been a guest at Broadoaks. And when it was time to leave, he had signed the leather guest book saying how much he had enjoyed the leisure of the place.

She went over and over it, the night of the big party. Like most of the lake parties of the time, it had been extravagant. The women wore gowns so sheer you could have pulled them through a wedding band, and there was a full orchestra and the buffet was simply heaped.

But Isabelle had not been hungry as the guests flowed in and out of the house, weaving through a common conversation, trying to rise above the heat of the night and the bother of mosquitoes. Hanging lanterns had been strung down to the lakefront, and the big launch had been tied to the dock so the younger people could rest there. Helen had been spending a great deal of time with the young Leonard Faithorne, and their union seemed natural and didn't upset anyone.

Isabelle lingered back by the punch bowl, smiling with an effort and trying to look invisible. Then the dark, striking Joshua had come up and found her, feeling not quite a part of all the commotion. After all, it was tiring for him to meet so many gay young women, and he didn't feel the same giddy strain coming from Isabelle.

So he had searched her out, though she thought he was just thirsty. He was more handsome than any of them, though they thought he looked "unusual." But that such a man should pay her this attention was alarming, for he could hold the floor in any conversation, but he preferred not to, preferred to share it with her, who did not know how to say anything without making it sound queer, as if she had just upped a little something and had to quickly cover over. Even if no one heard her, she felt sick just the same.

And so he had come to dip the silver spoon into the punch with its heart-

shaped ice cubes, and with the bowl of the ladle, which had the carved en-
gravings of a seashell, he had filled her little glass almost to the brim. She was
glad he hadn't scooped out one of those silly looking ice cubes because she
couldn't bear ice – she had sensitive teeth.

He offered her his arm, meaning to walk her away from the party – the
lights, the leaves, and her mind seemed to flutter as they walked the stone
path, and he said things privately to her, that Helen was indeed lovely,
she would make a fine mother, but that she, Isabelle, could be a painter's
inspiration.

This had made her heart so confused, she couldn't even think. He had
such a radiance, as dark as he was. A density surrounded him, but his words
seemed to burn in the air like Roman candles – they didn't sputter out. She
felt his eyes sweep over her as he took her chin in his hand, but how could
she, she felt, *Isabella Wells*, ever *be* such a thing?

When she did look, just for an instant, as he framed her face with both of
his hands, his look had been soft, almost softened by love, or, *No*, she thought
– he just feels sorry for me! And then wasn't she ashamed, horrified and foolish, running up that hillside, up the stairs into her room.

No, she could not allow herself to flower for this Joshua, for she was like
the moonflower opening only to herself, in her thoughts or in a dream, in the
middle of the night, and though the dream had been for him, he had never received it, this young and daring man whose last name Casey couldn't quite
make out, as if it had been worn from too much contemplation, like the material of an armchair, naturally fading.

We knew that Auntie's life had been lived in the shadow of the father, of
the house, of the oaks that were always in perpetual motion, the shadow a sister casts onto the life of a sister.

Auntie once said how our grandmother, Helen, didn't have a shadow to
her. It must have appeared that she always stood at that certain point of light
that keeps the body in its body, and doesn't spread itself out, elongated and
ghostly, trailing along behind in a kind of distortion. No, Helen had been all
of a piece, in herself, right there in her body. She wasn't afraid of her own
popularity. She stood in the center, at noon, without shame, and Auntie was
somewhere back, on the edge, the periphery.

CHAPTER FIFTY

Jetner, Auntie's housekeeper, was as cranky and protective as a well-trained guard dog. She tried to discourage me from visiting my aunt, saying it would be a strain. "She's probably sleeping, and she should sleep." Jetner stood there in her bedroom slippers, blocking the way, but I nodded and stepped around her. "She sleeps twenty hours a day now," Jetner warned me, "so don't go expecting anything." I didn't follow up on that comment, so she shuffled on back toward the kitchen, muttering as she went.

Going up the front stairs, I wondered how much I should ask of my aunt, and why I hadn't asked sooner. At the top of the stairs, I saw her bedroom door was cracked. Going over, I pushed open the heavy door, and for a second I was startled. She looked so utterly asleep, her small body dwarfed by the size of the bed, and her hands lay bonily upon her chest in the typical funereal position. I wondered if Jetner had placed her head right there on the pillow, for it looked as though she had not made any effort to stir from that placement. The covers were so neatly tucked in that she must have felt swaddled.

Walking in, I gazed at the familiar objects on her curio stand – the tiny ivory children on their ivory teeter-totter, placed beside an object that resembled an anemone, beads of concentric turquoise blooming all over it. There was a crystal ball, which I used to hold in my hand despite the fact that it was solid crystal and could be dropped. It rested on the necks of three bronze storks, who were obediently holding their heads in the proper balancing position.

Sitting down in a chair by the window, I wondered if Jetner had not been right – that this would be a fruitless visit. I gazed at the painting that had been creating a family stir. Someone had discovered its value, though to me it simply looked like a pleasant winter picture, the sun warming a stream that ran through a snowy hollow. When my great aunt died, it would be passed on to my father's generation, and there was already some dispute as to what they should do with it.

"Are you here to see the painting?" my great aunt asked. I looked over at her head on the pillow and wondered if that had actually been her voice, because her eyes were still closed and she looked exactly the same, but then she continued. "I think we should give it to the art museum."

The room was warm, no window had been opened to release the odor of closeness. "Mrs. Jetner thought you might be too tired to visit."

"Tired of waiting, perhaps. You must excuse Jetner, she does mean well. So how is your mother?" she added, which surprised me, because I had come to ask about my mother, in part.

When my grandmother died, I had found a letter that was disturbing. It appeared that the family had been investigating my mother's background, as if they were doing a title search on a piece of property. There was some question about my maternal grandmother's name, and I found the tone offensive.

My mother's family had not been wealthy. Her father was a postman, and she had been raised a Catholic. Her father had been devout, and her mother had converted, but there was an allusion to something else. "So many unfortunate traits can be passed down through heredity," and there was exceptional pondering over my grandmother's maiden name.

"I've been trying to figure out this family, my parents," I confessed to my aunt, pulling my chair a bit closer. "I wish things made more sense."

"Your parents." She paused. "That relationship was never very clear. I don't know what brings two people together like that, but they certainly let the sparks fly."

"She never felt accepted by the family. I always wondered what went wrong."

"So no one ever told you?" my aunt said slowly. "I thought you must know by now." I didn't know what she was talking about, but I didn't want to push her. She paused then, as if deciding. "Your mother's side was Jewish."

I felt like a sheet had been pulled from some invisible form, and suddenly I saw the statue, saw the curves of naked truth. I was astonished, offended, and relieved. Why hadn't anyone told me?

"We decided to keep it a secret," my great aunt explained. "Your father was set on marrying, and things were much different in those days. Your mother had to enter society. I believe it was difficult for her – not only that, but a Southerner." I could tell my great aunt was struggling to relay all this. She was making an effort, but also taking her time, pacing herself pretty well.

"She felt particularly at odds with my sister, though Leonard was actually the one against that sort of mix. I always thought you were rather lucky though," Auntie went on, "for the Jews supposedly have great intelligence, and that should be passed on down to your children."

"I can't believe this," I said, though suddenly so much fell into place. I'd never even seen a photograph of my maternal grandmother – I had always thought my mother hated her.

Auntie recalled the days when my mother was a bride. She had just moved up from Savannah. She was a beautiful woman, and when Alden brought her home, it was as if they were breaking and entering. "People felt a certain – violation, you know. The men all found her appealing, and that didn't sit well. I liked her, though. I genuinely did, once I got to know her. I always thought she was a real person."

But something else went wrong, something at the very beginning. Auntie believed it had something to do with bats. Oh yes, and my father's attitude. He wasn't sympathetic, or he liked to see her upset. It had something to do with her irrational fear, her tremendous fear of those creatures. Of course, they were quite nasty, but possibly there was something more fundamentally wrong.

"I remember a dance we had out here. Jonathan Bloodgood used to lead the cotillion, and it did make a difference to have someone there with his command and grace. He'd have these figures forming, you know, people circling in and out – there were favor tables, just little trifles, but goodness it was so gay." She paused for a moment, her eyes still closed. "I could tell your mother was disturbed as soon as she walked in – apparently she'd come upon a bat. Your father tried to hush her up, but she kept picturing it dangling beneath her dressing table, like a little broken umbrella. All the gentlemen seemed delighted and had their own personal stories – somebody had just stepped on one in the shower, and another had come upon one clinging to a porch screen – you know how they do, like a mud pie."

It was true, my father liked seeing her upset. He even kept a bat net beside their bed, and made a big joke about it.

"People get fixed on such unusual things," my great aunt continued. "When I grew up, we had a servant named Angeline, and we had to ignore half the things she said. Once she announced that she'd seen a ten-foot snake come out of the drainpipe that feeds into the lake, fat as the pipe itself. I don't know, but when someone tells you something like that, even if you don't believe it, something in you does. The crazy are convincing."

"But I don't think my mother is crazy."

"Your mother? No, she's just high-strung. The craziness, in fact, is on your father's side. You know there is a history," she continued, "a history of insanity in the family. Not the Faithornes, but on the Peckham side."

I stroked down the blue satin ribbon that had been sewn into the coverlet. The sheet, folded over, looked pressed, and I noted the tiny cobwebbed effect of mending, as if tiny holes had grown back together with little white spidery threads.

"The reason I bring it up is that there was some dispute over the final division of the Peckham estate, and now that I'm getting older, I certainly don't want my passing on to have the same effect. I want to leave everything settled. Oh, you know these things do go way back, but I tend to believe in heredity, the passing on of certain gifts, as well as these strains of abnormal behavior."

I asked her what had happened to them, and she explained that one of the Peckham boys, who had chosen a rather modest life as a professor, but who was fairly accomplished in his field, had simply gone off the deep end. "When he didn't get the inheritance he thought he had coming, he simply went berserk."

"Did they lock him up?"

"They didn't have to. He went home and murdered them all. The wife, the children, and then finally himself."

"Well let's hope that tendency's passed out of the family bloodstream." I hardly knew who the Peckhams were, some distant relatives.

"Let's hope," she repeated with a laugh. "Though there were other incidents as well. I don't even know why I brought that up."

"Because of the bats," I reminded her.

"Oh, yes," she said, remembering. "It was after your brother was born, and your father was away, in Korea. Your mother was pregnant, with you, I believe – that might have made her emotional. But my sister, Helen, heard her screaming one night. She heard it all the way up at the big house, and when she rushed down to the cottage, she found your mother in the hallway. Apparently she'd encountered another bat. She hadn't exactly *seen* it, but she'd felt it, in one of her slippers. Well these things didn't bother my sister much. So she offered to go in and get rid of it, but when she went into the bedroom, there was nothing flying about." No jerking or dashing of wings, no black patches of terror at all. "She peered into the closet, and crouching down, she lifted the pink leather slipper, but there was nothing inside. Nothing in the other one either. So she took both slippers into the bathroom, stood over the toilet bowl, and whacked them together. She told your mother that she'd gotten rid of it, and suggested that they throw the slippers down the incinerator."

From that moment on they were enemies. "Helen *was* mystified. Usually she managed everything so well." My great aunt paused then, as if catching her breath. "Did you know I was with her for her entire life? Why should that seem so astounding. I was here at Broadoaks when my sister was born." Her eyes traveled to a photo of Great Grampa Felton proudly holding up a tiny baby. "It *is* almost odd, but I can still remember Reusner, how she tried to get me take Tai out for a walk, so I wouldn't hear anything, upstairs, you know, the labor. But I was determined to stay, and I pushed that old chow dog outside, out the mud-room door. I can still almost see her, that deep red bundle of fur. . . . I didn't want to go out, you see, I was so upset about Mother. But I must have fallen asleep right there, because the next thing I knew Fraulein

Reusner had found me, and she was in such a flurry – I must have started bawling, for a moment I thought she meant Tai had brought back another half-dead chicken from Vintry's, but then I remembered what was going on and I ran up those stairs so fast.

"You know, Julia, your coming up here, when I first saw you, standing outside in the hallway there, something about you . . . I don't know why, because I was so happy, and yet I was afraid to go into my mother's room. Father must have plucked me up and stood me next to the bed, because there she was, almost buried in pillows and blankets and tired arms – my little sister. I was so pleased! Right away I planned, oh – I had a million ideas for us. You should have seen her, at all of the dances, with her large circle of friends, she was like the maypole in the middle of them all. And Leonard, how perfect he was for her. I never had anyone else like her in my life."

Stopping with those words, she turned her head and stared out the window, letting her thoughts ride in the whorl of leaves. "I know, there was something special there, between you too. We all do it, don't we. We can't help but choose certain people, loving them a little bit more, even when it comes to our own families. But now I'm talking too much. You must have something else you wanted to tell me."

"Yes," I answered. "I'm in love. Do you remember Lionel Ulrich?"

"Wasn't that Joseph Ulrich's grandson? He was always considered a bit of a delinquent. That must make him an interesting man. Let's hope he hasn't gotten you with child."

"You don't have to worry about that," I assured her. "I *am* a modern woman. Yours was a different age."

"Was it?" she said shrewdly, but without much force. "You might be quite right there, but it seems to me that it has always been one of the great preoccupations of women, and has been throughout time."

Then her face seemed to withdraw back into her face, as if that last effort to speak had taken too much from her. I could see her trying to shift her weight, and I was about to help when she settled back down. "Your parents were infatuated because they were so different. You'll have the advantage of a similar background."

I waited for her to say something else, but she was quiet for a time. My great aunt had never been married, so I wondered how she had insight about such things.

"It was good of you to come," she said, as if from the rim of sleep. "You always were an attentive child." Leaning over, I kissed her on the forehead, then left her room exactly as I had found it.

357 ꙮ

CHAPTER FIFTY-ONE

*Y*ou could say that growing up on Nogowogotoc Lake must have been heaven on earth, or you could say nothing, and disbelieve such truck.

Joey's father, Joseph Ulrich, had been the prize of the family, the brightest, most handsome Ivy League prince, who was to carry on the family name and further the family industry. But death occurs, untimely, and Joey had been left without a father while still an infant, left with a mother who was known for her beauty, the kind of woman who paraded her son in front of friends, having him "do the rounds," kissing everyone goodnight, but as soon as dinner was announced, she would curtly dismiss him as if he belonged elsewhere.

He would go into the living room and, one by one, empty all the cocktail glasses. Lingering half-smashed on the upstairs landing, he listened to the roar of their laughter as it subsided and rose through the overall murmur, his mother's voice sparkling at the center of it all. She seemed so happy when candlelight tripled in the mirror behind her, and she could delight her friends with something unusual, a yellow-tomato aspic, or a lilikoi sorbet, served to clean the palette between the fish course and the meat.

Alicia Ulrich, Joey's mother, "looked like a movie star," my father searched for a way to describe her superlative figure and terrific legs.

Even at seventy years old, Alicia knew how to slide sideways disembarking from a car, knees together, feet first. "You should have seen Elisa," Joey described how his daughter had run to greet her grandmother, and how the old woman had said – "I'm not here to visit you. I've come to see my grandson."

Elisa, now thirteen, escorted by her father, had come to join my father and me at The Blackstone in Chicago. Elisa displayed the delicate ring her father had purchased for her that afternoon – it had two combining curves, one silver and one gold. Her pale blue eyes were wide and shining, and her hair was blonde to the scalp.

"Does Elisa resemble your mother?" I asked. She was the second child of Joey's third marriage, and seemed completely without tarnish, turning her adoring eyes toward her father as he finished his second glass of wine. Normally Joey only drank Kreuser Beer, but tonight my father had ordered something special.

"My mother had long, dark auburn hair," Joey said. "And Elisa is beautiful on the *inside* too."

She was pleased, yet shy, as we drank to her health, to youth and love and – good investments. She told me she didn't have a boyfriend, yet.

"Is it true," I asked Joey, "that your mother had an affair with Walter Schraeger?" My father had told me about it, saying that Walter had kept up the pretense of being a family man by keeping his wife constantly pregnant, but then he would waltz into the Lake Club with Alicia on his arm.

"What's sad," my father added, "was that Schraeger's son was so good looking, while all the girls were big and unattractive."

Elisa turned her amazing flower-like face up from her soup bowl – she had never heard about this.

Walter used to fly his pontoon plane into the factory every morning, Joey told us, landing at the Milwaukee Yacht Club. Returning to the lake every evening, he would often land before Alicia's pier, hitching up the plane at the end of the dock as she ran down the hill to join him. Sunset was their appointed hour.

Once, early in their affair, he had asked her, "Do you want to see the sun set twice?" They were standing by the shoreline, watching the sun burn into the smoothness of the lake – how calm it became, uncanny. He said it was because they were together now, and she could stop stirring things up. He let his lips rest calmly in the hollow of her neck – the glowing pathway seemed to burn straight through her. He helped her step into the co-pilot's seat before they skimmed over the water, lifting up, rising like some apparition, until they saw that fireball reappear – there on the curve of the horizon, and flying together they witnessed the sun descend a second time – and she felt the pang of it even deeper.

At moments like this, she forgot she even had a child, forgot about everything else, that he had a wife and five children, as if a separate history did not exist, shouldn't exist, as if he wouldn't be standing there with the whole line-up for the next Christmas card, each face like a bulb on O *Tannenbaum*.

Alicia wasn't ashamed of her claim on Walter Schraeger, though as time went on, she felt she deserved more, or at least that their love deserved to be honored – she wanted to be recognized as his true and only match. She could not bear exclusion, this part-time life, adored one moment and ignored the next. Their time together began to feel like an insult, but whenever they argued about it, he said that it couldn't be helped.

Joey began to see Mr. Schraeger as a father figure. He was a big, strong man, and he often stopped by the house. He even ate meals with them on occasion. He liked to take Joey up on his shoulders and run with him around the room. Though Joey was just a child, he sensed the feeling between this man and his mother, that it was something warm, yet partially hidden, like the hearth fire burning behind the screen with the seven painted pheasants.

As the years went by, Joey came to know Wally Schraeger – the boys were about the same age, and Walter took them both sailing, taught them how to stand on the sideboard of his E boat, told them when to shift to port, pulling in the slack. Joey always liked it when they cruised downwind with the big sail filling, the boat gliding flat and fast.

Walter promised to take his two little skippers fishing up north. "Great fishing up there at the Brule. We can stay in our cabin, just the three of us."

Joey didn't tell his mother this plan, but it was a dream he lived with daily, tying delicate fly creations, putting each one in an individual niche in his tackle box. He practiced casting off the end of the pier with a wet line, and caught lake bass and perch but mostly little throwaways.

Then one morning Mr. Schraeger's blood-black Pierce Arrow pulled up in the drive. It seemed awfully early for him to come visit. Joey listened as his mother descended the stairs in her shiny peach-colored bathrobe. Mr. Schraeger was dressed in khaki. He had on that vest with the pockets all over it. He only came as far as the entry, and Joey heard, "Sweetheart, you've got to forgive me," and, "We won't be gone long." Then the car pulled out of the driveway, and he saw Wally there in the backseat, sitting next to his father. A shock of heat passed through him.

Joey dreaded to ask his mother, but he had to know where the car was going. He startled her as she came up the stairs.

She sensed his strange excitement, but she was more concerned with her own disappointment, for Walter had promised to spend the weekend with her. She repeated his question – "Where are they going?" She seemed disgruntled, half asleep. "Oh, just up north, some silly fishing trip."

Something inside of him stopped. He walked to his room and scanned his possessions, as if they might support him, but they were all foolish, stupid toy soldiers – all of it seemed fake – the little theater with the Steiff hand puppets, the row of china dogs, the hand-carved wooden beer wagon with its fourteen kegs. He had his own three-speed, bright blue Schwinn, and a pair of New Forest ponies, but he didn't have the most important thing. Not even a pretend father.

Joey went downstairs, got out his BB gun, took it outside, and went over to the woods where they'd made a mesh fence for his pet mud turtle. He aimed his gun and sent a ball of lead through the top of its dark brown shell. He didn't know why he'd done that, but it seemed to make perfect sense.

Joey took the dead turtle inside to his mother, handing it to her as she sat at her vanity. She screamed and let it drop to the floor, where it rolled in place like a china saucer. "Go to your room!" she yelled at him. "Just go to your room and stay there!"

He made a moist X on every pane of the leaded-glass windows, for everything had changed. But some things repeat and continue. The mud turtle goes on, sleeping in the heart of childhood, and innocence leaks from its wound.

"Why am I telling you all this?" Joey said to me, as he finished off the bottle of wine. My father raised his hand to order another. "This is bringing up feelings I don't even want to have."

I looked at his daughter, who was gazing down as if she shouldn't have heard all this, but then she said, "I remember sitting in this duck blind with Joe, and we were supposed to be real quiet, and then he slugged me, right in the stomach – for no reason. It knocked the wind right out of me."

"I never heard that," her father responded, with too-late, mock protectiveness.

"Then he said – Now you're going to cry, aren't you. I bet you're going to cry. But I wouldn't, I wasn't going to."

Joey put his arm around his daughter, kissed her on the temple as if to comfort her now. But maybe that shock to the gut was as necessary as other changes, bloody cramps, broken illusions.

And what about that first true love for the father in its oval silver frame? When does that start needing polish? Those juicy family jewels can't be hidden forever in the safe-deposit box of a sealed sex. And when the child mind begins to open, as if with a clam knife, a tight slit of consciousness comes. Elisa was beginning to see some things, that charm and easy affection had something to do with alcohol, and though she would always adore her father, when the hinge was broken and the meat forced out – would she taste it or turn away?

Joey wanted to tear down Topside, the family home, and build a reasonable house.

Lionel, second son of Joey's first marriage, was violently opposed to this plan. A shadow of the past fell over Elisa as well, because, as she said, "That's my childhood."

"I just want to be able to leave the place, push a button and have the house lock up. Do you know what it costs to heat that house in the winter?"

"Still," she said.

"Nobody lives that way anymore," my father tried to explain, adding that they closed up their lake home every fall and spent the winter in a Milwaukee apartment. But that wasn't the point. Her feelings had to do with memory, with divorce and the dislocation of things. We were drinking a 1970 B.V.

Cabernet Sauvignon, and my father said it was probably the most significant wine we would ever taste in our lifetimes.

"My most painful memory," my father wanted to participate, "was actually hurting someone else." So why did he have that look on his face. "I said to my brother Carl Merrick, who was two years younger – Stick out your foot – and then I slammed down an ice pick and he pulled his foot away. So I taunted him, saying – *Scaredy cat, scaredy cat*, stick out your foot – can't you be brave? So Merrick put out his foot again," my father paused, "and I lifted the ice pick and then plunged it down, right through his shoe and sock and foot and everything."

"Gross," Elisa said, and I agreed.

Only later did my uncle tell me that the pick had actually gone between the toes.

I couldn't stand the thought of another winter coming on, and asked Mr. Ulrich, "Don't you get lonely out there?" We were all drinking too much, a port wine now, as if to fill up some empty place inside with red-black, port-wine heat. I started to think about summer, how I used to pick at my knees, wanting to see the fresh pink meat beneath the scab, the way I imagine the flesh of a turtle.

"So what do you think happened," my father said to us, always liking the underside of a story, as if exposure brought comfortable darkness rather than light on the matter. "Walter Schraeger went down. He crashed his pontoon plane right into the lake, killing himself and Walt Junior. Can you imagine? Leaving his wife with all those girls?"

"He left two widows," Joey said. But he only killed one son.

CHAPTER FIFTY-TWO

*I*f you go," Lionel said, "you can't believe a thing she says. They're torturing her over there, you know, or so she claims. Torturing her probably because no one has to listen to her bullshit anymore."

Still, I was inclined to visit. I took the old twenty-five horsepower Evinrude attached to the fiberglass rowboat and headed out toward the center of the lake. The wind was full in my face, my hair blown back, the wide bow smacking the water. Turning into the bay, the old monastery loomed straight ahead. "Home for Unwed Fathers," Lionel liked to say, and then the new Goldenbank behind it. Lucy Knobloch had left several million in her will for the creation of this new nursing home complex.

Though the place appeared modern and well thought out, a single story of white painted brick, once I entered the sliding glass doors I was overwhelmed by a smell that seemed a mixture of baby powder moistened with formaldehyde. I noticed a plaque by the door that read *In Memory of our Loving Mother, Lucy Smythe Schraeger Knobloch.*

When I tapped on Alicia's door she answered as if she'd been expecting me. She was sitting in a high-backed Edwardian chair, placed at an angle in the corner. It was hard to believe that this bird-like woman with the wizened arms and thin gray hair had ever been considered a beauty. She was wearing large sunglasses, which lent an aura of glamour, and her manner was both distancing and familiar.

"It's been arranged just like my bedroom at home," she informed me, and I wondered how they had managed to get the canopied bed and bureau to fit. At least she had a corner room, and the light streamed in the windows. "They're stealing everything I have," she went on, "right out of the drawers. But they can't waltz off with this furniture."

"Too heavy," I agreed, "and traceable." I paused for a moment, then decided to tell her my news. "Lionel and I are getting married this summer. I hope you'll come to the wedding."

"Lionel Hewitt's a terrible womanizer," she responded. "He cares more about oatmeal than he does his own wife. But then he always was considered a simple man."

"And you were considered quite beautiful," I added.

"*Hmph*," she agreed. "Well, that doesn't last. They pickpocket everything that isn't tied down. Can you look in that top drawer and get me a scarf? Rather cold in here, don't you think?"

I did as she asked, but saw nothing but one drab, navy muffler. She accepted it as if it were pale peach chiffon. "Are you here from the newspaper? There was a woman last week doing research on all the big families of the lake. So much misinformation. Not that I corrected her."

"I'm not doing research. I'm visiting you. I was curious, though, about certain stories."

"Yes?" she replied. "That's what I prefer." But then her face fell and she looked toward the window. "You probably want to know about the fire. They all want to know about that."

I was surprised that she had brought it up, but yes. "That fire so long ago."

"It wasn't *that* long ago. When you get to be my age, the past is often more apparent than the present. Would you care for some fruit punch? That's all they serve in this place. Joseph gave me this scarf – it's French, I believe. He never comes to see me."

Lionel had told me his father visited every day, and brought fresh flowers at least once a week. There was a bunch of hand-picked black-eyed Susans on the sill. Lionel had said I shouldn't bother bringing anything, because she wouldn't remember that I'd even come. That seemed harsh, even if Alicia had been mean to everybody – especially to Lionel's mother, Siobhan.

I slipped a pint of ripe strawberries from my tote bag, along with a box of Heineman chocolates. She eyed the booty, but remained discreet and did not make a move.

"Do you think I started the fire?" she asked, not waiting for my response. "That woman from the paper thought the name of our place was *Mon Bijou*, that father had been smoking in bed. Fireworks, also. They supposedly went off in the basement. What nonsense. For one thing, he never smoked in his bedroom. He was particular about his linens, and it was dynamite that was ignited, downstairs."

"Dynamite?" I asked. "That's curious."

"Oh yes, he collected everything – guns, pistols, ammunition. It was a hobby of his."

"But *you* didn't start the fire, did you? You were over at some party, across the lake. That's what I was told."

She leaned toward me then and said quite cogently, "You can cook a meal and then have it served." She sat back, still eyeing the saran-covered berries, which I proceeded to unwrap, offering her one.

"I hope you don't torture your children." She paused, savoring the berry as if she had not tasted fresh fruit in months. "He used to lay his pet alligator down on my bed. I never liked reptiles of any sort, and that thing made my skin crawl." She paused for the briefest moment, and then asked, "What do you see in my grandson?"

I had the feeling she didn't really want to ask me questions, but would rather reveal more about herself. Of course, anything I might tell her would only remind her of her own experience, and that's what I had come for, really. I didn't know how to answer her question, but said the first thing that came to mind. "I think we were made for each other."

"*Ahhh*," she responded, "made for each other. That is quite an accomplishment. You might be the first in five generations to succeed at that. I was meant for one man as well, but he was never meant for me. He gave me this ring for my birthday." She held out her hand. "It's the only piece of jewelry I have left." I peered forward to see the creamy, oval stone, tiny diamonds running all around it. The smooth, milky stone was shot through with lights – turquoise, yellow, and orangey-red. "He always said the opal suited me, because it was magic, like fire on water. Such a horrible, horrible death. And to think I almost married that awful man just to make Walter jealous."

She paused for a moment before going on. "You have to grab what love you can in this world. Love yourself, young lady, or no one else will. I was lost, simply lost without Walter. It's cold in here, don't you think?" She wrapped the navy muffler around her shoulders. "I'm afraid they can't afford much fuel in this place."

A rather wrecked-looking image of a pretty child hung in a great gilt frame above the bed. The boy had long golden curls tied with a ribbon, a bonnet gripped in his serious little hands. It looked as if someone had kicked the face in, and it had been smoothed out and repaired from behind. The portrait on the opposite wall showed Alicia in all her glory, dressed in a gold-and-crimson gown. I wanted to pay her the ultimate homage. "I can see why they say you have beautiful legs."

"Yes," she admitted, "I can still walk across a room." Now she wore strange wedge-soled shoes, short pink socks pulled over her stockings. She was so thin, she might have only weighed eighty-five pounds, but her presence had not diminished.

"When you were a girl, you liked to ride, didn't you?"

"I liked the socializing more than the hunt," she responded. "You see, horseback riding was the only way to see a man without a chaperone, and that put a good many girls in the saddle. One inevitably tumbled off and had to be rescued – we did have some glorious rides out across the farm. I suppose you've heard of my son's intentions, chopping up Topside into little tiny bits. An entire new town where they used to grow corn. Our estate will be a subdivision."

Lionel had been incensed by this plan, but there was nothing he could do about it. The Village Board had given its approval, and the Waukesha County Park and Planning Commission had found the design "nonobjectionable." Many Nogowogotoc estates were yielding to taxes – but once Topside was gone, there would only be money in the bank, paper stocks and paper bonds, holidays in strange places.

"Do you know what they had the gall to say? That they'd maintain the appearance and character of Topside by having no curbs or gutters. Thank God for that! No curbs or gutters. Nothing will really be changed, not that I care. Get rid of the place, knock it down. Forget the past is what I say, not that you'll ever get it back again. Maybe my son will make a pretty penny, and then he can take care of me properly, hire back my personal maid." She thought for a moment about that, then added, "My butler, chauffeur, and my maid, they were the only ones who ever cared about me. There *is* no society anymore. You don't have to be invited to Newport, you just have to buy up some art. Clutter your house with it, give cocktail parties. That's how one shines in society today. You don't have to be anybody." She paused. "People give a party, and ask their guests to bring the food. I hope you're not that sort. You must have a lavish wedding. Lots of champagne."

I doubted if it would be very fancy, but we would give them something to remember.

"That's the one thing you can't find around here. As if we weren't old enough to drink. *What kind of juice do you want with your dinner?*" she imitated the voice of some nurse. "I want Möet Chandon, I say, not milk with a straw. Chocolate soufflé, not pudding an' pie fill. They can take away almost everything, but not your good taste. That lasts to the end even if nobody notices."

She paused again, as if she were waiting for me to take notice of some particularly fine thing. A silver vanity set lay on top of her dresser, and I was about to comment on that when she went on. "Good taste isn't something you buy off someone else's wall. I've seen them do it too, buying up family photographs – Instant Relatives, for what I'd like to know. It happened at Yelping Hill with those Chicago dealers. Well, I outbid them, I tell you – I thought it utterly disgraceful. Not that I paid, why should I? They're probably still around in some old box. Maybe your children will be interested. Siobhan never gave a hoot."

I knew that Lionel's mother had cared. She had cared so much, she couldn't care anymore, but I didn't want to contradict Alicia.

"I'd take a look around if I were you, before the wrecking ball comes. He has plans, you know, plenty of plans, not that he remembers his mother."

I reminded her that she had been telling me about an alligator. "Did it ever grow up? To be – you know, very large?"

"He used to let the thing swim in the lake. But not without its leash, which he attached to the tail. It would have killed him to lose that old thing. It did get loose one time. Colin Hewitt found it, out by a buoy, bobbing around. Repulsive, really repulsive. After that my father kept it in his bathtub. He even thought it needed a night lamp to sleep, or maybe it was for warmth, I don't know. I'm sure it sounds peculiar, but my father couldn't tolerate dander. People keep animals for very odd reasons, don't you think? Lucy Schraeger had the most vicious Alsatians. Nobody understood why." She laughed.

"So your father kept this reptile in the bathtub – how did he bathe?"

"I never investigated *that*," she huffed, "thank you. He simply kept it in this old wooden tub, lined with copper – that's the way they were made in those days. We had one of the first, quite modern, and he kept a kerosene lamp on the edge, if you get my drift."

I didn't entirely, I had to admit, but she seemed eager to fill me in.

"The whole thing occurred to me when Haven Rose drove up – he was the Hewitts' chauffeur. I've often wondered if it happens that way with great artists – a sudden inspiration, like a flash going off. I wanted the fire to be like an opera. Haven opened the trunk – it was a brand new car – and there was this can, vivid red.

"I see," I said, not following very well.

"You see?" she repeated. "And what do you *see*." She leaned forward as if curious, or angry. Did I see a young girl filling up a wide-mouthed jar, hiding the petrol in the foundation planting? Did I see a daughter enraged by a little blonde tart who had cozied right up to that reptile? "She never even came to the funeral, and she almost got her hands on Bon Pres."

"Your father was about to remarry?"

"The woman was of no account," Alicia said curtly. "She managed to get away, that was all."

"Away from your father?"

"No, from the fire. She had returned to Chicago for a fitting. You can guess who was paying for that. You really don't get it, do you."

She had to explain how she had gotten the gasoline out of the Hewitts' new car, then instructed the houseman to fill the alligator's night lamp. He had never known what he was doing. The lantern was empty. It had to be filled. That much at least was obvious. She had purposefully given the old man the evening off, and he had gone to Broadoaks to play cards with his sister. While Alicia was over at the Hewitts' party, her father went into the bathroom as usual to sat goodnight to his reptile, and then, taking a single wooden match from the box, he leaned down and lit the lamp.

"What an explosion! The fire consumed everything. It was spectacular. The police weren't terribly bright or suspicious, not like they are today." She sat there calmly, watching me, as if to record my reaction. "I stayed at the Ulrichs' that night, in the green room. He was a very good husband, crazy about me, though of course he didn't have an inkling. Would you like a peppermint?"

I accepted the candy from her little glass bowl, though it looked like it dated from another season. "How is Kurtz, that gardener of yours? There are so many people I wonder about now. I'm probably one of the last. Not everyone's as strong as I am." She paused then to sample a piece of the bittersweet chocolate. I could tell she approved. Then she suddenly asked me, "Do you think they'd call it first degree?"

"Well, it was premeditated," I had to acknowledge. "But if I were on the jury, and heard the whole story, I might be inclined to pardon you."

"Why be so lenient!" she demanded. "Do you think I want to stay shut up in here for another two decades? Don't you realize what she's trying to do?" Mrs. Ulrich leaned so far forward I could see the white roots of her thinning hair. "You know who owns this place, don't you? Lucy Smythe. I was her greatest rival. Now she has me locked up in here, out of the way. She'll never let me out."

I didn't tell her that Mrs. Knobloch had died of colon cancer three years before. If Alicia did not know that much, I was not sure that I should say anything. I thought perhaps it was better to have a reason for one's imprisonment, rather than to have no reason at all.

CHAPTER FIFTY-THREE

*H*aving a purpose for once certainly put my mother in an excellent mood, or maybe I was so in love, even she had begun to amuse me. She rushed through the house in a frenzy, looking for that Tiffany vase she always used for lilies. "Where did he put that damn thing!" She was in charge of the wedding.

It pleased me that she finally had to admit that Lionel Ulrich wasn't all that bad. Growing up, she had never trusted him, thought he was trouble with a capital *T*, but then the men I'd dated in the past ten years made Lionel look like a miracle.

She had hired a trio of musicians who would play from the upper level of the boathouse, and Mrs. Vogel from Spruce Lake was refurbishing the brougham. It had been standing in the corner of the garage, up on blocks, since my great grandmother's day.

As children we weren't allowed inside it, but Lionel and I used to pull off the covering, letting the carriage shine like a hearse of wet licorice. I'd pull the tassels that closed the rotting shades till it was dark as a bedroom in there. A small round window with a black cushioned cover was a disguised peephole for escaping lovers.

Looking back, I think his love had been there from the beginning, that this marriage was like finally coming home, which was why it seemed slightly incestuous. We existed side by side, no quarrel about freedom, no struggle of wills, only a harmonized impulse. I believed he was probably the only man who could accept me for who I was, and what I would become. I wanted everyone to witness it.

When I first met Lionel, I was running water from the big house down the sidewalk to the lakefront, and he joined in. A wet-lipped river began pushing along on the gray cement, breaking new ground, circumnavigating twigs, and I was above there, watching, guiding, as the water dipped into a groove or flipped over an edge – a lot like the forming of a life as I see it now – you create this path once and then the river just continues.

That boy, indeed, was on the lip of my experience, beneath the catalpa, dropping orchid boats. We were ten years old, both second-born and at the mercy of our older brothers. I still have a photograph of myself at that age, wearing a sleeveless daisy dress with the pure golden smile of a winner, having guessed the exact number of flashbulbs in the big cardboard box during Maxwell Street Days, one hundred and fourteen, for this portrait.

Lionel and I took refuge in each other and headed for the playhouse down by the water, imitating adults with our little brooms and bickering, draining the magic cup of its red, red liquid, only to watch it fill again. I collapsed on the horsehair mattress with its two-foot headboard and appropriate pillows – wonderful to feel the dimensions fit your body as a child – then, sitting in the small wicker armchairs, I'd say, "Do you want to play murder, fire, or divorce." A couple of years later he was lying on top of me, but still we only kissed.

Lionel and his brother were attracted by all the commotion over at our place. We called Springwood Lee a camp without counselors, but it was also a zoo without walls. We had every kind of animal you could think of, but mainly there were lots of long-legged, blonde-headed Amazon girls, aching to get pushed in.

Lionel had his own sterling silver lighter with his initials on the side. He told me what it meant to blow smoke in someone's face, and the nicotine feeling sank down into me, made me dizzy as those drunken flies on the windowsill, wanting to try out the twin-sized bed in his boyhood room though something inside me said not to – Don't unpeel that golden coin, your currency, it's such a thin wafer to dissolve in your mouth or get stuck on the roof with port wine, the body and blood of my boyfriend, there on my knees, untasted.

We paddled off to the Ulrich Canals, where the slowing squish of seaweed dragged beneath the bow – he'd push on through, gondolier style, parting the mass of waxen water-lily flowers – or we'd sit in the darkness of the abandoned squash court, secretly, one to one, hiding out, barely kissing, lips innocent unto lips – then we'd rush back out into the shock of daylight, leap into our boats, and race across the lake, the batting rhythm of the bows slapping water, feet flat on the vibrating Plexiglas, how nothing seemed to matter other than the great indivisibles of sun, water, love, and lake air.

"Isn't he wonderful?" I said to my mother, holding up his black-and-white photograph.

"Men often improve with age." But even she couldn't deny those eyes, which would be hazel, and that head of auburn hair.

"He looks like a prince in a story," Mrs. Seher, the seamstress, said. They had to take in the bust of my grandmother's wedding gown and fit it around my waist.

"He looks like an Italian count," my mother surprised me with her generosity. Compliments always seemed false coming from her. "A bit degenerate."

"I just hate the fact we wasted so many years. I should probably blame that on you."

"Well," she huffed, "you always have."

"Mothers seem to have that role," Mrs. Seher said cheerfully. "Not just to cook or sew, but to take the blame."

"Exactly," my mother agreed, plucking at the loose material.

"Uncle Eddie is coming," I announced, to bait her. "He always predicted we'd get married someday."

"I'm sure *he*'s someone to listen to." She considered the trailing effect of the gown, sounding more like the woman I was used to. Everything was making me happy.

I felt as I had as a child when we lay down in the field by the old stone wall and pricked our fingers to merge blood. We were matching halves, and looking back, I saw the inevitability of our coming together. How lucky to be marrying my sweetheart. Most people married a total stranger and ended up with disappointment, while I had been getting ready for Lionel all my life.

Lionel and his mother, Siobhan Alair, would be flying in from Dublin for the rehearsal dinner. His mother had moved abroad after divorcing Mr. Ulrich. Lionel was spending the week with her, and I wanted this time with my family too, greeting carloads of cousins, siblings, nieces, and nephews – the tribe had certainly multiplied, and the air felt thick with life and laughter. Sometimes it was almost too much.

I wanted to crawl back into our golden pasture, bare arms gleaming in the summer sun. We used to lie in the warm, high grass, looking up, imagining mythic scenes, huge white horses, warriors colliding, but now I sensed something strange. Sitting up, I saw my great great grandfather, William Felton – I knew him from the painting in the department store. He was wearing a peculiar hunting outfit and a long gray beard. I waved but he ignored me, aiming his gun at the old stone wall. My blood ran cold as any animal's aimed at, knocked off balance, and I wanted Lionel lying down beside me, giving me a thousand of his eager, boyish kisses. I wanted to lead him back into the cool, dark places of our childhood, back down those slippery steps into the lower level of the boathouse, where we'd lean into the damp smell of mud-filled shells and boat-bottom slime, sitting on rotten orange life preservers. We'd take turns lighting matches, the air so dense it seemed like a gas that might explode.

"It's not that I'm a cynic, or an atheist," Lee said, "I just wonder about taking vows when you've already broken them once."

"Maybe commitment should have a date on the side. You know, when it's bound to go bad."

Lee's marriage had been smelling rather sour for some time, and she was turning things over in her mind too much, trying to figure out how she could get him, pay him back – "I'm going to use the worst *shyster* lawyer, I tell you that. *He*'ll probably hire a woman, someone who doesn't even *have* children."

Lee was my closest girl cousin, oldest daughter of Uncle Merrick and Aunt Evelyn. We were always together growing up. Lionel had completed one part of me, but Lee had mirrored another. She had been one of three girls, and now she had three of her own. She managed them with incredible calmness, unlike her mother, who had to label everything in order to keep a grip on order.

Lee and her sisters used to have to hang up their clothes, just so, down in the bathhouse. Each family had a changing room, and it was there that my mother tried to imitate Aunt Evelyn's organizational mode, getting out her shocking pink nail polish and dashing out our names over ascending hooks, but we were a disordered, random lot, too much for her to handle, and our underpants usually ended up on the floor, while our sandy wet suits became cold and clammy, impossible to put back on.

"They disproved that theory about swimmer's cramp," Lee informed me. Her girls were diving off the posts of the pier, like we used to do, but just then I thought I saw our great grandmother Sarah cruising by in the electric launch, as silent and surprising as my mother's golf cart, but she looked serene and didn't turn her head.

Lee had brought their old wicker basket with the painted flowers down to the dock. She used whole wheat now instead of white, but everybody still loved Hellman's, grapes, Wisconsin cheddar, and potato chips. We'd been

371 ↰

hungry but generous children, with an eye to the small fish cruising below us, turning together in the yellow-green shallows – how quickly they nibbled up Wonderbread, while we dripped explosions of milk through the planks and sank our eyes into the world of water. I didn't see any fish swimming now. They'd been spraying the lake for weeds.

"Remember when we had to lie down for half an hour? Well, it's just not true – you *can* swim after eating."

"They probably just wanted us to shut up for a while, to give themselves a break." I understood it now, witnessing the commotion at the end of the pier. Vernon's wife had just arrived with her two boys, an armful of magazines, and a thermos of wine cooler. There was much family concern about her drinking while pregnant, and her boys always brought an additional dimension of chaos, *shrieks*, "No pushing!" But after handing out the waterwings, she plunked herself down and immediately began to read.

I wanted to bake my backside, but Lee persisted in drawing letters on my skin, to remind me of the game we played as children. She couldn't relax, and kept thinking about Adam. "He always hated this place. Do you know what he said? He said, next time I'm going to marry one of my *own kind*. Another asshole, I suppose."

Wanting to change the subject, I pointed out the willow down near the Hawkshursts'. Lee and I used to have a hiding place there. It was well protected, yet close enough to the liquid lap of the foam-scum shore to see what was happening, away from our pier and the boats that delivered younger sisters and brothers to the screened sandbox and babysitters. We always liked spying, being on the outskirts, climbing that maple with the limbs set perfect. We would get so high even we were unnerved. Lee and I used to crawl all over the roofing tiles of the barn, the loft, the old gymnasium, usually hiding from someone. It was only when we came back down to earth that we fought to kill, like the time Lee and I camped out on Auntie's property – we nearly murdered each other over a plastic pad of fake butter.

Just then I noticed Goetschie standing on the porch to the big house. I was startled, as if I'd seen an owl sitting right above me. She was looking out over the lake in the classic hand-over-the-eyes pose. It gave me a thrill that so many people were appearing, even coming back to life.

"Did you get your wedding gown at Felton's?" Lee asked.

"I'm wearing my grandmother in Georgia's." I never shopped at Felton's anymore, now that we didn't get our discount. Uncle Wink was negotiating the sale of the downtown store. The land was more valuable than the retail business. The branch stores would remain open in various shopping centers, but it wouldn't be the same with the main store gone. It was the only one with any elegance, though they had recently covered up the old wooden floor and removed the stools before the glove department, upgrading the decor to a more modern look.

It was now nap time, and Lee had to corral all three daughters. Their lips were blue from the extended swim, and their skin was slippery cold. She rubbed a towel over the youngest one's shoulders and steered them in the direction of the loft.

I wondered if I should tell Lee about the spooks, for there was long-gone Kirchner in his overalls, walking so slowly, it was as if he were moving the entire world in his gray wheelbarrow. Lee almost walked right through him.

"They used to pack hunks of ice in here," Lee told the girls, showing them the walls of the ice house, eight inches thick. With the door bolted shut, you couldn't see a hand in front of your face. My father had once locked Uncle Eddie in here and gone off to eat Sunday supper. As Lee pushed back the heavy door, there stood the E boat, *Bottoms Up*, as well an old wooden canoe and a bunch of snow fence.

Lee checked her watch, concerned about the schedule. Even as a child she had organized things. One summer she went so far as to usurp my control, getting everyone to ditch me and join her in the Bunny House – that was their club, by the compost heap, which took up a serious quarter acre. It was all a big secret, and that summer I hated her. They had pictures of horses concealing naked girls tacked up on the walls, and special rules, like walking in order and where to run if they were attacked. She taught them all how to play strip poker, explaining intercourse and "the curse" all wrong, but I got her back later when I told the girls on the bus that her mother wore falsies. Aunt Evelyn called up and said, "That's not nice. You know the family has to stick together."

Sure, I thought, by despising each other.

My mother hated almost everyone a little, but mostly she hated living in such close proximity to so much family, sharing everything, like communists. She was mainly engaged in serious warfare with my grandmother, who liked to serve weird food at family dinners – kidneys, kohlrabi, sweetbreads, squash – but I liked the commotion, and there were slabs of tomato we could smother with sugar, pieces of white bread we could cut even thinner, stuffing the insides with marmalade. We plunged silver prongs into the baby bantam corn, till Kirchner died, and the new idiot gardener threw the chickens our seed corn.

"Remember when Grampa told David Jerome to take a long walk off a short pier?"

"That was the only cruel thing your grandfather ever did," my mother answered. "Some people make a habit of meanness."

Jerome did not recall this incident, but he did remember one housekeeper who made us eat raspberries crawling with ants. "She was some witch," he grimaced.

I remembered counting June bugs on the screens with him, wondering whose car was coming up the drive, how we'd leap to lower the green canvas shades when a downpour came, jumping back and forth from bed to bed over the gray floor we called "Spit Sea."

"You know, Jerome," Lee said to him, "you don't scare me anymore."

"Well you scare me," he chuckled, as if she were that ugly.

"Is the safe still there?" I asked my cousin Vernon. This dining room used to have a hand-painted landscape with beautiful pheasant in a forest of fern, until Aunt Carol's decorator had it all covered over with a small brown print that didn't correspond with the grandness of the room.

Vernon leaned back in his chair and thumped the hollow sounding wall behind him. "Good place to keep boys who won't sit still."

"You were the exact same way," Aunt Carol reminded him. She had always stood up for Vernon, no matter what he did, and now she was extending this generosity to her grandsons as well.

"Can I have another bratwurst?" Lee's littlest asked.

"No," Lee said. "They're not good for you."

Lee's girls were blonde, with straight bowl haircuts. "Do you want me to take them over to the barn?" I asked. She looked like she could use a break, and they wanted to go, so after coffee and brownies, we ran down the steps of the big house, across the nut-strewn lawn, to the path that crossed over to the Vintrys'. Snake grass grew there, tall hollow reeds. I taught the girls how to pull them apart and make necklaces with them. Then we walked the stone shore and I showed them where we had once made a fire, like Indian children. I promised them we'd cook s'mores one night, maybe look for lightning bugs. They were beautiful girls in their various sizes, like those dolls that stack neatly inside each other.

"Can any of you jump?" I asked, and they hopped in unison. "Not that, I mean on horseback." They shook their manes, no. They had only been on pony rides, city children. Just then, as we were about to cross Mixter Road, a vintage 1912 Packard drove down the driveway and turned in at Broadoaks. It was the same steel-gray as the other apparitions. I couldn't tell who was driving.

Clausen had been the last in the long list of chauffeurs. He drove Aunt Isabelle. Her car had a sliding glass panel between the front and the back. We used to push the button and ask him to sing – he wanted to be famous, to sing on the radio. Lee and I used to drop by the carriage house as if paying homage, but he drank red wine and I noticed the residue in those big Gallo bottles. He always seemed too familiar to me, up there in the semi-darkness of the garage apartment. Once he offered Lee a silver dollar if she'd touch something, but it looked all bruised. I said, "Let's get out of here." I think Lee was pretty tempted by the money, and she was no coward, but at that moment in time, she was my follower.

After he quit, Lionel and I snuck up those stairs to make out on the sofa bed. The place was falling apart, with animals in the walls, but Lionel liked it. Lee always picked the most unlikely partners, but she was physically daring, and let Cricket Harrison go all the way with her.

The girls were picking mulberries that grew over the gate that led to the garden. The latch on the metal gate felt like it always had, responding to a subtle squeeze of pressure. I didn't want to tell them what this garden had been like in its day – row after row of flowers and vegetables. Now only a few currant bushes grew along the edge of the abandoned asparagus bed, the crossing of the paths still visible, like a raised scar. "You know your great *great* grandmother used to order every single item from the seed catalogue. This garden was once a showplace."

We used to come here and pick those tiny yellow, squash-shaped tomatoes, eat crisp green beans that tasted like rain. We pulled carrots up from the easy loam, lima beans – my favorite, tender green and melting with butter – baby lettuces, small zucchini, prickling with hairs. I used to gather an armload of bright-colored zinnias, my feet sinking into black earth.

The girls were running for the greenhouse now, and on stepping inside, the same peat scent rose up to greet me. I remembered coming in here, late March, how the seedlings thrust their numerous heads up like froth. The smell of pure growth still bloomed in my memory, how Kirchner used to offer us Sen-Sen, and sometimes Lee would slip a cigarette from his pack of Pall Malls and we'd sneak down to the family dump, crouch behind a fresh pile of garbage and smoke, passing it back and forth. I remembered riding on the bed of the farm truck, how we'd hang our legs over the back and hold on. No one was ever afraid we'd get hurt.

Leading the girls on down the white-washed hallway of the chicken house, we opened one disappointing shelf door after another, exposing the bare, empty roosts, a few random feathers, but no warm brown eggs. The chickens had all died of some disease.

"When I was your age, Tully, the groom, taught me how to jump. He had me put pennies in my pony's water, to help calm him down. He figured Bunko and I were a pair – full of shenanigans." The barn used to have this cozy feeling of bound bales, with the mud nests of swallows glopped in corners, but the stable had burned down and the new one had too much height and space – a cold stretch of clean cement flooring. Even the tack room seemed overly generous, with its dark green rug. I liked to look at the old family pictures – Gramma and Papa with all four children, riding in a perfect line. That picture had been coupled with a western one from Jackson Hole – *Let each one say which he prefers, the English boot or riding spurs.* There were also more recent acquisitions, a photograph of a Roman-looking lad gripping the neck of his muscular white stallion, and other more stylized kitsch.

Back in my childhood, on entering the stable, you felt like you were entering another dimension of smells, a unique combination of lime and manure, leather and hay dust. The tack room was small but each saddle and bridle was marked with a nameplate. Tully would grab Bunko's jaw with his thumb and third finger, say – "Ah . . . if a horse bites you, you bite him back – that's number one lesson in learning how to jump." One day Tully quit, or he was fired, I didn't know, but it made me feel strange, that life could get twisted all around wrong like leather. It seemed like such a comedown to do lawn work at the neighbors'. I always looked for him when I rode through the Ulrichs', and he'd be sitting up on the big red lawnmower, cutting swaths. When he saw me, he'd come over, put his hand on Bunko's neck, spit, and laugh his horsey laugh. But one time, riding alone after a heavy rain, I was walking Bunko silently across the lawn and I saw him speaking to the bushes, rubbing them down with his hand.

We walked through the pole barn reading the names of the horses. I held the littlest girl up so she could give the mare oats. "Keep your thumb right next to your fingers." I showed her how to keep her hand held flat and told her some of the names of the horses when I was growing up, "Busytown, but he was so tall we could hardly get up on him, and Lady, who was no lady at all." She'd put back her ears and chase us through the pasture. Then there were the Shetlands and Papa's gray gelding, Honoré. Just at that moment, I saw the exact same horse in the end stall. It gave me the chills, for that was the one that had fallen down on Papa and caused his second, fatal heart attack.

"Papa never fell off a horse," Jerome said that night at dinner, as Aunt Carol tripped onto the porch carrying a round glass tray, full and clinking.

"Don't spill it, dear."

"I didn't, darling."

Jerome was sitting next to his girlfriend, Linda, who was blonde, petite, and very pretty. It seemed unnatural for any girl to join forces with Jerome, but she was doing her best to fit in. "Where should I sit?"

"Where would you *like* to sit?" Aunt Carol was not big on organizing anyone.

"Where would you like me to sit?"

"Just sit down," Jerome growled.

"Is that true?" I asked Aunt Carol, meaning about Papa never falling off. She paused for a moment before setting down the tray of instant iced tea, recalling many rides with her father.

"Yes," she finally answered.

"Yes *what*, Carol."

"Yes, he did fall off," she remembered. "But he always picked himself up like a gentleman."

"I've never fallen off, either," Jerome announced. Being a man meant staying on.

"Gramma always said you weren't a real rider unless you'd fallen off at least three times."

"I guess you're marrying a real rider, then." Jerome was such a pain.

I would have traded my dimes for Jerome's nickels any day, but there was no way to earn his approval. It was not even subtle, his version of torture, he would either lock me in the basement, in the salamander pit, or push me into Spit Sea. Then he'd give me a snake bite or knuckle sandwich. I was not allowed to be a tattletale, so I took it out on Vernon or Casey or Lee, who would pick on younger siblings. The last-born children seemed to get off easy. They were considered the babies and not in the thick of things, but everyone did think it pretty amazing, how our cousin Fifield could do the monkey walk. Aunt Carol tried to get him to stop it, but he'd throw himself down and gallop across the lawn, Jerome laughing loudest of all.

Lionel and I had selected Motown oldies to play in the big tent during the reception. Our generation would dance up a storm, while the older set had a trio of musicians for the intervals. I looked through our old 45 collection. "Get Ready" was on top, but I did not feel prepared for this at all.

My mother was letting her best colors shine. This role of mother-of-the-bride was keeping her so manic, she was either in overdrive, telling the workmen where to put the seventy white chairs, or too exhausted to bad-mouth anyone. Luckily, she didn't notice Gramma, standing beneath the grape-covered pergola. Gramma was simply observing the progress of events as if they were only mildly interesting. I longed to go up to her, to give her a hug, but I knew that she was off limits. None of these apparitions seemed to display much energy or emotion. It was more as if they were watching, like guards at a museum.

"Why are *you* just standing there?" My mother turned toward me. "Shouldn't you be writing some thank-yous?"

I wandered down in the direction of the pier. Naked blond babies were playing in the shallows, digging sand and throwing small, smooth stones. The older boys dragged each other off the pier. There were always eruptions down on the dock, dog fights and minor squalls between siblings – someone getting shoved or dunked or splashed, falling on the sand-coated planks and then bleeding, the loser always louder right after some disaster. Boats zoomed around with water-skiers, sailfish were pulled behind outboard motors – a gush of water shooting up the centerboard slot – cub boats turned together, *Comin' around port*, while Valdemar attacked Beau Jacques.

We came back to Nogowogotoc to swim every day in the warm, green water, walking overgrown paths to the remains of hiding places. We came back to smell the algae and water-logged planks of the boathouse, to feel the same old bounce in the yellow metal tennis chairs. We came back to feel the heavy, humid air blanketing the grass next to the cool dark places, the lake with its levels of temperature. Touching the rooty dry snarls of the grapevines that draped themselves over the pergola, we returned to the statue of the waterboy holding up his shell – how often we used to bathe his small molded form, tufts of hardened hair, wanting him to be completely wet all over before the sun sucked him back to that gray dusty color.

My father once said that when things were too perfect, he felt this compulsion to mess them up. So I was almost relieved when the afternoon light shifted darker and lit up the color of everything, making the surface of the water a strange teal blue. We were in for a good storm. I was supposed to see Lionel that evening at the rehearsal dinner, but it didn't seem real. I felt like I'd be waiting forever. A gray sheet of water advanced across the lake and the trees bent down before the force of the wind. I ran for the big house, where the tables were set up, sliding the glass panels closed. Then I rushed back outside and let the storm shower over me, deafening, wet, the strikes coming closer, close to my nature – counting the seconds until the big one fell – how we used to walk the length of a fallen elm tree smelling the fresh ripped scent of wood pencils.

The storm cleared the air, but it also delayed Lionel's arrival in Chicago. I hoped he and his mother would join us in time for dessert, but no one at my table that evening seemed to believe it. The food was excellent, unusual for the Lake Club. But it's hard to ruin lobster, and the champagne did flow. My brothers took turns, making humorous toasts, how we'd better remain heartily hopeful until we saw the groom. Joey Ulrich repeated a saying he remembered from his own first wedding – "May *his* arms be her defense and *her* arms his recompense."

Dad stood to announce, "You know, it seems like only yesterday when my lovely little daughter burst into tears because the Lake Club was out of *schaum torte*. Well, tonight we're going to make it up to her!" He turned in my direction, and everyone applauded. "I think you all know that a dinner invitation, once accepted, is a sacred obligation. If you die before the dinner party takes place, your executor must attend." Everybody laughed. "And yet I believe," my father continued, "that if Mr. Lionel Ash Ulrich manages to make it to the altar tomorrow, *all* will be forgiven." More cheers.

Lee gave me a look that said – I wish he would get here. Casey shrugged. Everyone was priming Fifield to do the monkey walk, for there he was in the good ol' home movies, galloping across the lawn, and there was Vernon sitting on the pier with his foot in his mouth, looking at the camera sideways – I give him a kiss and he topples over – then Lee begins bossing her sisters, trying to make them salute in a line – Jerome's croquet mallet whacks me on the head, and I stumble off across the lawn – but no, I recover, a true survivor, for there I am swimming Bunko bareback, gripping his mane – he trots out of the water and shakes so hard I vibrate – I laughed until I had to wipe my eyes.

I wanted to believe that Lionel would suddenly appear, rushing in with an armload of drenched red roses, but word was passed back to me through my mother who had gotten a telephone message from home that someone had called from Chicago to say that their plane was expected around midnight. Lionel and his mother would drive up then. It was probably for the best, for if he had arrived on time, he would have tried to sneak into my bedroom, ruining this delicious build-up, and I wanted to sleep my last night alone.

Lee and I went swimming that evening – lightning bugs and small brown bats swooped in our direction, while our sticky bodies made cool slices into the water. It let us enter like pieces of heavy silver, dipped and polished. Then holding my body in a ball underwater, with an endless effortless breath, I was slung in the primal fluid, my hair spreading over the surface, weightless as a stone.

Coming back to my sleeping-porch bed refreshed, I lifted the bamboo shade to see how many bugs were still clinging there. Their presence didn't disturb me. They were just the closest proof that night was all around and that I was safe from it. I was in no hurry to succumb to sleep, not until I'd listened for a long, long time to the crickets in their keen, sonorous unison, and then marked the hour of the bell as it gonged from across the bay, the sound of it so clear because the tower that held it stood down by the water, where the air was undisturbed, and where everything could be heard more easily, but especially the sound of that bell, way past midnight.

But then, from as far away as Wahcheetah, I heard the haunting, grinding churn of the train as it came on beside the corn fields, an eerie embrace for me, that sound, and I let it rouse my being with a comfort that could only be called amniotic in comparison, as it seemed to repeat itself over the tracks, moving along on the heat of the heart, held in by the sound of the moving train, grinding, pounding ahead.

I woke thinking about the truckload of cows that had recently tipped over on the highway. I had no desire for breakfast, and there was a murmuring about another delay, that Lionel and his mother had decided to sleep at an airport motel rather than trying to drive up jet-lagged. Nobody would let me speak to him.

"Didn't you know that that's bad luck? Adam and I had a fight on the morning of our wedding, and I'm sure that jinxed us." Lee was my maid of honor, but she didn't feel young enough to be a maid of anything. My sister and she were both wearing pale pink dresses that exposed their shoulders. Casey kept checking the time out of the corner of her eye, like a therapist might toward the end of a session, and it was beginning to get on my nerves.

"Would you at least go and see if he's here?" I asked my sister.

"Of course he's here. Where else would he be?"

I could think of about a hundred places.

Casey went as far as the bedroom door, as if I might escape if she weren't on duty. She called out to our mother, "We need some confirmation up here." The commotion of people gathering outside could easily be heard and I did not feel well.

Finally, Mother came to the door. "Why aren't you ready?" she glared at me. "Do you know what time it is? Of course he's here. Take that gum out of your mouth. Your pearls aren't even on! Do you know who your father invited? That horseback rider, Leslie Thomas. This was supposed to be a *family* wedding. Why do I have to do everything?"

Casey held up the pearls. They were tiny and beautiful, three delicate strands, all swooping together. They were a creamy white that went well with the old satin wedding gown. "There," Casey hooked the antique clasp, then she hugged me from behind and began to sniffle.

"Don't start," I told her, "or you'll get me going."

"I feel sad too," Lee's face clouded over. "You really look beautiful. Shit."

"If you make me cry, I'll slug you. Come on." It was eleven-thirty exactly, and we were going to be punctual, ready or not. I walked out into the hall, indicating that they should both go ahead of me. I felt rather sick, as if a red leather wallet had gotten lost in my stomach, misplaced credit cards, stolen cash. I peered out the little mullioned window toward the lake, and could see my brother escorting our mother down to the front. On the other side were Lionel's relatives, the living and the dead, turning in their seats to watch the procession. A chilling sweat broke over me when I saw Lionel standing there talking to Heinrich Ulrich. They seemed to be agreeing on something. The old man pointed across the bay, and when I looked in that direction I saw a large white stag standing on the bank. But then Lionel glanced up and I was sure his eyes had found me. He could see me and know me through the walls of this house, and I knew that I had to go to him.

My father was parading around downstairs, and as I took his arm the musicians paused and then began a new piece as we stepped onto the lawn. I was in a state of shock now. Lee and my sister were walking down the slope at intervals. Helen, my flower girl, was dropping pale rose petals. A murmur of amusement moved through the crowd when she stopped and dumped the remainder out. It really was a beautiful morning, perfectly clear. A flock of sailboats was moving far out on the water, then one after another, their white sails turned – a light wind waved in the oak leaves – and a long stretch of gradually sloping lawn took me down to Lionel. Everybody's eyes were turned uphill. My cousins were smiling yet serious. There were Mildred and Morvan in their Sunday best, Gramma and Papa and my Great Aunt Isabelle, Alicia in her wheelchair, ancestors scattered amongst the living.

As I stood before Lionel, it felt like that second before you swallow a fish bone – you know it is there and about to go down, but you can not stop the impulse. But then he reached out and took my hand and all my fears just melted. He was once again my darling, as real and wonderful and handsome as ever. There was an intense kind of calm in his eyes. I was sure it was a reflection of something so powerful it was burning us clean, leaving us like softened embers. This must be like walking on coals, I thought.

I repeated that I would love him and cherish him, in sickness and in health. I gave him my hand for the plain gold wedding band, then the minister told him he could kiss the bride. Pausing for a moment, he took a deep breath and then, bending me backward, we kissed. The warmth of his kiss sank into me like hot sand running through my arms into time, but then, lifting me back to my senses, he whispered, "Let's get out of here."

"Now?" I asked.

He had taken a silver stopwatch from his breast pocket, and pressing the little button on top he said, "Now."

So I kicked off my shoes, threw my bouquet in the air – Lee grabbed it –

my mother was crying. I could see the horses were ready to go, even the musicians began playing impromptu as we ran up the hill. Everyone was left perplexed, but then these family weddings always were a bit peculiar – you never could tell what would happen. As I climbed into the brougham, I heard Aunt Evelyn's whistle, a chorus of female *Ooo-ahhs* before our sudden departure, assuming quite rightly that we'd been patient long enough – or perhaps they were hooting for Fifield, who was galloping up the lawn at tremendous speed, trying to overtake us.